# A Primer of Population Dynamics

Krishnan Namboodiri
*Ohio State University*
*Columbus, Ohio*

Plenum Press • New York and London

**Library of Congress Cataloging-in-Publication Data**

Namboodiri, N. Krishnan (Narayanan Krishnan), 1929-
A primer of population dynamics / Krishnan Namboodiri.
p. cm. -- (The Plenum series on demographic methods and population analysis)
Includes bibliographical references and index.
ISBN 0-306-45338-X
1. Population--Miscellanea. 2. Demography--Miscellanea. I. Title. II. Series.
HB849.4.N363 1996
304.6--dc20 96-35755
CIP

ISBN 0-306-45338-X


A Division of Plenum Publishing Corporation
233 Spring Street, New York, N. Y. 10013

10 9 8 7 6 5 4 3 2



Printed in Great Britain by IBT Global, London

To Ronald Freedman, whose course on population problems at the University of Michigan was my first exposure to a substantive course on the subject. As a teacher and scholar he has been a model for all of his students.

# Preface

This book has been prepared for readers with no formal exposure to the scientific study of population. The emphasis is on presenting information in a readily retrievable form. A question-and-answer format has been chosen with this purpose in mind. The index and the extensive glossary also enhance retrievability of information.

My experience in teaching introductory population courses over the past thirty years has sensitized me to the need for such a presentation. Students of varying background who take such courses often want to know what their focus should be when they read a prescribed text, especially when they begin hurriedly preparing for the mid-term or final exam. A question set covering the readings and lectures seemed to help them a great deal. Furthermore, with this information in their hands, it would be possible to cut down lecture time somewhat to accommodate class projects and discussion.

Those without any exposure to demography are likely to find the book useful as an introduction to the basics of population studies; those with some exposure to the field may use it to test their grasp of the basics. The questions and answers may be of interest to instructors of population courses and to graduate students preparing for their doctoral exams in demography.

An effective way to use the book is to indicate your answer(s) beside each question and then spend as much time as necessary verifying the answers and carefully reading the explanations. Also consult the references cited if additional information is desired. Going over the questions a second time is highly recommended.

I have benefited from the comments, criticisms, and suggestions of many students and colleagues. I am especially indebted to Joyce Abma, Linda Dorston, and Luying Wie for sensitizing me to the concerns of students in population courses. Luying Wei rendered invaluable help with computer graphics. Among my colleagues in the department of sociology at the Ohio State University, I should single out Bill Form, who has been very generous with his time in discussing with me his views regarding the linkage between population dynamics and the various dimensions of societal change. I have drawn inspiration from my teachers Ronald Freedman and Amos Hawley.

# Contents

# *A Primer of Population Dynamics*

# CHAPTER 1

# *Introduction*

Many people think of demography (population studies) as a number-crunching, dry subject. Most of them usually change their opinion when they realize that population is a factor that affects, directly or indirectly, almost everything that goes on around them, especially in a modern world that is relentlessly converging to an interdependent whole.

## *1.1. POPULATION AS A PROBLEM AND A RESOURCE*

There are those who subscribe to the catastrophic view that rapid growth of the population is what causes many of the major problems such as hunger and malnutrition, air and water pollution, vice and misery, sickness and poverty, international aggression, and internal dissensions. At the other extreme are those who believe that the "more-the-merrier" principle applies to population too. Their argument is that the physical and economic well-being of the world's population has been constantly improving as a result of technological and socio-economic progress stimulated and facilitated by population increase and that this relationship will continue indefinitely. In a poem titled "Man's March to 'The Summit,' " Kenneth Boulding (1955, 1995) summarized the long-standing debate between the conservationist and the technologist. The conservationist laments that people are plundering the planet and that soon there will be nothing left for our descendants—no coal, no oil, no forests—except polluted air, depleted ores, sinking land, and eroding soils. To this the technologist replies that human beings are resourceful; they cultivate knowledge, which, in turn, help them solve almost all problems—food can be obtained from yeast and algae, for example, and almost everything else we need from granite.

Historically, opinions have swung back and forth between such extremes more than once. During the 1930s, for example, the dangers of underpopulation were the main worry of those writing on population matters. In the post-World War II years, however, it became fashionable to cry about the untoward consequences of overpopulation. In 1945 Kingsley Davis wrote, "Viewed in the long-run, earth's population has been like a long, thin powder fuse that burns slowly and haltingly until it finally reaches the charge and explodes." (Davis 1945, p. 1) In Paul Ehrlich's *Population Bomb* (1968), worldwide famine and war were seen as almost inevitable, given the continued increases in the world's population. In 1970, Harrison Brown wondered whether the poor countries of the world, fed up with the increasing economic gap between themselves and the rich Western nations, will "resort to rebellion on an unprecedented scale," and "drag the rich down with them." (Brown 1970, p. 12) In 1973, Robert McNamara, then president of the World Bank, likened the "threat of unmanageable population pressure" to the threat of nuclear war. In the midst of such pessimism, Donald Bogue (1964), addressing the Population Association of America as its president, expressed extreme optimism that the world was about to bridle the runaway population. Three years later in a paper published in *The Public Interest*, he declared that "the world population crisis is a phenomenon of the 20th century, and will be largely if not entirely a matter of history when humanity moves into the 21st century." Bogue's optimism was based on his conviction that family planning programs were producing the desired fertility reduction in low income countries. But no one seemed to be as optimistic as Julian Simon (1981), who tried to popularize the idea that population is the ultimate resource. By the mid-1980s the extreme views had given way to more moderate ones, emphasizing that population growth has both positive and negative implications for social and economic change, and that in certain circumstances one set of implications may dwarf the others.

## 1.2. INDIVIDUAL-LEVEL AND AGGREGATE-LEVEL VIEWS OF DEMOGRAPHIC PHENOMENA

To those who are not interested in such aggregate-level phenomena as the population–development or population–environment relationships, demography offers an opportunity to think about trends and differentials in age at marriage, family size, length of life, and risk of divorce. Demographers analyze marriage histories, pregnancy histories, job histories, migration histories, and the like. Often such histories are put together from the experiences of people at different stages in their career, e.g., marriage histories from data for women with different marriage durations. Based on marriage data of people at different ages, for example, demographers discuss the probability that a 15-year-old will ever get married, and, for those who enter matrimony, the average age at marriage, the chance of getting divorced, and expected fraction of the total lifetime spent in widowhood. The same perspective can be applied in analyzing many other topics. For example, using the same approach, one could analyze passage of students through successive grades, taking into account dropouts and reentries, or the working life of people, taking into account unemployment and retirement.

Thus demographers deal with large- as well as small-scale units of analysis. Examples of large-scale units of analysis include the world as a whole, major population areas such as continents and nations, and subnational aggregates (such as regions). Among the small-scale units of analysis are individuals, couples, families, and households. In studying deaths, for instance, one may focus on death rates (number of deaths per 1000 persons) of large-scale units and examine how these rates are affected by a given set of public health activities, such as vaccinations or sanitary improvements. Alternatively, one may investigate the propensity of individuals to take preventive health measures, such as eating properly and exercising regularly, or to seek prompt medical help when indicated. Similarly, in studying reproduction, one may focus on birth rates (number of births per 1000 persons) of large-scale units and discuss how social change such as empowerment of women influences the birth rate, or at a less aggregate level, focus on parents' decisions regarding whether and when to have another child. In analyzing migration, one may focus on the association at the regional level between lack of job opportunities and net out-migration and, similarly, between abundance of job opportunities and net in-migration; at the individual level one may focus on migration-related decision-making.

At the aggregate level, demographic accounting focuses on how the three basic processes just mentioned, fertility, mortality, and migration, singly or in combination, change the size of the population of an area (e.g., region, nation) or segments of it (defined, for example, in terms of racial/ethnic group membership, rural versus urban residence, male–female distinction, or age categories). Based on such accounting, demographers can speculate, for example, about the possibility that Hispanics in the U.S. will within the next few decades outnumber African-Americans.

The characteristics age and sex enter demographic analysis at the aggregate level and individual level. At the latter level, more than any other characteristic, those of age and sex affect a person's survival chances, migration propensity, reproductive proclivity, and a host of other things. Therefore at this level, one thinks of age and sex as independent variables affecting the propensity to shift residence within the year, the probability of dying within the next 5 years, and so on. At the aggregate level demographers speak of the age–sex structure—the classification of people by age and sex—and its demographic, social, and economic implications. For example, a population with a younger age–sex structure (one with relatively numerous children under 15 years of age) has a built-in tendency to grow.

There are many characteristics other than age and sex that enter demographic analysis at different levels. Among these are race/ethnicity, education, literacy, occupation, income, marital status, employment, and residence (e.g., rural or urban; size of place). At the individual level, analysis of any of these may enter as an independent variable when analyzing survival chances, reproductive behavior, or mover–stayer tendency with respect to residence or a social-economic trait itself. At the aggregate level the focus may be on the composition of the population with respect to these characteristics, singly or in combination, or on the demographic, social, and economic implications thereof. For example, in what direction is the racial/ethnic composition of the U.S. population changing, and what implications, if any, does such a change have on the U.S. income distribution? In particular, is income inequality likely to increase along with the changing racial/ethnic makeup of the population? To give another example, in what way are the residential distributions (say, by city, suburb, rural area) of different racial/ethnic groups in the U.S. population changing and what are the implications of these changes for the prevalence of urban poverty in the United States?

## 1.3. THE SCOPE OF DEMOGRAPHY

In summary, demography is the study of the nature, components, and consequences of population dynamics (changes in population size and structure). The aim of this book is to give a coherent overview of population dynamics, from the world, regional, and individual country perspectives. The emphasis is on presenting the current knowledge regarding the size and structure of populations, changes therein, and their causes and consequences. In such an undertaking selectivity of topics and treatment is unavoidable. The selections reflect my conviction regarding what is essential in an overview meant for readers with little formal exposure to the scientific study of population dynamics.

## 1.4. ORGANIZATION OF THE BOOK

The presentation of the material in this book follows a somewhat unconventional format. Each chapter begins with a summary presentation of a set of basic material. This is followed by a set of questions and answers, covering many details. The paragraph-length explanations are designed to reinforce and supplement the information tested by the questions. Textbooks, journal articles, and other publications cited in the explanations are sources that contain additional information about the material covered.

Chapter 2 provides an overview of the ideas contributed by different authors toward developing a set of principles of population dynamics, its causes and consequences. Chapter 3 is a primer on demographic data and the nature of population change. Chapters 4, 5, and 6 deal with the three basic demographic processes, mortality, fertility, and migration. The remaining chapters, except the last one, are devoted to the implications of the basic demographic processes or of the resultant population change. Chapter 7 deals with population composition, Chapter 8 with spatial distribution, Chapter 9 with family, household, and women's status, Chapter 10 with food production, and Chapter 11 with economic development. Chapter 12 is devoted to population policies and programs.

CHAPTER 2

# *Population Theories and Conceptual Schemes*

Understanding population dynamics involves studying the particulars as instances of some general principles. A search for general principles of population dynamics has been going on for a long time. No one has discovered a definitive, all-encompassing, space-and-time invariant set of principles of population change, but many have contributed interesting ideas. A familiarity with some of the well-known ideas is expected of all population students. Let us start with Malthus. We will then go on to Marx and others, including the contributors to the formulation and reformulation of what has come to be known as the demographic transition theory.

## *2.1. MALTHUSIAN THEORY*

Thomas Robert Malthus (1766–1834), an English clergyman, became famous among population students for his *An Essay on the Principle of Population* (1798). In this essay, Malthus started with the following two postulates: "First, that food is necessary to the existence of man. Secondly, that the passion between the sexes is necessary, and will remain nearly in its present state." He then declared, "assuming then, my postulata as granted, I say that the power of population is indefinitely greater than the power in the earth to produce subsistence for man. Population, when unchecked, increases in a geometric ratio. Subsistence increases only in arithmetic ratio."

The main ideas of the Malthusian theory include the following: (i) for humans fecundity (biological capacity to reproduce) is great enough to permit the population to double in size each generation, (ii) actual fertility has never been as high as the fecundity, (iii) the checks on population growth imposed by reduced fertility tend to be less important than those imposed by mortality, and (iv) actual or threatened shortage of food had been the major force behind the checks on population growth (Petersen, 1975, p. 184).

The first two apply to all societies at almost all times. The third was generally true as of Malthus's time, although postponement of marriage and non-marriage were common then and they had significant effects on fertility. Malthus underestimated the extent of marital fertility control that was to become a major factor affecting population growth patterns. Malthus also failed to recognize that control on the timing of marriage was enforced through institutionalized regulations concerning such things as who inherits family property and when. This failure is reflected in the fourth idea.

Among the strengths and weaknesses of Malthus's essay are the following: (i) it described rather well the relationship between population change and economic growth in pre-industrial societies, (ii) The confusion between "what is" and "what ought to be" is a major problem in the essay, (iii) the full implications of the technological revolution underway in Malthus's time escaped due recognition in the essay. [With respect to (ii), note that Malthus disapproved of contraception "both on account of immorality and their tendency to remove a necessary stimulus to industry," and he automatically assumed that contraception, since it ought not to become popular, would never, in fact, be popular.]

Malthus wrote his essay in an era of rural societies, and his ideas still apply to such societies (Nam, 1994, p. 70). The moralist in him made Malthus discount the possibility that people might use birth control. What goes in a society need not always be consistent with "what ought to be" (Petersen, 1975). "He was aware ... of the Industrial Revolution, but he was skeptical of its long-run value." (Weeks, 1994, p. 65) "There are good reasons for using Malthus as a point of departure in the discussion of population theory. These are the reasons that made his work influential in his day and make it influential now." (Davis, 1955, p. 541)

Malthus has not been given due credit for some of the ideas he expounded in his writings. As Petersen (1975, p. 155) pointed out, Malthus did subscribe to the notions that: there is a negative association between fertility and socio–economic status, workers who move into middle-class income bracket would acquire middle-class values, and universal, free education is a sure way to improve the lot of the poor.

Neo-Malthusians subscribe to the idea that the world is overpopulated, advocate the practice of birth control, are pessimistic regarding the availability of resources for future economic growth, and are in favor of government-sponsored action programs to control population growth.

## 2.2. MARXIAN THEORY

According to the Marxian (1887) position with respect to the population question, (i) there is no "law of population" that applies universally to all societies all the time, (ii) poverty is the result of poor organization of society, and (iii) poverty is inevitable in capitalist societies.

An essential part of Marxian thesis is that poverty among the working class is attributable to the exploitation of the working class by the owners of capital. Marx and his colleague Engels believed that technology could help produce more food and other goods as needed. The Marxian position that organization is a major factor in population dynamics (Hawley, 1950, p. 152) continues to influence theory building even today.

## 2.3. COMPARISON OF THE MALTHUSIAN AND MARXIAN POSITIONS

By way of comparison and contrast, the Marxian position was optimistic while the Malthusian position was pessimistic with respect to economic development and improvement of living conditions, Marx treated population as a dependent variable whereas Malthus treated it as an independent variable, both Marx and Malthus allowed their perspectives to be colored by their ideological positions, and both continue today to influence the thinking of population matters (Nam, 1994, pp. 68–73). Note however, that some demographers have called upon their colleagues to "bury" the population theories of both Malthus and Marx (see e.g., Bogue, 1969, p. 17).

## 2.4. OTHER CONTRIBUTIONS TO POPULATION THEORY

Another contribution to population theories during the 19th and early 20th centuries is Dumont's *Principle of Social Capillarity* (1890), according to which people with mobility ambition restrict their fertility to enable them to take advantage of opportunities to move up the social ladder (Nam, 1994, p. 73).

In the 20th century, descriptive analyses of fertility, mortality, and migration differentials began to receive considerable attention; the so-called demographic transition theory was formulated and repeatedly reformulated; the use of typologies in developing conceptual schemes was proposed; causal modeling became popular; and a distinction was drawn between macroscopic models and microscopic models.

- Socioeconomic differentials in mortality, religious differentials in fertility, and marital status differentials in migration are examples of demographic differentials. The focus on descriptive analyses, particularly the documentation of differentials of the kind just mentioned, was prompted by the understandable tendency to put the search of "what" before that of the "why."

- An example of a typology is one that Petersen (1958) developed for migration, combining the forces or circumstances that caused the move with the change, if any, in the way of life of the mover, an instance being a change from farm to non-farm type occupation.
- Causal models are the same as the simultaneous-equation models in econometrics, although econometricians seldom use causal (path) diagrams connecting causes to effects by means of arrows.
- Macroscopic models focus on aggregate-level regularities whereas microscopic models focus on individual-level regularities (Nam, 1994, pp. 74–84). Malthusian theory; Marxian theory; the sociocultural approach that emphasizes, among other things, that the type of social and cultural systems in an area shape population processes; and the human ecological approach that focuses on the interrelationships among population processes, social organization, environment, and technology are all examples of macroscopic models. Decision-making models, built on the postulate that people are choice-makers and that they behave rationally when choosing between alternative courses of action, illustrate the microscopic approach. Demographers have given considerable attention to the impact of macro-level forces on individual-level behaviors.

Davis's (1963) theory of demographic change and response, for example, is concerned with how individuals respond to macro-level demographic changes such as a significant decline in mortality. Families with too many children find themselves under what might be called economic strain, inhibiting the ability of its members to take advantage of the opportunities to improve their economic well-being and relative socio-economic status, or prevent them from getting worse. Those who are at the early childbearing age, seeing this writing on the wall, take steps to protect their (economic) interests. Among the steps they might take are: postponement of marriage, remaining unmarried, migration, use of abortion, practice of infanticide, and use of contraception. (It is assumed that people are, in general, eager to improve their lot and in any case to avoid a fall in their relative socio-economic standing. It is further assumed that the conditions that produced mortality reduction also generated opportunities for individuals to improve their station in life.)

An example of a model that can be used to examine data at the macro and micro levels is Easterlin's (1973) relative income hypothesis, according to which fertility varies with relative income, i.e., the level of people's economic well-being relative to the one they have been accustomed to, e.g., when growing up. Survivors of small birth cohorts when they reach working age face relatively little competition and are likely to have higher fertility because they will be economically better off than they were accustomed to when growing up. Similarly, survivors of large birth cohorts when they reach working age usually face intense competition and will probably have lower fertility because they are likely to be economically worse off than they have been accustomed to when growing up. At the macro level the hypothesis has received some support, but much less so at the micro level (Nam, 1994, p. 208; Weeks, 1994, pp. 82–83).

## 2.5. DEMOGRAPHIC TRANSITION THEORY

The classic version of the demographic transition theory states, among other things, that in low-income, agrarian societies, fertility is high and stable whereas mortality is high and fluctuating; that with economic development, mortality begins to decline while fertility lags behind, although eventually it also begins to decline; that as further reductions in mortality become difficult to attain, the fertility level approaches equality with mortality level; and that when fertility and mortality levels are low, the latter remains stable and the former fluctuates, increasing in "good" times and decreasing in "bad" times.

There are demographers who hold that demographic transition theory is almost dead (see e.g., Alter, 1992). A number of alternative theories have been proposed in the literature to take the place of demographic transition theory, but none of them has gained wide acceptance (Hirschman, 1994, p. 214).

Among the weaknesses of the classic version of the demographic transition theory are the following: (i) The framework failed to recognize that fertility level may rise before falling and may start declining even before mortality transition starts. (ii) The framework ignored migration altogether. In a number of countries, such as Ireland, emigration played a major role in tempering the mortality and fertility transitions, as Davis, 1963, pointed out. Rural-to-urban migration within

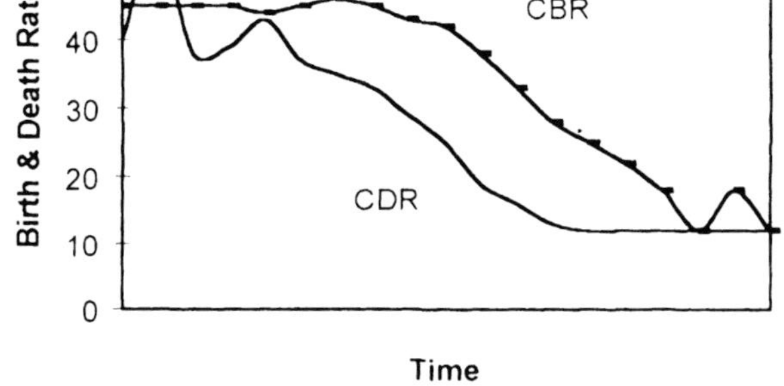


*Figure 2.1.* Classical Demographic Transition.

countries was also a factor in shaping the fertility and mortality patterns in early stages of transition (Friedlander, 1969). (iii) The framework is based on the untenable assumption that there is a simple association between economic development and demographic change. In France the demographic transition got well underway long before industrialization took hold. In England, on the other hand, industrialization was well underway before sustained fertility decline started. (iv) Furthermore, the timing of the onset of mortality and fertility decline cannot be predicted from the framework.

It has long been recognized that the classic version of demographic theory was an abstraction from the European experience. It did not precisely fit any country's actual experience. The general idea that in all societies fertility and mortality make the transition from high levels to low levels with social and economic development is valid. The framework serves as a model with which the actual experience of any country can be compared. Focus may then turn to accounting for the differences identified. In fact, it is this strategy that led to identifying the so-called weaknesses of the classic statement.

### 2.5.1. *Caldwell's Modification*

One of the attempts to modify the classic version of demographic transition theory was undertaken by Caldwell (1976). His "wealth-flow" hypothesis holds that in pre-industrial societies the lifetime benefits that parents receive from their children far outweigh the cost of bringing them up and that this direction of flow of net benefits reverses itself with economic development, but it may also do so in the absence of economic development, e.g., through "Westernization," which occurs by exposure to Western ideas. When parents stand to derive net benefits from their children, fertility remains high, and when they do not (that is, when the costs of raising children far outweigh the actual or potential benefits parents could expect from raising children) fertility declines. Note that "wealth flow" is a difficult variable to measure because it has economic as well as non-economic components, the latter including services, deference, obligations, and emotional gratification. Caldwell has taken the position that the way to empirically examine his theory is to use ethnographic investigations, which involve talking to people informally.

### 2.5.2. *The European Fertility Project*

Among the empirical studies that picked holes in the classical version of the demographic transition theory, the European Fertility Project was by far the most ambitious. The project, undertaken by scholars associated with Princeton University, led to identifying a number of important findings. One of these was that economic development was not a necessary condition for fertility to start declining in Europe. The spread of secularization was identified as a precursor to fertility decline. To give one example, Belgium is a small country, consisting of the French-speaking south with heavy industry and mining and the Flemish-speaking agriculturist in the north. In examining the fertility decline on the basis of small administrative units called arrondissements, Lesthaeghe (1977) found the expected north–south differences. Lesthaeghe then constructed a variable he called secularization, and interpreted its relationship with fertility to mean that the rejection of traditional values and modes of thinking explained a substantial fraction of fertility differences between arrondissements. Secularization was measured by percentage vote non-Catholic.

### 2.5.3. Coale's Necessary Conditions

According to Coale (1973), the necessary conditions for any sustained fall in marital fertility are that birth control (within marriage) must become a matter of choice, must appear attractive, i.e., bringing in net benefits, and must be practicable (e.g., in terms of knowledge and mastery of means). The second condition is given implicit attention in the demographic transition theory, which holds that socioeconomic changes alter the cost–benefit mix of childbearing.

## 2.6. QUESTIONS AND ANSWERS*

**FOR EACH OF THE QUESTIONS IN SECTIONS 2.6.1. TO 2.6.5., STATE TRUE OR FALSE AND EXPLAIN.**

### 2.6.1. Malthusian Theory

1. Malthus wrote his essay in reaction to the speculations of some of his contemporaries regarding the perfectibility of humans.
2. One of the postulates Malthus used in developing his theory was that the power of population is far greater than the power of the earth to produce food for all.
3. Malthus used the term positive checks to refer to causes of death and preventive check to refer to practices affecting fertility.
4. Malthus assumed that it is pain–avoidance rather than pleasure–pursuit that stimulates actions in life.
5. One of the most strongly criticized aspects of Malthusian theory is the conclusion that poverty is an inevitable consequence of population growth.
6. Marx and Malthus were contemporary demographers.

*Answers start on page 18.

### 2.6.2. Marx versus Malthus

7. Marx took exception to the Malthusian conclusion that population tends to outstrip resources.
8. Malthus virtually ignored technological development while Marx recognized its potential.

### 2.6.3. Influence of the 19th Century Theories on the 20th Century Actions and Research

9. Marxist countries started in the latter half of the 20th century to approve the neo-Malthusian approach involving governmental intervention in population matters.
10. Dumont's social capillarity theory was influential on 20th-century research on the social-mobility hypothesis of fertility.

### 2.6.4. Demographic Transition

11. Warren S. Thompson was the first to outline what later on became known as the demographic transition framework.
12. Frank Notestein supplied the linkage of fertility and mortality transitions to modernization.
13. In the classical formulation of the demographic transition theory, only three stages are distinguished.
14. The term "second demographic transition" is used in the writings on the fertility and mortality transitions that currently occur in the less developed countries.
15. The specific factors and forces that produce transitions of fertility and mortality from high to low levels are likely to differ from one country to another.
16. Among Asian countries, Japan, Hong Kong, and Singapore have completed demographic transition; India and Iraq are at about the halfway mark; and Afghanistan is way behind all others.
17. The demographic transition theory has been criticized for ignoring migration altogether.

### 2.6.5. Other 20th Century Theories

18. Davis's theory of demographic change and response holds that population pressure prompts people to panic.

19. Demographers use the term secularization for people's tendency not to vote for candidates with affiliations to religious organizations.

20. Easterlin's concept of one's relative income means income of one's close relatives.

**IN EACH OF THE QUESTIONS IN SECTIONS 2.6.6. TO 2.6.10., FOUR ANSWERS ARE SUGGESTED, AT LEAST ONE OF WHICH IS CORRECT. IDENTIFY THE CORRECT ANSWER(S) AND EXPLAIN**

### 2.6.6. *Malthusian Theory*

1. Which of the following are the postulates of the Malthusian theory?
   A. Food is necessary for survival
   B. Population's power to grow exceeds the earth's power to supply food
   C. The "passion between the sexes" is necessary and time-invariant
   D. Population when unchecked increases in geometric ratio

2. According to Malthus:
   A. Fertility is negatively associated with socio-economic status
   B. Upwardly mobile people acquire the values of the class of their destination
   C. Educating the poor is a sure way to improve their lot in life
   D. Real populations increase exponentially

### 2.6.7. *Demographic Transition*

3. Among the weaknesses of the classic version of the demographic transition theory are:
   A. Descriptively it does not fit with the experience of any real population
   B. A simple relationship is assumed between population change and economic development
   C. Its predictive power is limited
   D. The theory is an empirical generalization rather than a deductive one

4. Which of the following illustrate "exceptions" to the expectations derived from the demographic transition theory?
   A. In France demographic transition got well underway long before the country started industrializing
   B. In some countries fertility began to fall before sustained reduction in mortality started
   C. In some countries fertility rose before it started its sustained downward course
   D. Sri Lanka has almost completed demographic transition

5. Which of the following are the necessary conditions for sustained fertility decline, according to Coale?
   A. The acceptance of calculated choice as a valid element in marital fertility
   B. The perception of advantages from reduced fertility
   C. Knowledge and mastery of effective means of birth control
   D. A well-organized family planning program under the government auspices

### 2.6.8. *Marxian Theory*

6. The Marxian position with respect to the population question is:
   A. There is no "law of population" that applies universally to all societies all the time
   B. Poverty is the result of poor organization of the society
   C. Poverty is inevitable in capitalist societies
   D. Malthus erred in his notion of how or why population grew

### 2.6.9. *Macro-Micro Distinction*

7. Which of the following are macroscopic approaches to population analysis?
   A. Malthusian theory
   B. Marxian theory
   C. Human ecology
   D. Decision-making models

### 2.6.10. *Davis's Theory of Demographic Change and Response*

8. Which of the following apply to Davis's (1963) theory of demographic change and response? When confronted with population pressure
   A. As a first response people begin working harder
   B. Some family members migrate
   C. It is the prospect of rising prosperity rather than fear of poverty that motivate people to limit fertility
   D. People will respond to mortality reduction only if they are aware of it

**FOR EACH OF THE QUESTIONS IN SECTIONS 2.6.11. TO 2.6.14., FIVE POSSIBLE ANSWERS ARE GIVEN, ONLY ONE OF WHICH IS CORRECT. IDENTIFY THE CORRECT ANSWER AND EXPLAIN.**

### 2.6.11. *Malthusian Theory*

1. Malthus was reacting to the writings of
   A. Marx

B. Mills
C. Godwin
D. Plato
E. Ricardo

2. Malthus saw population pressure inevitably leading to
   A. poverty
   B. paternalism
   C. war
   D. communism
   E. capitalism

3. Malthus used the term moral restraint to mean which of the following?
   A. Postponement of marriage and avoidance of pre-marital sexual gratification
   B. Living according to the Biblical rule: "be fruitful and multiply"
   C. Teaching children proper behavior
   D. Avoiding extremes of all kinds
   E. Showing the left cheek when slapped on the right

4. A statement inconsistent with Malthus's theory is:
   A. Food is essential for survival
   B. The passion between sexes is necessary and time-invariant
   C. Food production increases in arithmetical progression
   D. Population size increases like the numbers 1, 2, 3, 4, 5, 6, 7
   E. Population is kept within the limits of subsistence by positive and preventive checks

5. In his essay, Malthus is not guilty of which of the following?
   A. He ruled out widespread usage of contraception
   B. He underestimated the power of technological change
   C. He confused "what will be" with "what ought to be"
   D. He gave more importance to mortality than to fertility
   E. He overemphasized the role of politics on population matters

### *2.6.12. Marxian Theory*

6. According to Marx's interpretation, Malthus's theory applied, if at all, only to:
   A. Communist countries
   B. Socialist societies
   C. Capitalist societies
   D. Military dictatorships
   E. Colonies of imperial powers

### 2.6.13. Demographic Transition Theory

7. At which stage of the demographic transition should one expect accelerating population growth?
   A. At at no stage
   B. During stage I, when both fertility and mortality are high
   C. During stage II, the transition stage
   D. During stage III, when both mortality and fertility are low
   E. At all stages

### 2.6.14. Easterlin's Relative Income Hypothesis

8. Easterlin's relative income hypothesis relates fertility to the ratio of your income to:
   A. The average income of your relatives
   B. Your parents' income when you were growing up
   C. The average income of your friends
   D. The average income of your community
   E. The average income of your country

❖ ❖ ❖ ❖

### 2.6.1. Answers

1. True. The first edition carried a sub-title: With remarks on the speculations of Mr. Godwin, M. Condorcet, and other writers. In the introduction, he explicitly stated that while he read with great interest some of the speculations on the perfectibility of human society, he saw great difficulties in achieving them.
2. False. His two postulates were about the need for food and the urge for sex. The statement about the power of population was not put forward as a postulate. "Assuming then, my postulata as granted, I say that the power of population is indefinitely greater than the power in the earth to produce subsistence for man. Population, when unchecked, increases in a geometrical ratio. Subsistence increases only in an arithmetical ratio...." (Malthus, 1798, pp. 11)
3. True. Positive checks include "wars, excesses, and many others which it would be in our power to avoid," but lack of food is often a major factor that weakens and destroys the human frame. The principal "preventive check" is "moral restraint" (postponement of marriage with no extramarital sexual gratification). Other preventive checks include promiscuity, homosexuality, adultery, contraception, and abortion.

4. False. "... if he has the opportunity of exchanging his superfluous food for conveniences and comforts, he will acquire a taste for these conveniences, and his habits will be formed accordingly." So wrote Malthus in his *The Principles of Political Economy* (pp. 224–225). He did subscribe, however, to the view that an actual or threatened shortage of food was the most important reason for late marriage and high death rates. One could argue, therefore, that in his view, satisfying necessities of life such as food was paramount in people's minds; when necessities are satisfied, however, other considerations begin to influence behavior.

5. True. Marx among others maintained that poverty was not the end result of population growth, instead poorly organized society was to be blamed for it.

6. False. Karl Marx (1818–1883) was a teenager when Thomas Robert Malthus (1766–1834) died. Although the writings on population form only a very small fraction of Marx's total scholarly output, whatever he wrote has been highly influential. Malthus is regarded as one of the most influential figures in the development of population studies. He was also a major figure in the development of economics.

### 2.6.2. Answers

7. True. Marx did believe that technological development would increase the availability of food.

8. True. In fact, one of the criticisms of Malthus has been that he underestimated the implications of the Industrial Revolution that was underway during his lifetime.

### 2.6.3. Answers

9. True. China provides an example. In 1949 Chairman Mao made his famous statement that people are the most precious of all things. This was consistent with the usual denial of the existence of any population problem. But the results of the 1953 census, revealing that the population was growing at the annual rate of 2%, led to the adoption of measures (e.g., relaxation of restrictions on induced abortion) to control births. By 1956, birth control as a national policy seemed to have been firmly established. But with the introduction of Mao's program of Great Leap Forward in 1957 the government's position swung to the pronatalist side. Early in the 1960s, the campaign to promote birth control was resumed. However, this was virtually abandoned in 1966, this time because of the Cultural Revolution. In 1970 the country

embarked upon the current population control program, which has turned out to be one of the most effective ones in the world (Cho, 1984).

10. True. See, for example, Westoff (1953) for a discussion of the influence of Dumont's ideas on the development of the social mobility hypothesis as a new focus in fertility research. This thrust was very pronounced in the design of the Family Growth in Metropolitan America study (Westoff *et al.*, 1961).

### 2.6.4. Answers

11. True. Thompson (1929) tried to generalize the European experience by classifying European countries into three groups according to the levels of birth and death rates.

12. True. Notestein (1945) placed the three stages of the demographic transition in the broad context of modernization.

13. True. Notestein (1945) named them high-growth potential, transitional, and incipient decline.

14. False. Van de Kaa (1987) has discussed under the heading of "Europe's second demographic transition," the implications of low-fertility in Europe, in particular the imminent population decline in the absence of net immigration.

15. True. As Nam put it, all societies make fertility and mortality transitions from high to low levels, but "each society may have a unique combination of factors that produces it and a varying time period during which it occurs." (Nam, 1994, p. 40. Also see Freedman, 1995).

16. True. Demographers frequently have estimated how far different countries have come in respect to completing the demographic transition. One of the latest such exercises is that of Tanaka (1989), according to which, Japan, Hong Kong, and Singapore have completed the transition; Cypress, Israel, Korea, and China are nearing completion; Sri Lanka, Malaysia, and Thailand are among those that are more than three-quarters of the way there; India, Iran, and Iraq are halfway through; Pakistan, Bangladesh. Jordan, Syria, Saudi Arabia, among others, are far behind; and Afghanistan is still close to the starting point. (Also see Freedman, 1995).

17. True. Davis (1963), discussed the part migration played in the case of Ireland and Friedlander (1969) pointed out that rural-to-urban migration within countries was an influential force in determining the course of fertility and mortality in the early stages of the demographic transition. To Nam (1994, p. 36), leaving "migration out of the transition framework is thus both conceptually unsound and empirically fallacious."

### 2.6.5. Answers

18. False. Davis (1963) did emphasize that there are many possible responses to population pressure, but panic is not one of them. Among the usual responses are, working harder, postponing marriage, remaining unmarried, and migrating in search of opportunities.

19. False. The demographic usage is consistent with the dictionary definition of the term: imbued with secularism, i.e., indifference to or rejection of religion or religious considerations, particularly the idea that living things are under the influence of other-worldly powers. Measuring it is not easy, however, especially when one has to do it on the basis of secondary data.

20. False. The reference is to one's income as an adult in relation to the income level one is accustomed to when growing up (i.e., the income level of parents when one was in late childhood).

### 2.6.6. Answers

1. A and C. The others are deductions.

2. A, B, and C. Malthus has not been given due credit for espousing these ideas, perhaps because these ideas were discussed not in his essay but in the *Principles of Political Economy*. See, however, Petersen (1975, p. 155). As for choice D, note that Malthus maintained, on the contrary, that actual populations tend to oscillate around its means of subsistence? increasing in "good" times (when food is plentiful) and decreasing in "bad" times (when food is scarce).

### 2.6.7. Answers

3. A, B, C, and D. It should be recognized that no abstract model fits individual instances perfectly. But in this case the complaint has been that the model failed to recognize factors such as that fertility rose at first in some countries before starting on a declining course and fertility decline started well before industrialization got underway. Another complaint has been that it is an inductive model, patched together from the historical experiences of various countries, rather than a deductive one, based on a set of postulates. It has also been a concern that the model is not of much use in predicting precisely what is likely to happen in countries that are yet to start demographic transition or are on the way.

4. A, B, C, and D. In contrast to the situation in France, industrialization in England was well underway when demographic transition started. With respect to choice D, note that Sri Lanka's total fertility rate as of 1994 was 2.5 children per woman and life expectancy at birth is 73 years. What is significant about this

case is that this is an instance of a poor country moving steadily through the demographic transition.

5. A, B, and C. That choice D is not a necessary condition is obvious from the fact that sustained fertility decline started in Europe and America long before the invention of family planning programs.

### 2.6.8. Answers

6. A, B, and C. Marx did not quarrel with Malthus regarding how or why population grew.

### 2.6.9. Answers

7. A, B, and C. Decision-making models are microscopic models, because they emphasize how each individual makes choices between alternative courses of action. Many such models assume that people approach such situations rationally. Some models use the idea that when people make choices they maximize, subject to resource constraints, the overall satisfaction, considering the consequences of each course of action, their probability of occurrence, and their desirability.

### 2.6.10. Answers

8. A, B, C, and D. The emphasis on the link between changes in the social environment and the deliberate behavior on the part of the individuals implicitly requires that people become aware of the changes in question.

### 2.6.11. Answers

1. C: Malthus was reacting to the writings of people representing what has come to be called the utopian thought. Godwin was one of the representatives. In Godwin's view there was no question that food production will keep up with population increase. He believed that in the far future when zero population growth would be necessary, the world would achieve it with no births and no deaths—sexual urge would be dissipated and conquest of death would be complete (see Petersen, 1975, p. 150–151). It was to this type of utopian thought that Malthus reacted. Just as Godwin overemphasized the power of reason to control human affairs and transform society, so did Malthus overemphasize the imbalance of two biological drives, hunger and sexuality (Petersen, 1975, p. 151).
2. A: Poverty, which according to Malthus was a natural consequence of his "principle of population."

3. A: Postponement of marriage, with no pre-marital sexual gratification.

4. D: As Malthus put it "the human species would increase at a geometric rate, doubling every 25 years or so, while under the most favorable circumstances, food production would increase as in an arithmetic progression, with constant additions every 25 years, resulting in within two centuries a population-to-food ratio of 256 to 9."

5. E: He did, however, oppose the English poor laws, which provided welfare benefits to the poor. His reasoning was that such programs undermine work ethics and discourage prudence. We hear similar arguments today: "Poor people who get support from others have no incentive to work hard or to be prudent about having children."

### 2.6.12. Answers

6. C: The argument is that the organization of production in capitalist societies creates unemployment and keeps wage rates low, thereby perpetuating poverty among the working class.

### 2.6.13. Answers

7. C: When both fertility and mortality are declining, with the former lagging behind. the rate of population growth would increase, reach a maximum, and eventually decrease.

### 2.6.14. Answers

8. B: Your parents' income while you were growing up determined your tastes and preferences. When you start thinking about raising a family, you think about the family size you can afford if you want your family to have the same standard of living that you were accustomed to when you were growing up.

CHAPTER 3

# *Demography, Demographic Data, and the Nature of Population Change*

As Shakespeare said, all the world is a stage and we people are the actors. Each of us enter the stage at birth and exit from it at death. We play many parts, such as getting ill and getting well, getting married and getting divorced, staying in a place or moving out of it, climbing up or sliding down the social ladder, and all the time getting inexorably older. Demography is the scientific study of this ageless drama. Demographers focus on certain features of us, the actors, and the drama we play. How many of us are around at any given time? Are our numbers growing, declining, or unchanging? How diverse are we in our traits and roles? How does this diversity change over time and space? How are such changes (in size, makeup, and diversity) produced, with what consequences? To study such questions, demographers use data collected in censuses, registration systems, and sample surveys as well as materials assembled by administrators to keep track of what they do.

## *3.1. THE FIELD OF DEMOGRAPHY*

Demography is the scientific study of the size and structure of populations and the components, causes, and consequences of changes in these. Population structure stands for composition (makeup) and spatial spread of people. Fertility, mortality, migration, and social mobility are different processes which separately or in combination produce population change.

Fertility process adds members to the population through reproduction; mortality process takes away members through death; geographic mobility redistributes population spatially; and social mobility process (involving change of status of people, e.g., from being single to being married) relocates population socially.

Changes in population composition and distribution are a result of the combined operation of fertility, mortality, migration, and social mobility. To understand this, consider the age composition of a population. Suppose a population was counted twice, say, 10 years apart, each time recording the age of each person. Suppose at the second time there was a higher percentage of people in the older ages (say, 65 years and older) and a lower percentage at younger ages (say, under 10 years of age) than at the first counting. If migration was not a factor, a drop in fertility during the 10-year-period and a drop in mortality that disproportionately favored the elderly could have produced the observed change in age composition. If migration was a factor, then the age pattern of movement in and out of the population is relevant. For example, if disproportionately more young people moved out and disproportionately more old people moved in, that combination would partly account for the change in age composition observed. All these processes usually operate simultaneously and in any of a number of possible combinations, and one would have to examine the net result in order to account for the change in age composition observed.

To account for changes in racial/ethnic composition, one starts with a study of the factors (fertility, mortality, and migration) responsible for changes in the membership of each racial/ethnic group. This reveals which racial/ethnic group is growing faster and which one is growing slower. Differential growth rate produces shifts in their relative numbers, i.e., in their composition. To account for changes in marital status composition, one examines, mortality, migration, and changes in marital status.

Demographers usually go beyond the kind of demographic accounting just described. If a fertility level is dropping, for example, demographers ask, why it is doing so? If a mortality level worsens for a group, one would want to know why. In the study of causes and consequences of such changes, demographers use ideas borrowed from social and biological sciences.

## 3.2. DEMOGRAPHIC DATA

The major sources of demographic data are censuses, registration systems, sample surveys, and administrative records.

### 3.2.1. Censuses

According to a standard definition, a population census is "the total process of collecting, compiling, evaluating, analyzing and publishing or otherwise disseminating demographic, economic and social data pertaining, at a specified time, to all persons in a country or in a well-defined part of a country." (United Nations, 1980)

Among the essential features of a modern census are: universality, simultaneity, individual enumeration, and defined periodicity. The census should include everyone who is supposed to be included. The census count must pertain as nearly as possible to the same well-defined point of time and information recorded must pertain to the same well-defined reference period (e.g., income during the 12 months preceding the census date). Each individual and their living quarters must be enumerated separately and their characteristics recorded accordingly. Put differently, group enumeration, i.e., ascertaining the number of persons in different specific groups (e.g., age-sex category) is not enough. Finally, censuses must be taken at regular intervals, e.g., every 10 years.

Errors are not rare in census data. Failure to enumerate some people who should have been enumerated and enumerating some people more than once constitute coverage errors and recording wrong information (e.g., incorrect age) about anyone who is enumerated is a content error. To check the accuracy of census data the U.S. Bureau of the Census uses (i) post-enumeration survey, (ii) post-censal local review, (iii) statistical follow-up of births which occurred in the previous year, people enumerated in a previous census, etc., and (iv) case-by-case matching. Post-enumeration survey is very much like repeating the census in a sample of areas using highly skilled interviewers. This method is used by almost all modern censuses. Post-censal local review involves submitting census counts for review by local (e.g., city) authorities who generally have their own estimates of the population count in the area under their jurisdiction. As for the follow-up procedure, one could use the simple fact that, except for deaths and migration, all those enumerated at the last census must be enumerated at the current census. For example, when censuses are taken every 10 years, those who had been enumerated in the age group 10–14 at the last census must be enumerated in the age group 20–24 at the current census, except for those who died and those who left to take up residence elsewhere. Finally, for matching on a case-by-case basis, one could use existing lists such as that of people receiving benefits from the Social Security system.

Two different ways of attaching people to places are distinguished in modern censuses. The *de facto* count is the number of people enumerated in a census according to where people are on the census date (e.g., April 1, 1990) or the census moment (e.g., at the start of April 1, 1990). This count is distinguished from the *de jure* count, which is based on attaching people to their legal (usual) place of residence. The *de facto* count is more common on a worldwide basis than the *de jure* count. The latter concept is somewhat ambiguous. Legal residence, usual residence, and other criteria could be used to determine where a person "belongs." But even these run into difficulties. For example, in some countries there is no unique definition of "legal residence." (Shryock and Siegel, 1971, p. 94)

### 3.2.2. Registration Systems

Vital registration systems keep a continuous record of vital events such as births and deaths in a defined territory. They first began in Europe as an ecclesiastical function of maintaining weekly records of baptisms, weddings, and burials. They are more complete in economically advanced countries. When complete they are an important source of information for making population estimates for intercensal or post-censal dates. To make such estimates one also needs migration data. Migration is not recorded as part of the usual vital registration system. There are, however, countries that maintain what are known as population registers (see below), in which demographic and socio-economic data, including migration, are recorded continually.

Before turning to population registers, a few more comments about vital registration systems are in order. As originally conceived by William Farr in the 1830s, vital events referred to transitions involving health, sickness, diseases, or death. Later the concept was also extended to cover births. Today, however, the term is used broadly to cover marriage, divorce, annulment, separation, adoption, and legitimation, in addition to birth and death. Some writers apply it to migration also.

Population register, as just mentioned, is a system of data collection that records, on a continuous basis, demographic and socio-economic characteristics of a population. Typically, at birth or at the time of in-migration a card or a file is opened for each person, which is updated whenever the person experiences important events such as changing residence or getting married. This updating continues until the person dies or leaves the area. Many countries in Europe (e.g., Norway, Sweden, Denmark, Finland, the Netherlands) and a number of countries outside Europe (e.g., Israel, Taiwan) maintain population registers. When complete, the population register combines the functions of censuses and vital registration systems; i.e., from the population register, if it is complete, one can obtain a snap shot of the population at any given time point as well as the flow data on such events as births, deaths, and migration during any given time interval. The Netherlands chose to bypass the census scheduled for 1980 on the ground that the population register supplied the kind of data the census was expected to provide.

### 3.2.3 Sample Surveys

The sample survey is a widely used research strategy that collects information about a part of a population with a view to making inferences about the whole. Sample surveys are cheaper than censuses, for determining a given amount of information. Examples of sample surveys include the following: The U.S. government conducts (within the U.S.) the monthly Current Population Survey, the continuous National Health Interview Survey, and many other sample surveys.

Multinational surveys include, the World Fertility Survey (1974–1982) and the Demographic and Health Surveys (since mid-1980s).

Estimates from sample surveys are subject to sampling errors. To see this, imagine calculating the U.S. average family income from different samples of the same size, each drawn according to the same procedure; the estimates vary from sample to sample and none of them may be the same as the average calculated without content or coverage errors from a census.

Sampling is involved in many modern censuses. Because of the burden placed on respondents and because of cost considerations, it has become a common practice to limit the number of questions to be asked of everyone to a few basic ones and ask a greater number of questions to a sample of persons.

When, as is often the case, investigators find that they need their own primary data to examine their research questions, they collect the needed data using sample surveys. To give one example, in 1938 a committee was formed in the United States to launch an inquiry into the social and psychological factors affecting fertility. The efforts of this committee led to a sample survey and a series of research reports constituting what has come to be known as the Indianapolis Fertility Study (Kiser and Whelpton, 1953). To give another example, a conference in the mid-1950s sponsored by the Milbank Memorial Fund initiated plans for a study of urban fertility in the United States. The first phase of the resultant research involved interviewing 1165 couples, each with a very young second child and residing in one or another of the large metropolitan areas of the United States. Later on the couples were interviewed a second and a third time. (See Bumpass and Westoff, 1970, for the final report of the study, which investigated the question why some couples have more children while others have few.)

### 3.2.4. *Administrative Records*

As mentioned, census and the so-called population registers belong to the category of administrative records, because they have been created with some administrative purpose in mind. Examples of other administrative records that provide demographic information include immigration and emigration records, passport statistics, and records on social security recipients. Mention must be made also of medical records and records kept by birth control clinics. These are especially interesting if they contain follow-up information.

## 3.3. PUBLICATIONS CONTAINING DEMOGRAPHIC DATA

Each country has its own program for publishing demographic data. For example, the sources of population data for the United States include census reports and *Current Population Reports* published by the U.S. Bureau of the

Census, *Monthly Vital Statistics Reports*, and annual summaries of them published by the National Center for Health Statistics.

International compilations are available in sources such as the *United Nations' Demographic Yearbook*, which, as the name suggests, is an annual publication. In some years special attention is given to a particular topic, e.g., mortality or fertility. There is virtually no other publication that brings together as much demographic information for as many countries as does the *U.N. Demographic Yearbook*.

There are many professional journals that publish studies on population dynamics. Among those in English are *Demography*, *Population Studies*, *Studies in Family Planning*, *Population and Development Review*, *American Demographics*, *Social Biology*, and *International Migration Review*. Many professional associations have their own official journals. For example, the Indian Population Association publishes *Demography, India*. A quarterly called *Population Index* publishes annotated bibliography of population-related publications. Sociological, economic, and statistical journals also publish materials on demography. Examples are *American Sociological Review*, *Journal of Political Economy*, and *Journal of the American Statistical Association*. It should be emphasized that with the development of computer technology, demographic data in machine-readable form have become readily available. Government and private agencies make such data files available to users.

## 3.4. USERS OF DEMOGRAPHIC DATA

Demographic data are used by many people for many purposes. In the United States, several government agencies are mandated to use demographic data: federal funds are allocated to states and state funds are allocated to counties for various purposes on the basis of population size or composition. Insurance companies fix premiums on the basis of mortality data. Demographers and social scientists use demographic data to study how population dynamics are interrelated with social and economic dynamics. Marketing specialists use demographic data to forecast demands for various goods and services.

## 3.5. DEMOGRAPHY VERSUS POPULATION STUDIES

Some writers (e.g., Petersen, 1975) distinguish between demography and population studies; many do not (e.g., Weeks, 1994; Nam, 1994). Those who do think of demography as little more than gathering, compiling, statistical analysis, and technical presentation of population data. In their view population studies has a broader scope, placing population in its social and economic context.

According to Bogue (1969, p. 4), however, efforts to make such distinctions have met with little success.

## 3.6. NATURE OF POPULATION CHANGE

### 3.6.1. Changing Size

The size of the world's population can only be roughly guessed for very early times. More credible estimates are available for recent dates. About 6000 years ago, the size of the world's population was most probably less than 100 million. It grew to about 300 million by the beginning of the Christian Era and to one-half of one billion by the beginning of the 16th century. The one billion mark was hit early in the 19th century.

Thus, it took all of human history, up to the beginning of the 19th century, for the world's population to reach one billion. But each successive billion was added in progressively shorter time: the two billion mark was reached around 1930, the three billion mark around 1960, the four billion mark by 1975, and the five billion mark by 1987. It is almost certain that there will be more than six billion of us around when the 21st century arrives.

The world's population was growing very slowly for most of human history because of high and widely fluctuating death rate (the number of deaths per 1000 persons). When people began to settle down in stable farming communities about 10,000 years ago, the world's population growth is believed to have started to accelerate slightly. The speculation is that stable food supplies probably increased birth rates (the number of births per 1000 persons) slightly and had a depressing effect on death rates. But the relatively more dense settlement pattern is believed to have helped communicable diseases to spread more quickly, and as a consequence

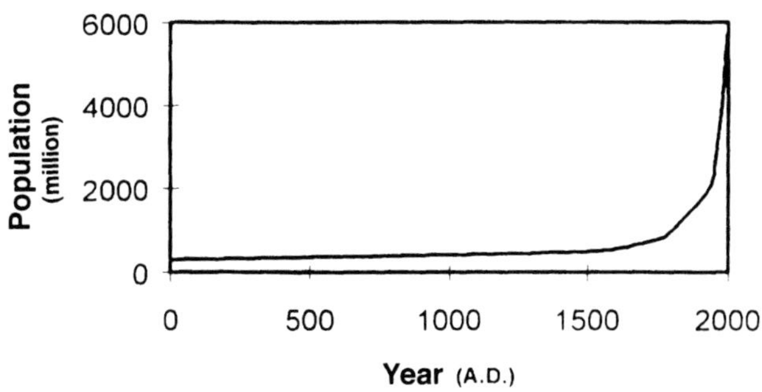


*Figure 3.1.* World's population from the beginning of Christian era.

death rates may have increased. On balance, however, the result was probably more births than deaths (Weeks, 1994, p. 32).

### 3.6.2. Changing Distribution

Some regions were able to achieve sustained mortality decline earlier than others. Those regions where sustained mortality decline started first were also the first to experience accelerated population growth. Northern and Western Europe and North America were in the forefront in these respects. They were followed by the Southern and Eastern European countries (with a time lag) and still later by the currently less developed countries. A consequence of this regional difference in population growth rate pattern has been that the geographic distribution of the world's population (by major regions) has undergone drastic changes (see Table 3.1).

Asia's share of the world's population in 1750 was 65%, which declined to 55% by 1950 and has increased since then. The combined share of Europe and North America was 20% in 1750, 26% in 1850, 29% in 1950, and has declined since then. Africa's share was 13% in 1750, 8% in 1850, 9% in 1950 and has increased since then. Latin America's share of the world's population has been increasing since 1750. The combined share of New Zealand and Australia (not shown) was 0.27% in 1750, 0.17% in 1850, 0.52% in 1950 and has remained close to 0.5% since then.

### 2.6.3. Growth Cycles

In discussing population change, the concept of growth cycle is helpful. See Table 3.2 for a hypothetical example. A growth cycle could result from a combination of a time-invariant birth rate and a temporary decline in death rate.

A similar scenario is shown in Table 3.3, in which the growth rate declines

*Table 3.1.* Major Regional Shares of the World's Population: 1650–2000[a]

| Year | World | Europe & North America | Latin America | Africa | Asia |
|---|---|---|---|---|---|
| 1650 | 100 | 0.191 | 0.022 | 0.183 | 0.600 |
| 1750 | 100 | 0.199 | 0.015 | 0.130 | 0.652 |
| 1850 | 100 | 0.256 | 0.028 | 0.081 | 0.633 |
| 1950 | 100 | 0.294 | 0.066 | 0.088 | 0.547 |
| 2000 | 100 | 0.178 | 0.086 | 0.143 | 0.588 |

[a]Calculated from Weeks (1994, Table 2.3, p.47)

*Table 3.2.* Hypothetical Examples of Growth Rate Cycles, when the Birth Rate Remains Time-Invariant at 35 Births per 1000 Persons Per Year, while the Death Rate First Decline and then Increases

| Year | 1990 | 1991 | 1992 | 1993 | 1994 |
|---|---|---|---|---|---|
| Death rage | 35 | 34 | 33 | 34 | 35 |
| Growth rate (%) | 0.0 | 0.1 | 0.2 | 0.1 | 0.0 |

and then returns to its original level of 0.0, on account of a rise followed by a fall in the death rate. In another scenario, the death rate remains time invariant, while the birth rate increases and later returns to the original level. The post-World War II "baby boom" approximated this pattern. Yet another scenario is for both the birth and death rates to decline from a high-but-equal state to a low-but-equal state, with the birth rate lagging behind the death rate during the transition (see Table 3.4).

### 3.6.4. *Migration as a Factor*

Migration from Europe started with the European voyages of discovery and conquests in the 16th century. Before 1800, however, this movement was of relatively small volume. Emigration played a major part in some countries, such as Ireland, to temper the mortality and fertility transitions (Davis, 1963; Nam, 1994, p. 36). Emigration potential is high in countries such as China and India today. But there are no countries that match these with immigration potential. Hence the prospects of large-scale emigration from such countries as China and India seem to be low.

*Table 3.3.* Hypothetical Examples of Growth Rate Cycle, when the Birth Rate Remains Time-Invariant at 35 Births per 1000 Persons per Year, while the Death Rate Increases and then Decreases

| Year | 1990 | 1991 | 1992 | 1993 | 1994 |
|---|---|---|---|---|---|
| Death rate | 35 | 36 | 37 | 36 | 35 |
| Growth rate (%) | 0.0 | −0.1 | −0.2 | −0.1 | 0.0 |

*Table 3.4.* A Hypothetical Example Showing a Combination of the Death Rate and Birth Rate Transitions (from High to Low Levels) Producing a Growth-Rate-Cycle

| Year | 1940 | 1950 | 1960 | 1970 | 1980 | 1990 |
|---|---|---|---|---|---|---|
| Death rate | 30 | 20 | 15 | 10 | 10 | 10 |
| Birth rate | 30 | 25 | 21 | 14 | 12 | 10 |
| Growth rate (%) | 0.0 | 0.5 | 0.6 | 0.4 | 0.2 | 0.0 |

## 3.7. QUESTIONS AND ANSWERS*

**FOR EACH OF THE QUESTIONS IN SECTIONS 3.7.1. TO 3.7.10., STATE TRUE OR FALSE AND EXPLAIN.**

### 3.7.1. The Beginning of Demography

1. John Graunt is regarded as the father of demography.

### 3.7.2. Population Censuses

2. Early censuses were mainly concerned with determining such things as a tax base or potential recruits for the army.
3. A modern population census requires that each person be interviewed face-to-face by a census taker.
4. The 1990 U.S. population census collected detailed information using the "long form" (as opposed to the "short form" that contained questions asked of everyone) from only one-eighth of the households.
5. The 1790 U.S. census is regarded as the first modern census.
6. The U.S. constitution requires that a population census be taken every 10 years.

### 3.7.3. Vital Registration Systems

7. The term vital events refers to events that have life-and-death implications for the individual members of a population.
8. The term vital statistics was coined by William Farr of Britain's General Register Office.

*Answers start on page 46.

### 3.7.4. Population Registers

9. Population registers combine the functions of censuses and vital registration systems.
10. Population registers are maintained for certain Indian tribes in the United States.

### 3.7.5. Censuses and Registration Systems Compared

11. The census is analogous to the business practice of periodic stock taking, whereas the registration system is more like keeping a record of inputs and outputs.
12. Sampling is used in modern censuses but not in vital registration systems.
13. The origin of population censuses is political, whereas that of the vital registration system is ecclesiastical.
14. Errors are rare in registration data, but are not rare in census data.

### 3.7.6. Sample Surveys

15. The U.S. Bureau of the Census was responsible for coordinating the World Fertility Survey.

### 3.7.7. Population Size and Growth Rates

16. The world's population is now more than 5 billion and is increasing at an accelerating rate.
17. The world population has a history of different surges of growth.
18. The best guess is that the rate of growth of the world's population will progressively slow down and the population size will stabilize under 13 billion, many decades from now.
19. If a population grows in size at the annual rate of 1%, it will double its size in 70 years.
20. All along, the least-developed regions of the world had the fastest growing population.
21. In the colonial period, in North America, almost all colonies had about the same rate of natural increase (i.e., birth rate − death rate).

### 3.7.8. *Components of Change*

22. The balancing equation expresses population change as the sum of natural increase and net migration.

23. India's birth and death rates are higher than the corresponding rates for China.

### 3.7.9. *Population Distribution*

24. Asia currently houses two-thirds of the world's population.

25. Two out of every five humans alive today is either a Chinese or an Indian.

### 3.7.10. *Population Composition*

26. In 1650, the European colonists in North America were outnumbered 20 to 1 by native American Indians.

**FOR EACH OF THE QUESTIONS IN SECTIONS 3.7.11. TO 3.7.20., FOUR ANSWERS ARE SUGGESTED, AT LEAST ONE OF WHICH IS CORRECT. IDENTIFY THE CORRECT ANSWER(S) AND EXPLAIN.**

### 3.7.11. *The Scope of Demography*

1. In demography one studies:
   A. Population size, structure, and changes
   B. Fertility, mortality, and mobility processes
   C. The causes and consequences of population structure and change
   D. The ups and downs of political parties in a country

2. Which of the following are macrodemographic issues?
   A. The effects of vaccination and public health measures on death rates
   B. The considerations that prompt a person to seek medical help
   C. The issue of whether economic development is a necessary condition for the onset fertility decline in a society
   D. Factors that enter into an individual's decision to move from the current place of residence

3. Which of the following variables are of interest to demographers?
   A. Age
   B. Sex
   C. Religion
   D. Color of hair

### 3.7.12. Population Censuses

4. Errors in census include
   A. Omission
   B. Multiple counting
   C. Recording incorrect information on those enumerated
   D. Failure to interview each person face-to-face

5. Of the *de facto* and *de jure* methods of census taking:
   A. The results of one may differ from those of the other
   B. The former is easier to use than the latter
   C. Both can be used in the same census
   D. The former is more common on a worldwide basis than the latter

6. Which of the following apply to content errors in censuses?
   A. They refer to incorrect information on individuals or living quarters
   B. They could occur at the collection stage or later on
   C. Their presence could be detected sometimes by examining whether the tabulated data "look reasonable"
   D. They are a subset of coverage errors

### 3.7.13. Vital Event Registration System

7. Vital event registration systems:
   A. Tend to be defective and incomplete in less-developed countries
   B. First began as an ecclesiastic function
   C. Supply population data analogous to inputs and outputs
   D. Were invented by John Graunt

8. The so-called vital events include:
   A. Graduating from college
   B. Births and deaths
   C. Changes in occupational status
   D. Changes in civil status

### 3.7.14. Population Registers

9. Population registers:
   A. Contain stock-and-flow data
   B. Combines the functions of censuses and vital registration systems
   C. Are maintained in a number of countries in Europe and Asia
   D. Can be found in parts of the United States

### 3.7.15. Sample Surveys

10. Sample surveys:
    A. Are used for making estimates for a whole from data for a part only
    B. Are cheaper than the corresponding censuses, for a given amount of information
    C. Yield results that are subject to sampling errors
    D. Are used only in countries were census taking and vital registration systems are defective

11. Sample surveys:
    A. Are never combined with censuses
    B. Require face-to-face interviews
    C. Became a frequently-used research strategy since the turn of the 19th century
    D. Are nowadays used by government agencies, market researchers, opinion pollsters, social researchers, and many others

12. The World Fertility Survey:
    A. Was conducted under the auspices of the United Nations
    B. Covered only English-speaking countries
    C. Was confined to the industrialized nations
    D. Provided useful, comparative information for the countries covered

13. The U.S. Current Population Survey (CPS):
    A. Is conducted every month
    B. Collects information from residents of a very large sample of housing units each month
    C. Provides data on a variety of topics
    D. Has the same legal status as that of the U.S. Population Census

### 3.7.16. Published Sources of Demographic Data

14. International compendia of population data include which of the following?
    A. The U.N. Demographic Yearbook
    B. The U.N. Statistical Yearbook
    C. The UNESCO Statistical Yearbook
    D. The Population Reference Bureau's World Population Data Sheet

15. The sources of population data for the United States include:
    A. The U.S. Demographic Yearbook
    B. The U.S. Census Bureau's census reports and the Current Population Reports

C. U.S. Population Register Abstracts
D. Monthly Vital Statistics Reports published by the U.S. Department of Health and Human Services

### *3.7.17. Users of Demographic Data*

16. Among those who use demographic data are:
    A. Governmental agencies
    B. Insurance companies
    C. Demographers and social scientists
    D. Market researchers

### *3.7.18. Population Size and Growth Rates*

17. The world's population:
    A. Probably numbered less than 100 million, 4000 years before Christ
    B. Numbered about 300 million by the beginning of the Christian Era
    C. Reached the 1 billion mark by the early part of the 19th century
    D. Reached the 5 billion mark by the beginning of the 20th century
18. Historical evidence indicates that the world's population had different surges of growth, coinciding with:
    A. The revolution that brought tool making
    B. The agricultural revolution that began about ten thousand years ago
    C. The Industrial Revolution that started in the eighteenth century
    D. The computer revolution of the 20th century
19. Estimates of the world's population at different dates show that
    A. It took most of human history for the world's population to reach the 1 billion mark
    B. The second billion was added in only 130 years
    C. The third billion in only 30 years
    D. The fourth billion in only 15 years

### *3.7.19. Population Distribution*

20. The changes in the geographic distribution of the world's population since 1750 involved decrease-and-then-increase pattern for:
    A. Africa's share
    B. Latin America's share
    C. Asia's share
    D. The combined share of Europe and North America

21. Geographic distribution of a population may change because of differences between the geographic areas in:
    A. Natural increase
    B. Gains and losses due to migration from one area to another among them
    C. Immigration and/or emigration
    D. Because of territorial changes

### 3.7.20. Components of Population Change

22. The basic components of change in population size of a country are:
    A. Births
    B. Deaths
    C. International migration
    D. Internal migration

23. The components of population change in a political unit such as a city or a country are:
    A. Natural increase
    B. Net migration
    C. Annexation of territory
    D. Social mobility

24. Factors contributing to the risk of death at any given age may be:
    A. Biological (e.g., genetic makeup)
    B. Socio-economic (e.g., income)
    C. Environmental (e.g., air quality)
    D. Behavioral (e.g., smoking)

25. Factors contributing to having a birth may be:
    A. Biological
    B. Psychological
    C. Social
    D. Political

26. Migration propensity is associated with factors that are:
    A. Geographical
    B. Social
    C. Psychological
    D. Biological

27. Which of the following combinations of births, deaths, and migration result in zero population growth?
    A. 400 births, 200 deaths, and 200 net out-migration
    B. 0 net out-migration, 400 births, and 400 deaths

C. 200 births, 400 deaths, and 200 net in-migration
D. 100 births, 150 deaths, 25 out-migration, 175 in-migration

28. With respect to migration as a factor in population growth or decline, which of the following statements are true?
   A. Migration from Europe started in the 16th century with the European voyages of discovery and conquests
   B. The peak period of European emigration to overseas destination occurred early in the 20th century
   C. During the latter half of the 20th century the direction of the net flow of migration changed, making the more developed countries the gainers
   D. In the next two decades, international migration is unlikely to play any significant role in population change of India

29. With respect to the time trend in birth rates, which of the following statements are true?
   A. In the 1930s there was widespread concern in Europe and North America over a potential population decline because of low fertility levels
   B. The post-World War II "baby boom" was of more or less the same duration in all countries
   C. A "baby bust" followed the post-World War II "baby boom" in the United States
   D. A "baby boom" is expected in the United States at the turn of the 21st century

30. The so-called balancing equation for population change has which of the following components?
   A. Births
   B. Deaths
   C. Net migration
   D. Social mobility

**FOR EACH OF THE QUESTIONS IN SECTIONS 3.7.21. TO 3.7.28., FIVE POSSIBLE ANSWERS ARE GIVEN, ONLY ONE OF WHICH IS CORRECT. IDENTIFY THE CORRECT ANSWER AND EXPLAIN.**

### *3.7.21. The Beginning of Demography*

1. Who is commonly thought of as the father of demography?
   A. Graunt
   B. Malthus
   C. Gini
   D. Plato
   E. Farr

### 3.7.22. The Scope of Demography

2. The size of the population of an area is not directly affected by which of the following?
   A. Births occurring in the area
   B. People who move into the area
   C. People who move out of the area
   D. Deaths among the people of the area
   E. People of the area who become divorced

3. Which of the following is not among the findings of historical demography?
   A. Pre-industrial Western Europe had a high proportion of women not marrying
   B. Nuclear family was typical of England as early as the sixteenth century
   C. Throughout pre-industrial Europe, fertility level remained uniformly high and stable
   D. Immobile peasantry tied to the land was not necessarily the universal pattern throughout pre-industrial Europe
   E. Industrializing Europe did not provide any clear-cut evidence to support a simple relationship between fertility decline and social and economic development

### 3.7.23. Population Censuses

4. The first population census in the United States was taken in:
   A. 1690
   B. 1750
   C. 1790
   D. 1850
   E. 1890

5. During the first ten U.S. censuses, the census enumerators were:
   A. School teachers
   B. U.S.marshals
   C. National Guards
   D. Specially trained temporary census workers
   E. The heads of the respective households

6. In the 1990 U.S. census which of the following was not a 100% item?
   A. Age
   B. Sex
   C. Race
   D. Marital status
   E. Veteran status

7. The overall undercount in the 1990 U.S. census was:
   A. Less than 1%
   B. 1–1.9%
   C. 2.0–2.4%
   D. 2.5–2.9%
   E. Greater than 3.0%

### 3.7.24. Vital Events Registration System

8. Which of the following is LEAST likely to be a characteristic of a country with the most complete vital events registration system today?
   A. A well-developed communication and transportation system
   B. An efficient administrative system
   C. An educated population
   D. A high fertility level
   E. A low mortality level

### 3.7.25. Population Registers

9. Which one of the following countries does not maintain A country-wide population register?
   A. The Netherlands
   B. Denmark
   C. Norway
   D. Taiwan
   E. The United States

### 3.7.26. Sample Surveys

10. Which of the following statement is NOT true of the World Fertility Survey (WFS)?
    A. The WFS covered 62 countries—42 developing ones and 20 developed ones
    B. The project lasted about 10 years—1972–1982
    C. India was one of the countries covered by the project
    D. The data from the Survey shed considerable light on fertility dynamics in various parts of the world
    E. It was perhaps the largest project of its kind undertaken ever before

### 3.7.27. Population Size and Growth Rates

11. The size of the world's population now is close to:
    A. 3 billion

B. 4 billion
C. 5 billion
D. 6 billion
E. 7 billion

12. A population that grows at the annual rate of 1.4% doubles itself in:
A. 20 years
B. 30 years
C. 40 years
D. 50 years
E. 60 years

13. Since 1750, Latin America's share of the world's population has more or less been:
A. Steadily increasing
B. Steadily decreasing
C. Widely fluctuating
D. Remaining steady
E. Close to zero for most of the time

14. ——— is not among the currently five most populous countries of the world.
A. China
B. India
C. U.S.A.
D. Indonesia
E. Mexico

15. ——— currently has greater-than-world-average annual population growth rate.
A. Southern Europe
B. Western Europe
C. North America
D. Oceania
E. Southern Asia

16. Which of the following is true? India's current:
A. Birth rate is lower than China's
B. Death rate is lower than China's
C. Rate of natural increase is lower than China's
D. Population size is smaller than China's
E. Land area is larger than China's

17. With respect to the population history of what is now the United States, which of the following statements is NOT true?
A. There was a time when the country's birth rates were among the highest in the world
B. Now it is one of low-fertility countries of the world

C. Its population has grown largely as a result of natural increase
D. Currently it is one of three most populous countries in the world
E. It is expected to become the second most populous country in the world within the next 25 years

18. With respect to the population history of the world, which of the following statements is NOT true?
A. For most of human existence, the world's population grew very slowly
B. The so-called "population explosion" is a recent phenomenon
C. The world population's annual growth rate has been going down for some years now
D. Those who make population projections believe that the world's population will stop growing sometime between the years 2050 and 2200
E. The chances are that the world's population will quadruple its current size before it stops growing

19. With respect to the current demographic situation, which of the following statements is NOT true?
A. Most of the countries have achieved fairly low death rates
B. Many countries continue to have high birth rates
C. Among the major regions, Africa has the fastest growing population
D. Death rates have been higher than birth rates for some time now in a number of countries
E. Population growth rate of North America is lower than that of Europe

20. Which of the following statements is NOT true with respect to the history of change in the combined population of North America and Europe? (For convenience refer to this population simply as the NAE population.)
A. Before the 1930s, the NAE population was more rapidly growing than the rest of the world's population
B. During the 1930s, the growth rate of the NAE population was approximately the same as that of the remaining population of the world
C. Currently the NAE population is in the slow-growing camp
D. Early in the next century, the NAE population is expected to regain its status as the fastest growing population in the world
E. Among the member countries of the NAE population, several in Eastern Europe had, as of the mid-1990s, lower birth rates than death rates

21. With respect to India's population history, which of the following statements is NOT true?
A. The birth rate during 1951–1961 was relatively high
B. During the 1970s, fertility decline was more rapid than that during the 1960s
C. The rate of population growth remained above the world average during the 1980s

D. The population size was about 890 million now as of the mid-1990s.
E. It is speculated that before the year 2020, India will become the most populous country in the world.

### 3.7.28. Population Distribution

22. Compared to Europe, Africa's current:
    A. Share of the world's population is lower
    B. Population growth rate is lower
    C. Death rate is lower
    D. Birth rate is lower
    E. Proportion of the population under age 15 years is lower

### 3.7.1. Answers

1. True. John Graunt's (1629–1674) *Natural and Political Observations Made upon the Bills of Mortality* was first published in 1662. His development of the life table has led to his being called the "father of modern demography" (Glass, 1963). The term demography was derived by Guillard (1855) from the two Greek words, δῆμος, the people, and γράφειυ, to draw or write (Cox, 1976, p. 1). The first extensive use of the word "population" in its modern sense is credited to Francis Bacon, who in 1597 spoke of the "depopulation of towns and homes of husbandry," in connection with his opposition to land enclosures in England (Thomlinson, 1976, p. 5).

### 3.7.2. Answer

2. True. For example, the English *Domesday Book* was prepared in 1086 to determine the fiscal rights of the king. It provided a list of all taxable households as of that date. Charlemagne's *Breviary*, to give another example, compiled in the latter part of the 8th century a list of all males of military age in the empire. (See Hawley, 1950, p. 91).

3. False. In the 1990 U.S. census, for example, census forms were mailed to households with the instruction that it be filled out by one of the members of the household. Even when census takers visited each household, as was the practice in most countries until recently, the information on all members was collected from one of the adult members.

4. False. In 1990, five in six of all household received only the short form (asking information on household relationship, sex, race, age, marital status, and

Hispanic origin of each member of the household) while one in six received the long form, asking information on a number of social and economic characteristics (education, place of birth, residence in 1985, disability, fertility, veteran status, occupation, income in 1989, and so on).

5. False. The key part of the statement is "regarded as." Various censuses have been claimed as the first modern census. Examples include a 1665 census of Quebec and a 1703 census of Iceland (Cox, 1976, p. 28). At five-year intervals beginning in 1749, the Lutheran ministers of Sweden, who had long been keeping records of their parishioners, were required by the government to submit data from which population totals could be calculated (Petersen, 1975, p. 21). The oldest continuous periodic census is that of the United States, which has been conducted every ten years beginning in 1790. Except for the year 1941, a census has been taken in the United Kingdom every ten years since 1801.

6. True. In the United States the starting of the decennial census can be traced to efforts to establish the national government. Power was balanced between small and large states through a bicameral structure of the legislative body, consisting of the House of Representatives and the Senate. In the Senate all states have the same number of representatives, while in the other House, representation is proportional to the size of population. The number of representatives for different states had to be adjusted periodically to reflect population change, and the Constitution itself provided for a decennial count.

### 3.7.3. Answer

7. False. Vital events were originally defined as having to do with health, sickness, diseases and death. Later on the term was broadened to include births. According to the current practice, these events usually include live births, deaths, fetal deaths, marriages, and divorces. Some countries also include in the definition, adoptions, legitimations, annulments, and legal separations.

8. True (Petersen, 1975, p. 39). William Farr is credited with the first publication of vital statistics by a government office. He was appointed England's Compiler of Abstracts in the General Register Office in 1839, shortly after England's Registration Act of 1837 went into effect (Shryock and Siegel, 1971, p. 27).

### 3.7.4. Answers

9. True. Population registers provide information on both the stock of population (size, composition, and distribution) and flow of events, including births, deaths, and changes of residence.

10. True. An example is the Navaho (see Johnston, 1966; Petersen, 1975, p. 29.)

### 3.7.5. Answers

11. True. Censuses give stock data on a population while registration systems provide flow data that account for changes in the size, composition, and geographic spread of the population.

12. False. Sample registration areas as a means of obtaining estimates of vital statistics have been used in several countries, including India, Pakistan, Turkey, and Peru. Intensive efforts are taken in the sample registration areas, selected using probability sampling methods, to make registration as complete as possible. From the data thus obtained, estimates are made for the country as a whole or for different regions.

13. True. Early censuses were taken by rulers to assess their tax base or to identify potential recruits for their army. The origin of registration system, on the other hand, can be traced to the practice of recording in the parish register baptisms, burials, and weddings. In 1532 an English ordinance required weekly "Bills of Mortality" to be compiled by the parish priests in London and in 1538 every Anglican priest was required by civil law to maintain a register of weddings, baptisms, and burials (Shryock and Siegel, 1971, p. 27).

14. False. Errors are common in censuses as well as registration data. In many less developed countries the registration data are incomplete. Compare this to the coverage errors in censuses. Also, quite often the recorded information about the events (e.g., age at death, cause of death, age of mother at the birth of her *n*th child) may be incorrect. These are similar to the content errors in censuses.

### 3.7.6. Answers

15. False. The World Fertility Survey (WFS) was undertaken, with the collaboration of the United Nations, by the International Statistical Institute, in cooperation with the International Union for the Scientific Study of Population. Financial support was provided principally by the United Nations Fund for Population Activities and the United States Agency for International Development. The WFS had its headquarters in London, England.

### 3.7.7. Answers

16. False. It is true that the world's population is now more than 5 billion. But its growth rate peaked in the 1960s and has been dropping.

17. True. It is speculated (Brown, 1970, p. 4) that with the emergence of sophistication in hunting and gathering technology (clothing, fire, crude habitations, tools and weapons—the latter being first of wood and bone, then stone, and

eventually, metal), human habitations spread over the land areas of the world. If humans had continued indefinitely to live as hunters and food gatherers, the world's population would have leveled off at about 10 million (Brown, 1970). Around 10,000 years ago a new technology—domestication of plants and animals—began to appear. This new technology spread rapidly, and human population grew in size. Wandering tribes began to decrease in number and were replaced by settled farming villages, typically of 200–300 people, at an average between-village distance of a few kilometers (Brown, 1970, p. 5). Gradually it became possible to produce enough surplus food to support non-agricultural pursuits for a small fraction (perhaps a maximum of 10%) of the people. This led to the emergence of towns and cities, particularly in river valleys, taking advantage of water transport. The third surge of population growth has been associated with the Industrial Revolution.

18. True. The United Nations' projections indicate that by the year 2050 the world's population will reach slightly over 10 billion and will eventually stabilize between 11 and 14 billion. Note that this is only a guess. There are those who believe that the world's population will stabilize between 8 and 10 billion within the next 50 years (Keyfitz, 1995).

19. True. The quick formula for calculating the doubling time for a population at a given growth rate is to divide 70 with the given percent annual growth rate. This formula is based on the idea that population growth can be thought of in the same way one thinks of money deposited in a bank growing at compound interest. If interest is compounded at each instant, the amount at the end of a given period as a multiple of the amount at the beginning is, in the (natural) logarithmic scale, equal to the rate of growth times the length of the interval. Hence the doubling time is obtained by dividing the natural logarithm of 2 (i.e., 0.69315) by the rate of interest. This is the same as dividing 69.315 (or approximately 70) by the percent rate of interest.

20. False. During the Industrial Revolution the European population grew faster than the population in other parts of the world. At present, however, the less-developed countries are experiencing higher population growth rates compared to the more-developed countries.

21. False. For example, the New England colonies had higher rates of natural increase than their counterparts in the South, primarily because of differences in death rates.

### 3.7.8. Answers

22. True. The balancing equation ordinarily expresses population change during a time interval as the algebraic sum of (1) the difference, births − deaths, in the

interim and (2) the difference, in-migration − out-migration, in the interim. The equation is usually expressed as follows: population size at time 2 = population size at time 1 + births in the interim − deaths in the interim + in-migration in the interim − out-migration in the interim. Note, however, that for the world as a whole only the balance between births and deaths applies. For a local unit such as a city or a country, a third component may be relevant, namely addition or deletion of territory. For example, the population increase between 1950–1960 in the United States had this third component because Alaska and Hawaii joined the United States in 1959. Also note that some cities expand by incorporating adjoining territories.

23. True. China's birth and death rates as of 1994 were 18 and 7, respectively, per 1,000 population; the corresponding figures for India were 29 and 10, respectively (Population Reference Bureau's *1994 World Population Data Sheet*).

### 3.7.9. Answers

24. False. Asia's share was below 60% as of 1995. Two and a half centuries ago, however, Asia's share was close to two-thirds.

25. False, strictly speaking that is. The 1994 World population was 5,607 million. China and India together accounted for only 1,192 + 912 = 2,104 million (or 37.5 percent) of the world's population.

### 3.7.10. Answers

26. True. (See Snipp, 1989; Weeks, 1994, p. 38). The native Indian population in North America in 1650 numbered about a million compared to about 50,000 European colonists. During the 200 years that followed, warfare and diseases, the latter imported from Europe and for which the natives had very little immunity, took a heavy toll, dwindling the size of the native population to 250,000 by 1850. By that time the population of European origin had increased to 23 million.

### 3.7.11. Answers

1. A, B, and C: Demographers do not ordinarily study the ups and downs of political parties. However, if there are a large number of political parties in a country, they can be treated in the same way one would treat any population of formal organizations (e.g., business corporations). In such a case, the ups and downs of political parties can be viewed as a demographic topic analogous to illness and recovery of people.

2. A and C: Macrodemography deals with relatively large aggregates of people (e.g., cities, regions, states, nations, continents), whereas in microdemography the focus is on small units, particularly individuals.

3. A, B, and C: If a variable is associated with (as a cause or as an effect of) any of the basic processes, i.e., mortality, fertility, mobility, then that variable is of interest to demographers.

### 3.7.12. Answers

4. A, B, and C: No census system requires that each person be interviewed, let alone face-to-face.

5. A, B, C, and D: See Shryock and Siegel (1971, pp. 92–93). The difficulty with the *de jure* method is that although most persons will have little difficulty in stating their usual place of residence, confusion is likely to arise in some cases in which a person may appear to have two usual places of residence (e.g., students living at a school away from their parental home; employed persons who have a secondary residence close to their work place; a woman who has her own apartment, but spends almost all of her wakeful hours with her son's family next door.) To use both methods, the legal residence of each person enumerated is ascertained, and at the tabulation stage, persons are allocated to their legal residence, thus giving rise to two sets of tabulations, if desired, one (the *de facto* counts) according to the residence as of the census date and the other according to legal residence.

6. A, B, and C: Another term for content error is classification error. At the collection stage, such errors might occur from recording incorrect information. At the processing stage, errors may occur, for example, when information is transferred to the processing equipment. It is possible sometimes to detect the presence of content errors by examining whether the tabular data look reasonable. For example, the common tendency of age "heaping" (age preference, digit preference) in classifications of people by age is an indication of content error. The preference for the various ages ending in 0 or 5 is widespread, e.g., age 19 or 21 years reported as 20 (Shryock and Siegel, 1972, p. 204).

### 3.7.13. Answers

7. A, B, and C: In some less developed countries, as much as 50 percent of certain vital events go unregistered. See Question 13 in section 3.7.5 regarding the origin of registration systems. See Question 11 in section 3.7.5 regarding the analogy between census and stock taking and between registration data and the records of input-output flow.

8. B and D: William Farr originally defined vital statistics to include statistics on health, sickness, and disease. And since vital statistics is regarded as the end product of the collection, compilation, and presentation of data on vital events, one might think all health-related events as vital events. But as the term is currently used it covers births, deaths, marriages, divorces, and sometimes, adoptions, legitimations, annulments, and legal separation.

### 3.7.14. Answers

9. A, B, C, and D: Population registers are maintained in several European countries (e.g., the Netherlands, Belgium, Finland, Norway, Sweden, and Denmark) and a number of countries outside Europe (e.g., Taiwan, Israel, and for certain Indian tribes in the United States). In Europe, local registration bureaus maintain a separate card or file for each individual from the time of birth or in-migration until death or out-migration, recording in it changes in civil status and other demographic and socio-economic statuses. A population register when complete thus provides the information ordinarily provided by censuses and vital statistics, plus data on geographic mobility.

### 3.7.15. Answers

10. A, B, and C: For the same amount of information, sample surveys are cheaper than censuses. Sample surveys are used in less developed as well as more developed countries. They are frequently used in less developed countries to obtain information on vital events, where the registration system is not working well. Their use in the more developed countries is mainly for collecting data not usually available from the censuses or registration systems.

11. D: As mentioned, many modern censuses collect a minimal set of information from all the people and detailed information on a number of items from only a sample. Sample surveys collect data through mail or through telephone interviews and of course through face-to-face interviews as well. Survey sampling methodology has been developed over the past 100 years or so, particularly since the 1930s.

12. D: A total of 62 countries (42 from the less developed regions and 20 from the developed areas) were covered by the World Fertility Survey. Language spoken was not a criterion for inclusion in the survey. The interview questionnaires were translated into the local languages.

13. A, B, and C: The legal status of the Current Population Survey is that of any other survey, different from that of the U.S. population census, which has a Constitutional mandate. The CPS started in the 1940s and currently collects data from the residents of over 70,000 occupied housing units. Parts of the

sample are rotated; so certain portions of the sample reappear for several months. Items of education and income are included once every year. Labor force questions are asked every month. Special topics (e.g., smoking habits) are occasionally covered.

### 3.7.16. Answers

14. A, B, C, and D: The Statistical Office of the United Nations collects and publishes statistics on demographic, economic, and social characteristics of individual countries and regions. Among the publications are *Statistical Yearbook*, *Demographic Yearbook*, *Population and Vital Statistics Report*, *Compendium on Human Settlements Statistics*, *Compendium on Social Statistics*, *Yearbook of International Trade Statistics*, *Yearbook of Industrial Statistics*, and *Yearbook of Construction Statistics*. The same Office also publishes guidelines and methodological studies such as the *Handbook of Vital Statistics Systems and Methods*, Vol. 1 (1985), the *Handbook of Household Survey* (1984), and *Censuses of Population and Housing in Asia and the Pacific: Towards the 1990 Round* (1988). UNESCO publishes the *Statistical Yearbook*, and *Compendium of Statistics on Illiteracy*, among others. The population Reference Bureau in Washington publishes every year its *World Population Data Sheet* (among other things).

15. B and D: There are no U.S. Demographic Yearbooks and the United States does not have a Population Register covering the entire country. The *U.N. Demographic Yearbook*, however, also contains demographic information for the United States.

### 3.7.17. Answers

16. A, B, C, and D: Government agencies use demographic data to allocate funds to different states, counties, and other local units; insurance companies use them for fixing premiums, demographers and social scientists use them in their research work; and market researchers use them to determine demands for goods and services. Programs relating to education, taxation, social security, and farm production as well as determining the location of hospitals, schools, shopping centers, and the like are better shaped if the number and makeup of people involved are known.

### 3.7.18. Answers

17. A, B, and C: We have only rough estimates of the size of the world's population for very early dates. According to Durand (1967) there were probably 5 million people inhabiting this planet 8000 years before the birth of

Christ and 300 million at the beginning of the Christian Era. It is a good guess that midway between the two dates, the world's population was less than 100 million. We are on more sure grounds regarding the time when the world's population hit the 1 billion mark (early in the 19th century) and the 5 billion mark (1987).

18. A, B, and C: Lenski and Lenski (1987, p. 85) distinguish four major eras: (1) the hunting and gathering era (all of human history until 7000 B.C.); (2) the horticultural era (from 7000 B.C.–3000 B.C.); the agrarian era (from 3000 B.C.–A.D. 1800); and the industrial era (from A.D. 1800 onward). (The term horticulture, as Lenski and Lenski use it, stands for cultivation of small gardens using a hoe or a digging stick as the main tool. Agriculture is more advanced in that the main tool is the plow.) One of the main propositions of the "evolutionary-ecological" theory of societal change, used in Lenski and Lenski (1987), stresses a positive association between increases in population size and advances in subsistence technology.

19. A, B, C, and D: It took all of human history until the beginning of the 19th century for the world's population to reach the 1 billion mark. The 2 billion mark was reached in 1930, the 3 billion mark in 1960, 4 billion in 1975, and 5 billion in 1987.

### *3.7.19. Answers*

20. A and C: Since 1750, Latin America's share seems to have been increasing, and the combined share of Europe and North America increased at first and then decreased (see Table 3.1).

21. A, B, C, and D: One of the difficulties in studying geographic distribution of a population is that over time the boundaries of the areas used in data presentation change. India provides a good example. Starting with a few states at the time of independence, a number of reorganizations resulted in the creation of new states from the old ones. In such cases, a study of changing population would require estimating data for the new units from earlier data presented for an entirely different sets of units. This is often a difficult task because earlier data may not be readily available for the parts that were combined to form the new units.

### *3.7.20. Answers*

22. A, B, and C: Note, however, that in some instances cessation or accession of territories may be involved.

23. A, B, and C: Social mobility does not directly add to population size or deplete it. It may, however, affect fertility, mortality, and migration.

24. A, B, C, and D: Individuals vary with respect to frailty—some are weak, some are strong, and some in-between. Frailty has genetic and environmental components. Socioeconomic status affects access to, and utilization of, medical care. It may also influence behavior with health implications (e.g., refraining from smoking and excessive drinking, watching weight, exercising, eating right, sleeping enough, etc.).

25. A, B, C, and D: Some people are biologically incapable of having children. Social and psychological factors enter into decisions that affect fertility behavior. Thus, women who attach top priority to career development may decide to postpone childbearing. Political factors, such as laws restricting access to safe abortion, may affect fertility behavior at least temporarily. An example is Rumania in the 1960s, where the birth rate went up dramatically when the government restricted access to abortion.

26. A, B, and C: Migration is not considered to have a biological basis, unlike death and childbearing. Social and psychological factors affect migration propensity. Geographical factors such as elevation, nearness to the boundary of a continent, and climate, are known to attract or repel migrants to an area.

27. A, B, and C: Population change = births − deaths + in-migration − out-migration. All combinations except choice D give zero population change.

28. A, B, and C: In the foreseeable future no country is likely to have the immigration potential to match the emigration potential of large countries such as India, China, and Indonesia. International migration, nonetheless, is likely to be an important factor that keeps the populations of some of the industrialized countries from declining in size.

29. A and C: The "baby boom" lasted longer in the United States than in other, more developed, countries. The chances of another "baby boom" of the kind that occurred after the second World War are small.

30. A, B, and C: Social mobility is not part of the so-called balancing equation, which is concerned about the components of change in population size.

### *3.7.21. Answers*

1. A: Graunt.

### *3.7.22. Answers*

2. E: Changes in marital status, occupational status, educational status, or the like do not have a direct impact on the size of the population of an area. They may have indirect impact in that they may affect fertility, mortality, or mobility processes.

3. C: Fertility levels varied among population segments because of differences in such things as age at marriage and separation of spouses due to one reason or another, e.g., work-related migration.

### 3.7.23. Answers

4. C: 1790.
5. B: U.S. marshals.
6. E: Veteran status.
7. B: 1–1.9% (Weeks, 1994, p. 16). The overall undercount varies from census to census. In the 1970 U.S. census, for example, it was little over 2.0% (Weeks 1994, p. 11). The degree of undercount varies by demographic characteristics. For example, in the 1960 U.S. census, the undercount was only 1.1% among white males, 1.7% among white females, but 10.3% among nonwhite males and 7.1% among nonwhite females (Cox, 1976, p. 53).

### 3.7.24. Answers

8. D: High fertility level.

### 3.7.25. Answers

9. E: The United States. Note, however, that for some Indian tribes such as the Navaho in the United States, population registers are maintained.

### 3.7.26. Answers

10. C: India did not participate in the WFS. India did, however, participate in the Demographic and Health Surveys—the survey was conducted under the name National Family and Health Survey during 1991–1993.

### 3.7.27. Answers

11. D: The 1995 size of the world's population was 5.7 billion, growing at the rate of 1.5% per year.
12. D: 70/1.4 = 50, or more accurately 69.31/1.4 = 49.51 years.
13. A: Steadily increasing. See Table 3.1.
14. E: Mexico. The most populous ten countries of the world (as of 1995) are China (1.2 billion); India (931 million); U.S.A. (263 million); Indonesia (198 million); Brazil (158 million); Russia (148 million); Japan (125 million); Pakistan (130 million); and Bangladesh (119 million).

15. E: Southern Asia. The world population as of 1995 was growing at an annual rate of 1.5%. The corresponding regional growth rates were: Southern Europe (0.1%); Western Europe (0.1%); North America (0.7%); Oceania (1.2%); and Southern Asia (2.0%).

16. E: India's land area is 1,147,950 sq. miles whereas China's is 3,600,930 sq. miles. The crude birth rate is estimated to be 29 births per 1000 persons in India as of the mid-1990s compared to China's 18 per 1000 persons. The crude death rate is estimated to be 9 deaths per 1000 persons in India in the mid-1990s, compared to China's 6 deaths per 1,000 persons. The mid-1990s rate of natural increase is estimated to be 1.9% in India and 1.1% in China. As of the mid-1990s, India's population is estimated to be 931 million compared to China's 1219 million. The figures are from Population Reference Bureau's 1995 World Population Data Sheet.

17. E: China and India will remain the first and second most populous countries of the world for a number of decades to come. At present China is the most populous country in the world. Whether India will usurp that dubious distinction sooner or later is difficult to predict.

18. E: According to most projections, a doubling of the current size is expected.

19. E: North American population was, as of 1995, growing at the annual rate of 0.7% while the corresponding figure for Europe was only 0.1%.

20. D: The NAE population is expected to remain in the slow-growing camp in the foreseeable future. As for choice E, the Eastern European countries, Bulgaria, Hungary, Rumania, and Russia had higher death rates than birth rates, as of 1995.

21. E: It is speculated that before the year 2020, India will become the most populous country in the world.

### *3.7.28. Answers*

22. A: Africa's share of the world's population is lower than that of Europe. Africa's population size in 1995 was 720 million compared with 729 million for Europe. African population was growing in 1995 at the rate of about 2.8% per year while the European population was growing at about 0.1% per year (1994 population size was 728 million). In 1995, Africa had 41 births per 1000 persons compared to Europe's 11 births per 1000 persons. In the same year, Africa's death rate was 14 deaths per 1000 persons compared to Europe's 12 deaths per 1000 persons. Figures are from Population Reference Bureau's *1995 World Population Data Sheet.*

# CHAPTER 4

# *Mortality*

Demography started with a statistical study of mortality (Durand, 1962); however, the subject lost its priority on the way. After the routinization of data collection and compilation and the development of basic measures of mortality, demographers began to believe that most of what needed to be known had been discovered, and that not many challenges remained to be met in that quarter of demographic studies. Fertility started to receive increasingly more attention. Recently, however, mortality has staged a comeback and is no longer a neglected topic. The aging of the population in the more developed countries, the dramatic drop in mortality from certain causes of death, methodological developments, and the availability of new data (e.g., on multiple causes of death), are among the factors responsible for the renewed interest in mortality research.

When thinking about mortality, one is reminded of the fact that some people live long, some die young, the end is sudden for many, and a lingering one for others. Medical advances have made it possible to keep people alive. Some even believe that the time is not far off when almost everyone will live a long and healthy life with a disability period shrunk to a short span just before death. Be that as it may, there is no doubt that humanity has come a long way in gaining control over mortality. To appreciate this conquest, one needs to know certain basic concepts and measurements and the nature and explanations of trends and differentials in mortality.

## *4.1. CONCEPTS*

Death is defined as "the permanent disappearance of all evidence of life at any time after birth has taken place (post-natal cessation of vital functions without capability of resuscitation)" (United Nations, 1973). For legal and medical purposes the following definition of death has been proposed: the irreversible cessation of all of the following: (1) total cerebral function, (2) spontaneous function of the respiratory system, (3) spontaneous function of the circulatory system (*Dorland's Illustrated Medical Dictionary*, 25th Edition). Mortality is the process by which a population's membership is depleted via deaths.

Life span refers to the (not precisely known) maximum number of years a person can expect to live under ideal conditions. Weeks (1994, p. 159) refers to an authenticated case of a Japanese person who lived almost 121 years.

Life expectancy is the average number of years of life remaining for those who survive to a given birthday anniversary, assuming that this group is subjected to a given schedule of age-specific death rates (defined below.) For example, at the turn of the 20th century, the life expectancy at age 65 for U.S. white males was 11.5 years.

Cause of death is the combination of the specific exogenous and endogenous conditions producing death. The immediate cause of death is distinguished from the underlying cause, and these are distinguished from others in between:

$$\text{Underlying cause} \rightarrow \text{intermediate causes} \rightarrow \text{immediate cause.}$$

The disease or condition that just precedes death is the immediate cause. When all causes are arranged in sequence the one farthest away in the causal chain is the underlying cause, between the underlying cause and the immediate cause are the intermediate causes.

Epidemiologic transition is a term applied to the shifts in disease patterns that accompany mortality transition (from high to low levels). The classical western pattern involved a gradual process stretched out over a long period of time. A more accelerated pattern, made possible because of the transfer of knowledge from the west, was experienced by Japan, for example. The experience of the currently less-developed countries differs from both of these patterns in the widespread use of insecticides, antibiotics, and organized disease-eradication programs. Omran (1971) distinguished the following three main stages of epidemiologic transition: the ages of pestilence and famine, of receding pandemics, and of degenerative diseases and diseases of human origin.

Frailty refers to the strength and weakness of human body affecting the ability to resist disease and illness. It varies from one individual to another and it changes with age for any individual. In any population, there are frailty distributions for successive age groups.

Morbidity stands for the ill-well composition of a population (from the Latin *morbidus*: sick). When used with reference to a specific illness, the following concepts apply: incidence (referring to new cases), prevalence (referring to all cases), and duration, referring to the interval that has elapsed since the illness started for a given case.

## 4.2. MEASURES

The crude death rate (CDR) is defined as the annual number of deaths in a population per 1000 persons, using the mid-year population for the denominator. The adjective "crude" signifies that the measure does not take into account the substantial variation by age, sex, etc., of the chance of dying within the year. The CDR is a period rate because it measures the rate at which a population loses its members due to death during a specific period (e.g., a calendar year).

A measure that takes into account the differences by age in the chance of dying within the year is the age-specific death rate (ASDR). For each age or age interval, one calculates the number of deaths at that age per 1000 persons, using the mid-year population at that age in the denominator. The curve of the age-specific death rate is J-shaped when plotted using the arithmetic scale (Fig. 4.1.) and looks like a check mark (✓) when the semi-logarithmic scale is used (age on the horizontal axis, using the arithmetic scale, and ASDR on the vertical axis, using the logarithmic scale, see Fig. 4.2.). The CDR is a weighted average of the ASDRs in a given population, using the population's age composition for weights.

Age-standardized death rate is the CDR that results in a population if that population adopts the age composition of a "standard" population while retaining its own ASDRs. The age-standardized death rate of population A, using population B as the standard, is a weighted average of the ASDRs of population A using the age composition of population B as weights.

Standardized mortality ratio (SMR) is the ratio of the CDR in a given population to the weighted average of the ASDRs of a standard population using the given population's age composition for weights. Sometimes this ratio is

*Figure 4.1.* Age pattern of mortality: U.S. 1990 (Source: NCHS, 1995, Table 37).

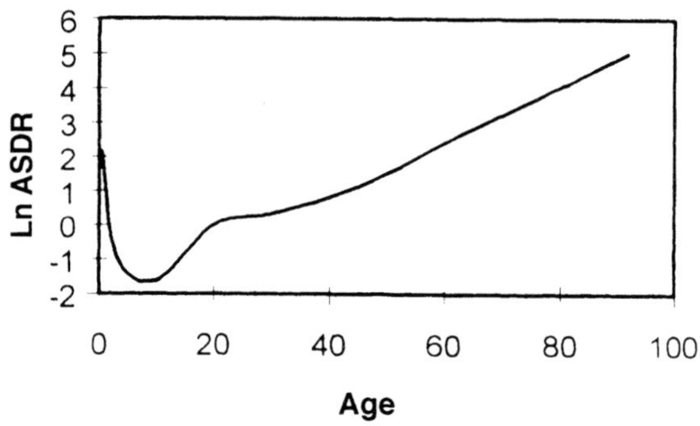


*Figure 4.2.* Age pattern of mortality, U.S. 1990 semilogarithmic scale (Source: NCHS, 1995, Table 37).

multiplied by the CDR of the standard population to obtain what is called the indirectly standardized death rate.

A life table is a statistical device to present the life and death story of a (hypothetical) cohort whose members are subjected to a given schedule of ASDRs. The story starts with an arbitrary number of births (usually a multiple of 1000) and follows the group until all of its members die. The life table shows how many in the starting group survive to specific birthday anniversaries, e.g., the first, fifth, ..., seventieth. A complete life table gives this information for each birthday anniversary, whereas an abridged life table gives this usually only for every fifth. The life table also gives the number of deaths in the group during each age interval, the probability of dying within the interval for those alive at the beginning of the interval, the total number of years lived by the group during each interval and beyond each given birthday anniversary, and the average remaining life time for those alive on a given birthday anniversary. The last is called the life expectancy at a given age. The life expectancy at birth is a widely used statistic.

Years of potential life lost (YPLL) per 100,000 persons under 65 years of age is a measure of premature mortality. YPLL is equal to the sum, over $x = 1, 2, \ldots 65$, of the product of $(65 - x)$ with the number of deaths in a given calendar year at age $x$. The YPLL rate = 100,000 times (YPLL / the number of persons under age 65), using mid-year population for the denominator. In the United States in 1991 about a third of YPLL rate was accounted for by unintentional injuries and cancer combined.

## 4.3. LEVELS AND TRENDS

Pre-industrial populations, uninfluenced by industrial populations, have very high and widely fluctuating levels of mortality—life expectancy at birth in the range 20–30 years and crude death rates fluctuating around 35 per 1000 persons. Not many such populations can be found today. Currently, the life expectancy at births varies from about 40 years in some countries in Africa to almost 80 years in some of the more developed countries. Wide fluctuations in mortality are things of the past. In terms of average life expectancy at birth, the following ranking holds currently: Africa (55), Asia (64), Latin America (68), and MDCs (more-developed countries) [Europe (73), North America (76), Australia (77), New Zealand (75), and countries in Asia, such as Japan (79)]. The world average (65) falls between the Asian and Latin American averages.

Morbidity data for Europe and North America indicate that long life does not necessarily mean healthy life. During the 19th century, when the life expectancy at birth was increasing, the age-specific incidence of disease and injury remained more or less constant, and the age-specific duration of disease and injury increased (Riley and Alter, 1989).

As the overall mortality level declines, the cause-composition of deaths changes drastically. At high mortality conditions, infectious and parasitic diseases are the major killers, accounting for about 45% of all deaths. At low levels of mortality, on the other hand, cancers and cardiovascular diseases become the major killers, accounting for almost two-thirds of the deaths (United Nations, 1963, see Fig. 4.3.).

Infant mortality (commonly measured by the annual number of infant deaths, i.e., deaths before the first birthday anniversary, per 1000 live births) is high when overall mortality is high. When life expectancy at birth is lower than 30 years, one fifth or more of infants die before reaching their first birthday anniversary. In 1990 Japan had the lowest infant mortality rate (4.60) and the highest life expectancy at

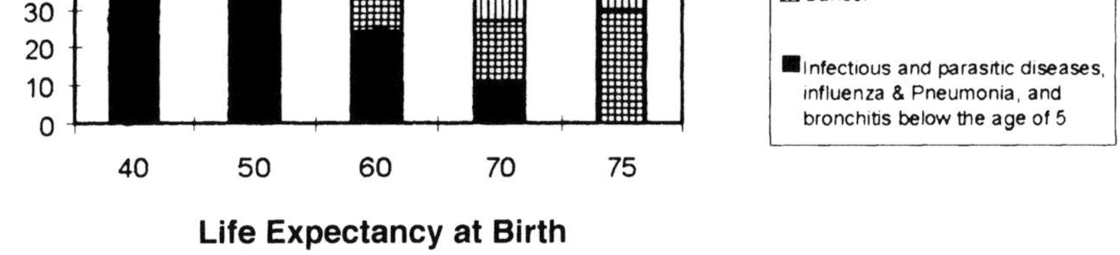


*Figure 4.3.* Distribution of deaths by cause of death (in groups) for different levels of life expectancy at birth (Source: Based on United Nations, 1963, p. 110).

birth (76.2 for males and 82.5 for females). The corresponding U.S. figures were 9.22, 71.8, and 78.9 respectively. Ranking of countries with respect to the overall mortality level more or less closely corresponds to the ranking with respect to infant mortality.

It is unlikely that the gains in mortality control is shared equally by all population segments in a country. For instance, in the United States infant mortality has been declining over the years, but considerable differences continue to persist between population subgroups. Socio-economically disadvantaged groups tend to have higher infant mortality (Fig. 4.4a). Various behaviors (e.g., smoking) of women during pregnancy, inadequate prenatal care, low birth weight (Fig. 4.4b), and absence of proper postnatal care are among the factors responsible for high infant mortality. The long drawn-out process that characterized the Western

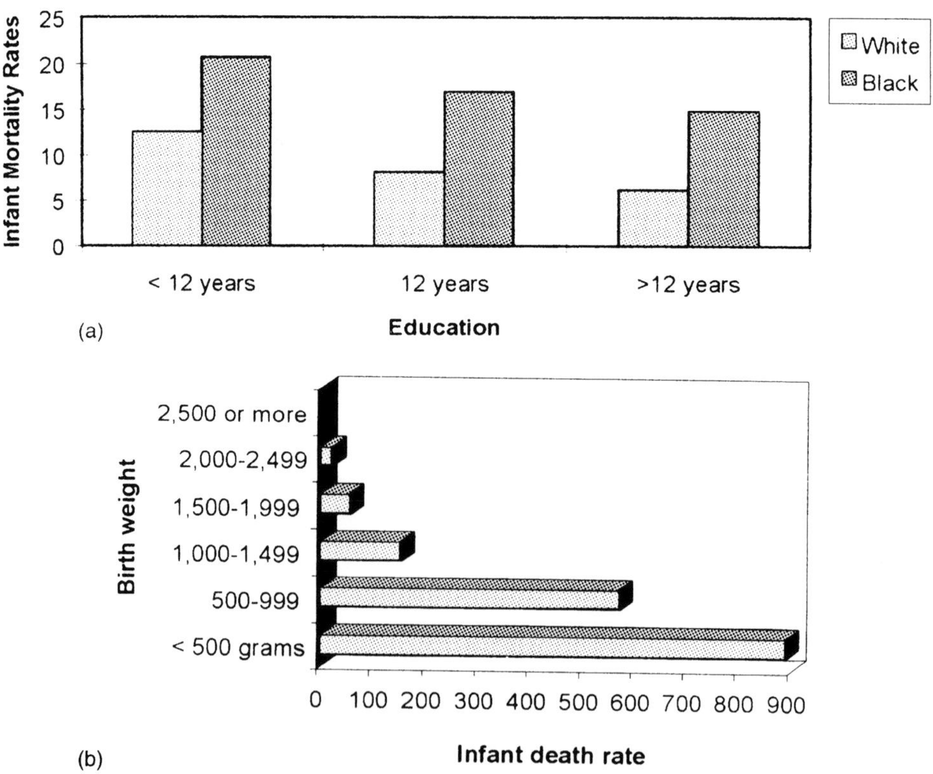


*Figure 4.4* (a) Infant mortality rates for mothers, age 20 years and older, according to educational attainment, selected states, U.S. 1986–1988 birth cohorts (Source: NCHS, 1995, p. 85). (b) Infant death rates by birth weight, U.S. 1983–1985 birth cohort (Source: NCHS, 1995, Table 22).

conquest of mortality can be illustrated by the case of Swedish. Sweden's infant mortality rates fluctuated around 200 infant deaths per 1000 live births prior to the turn of the 19th century. It took almost a century-and-a-half for the infant mortality rate in that country to drop below 20 per 1000 live births (by mid-20th century). By 1990 the rate had dropped to 6.76. Most of the currently developed-countries have had similar experiences.

Changes in maternal mortality (usually measured by the number of deaths to women from conditions associated with pregnancy, labor, and the puerperium per 100,000 live births) also parallel the changes in the overall mortality level in most populations. The world average now is about 300. In the 1920s and 1930s the European and North American countries had maternal mortality rate as high as the current world average level. Many of the LDCs (less-developed countries) have today double the world average rate. In the LDCs, close to a quarter of deaths among women of reproductive ages may be due to complications in pregnancy, labor, or the puerperium. The age pattern of maternal mortality is J-shaped: teenage mothers are at higher risk, those in the low twenties generally have the lowest risk, and beginning in the late twenties maternal mortality rates increase with age. As in the case of infant mortality, the level of maternal mortality tends to be high among socio-economically disadvantaged subpopulations.

Children of the age group 1–14 years deserve special mention. They have characteristically the lowest age-specific death rates, irrespective of the overall mortality level. In the United States in 1989–1991, unintentional injuries were the leading cause of death among children of this age group, and among the deaths from unintentional injuries for such children, about 50% were due to motor vehicle crashes.

The story of mortality control in the LDCs is remarkably different from that of the MDCs. Life expectancy at birth in the LDCs in the period 1935–1939 was about the same as that prevailed in the early 1800s in Europe (about 30 years). A precipitous decline in mortality levels started in the LDCs in the 1940s and many LDCs accomplished in a few years the same degree of mortality reduction that took many decades for the European and North American countries to accomplish. The following figures illustrate the contrast. As estimated by the United Nations (1963), the average expectation of life at birth for six European countries and the state of Massachusetts was 41.0 years in 1840; it took five decades for this average to rise to 47.1 years and another four decades to rise to 61.7 years. (1840: 41.0 years; 1890: 47.1 years; 1930: 61.7 years.) In contrast, in Ceylon (now Sri Lanka) the life expectancy at birth increased from 46 to 60 years in a matter of 8 years (1946 to 1954), and in Taiwan from 43 to 62 years in 19 years (1938 to 1957).

It should be emphasized that in Europe and North America, during early stages of mortality decline, improvements occurred disproportionately at the younger ages, especially at the very young ages. When mortality levels are low, however, gains are concentrated at the older ages. This is because in such populations, mortality at the not-so-old ages has reached very low levels. Such differences have implications for the effects of mortality decline on the population's age composition, a topic that will be discussed in Chapter 7.

## 4.4. MORTALITY PATTERNS AT DIFFERENT STAGES OF TRANSITION

### 4.4.1. Before Transition

The main factors responsible for high and fluctuating mortality levels in pre-transition periods were infectious and parasitic diseases, wars, natural disasters, and famine. Conquerors of distant people served as carriers of pestilence to their home land. Contact with colonizers exposed native people to new diseases.

### 4.4.2. Early Stages of Transition

A characteristic feature of early stages of mortality transition in the West was the lowering of peaks of mortality mostly due to improved food supply and overall better living standards and to a lesser degree due to medical progress, sanitation measures, or organized public health activities.

As time went on, however, new factors emerged to sustain the mortality transition. In England, for example, during the latter half of the 19th century, a substantial part in mortality control was played by public health measures such as purification of water, better sewage disposal, and more proper food hygiene. Respiratory tuberculosis, whooping cough, measles, scarlet fever, and diphtheria were brought under control long before medical interventions for their control were invented (McKeown, 1976).

In the United States, the transition from the stage in which infectious and parasitic diseases reigned supreme to the stage when degenerative and diseases of human origin became the major killers was mostly due to improvements in living standards, personal hygiene, and housing, as well as to recession of certain diseases (Omran, 1977).

The currently less-developed countries borrowed the mortality-control know-how from the West and have been able to bring mortality levels down without investing substantially in developing a health and medical infrastructure (hospitals, clinics, trained medical and public health personnel). It is doubtful, however, whether mortality reduction could be sustained without such infrastructure.

### 4.4.3. Later Stages of Transition

In the later stages of mortality transition, heart diseases, cancers, and stroke together account for two-thirds of the underlying causes of death. It should be noted that the paths to later stages of mortality transition have not been the same for all populations (Omran, 1977). As mentioned, the western model (involving a slow process) is distinct from the path followed by countries such as Japan and those of Eastern Europe and from the one followed by the currently less-developed countries.

Different populations completed the later stages of mortality transition at different paces. Some starting from behind overtook others. For example, four decades ago Japan was behind many of the Western countries with respect the overall mortality level and infant mortality level, but no longer.

Females have led males during the later stages of mortality transition. The male–female gap in life expectancy has widened in many of the Western countries (see Fig. 4.5.). Genetic factors probably had a small part in this development, but the main factors responsible have been socio-cultural and behavioral in nature (Lopez and Ruzicka, 1983).

Life expectancy at birth has continued to climb in developed countries with improvements in such practices as reducing the intake of dietary fats and salts, avoiding obesity, exercising, sleeping enough, eating regularly, keeping alcohol consumption to moderate levels, and refraining from smoking tobacco. In other countries with no such improvements, life-expectancy gains have slowed.

### 4.4.5. *After Transition*

In the post-transition populations, according to one view, disabilities caused by diseases are expected to be compressed to a short period just prior to death (Fries, 1987). Another view is that longer life brings with it longer period of disabilities (Kaplan, 1991; Manton and Tolley, 1991). There seems to be consensus on the point that in the post-transition stage, many people who are kept alive

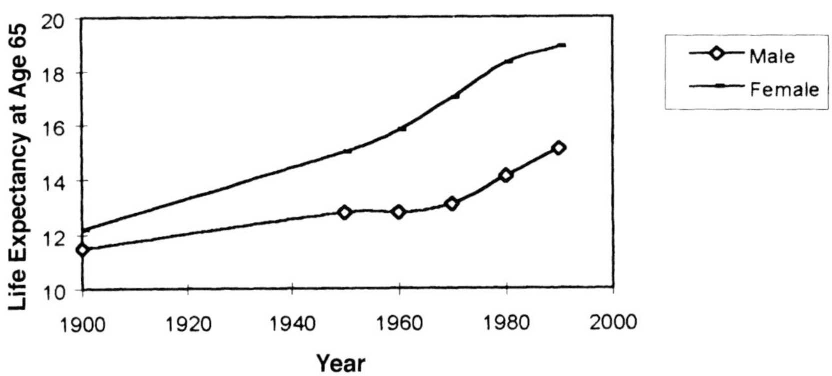


*Figure 4.5.* Life expectancy at age 65: U.S., all races combined (Source: NCHS, 1995, Table 30).

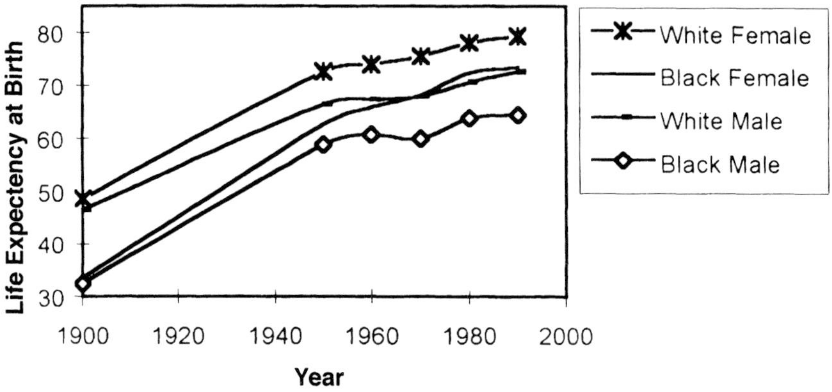


*Figure 4.6.* Life expectancy at birth: U.S. 1900–1990 (Source: NCHS, 1995, Table 30).

because of medical intervention, people who would have died otherwise, do not necessarily have optimal physical and mental well-being.

## 4.5. DIFFERENTIAL MORTALITY

Differential mortality refers to between-strata differences in mortality, when people are stratified (classified) by one or more demographic, social, economic, or behavioral variables. Mortality varies by age, sex, race/ethnicity, education and other socio-economic status indicators, marital status and "risk" behaviors such as smoking and reckless driving. The following patterns illustrate this point. (1) The age curve of mortality is J-shaped (Fig. 4.1). (2) Females have in most populations

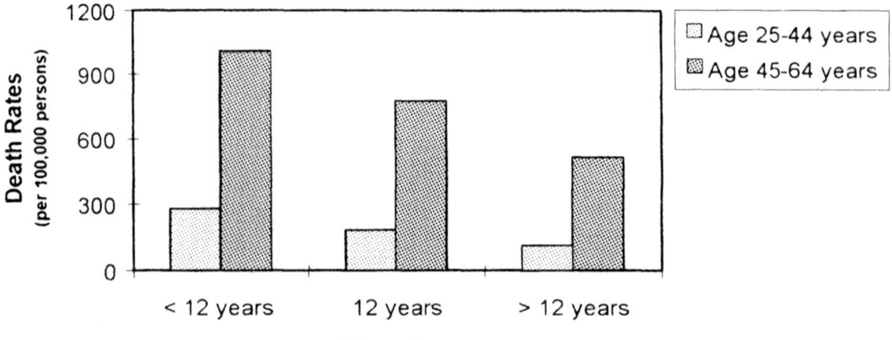


*Figure 4.7.* Death rates by educational attainment: U.S. 1990 (Source NCHS, 1995, Table 36).

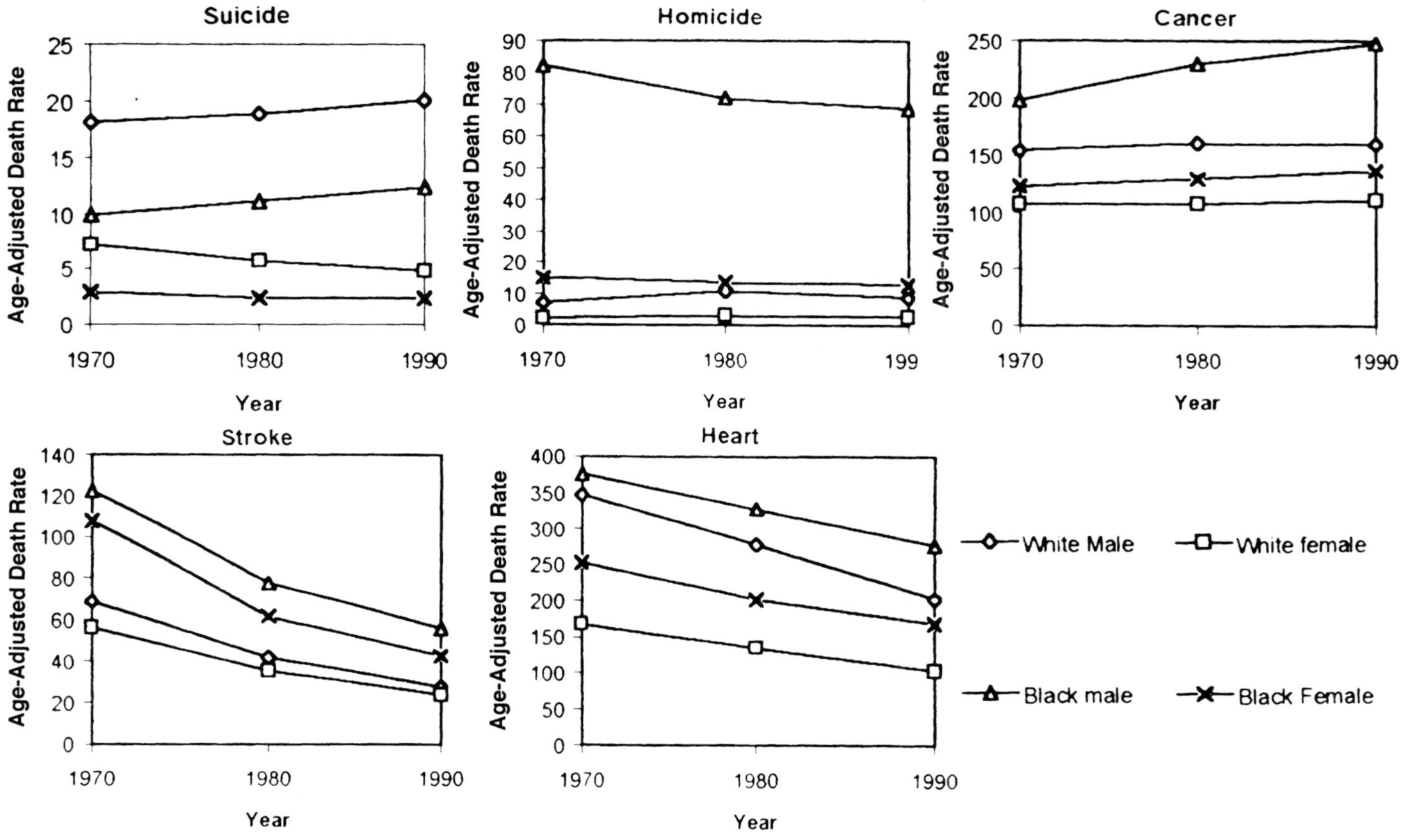


*Figure 4.8.* Age-adjusted death rates, selected causes, by race and sex: U.S. 1970, 1980, 1990. (Source NCHS, 1995, Tables 39, 40, 47, and 48.)

lower mortality than males, other things being equal (Fig. 4.6.). Part of the male–female differences in mortality under one year of age is generally attributed to biological sex differences. (3) People with poor resources and lower social-economic standing have higher mortality (Fig. 4.7.). Such differences are primarily a function of lifestyle and access to medical care. (4) Mortality due to certain diseases such as lung cancer tends to be higher for those who smoke than for those who do not. (5) Mortality tends to be lower for those who are married than for those who are single, widowed, divorced, or separated, other things being equal. Part of this difference is attributable to selectivity, people of poor health having a relatively lower chance of getting married, for example. (6) In the United States racial/ethnic group differences in mortality are pronounced (Fig. 4.6.), and these are believed to be largely due to the corresponding differences in resources, access to medical care, and "risk" behaviors (smoking, drinking, etc.). (7) In the United States in 1991: (a) suicide rates were higher among whites than among blacks, this being so for males and females, and higher among males than among females, this being so for whites and blacks (NCHS, 1994; Fig. 4.8a); (b) death rates due to homicide, unintentional injuries, stroke, heart disease, HIV infection, and lung cancer were higher for blacks than for whites, among males and females, and higher for males than for females, among blacks and whites (NCHS, 1994; Fig. 4.8b, c, d). (8) Social and economic differences in mortality persisted in many developed countries when overall mortality levels were declining (Lynge, 1984).

## 4.6. QUESTIONS AND ANSWERS*

**FOR EACH OF THE QUESTIONS IN SECTIONS 4.6.1. TO 4.6.4., STATE TRUE OR FALSE AND EXPLAIN.**

### 4.6.1. Mortality Levels and Trends

1. In the 18th century the life expectancy at birth in Europe was under 40 years.
2. Generally speaking, the level of infant mortality in a country is negatively associated with the level of economic development in the country.
3. In general, the rankings of countries with respect to the overall mortality level and infant mortality rate are correlated.
4. The U.S. infant mortality rate is the lowest in the world.
5. The global maternal mortality rate is currently about 300 per 100,000 live births.

*Answers start on page 82.

6. The plague called Black Death killed about a quarter of the European population.
7. The less developed countries of today made dramatic gains in mortality reduction beginning in the 1940s and 1950s, but the pace of improvement has slowed in many of them.

### 4.6.2. Mortality Control

8. Medical interventions were the primary factors responsible for mortality control in the beginning stages of the demographic transition in Europe.
9. Mortality control in the currently less-developed countries occurred primarily because of medical and public health measures.
10. Death control, once achieved, can be taken for granted.

### 4.6.3. Mortality Differentials

11. In general, death rates are higher for the socio-economically disadvantaged than for their better-off counterparts.
12. Universally, females have lower age-specific death rates at all ages than males.
13. Biological, socio-cultural, and behavioral factors account for the male-female gap in mortality.
14. The age-specific death rates tend to increase consistently with age.
15. The racial/ethnic differences in mortality can be explained mainly in terms of biological factors.
16. Married people tend to have lower mortality than divorced, separated, and widowed people.
17. Urban areas have lower mortality than rural areas in the same region; but it has not been always like that.

### 4.6.4. Causes of Death

18. As the mortality level of a population declines, the composition of death by cause is likely to change.
19. In the U.S., mortality rates from motor vehicle crashes have been highest among young males.
20. Nearly half of U.S. accidental deaths in the United States are caused by motor vehicle crashes.

**IN EACH OF THE QUESTIONS IN SECTIONS 4.6.5. TO 4.6.9., FOUR POSSIBLE ANSWERS ARE SUGGESTED, AT LEAST ONE OF WHICH IS CORRECT. IDENTIFY THE CORRECT ANSWER(S) AND EXPLAIN**

### 4.6.5. Concepts

1. The U.N. (1973) definition of death:
   A. Emphasizes permanent disappearance of all evidence of life
   B. Excludes fetal deaths
   C. Uses as a criterion the cessation of vital functions without capability of resuscitation
   D. Regards brain death as a sufficient condition

2. Mortality:
   A. According to the dictionary definition refers to the quality of being mortal
   B. Is treated by demographers as an aggregate phenomenon
   C. Is one of the components of population change
   D. Is no longer a subject of intensive demographic research

3. Life span:
   A. Refers to the maximum number of years a person can expect to live under ideal conditions
   B. Is higher than 120 years
   C. Does not vary from one population to another
   D. Is another term for the life expectancy at birth

4. Life expectancy at a given age ($x$):
   A. Is a concept developed in connection with the life table
   B. Invariably increases over time in a given population
   C. Varies from one population to another
   D. May take at $x = 0$ a value higher than the life span

5. Causes of death:
   A. Refer to the diseases, injuries, or complications that cause death
   B. Are routinely certified in the developed countries by a physician
   C. Are recorded on the death certificate in sequence beginning with the immediate cause and ending with the underlying cause
   D. Were recorded in the 17th century "bills of mortality" of some of the European cities

6. The term epidemiologic transition:
   A. Refers to shifts in health and disease patterns that occur over a long period of time
   B. Is a synonym for demographic transition

C. Was popularized by Abdel Omran
D. Refers to a topic that received no attention from demographers until the 1970s

7. As used in demography, frailty:
   A. Stands for the ability of human body to resist disease and illness
   B. Varies between individual members of a population
   C. Changes with age for any individual
   D. Is primarily a biological trait of individuals

8. Morbidity:
   A. Refers to the state of illness in a population
   B. Can be discerned from death certificates, hospital records, and returns from health interview surveys
   C. Is studied in terms of incidence and prevalence of specific diseases
   D. Is viewed by demographers as an individual experience rather than an aggregate phenomenon

### 4.6.6. *Measures*

9. Which of the following statements apply to age-specific death rates (ASDRs)?
   A. The ASDR has the same structure as that of the crude death rate (CDR), except that the numerator and denominator pertain to a specific age group in the case of ASDR and to the whole population in the case of CDR.
   B. It is possible for country A to have its ASDRs higher than those of country B, in each age group, and yet a lower CDR than in country B.
   C. When plotted on a graph using an arithmetic scale, the ASDRs exhibit a J-shape.
   D. The CDR is a weighted average of the ASDRs, with the age-composition of the population for weights.

10. The life table:
   A. Is a detailed statistical description of the survival versus nonsurvival experiences of the members of a hypothetical group of people born at the same time (e.g., in a given calendar year)
   B. Shows the probability of dying within specified time interval, such as five years, for those who survive to a given birthday anniversary
   C. Can be constructed from the age-specific death rates of a population for a given period (e.g., a calendar year)
   D. In a rudimentary form was developed first by Edmund Halley

11. Which of the following statements is (are) true with respect to either the measurement or the early 1990s levels of infant mortality?
   A. It is measured in terms of the annual number of deaths below one year of age per 1000 live births

B. Its average African level has been higher than the world average
C. Its average Latin American level has been lower than the world average
D. Its average Asian level has been lower than the Latin-American average

### 4.6.7. Levels and Trends

12. Which of the following statements apply to the life expectancy at birth at the global or major regional levels as of the early 1990s?
    A. At the global level it was about 65 years
    B. Asian and African levels were below the world average
    C. The Latin American level was above the world average
    D. Above-the-world average level prevailed in the developed countries

13. The historical morbidity data for Europe and the United States indicate:
    A. That the risk of dying declined sharply during the 19th century
    B. That the age-specific incidence of disease and injury remained unchanged for all practical purposes
    C. That the age-specific duration of disease and injury increased
    D. That longer life does not necessarily mean longer healthy life

14. Which of the following statements apply to mortality levels and trends in the less-developed countries (LDCs)?
    A. Life expectancy at birth in the 1930s in the LDCs was about the same level as that prevailed in Europe in the early 1800s
    B. A precipitous decline in mortality occurred in many LDCs in the 1940s
    C. Many LDCs accomplished mortality transition from high to low levels in much shorter time than the present MDCs did
    D. There is considerable homogeneity between the current LDCs with respect to their experiences in mortality transition

15. What do we know about the mortality situation in populations prior to the onset of mortality transition?
    A. Epidemics were prevalent even thousands of years ago
    B. Infectious and parasitic diseases, wars, natural disasters, and limitations of food supply together kept mortality levels high in the pretransition periods
    C. Conquests of distant lands and people often opened the gates for pestilence in the home land of the conquerors
    D. Contact with the conquerors exposed the conquered to diseases to which they had little immunity

16. Which of the following statements apply to the Western mortality transition during the eighteenth and early nineteenth centuries?
    A. The first noticeable development was a lowering of peaks of mortality rates

   B. Increased food supplies, improved nutrition, and overall better living standards were responsible for most of the early declines in mortality
   C. Medical progress and organized public health activities played only a minor role in the beginning of mortality transition
   D. It was the biological law of natural selection that made the early mortality decline possible

17. What lies ahead for low mortality populations?
   A. According to one view, in the not too distant future, everyone would live a long and healthy life, with disability caused by ill health confined to a short period before death
   B. According to another view, life expectancy may remain high, but long life may not necessarily be a long healthy life
   C. What is in store for the elderly will depend upon medical breakthroughs and control of risk factors, neither of which is predictable with any certainty
   D. William Godwin's prophesy would come true in the 21st century

18. Which of the following statements apply to U.S. infant mortality level?
   A. Infant mortality rate has been declining in the United States and has reached record low levels
   B. All major racial/ethnic groups now have more or less the same level of infant mortality
   C. The U.S. level of infant mortality is higher than that of many other countries
   D. Information regarding the covariates of infant mortality is scanty

19. Which of the following apply to maternal mortality rate?
   A. Its global level is about 300 deaths per 100,000 live births
   B. In less-developed countries maternal mortality accounts for close to a quarter of all deaths to women in reproductive ages
   C. In South Asian region, the maternal mortality level at present is about double the global level
   D. In the 1920s and 1930s the maternal mortality level in the United States was at about the present global level

### *4.6.8. Cause of Death*

20. The United Nations' analysis of cause-composition of death revealed:
   A. That at high mortality conditions, infectious and parasitic diseases claim about 45% of the deaths, and cancers and cardiovascular diseases claim another 20%

B. That at low mortality levels, infectious and parasitic diseases become almost insignificant, while the claims of cancers and cardiovascular diseases become quite high
C. That the fraction of death with causes unclassified or unknown is smaller when mortality is very low than when it is very high
D. That violence claims a higher proportion of deaths than cancers and cardiovascular diseases do in low-mortality populations

21. Regarding causes of death among children of ages 1–14 in the United States, which of the following statements are true?
A. Unintentional injuries topped the list of major killers
B. Homicide was close behind
C. Motor vehicle crashes were the major cause of deaths due to unintentional injuries
D. There were no significant racial/ethnic group differences in regard to death rates from the causes mentioned in choice A

### 4.6.9. *Mortality Differentials*

22. Which of the following statements apply to mortality differentials?
A. The term stands for differences in mortality between people classified by demographic, social, or economic characteristics
B. In the developed countries there are persistent, and perhaps increasing, socioeconomic differentials in mortality
C. Those who have fewer resources and lower social and economic standing have higher mortality levels
D. Racial/ethnic group differences in mortality are often a function of the corresponding differences in resources, access to medical care, and "risk" behaviors such as smoking and drinking

23. The statement "death rates from ______ were higher for males than for females among blacks and whites and higher for blacks than for whites among males and females" applies to which of the following causes of death in the United States in the decade ending in 1991?
A. Homicide
B. Unintentional injuries
C. Stroke
D. Suicide

24. The male–female gap in life expectancy at birth:
A. Has favored females in the developed countries
B. Has favored males in a number of less-developed countries until recently
C. Has been increasing until recently in the developed countries

D. Has been higher in the developed countries than in the less-developed countries

25. Regarding life expectancy at birth for U.S. black males and females and white males and females, which of the following statements are true as of 1991?
    A. White females outranked the other groups
    B. Black males had the lowest life expectancy at birth
    C. Black females outranked white males
    D. The 1991 life expectancy at birth for black males was a record high

26. Among behaviors that increase the chance of premature deaths are:
    A. Smoking and/or drinking
    B. Eating snacks and/or skipping breakfast
    C. Sleeping too little or too long
    D. Exercising too little or too much

27. Among the determinants of maternal mortality are:
    A. Delayed treatment for obstetric complications
    B. High fertility rate
    C. Nutrition that expectant mothers get
    D. Climate

**FOR EACH OF THE QUESTIONS IN SECTIONS 4.6.10. TO 4.6.14, FIVE POSSIBLE ANSWERS ARE SUGGESTED, ONLY ONE OF WHICH IS CORRECT. IDENTIFY THE CORRECT ANSWER AND EXPLAIN**

### *4.6.10. Concepts*

1. Which of the following is not studied under the topic of mortality?
    A. Infant deaths
    B. Abortion
    C. Mortality differentials
    D. Mortality trends
    E. Cause of death.

2. Which of the following terms most closely captures the human body's capacity to resist illness or disease
    A. Mortality
    B. Morbidity
    C. Mobility
    D. Disability
    E. Frailty

3. The crude death rate is called crude because:
   A. The risk set it uses in the denominator is not homogeneous enough to insure reliable inferences in comparative studies
   B. It ignores causes of death
   C. It can be calculated only in census years
   D. It is seldom used in developed countries
   E. It cannot be calculated for periods other than a calendar year

4. Life expectancy at birth is:
   A. A statistic readily available in a life table
   B. Equal to the life span
   C. Time-invariant
   D. Constant across population subgroups
   E. Never greater than the average remaining lifetime for those surviving to the first birthday anniversary

### 4.6.11. Levels and Trends

5. Since the 1920s, mortality levels in the currently less-developed countries have:
   A. Increased sharply
   B. Increased slightly
   C. Remained unchanged
   D. Decreased slightly
   E. Decreased sharply

6. Which of the following does not belong to the set of which the others are elements?
   A. High mortality level
   B. Low level of economic development
   C. High fertility
   D. Inadequate or incomplete demographic data
   E. Low infant mortality rate

7. Which of the following countries does not belong to the set of which the others are members (using 1994 life expectancy at birth as the membership criterion)?
   A. Singapore
   B. Malaysia
   C. Hong Kong
   D. Taiwan
   E. India

8. Which of the following regions does not belong to the set of which the others are members (using 1994 life expectancy at birth as the membership criterion)?

A. Northern Europe
B. Western Europe
C. Eastern Europe
D. Southern Europe
E. North America

9. Of the countries, ______ had in the mid-1990s the lowest life expectancy at birth.
A. Sri Lanka
B. The Philippines
C. Malaysia
D. Thailand
E. India

10. Which of the following regions does not belong to the set of which the others are members (using for the membership criterion the 1994 level of infant mortality)?
A. Northern Africa
B. Western Africa
C. Eastern Africa
D. Middle Africa
E. Pakistan combined with Afghanistan

11. Among the following regions, which one has higher infant mortality rate than all the rest?
A. Northern Africa
B. Southern Africa
C. Middle Africa
D. Southern Asia
E. Eastern Asia

### *4.6.12. The Role of Different Factors in Mortality Control*

12. Which of the following is not regarded as a major factor in producing mortality decline before the 20th century?
A. Improved food supply
B. Better living conditions
C. Use of soap
D. Advances in medical technology
E. Improved clothing

13. Which of the following factors contributed in a major way to the dramatic mortality decline in the less-developed countries during the 20th century?
A. Public health and medical services
B. Improved level of education

C. Improved nutrition
D. Reduction in smoking
E. Weight control

### 4.6.13. Causes of Death

14. Which of the following was not among the leading five causes of death in the United States as of the early 1990s?
    A. Heart disease
    B. Cancer
    C. Stroke
    D. Unintentional injuries
    E. Suicide
15. Which of the following causes of death is (are) associated with alcohol consumption, smoking, and other things that are ordinarily thought of as part of lifestyle?
    A. Heart disease
    B. Diabetes mellitus
    C. Cirrhosis of the liver
    D. All of the above
    E. Only A and B
16. In the United States, the group at highest risk of committing suicide is:
    A. Teenagers
    B. Older white males
    C. Middle-aged black males
    D. Older black males
    E. Older white females
17. Currently, in the United States the leading cause of death is:
    A. Cancer
    B. Heart disease
    C. AIDS
    D. Stroke
    E. Unintentional injuries
18. Which of the following does not belong to the set of which the others are elements?
    A. Infected fleas
    B. Lice
    C. Ticks
    D. Mosquitoes
    E. Alligators

### 4.6.14. Mortality Differentials

19. In the United States certain minority groups have a higher life expectancy than whites. An explanation for this can be found in:
    A. Social and economic factors
    B. The influence of minority status on behavior
    C. Biological factors
    D. Geographic factors
    E. Climate

20. Which of the following is NOT a characteristic of a currently developed country?
    A. Birth to age 1 is the riskiest age interval under 65 years
    B. The vast majority of infant deaths are accounted for by prematurity or low birth weight
    C. A J-shape for the age pattern of age-specific death rates
    D. Preponderance of deaths from cardiovascular disease at older ages
    E. Higher mortality rate in urban than in rural areas

**FOR EACH OF THE QUESTIONS IN SECTION 4.6.15., STATE TRUE OR FALSE AND EXPLAIN (THESE QUESTIONS MAY BE MORE DIFFICULT THAN THOSE INCLUDED IN SECTION 4.6.1. TO 4.6.4.)**

### 4.6.15. Concepts

1. In demography "bills of mortality" means the hospital bills for the treatment given to those who died while hospitalized.
2. Cardiovascular disease means disease of the heart and blood vessels.
3. Case fatality rate is a crude death rate for persons contracting a specific disease.
4. Cohort life table is another name for the ordinary (period) life table in which a hypothetical group of lives is followed up until no survivor is left.
5. The complete life table is so named because it has all the columns that a life table is supposed to contain.
6. Mortality crisis means a sudden sharp rise in death rate.
7. The crude death rate is strongly influenced by the age structure of the population.
8. Stillbirth is not a death, according to the WHO definition.
9. Abortion is not a death.

10. Differential mortality refers, among other things, to cross-national comparisons of mortality.

11. The directly standardized death rate of population A, using population B as the standard, is the crude death rate in population A that would result if population A retains its own age-specific death rates, but adopts the age composition of population B.

12. A disability in demographic usage refers to any reduction of a person's activity because of an acute or chronic health condition.

13. The term endogenous mortality refers to mortality attributable to environmental forces.

14. Epidemics and endemics mean the same thing.

15. Epidemiology is the scientific study of epidemics.

16. Ischemic heart disease is due to the deficiency of blood reaching the tissues of the heart.

17. The terms "incidence rate" and "prevalence rate" are synonyms in epidemiology.

18. The most common measure of death in infancy is the infant death rate.

19. Infectious disease is a disease caused by invasion and multiplication of microorganism in body tissues.

20. Instantaneous death rate is the crude death rate for instant deaths, the extreme opposite of lingering deaths.

21. Life expectancy is current age plus the remaining lifetime.

22. The term "life table functions" refers to the various uses of the life table.

23. At low levels of infant mortality, neonatal deaths account for most of infant deaths.

24. Pandemics are diseases of pandas.

25. The interaction between infectious disease and malnutrition helps to account for the high levels of infant and child mortality in low income countries.

❖ ❖ ❖ ❖

### 4.6.1. Answers

1. True. Throughout the long span of history until about 1650, the average life expectancy at birth was probably 25 years or less. Durand (1960), after

reviewing various attempts to estimate the life expectancy at birth from Roman tombstones, came to the conclusion that in the Roman Empire life expectancy at birth averaged between 25 and 30 years. By about 1840, when the first reliable life table became available for Northwestern Europe, the life expectancy at birth had risen there to 41 years.

2. True. This is perhaps one of the major reasons why in some cross-national studies, infant mortality is used as an indicator of development.
3. True. To give a numerical illustration, in 1995, Canada had lower infant mortality rate and higher life expectancy at birth than the United States (7 versus 9 and 78 versus 76 years); India had lower infant mortality rate and higher life expectancy rate than Bangladesh (74 versus 108 and 60 versus 55 years); and so on. Of course all paired comparisons would not give consistent ranking on both infant mortality rate and life expectancy at birth.
4. False. Denmark (5.7); Finland (4.4); Ireland (6.0); Norway (5.8); Sweden (4.8); United Kingdom (6.6); Austria (6.2); France (6.1); Germany (5.8); the Netherlands (5.9); Switzerland (5.6); Spain (7.6); Australia (6.1); New Zealand (6.9); Canada (7.0); and Japan (4.3)—all had infant mortality rate lower than the U.S. rate (8.0) in 1995 (see Population Reference Bureau's 1995 *World Population Data Sheet*).
5. True. For the United States it was 7.2 in 1991. (Nam, 1994, p. 149; NCHS, 1995, p. 128.)
6. True. The Black Death, as the plague that ravaged Europe between 1347 and 1351 came to be called, is believed to have killed about 25 million people, almost a quarter of the European population, during its short spell.
7. True. In the 1940s and 1950s many of the less-developed countries embarked upon mortality control programs based on technology borrowed from the more-developed countries. The rate of reduction in mortality levels was so dramatic that it was impossible to keep it up for a long period of time. When the easier-to-handle causes of death were brought under control the remaining task became naturally tougher, requiring not only more expensive programs, but basic improvements in the standard of living and alterations of the lifestyle.

### 4.6.2. Answers

8. False. The early stages of mortality reduction took place in Europe during the 100 years or so starting with early 1700s. Control of epidemic diseases produced the first gains. One opinion is that population that survived the epidemics developed resistance to many infectious diseases (McNeil, 1976).

Another opinion is that improvements in food supplies and nutrition and the betterment of living standards were the factors responsible for the early reduction in mortality in Europe (McKeown, 1976). In countries where the quality of rural life improved, mortality declined; while in cities with rampant poverty, crowding, hazardous working conditions, and poor sanitation, mortality remained high (Kunitz, 1983).

9. True. Public health measures such as massive-scale immunization, malaria eradication programs, and the use of antibiotics and other "wonder drugs" helped the less-developed countries to reduce their death rates dramatically.

10. False. The rise in death rates in some of the Eastern European countries and the former Soviet Union illustrate the point. One should not expect the mortality conditions to remain immune to the worsening of social and economic conditions in a country. Also note that even in countries where the social and economic conditions appear good on surface, the mortality level of some population groups may worsen, as illustrated by the decline in life expectancy at birth for U.S. black males from 65.3 years to 64.3 years between 1984 and 1989 (NCHS, 1995, p. 96).

### 4.6.3. *Answers*

11. True. People who have fewer resources and lower social and economic standing have higher mortality than their counterparts who are socio-economically better-off. Differentials in mortality have been reported in terms of income, quality of housing, household amenities, educational attainments, occupational status, and others (Ruzicka, 1989; Lynge, 1984; Feldman *et al.*, 1989).

12. False. The main exception is in less-developed countries where maternal mortality rates are high. In such countries, age-specific death rates have often been higher for females than for males in certain age groups (when women are at the principal reproductive ages) and life expectancy at birth has been lower for females than for males.

13. True. Some causes of deaths are sex-linked (e.g., deaths from pregnancy and related complications among females, prostate cancer among males). Even with respect to such causes of death as cardiovascular diseases, biological factors have been invoked in explaining male–female differences in mortality (Lopez and Ruzicka, 1983). Turning to sociocultural factors, it has been pointed out in the literature (Nag, 1991) that tradition tends to favor one sex over the other with respect to practices that have health implications (e.g., who gets better food; who gets involved in hazardous activities). Finally, behaviors

that have male–female differences with health implications include smoking, drinking, drug use, dietary habits, health care, and exercise.

14. False. The age pattern of death rate is J-shaped when plotted on arithmetic scale and looks more like a check mark (✓) when plotted using a semi-logarithmic (arithmetic on the horizontal for age and logarithmic on the vertical for age-specific death rates) scale (see Figs. 4.1 and 4.2).

15. False. Most of the racial/ethnic group differences in mortality are accounted for in terms of socio-economic factors (affecting resources and access to health care) and behavioral factors affecting lifestyle.

16. True. Usually, divorced males have higher death rates than their counterparts in any other marital status. There is a certain amount of selectivity involved with respect to the health status of those who get married—people who are physically handicapped or in ill health may have a lower chance of getting married and a higher death rate. With respect to mortality from diseases that require long-term care, a person with a spouse has generally an advantage. Behavioral factors such as excessive alcohol consumption and smoking also help explain some of the marital status differences in mortality. Single and divorced males have higher death rates from cirrhosis of the liver, associated with heavy drinking, and from lung cancer, associated with smoking.

17. True. There was a time when mortality rates in urban areas were higher than those in rural areas of the same region. Crowded living conditions, lack of protected water supply, open sewage systems, and the like put urban dwellers in a higher risk category.

### 4.6.4. Answers

18. True. When life expectancy at birth is low (e.g., 40 years), infectious and parasitic diseases, influenza and pneumonia, and bronchitis below the age of 5 years, account for about 45% of all deaths in a population. As the life expectancy increases, the proportion of death due to cancer and cardiovascular diseases and bronchitis above the age of 5 years increases progressively. (United Nations, 1963, p. 110; Lopez, 1990; see also Fig. 4.3).

19. True. In the United States, the motor vehicle crash-related mortality rate (per 100,000 persons) for the period 1989–1991 was 33.6 for the age group 15–24 years, while the corresponding figures were 6.1 for those of age 1–14 years, and 19.8, 15.3, and 23.0, respectively for those in the older age groups, 25–44 years, 45–64 years, and 65 years and older (NCHS, 1994, p. 106). The pattern was the same, although the levels were not, for different racial/ethnic groups.

20. True. U.S. death rate for unintentional injures in 1992 was 33.8 per 100,000 persons and that for motor vehicle crashes (a subset of unintentional injuries) was 16.4 per 100,000 persons (NCHS, 1994, p. 139).

### 4.6.5. Answers

1. A, B, and C: According to the U.N. (1973) definition death is "the permanent disappearance of all evidence of life at any time after birth has taken place." The case in which the heart is pumping while the brain is dead is not death according to this definition. Fetal deaths are excluded because they occur prior to birth.

2. A, B, and C: Mortality is a process that depletes the size of membership of a population through death. Death occurs to individuals, but mortality is a collective phenomenon. There was a time when mortality was not given much attention by demographers. But at present it is a "hot" topic.

3. A, B, and C: Weeks (1994, p. 159) refers to an authenticated case of a Japanese person who lived almost up to his 121st birthday anniversary. This puts the lower bound of life span at 120 years. Life span and life expectancy at birth are not the same. The latter is the average length of life of a group of people born at the same time and die in accordance with a given schedule of age-specific death rates.

4. A and C: The life expectancy at age $x$ is the average length of life remaining for those who survive to the $x$th birthday anniversary among a group born at the same time and die in accordance with a given schedule of age-specific death rates. It varies from one population to another and over time in the same population. The life expectancy at age 65 was 11.5 years for U.S. white males at the turn of the 20th century and had increased to 15.5 years by 1992 (NCHS, 1994, Table 27; see also Fig. 4.5). But there is no guarantee that the life expectancy at birth will continually increase in a given population. For example, in the United States, the life expectancy at birth for black males dropped from 65.3 years in 1984 to 64.3 years by 1989 (NCHS, 1994, Table 30). Life expectancy at birth cannot exceed life span, the latter being the maximum possible length of life at ideal conditions.

5. A, B, C, and D: The disease or the condition that just precedes death is the immediate cause. Prior causes that led to the immediate cause are supposed to be listed sequentially on the death certificate. The last mentioned cause in the sequence is the "underlying cause." Under the WHO recommendation, only the underlying cause is included in the official cause-of-death statistics. As for choice D, it is known that London's "bills of mortality" of the seventeenth century contained classification of burials by causes of death (Wilson, 1985, p. 16).

6. A and C: Omran (1971) highlighted how health and disease patterns change with social and economic development. He distinguished three stages: the age of pestilence and famine, the age of receding pandemics, and the age of degenerative disease and diseases of human origin. Epidemiologic transition is basically the shifts in composition of death by cause. Reasonably good data on cause of death are available for all developed countries. But the available information is defective and incomplete for most of the less-developed countries. Hence most of the discussions have been based on materials pertaining to the currently more-developed countries. As for choice D, it should be noted that the interest in the shift in cause composition of death predates the popularization of the term epidemiologic transition in the 1970s (see United Nations, 1963; see also Fig. 4.3).

7. A, B, and C: Frailty does have a biological component inherited from parents, but it is influenced by the environment too. The annual chance of dying (the probability of dying within the year) is positively related to the frailty level. Those who are more frail die, on average, sooner than their less-frail counterparts.

8. A, B, and C: The dictionary definitions of morbidity include: (i) the condition of being diseased, and (ii) the ratio of sick to well persons in a community (*Dorland's Illustrated Medical Dictionary*). The latter, however, is a measure of morbidity rather than an indication of a conceptual dimension of the term. Demographers view morbidity as an aggregate phenomenon. As for choice C, epidemiology distinguishes the incidence of a disease from its prevalence. In the former the emphasis is on new cases identified during a given period, whereas in the latter the emphasis is on the number of persons ill as of a given time, irrespective of when their illness started or was identified.

### 4.6.6. Answers

9. A, B, C, and D: The explanation for choice B is in choices C and D. A simple numerical illustration helps to make the point. Consider the following sequences of ASDRs for populations A and B: (A) (0.005, 0.001, 0.05); (B) (0.008, 0.002, 0.06). Suppose the corresponding population age compositions are as follows: (A) (0.3, 0.1, 0.6); (B) (0.5, 0.1, 0.4). The weighted averages of the ASDRs using the corresponding age-composition as weights are 0.0316 and 0.0288, respectively. Thus we have in this illustration, population B having its ASDRs higher than those of population A in each age group, yet the CDR of population A is higher than that of population B.

10. A, B, and C: It was John Graunt who introduced the idea of the life table in a rudimentary form. Edmund Halley (1656–1742) published a life table based

on data on deaths for the city of Breslau (now Wroclaw in Poland). Halley's life table was the first one based entirely on data, and was an improvement on Graunt's, who supplemented actual data with hypothetical numbers. The first scientifically correct life table was that of Joshua Milne (1776–1851), who used deaths classified by age and the base population also classified by age to calculate age-specific death rates, from which probability of dying within a specified intervals for those alive at the beginning of the interval was calculated (Wilson, 1985).

There are two main types of life tables, the so-called complete and abridged ones. The latter gives information for each successive (usually five-year) age groups and for the beginning point of each age group. The complete life table gives information for each birthday anniversary and each individual age interval.

The following is a simple (complete) life table for an animal population with a life span of 4 years. The first column shows the birthday and the successive birthday anniversaries. The next columns shows the number alive on each birthday anniversary, starting with 1000 (an arbitrary number) at birth. The third column gives the probability of dying within the year for the just-born and for those alive at a given birthday anniversary. The next column gives the number of deaths in the group in each year. The figures in this column are the products of the corresponding figures in the second and third columns. Thus, 200 = 1000 × 0.02; 100 = 800 × 0.125, and so on. The last-but-one column gives the number of years lived during each age interval. These figures are obtained by counting 1 year each for those who survive the interval and ½ year each for those who die in the interval. Thus, 900 = 800 + (200/2); 750 = 700 + (100/2); and so on. The last column gives the life expectancy in years at birth or at a given birthday anniversary. The figures in the last column are obtained by cumulating the figures in the last-but-one column from the bottom and dividing the result with the corresponding figure in the second column. 0.50 = 175/350; 1.00 = (175 + 525)/700; 1.81 = (175 + 525 + 750)/800; 2.35 = (175 + 525 + 750 + 900)/1000. In this population the life expectancy at birth is 2.35 years. Those who survive to their first birthday anniversary can expect

| Age | Number alive | Probability of dying | Number of deaths | Years lived | Life expectancy |
|---|---|---|---|---|---|
| 0 | 1000 | 0.200 | 200 | 900 | 2.35 |
| 1 | 800 | 0.125 | 100 | 750 | 1.81 |
| 2 | 700 | 0.500 | 350 | 525 | 1.00 |
| 3 | 350 | 1.000 | 350 | 175 | 0.50 |
| 4 | 0 | | | | |

to live another 1.81 years on average. Those who survive to the second birthday anniversary can expect to live another year. And so on.

11. A, B, and C: The following are figures for 1994: world, 63; Africa, 92; North America, 8; Latin America, 49; Asia, 63; Europe, 11; Oceania, 27. (Population Reference Bureau, *1994 World Population Data Sheet*).

### 4.6.7. Answers

12. A, B, C, and D: The following are for 1993: world, 65 years; Africa, 54 years; Asia, 64 years; North America, 76 years; Latin America, 68 years; Europe, 75 years; Oceania, 73 years (Population Reference Bureau's *1993 World Population Data Sheet*.)
13. A, B, C, and D: Rilely and Alter (1989) found choices B and C true and Verbrugge (1984) concluded choice D to be true.
14. A, B, and C: With respect to choice C, one demographer put it thus, "nothing in the history would have prepared a pre-World War II or even a 1950 observer for the mortality trends that soon emerged" (Stolnitz, 1982, p. 465). The LDCs are not at all homogeneous with respect to the date when sustained mortality decline started or the time it took for them to reach moderately low levels of mortality.
15. A, B, C, and D: According to Zinsser (1934, p. 106), "it is certain that epidemics were prevalent thousands of years before Christ." According to Cartwright (1972), "By her contact with distant lands and peoples, Rome opened her gates to pestilence." The severe impact of the contact with the European colonizers on the mortality level of the native American Indians is well known (Snipp, 1989).
16. A, B, and C: When epidemics were brought under control, the peaks of mortality rates were lowered. With respect to choices B and C, see McKeown (1976). With respect to choice D, note that if natural selection were the underlying mechanism, sustained mortality decline would have occurred long before it actually did.
17. A, B, and C: For the position represented by choice A see Fries (1987). For the position represented in choice B see Kaplan (1991). No one among the contemporary demographers has as yet subscribed to Godwin's optimistic prediction that humanity would conquer death completely.
18. A and C: In 1991, the U.S. infant mortality rate was 8.9 per 1000 live births, which was indeed a record low. The figure for blacks was 17.6, while that for whites was only 7.3. Between 1985 and 1991, infant mortality declined 21% for whites and 7% for blacks. (NCHS, 1994, p. 1). The socio-economically

disadvantaged groups tend to have higher infant mortality rates. Also, it is known that among the factors affecting infant mortality rates are various behaviors (e.g., smoking of women prior to or during pregnancy, inadequate prenatal and postnatal care, and low birth weight).

19. A, B, C, and D: The global level of maternal mortality rate is currently about 300, that for the South Asian region is about double that. The European and North American level in the 1920s and 1930s was not much different from the current global level. The 1991 U.S. level was as reported in NCHS (1994, p. 127), 7.2 (5.0 for whites and 18.1 for blacks).

### 4.6.8. Answers

20. A, B, and C: Violence claims relatively a small fraction of all deaths (United Nations, 1963, p. 110). These patterns are discussed in several textbooks including Nam, 1994, pp. 141–145. (See also Fig. 4.3).

21. A and C: See NCHS, 1994, p. 28. Deaths from automobile crashes accounted for about 50% of all deaths due to unintentional injuries. Homicide was not an important cause of death, except among black children. There were marked differences between major racial/ethnic groups with respect to mortality from unintentional injuries. The 1989–91 average rates were 19.3 per 100,000 children among American Indians, 18.3 among blacks, 12.0 among whites, and 8.2 among Asians.

### 4.6.9. Answers

22. A, B, C, and D: Socio-economic differences in mortality have remained substantial even in many developed countries. For example, in France and the Scandinavian countries, among men of age 40–55 years, mortality was in recent times twice as high for unskilled workers as for professionals (Lynge, 1984). In the United States, reductions in mortality since the 1960s were more rapid among the better educated groups (Feldman *et al.*, 1989). In some of the Latin American countries, when infant mortality was declining in the 1970s, social class differentials were maintained (Guzman, 1989). In the United States, the difference in life expectancy at birth between black females and white females widened from 5.3 years in 1985 to 5.8 years in 1991; the average annual rate of decrease in the infant mortality rate was less rapid for black infants than for white infants during the 1980s (2.1 percent vs. 3.5 percent) and the 1970s (3.8 percent vs. 4.8 percent). (NCHS, 1994, p. 18).

23. A, B, and C: Throughout the decade in question, suicide rates were higher for whites than for blacks among males and females and higher for males than for females among blacks and whites. (NCHS, 1994, pp. 25–27).

24. A, B, C, and D: Women generally live longer on average than men do. The exception occurs in countries where maternal mortality is high. The female advantage over males in life expectancy at birth has been increasing in many of the more-developed countries until recently. In the United States, the gap was only 2 years at the turn of the century, and peaked at 7.8 years by mid 1970s; in 1992 the gap was 6.7 years (NCHS, 1994, p. 91). In 1994, the male–female gap was 7 years in the more-developed regions of the world and only 3 years in the less-developed regions (Population Reference Bureau's *1994 World Population Data Sheet*).

25. A, B, and C: The 1991 life expectancy at birth was 79.6 years for white females, 73.8 years for black females, 72.9 years for white males, and 64.6 years for black males. The 1984 life expectancy at birth for black males was 65.3 years. (NCHS, 1994, p. 1, p. 20).

26. A, B, C, and D: Good health habits include not smoking; not drinking alcoholic beverages (or at least keeping the consumption to a moderate level, e.g., not more than five drinks during a two-week period); keeping weight in accordance with weight–height standards; exercising regularly, but not overdoing it; eating breakfast daily; refraining from eating snacks; and sleeping about 6–7 hours each day (Nam, 1994, p. 140). The evidence for the health benefits of some of these habits are not strong.

27. A, B, and C: There are some writers who believe that natural factors such as climatic conditions affect mortality levels and trends (Perrenoud, 1984), but the view is not widely shared.

### *4.6.10. Answers*

1. B: Abortion, which is not regarded as death, according to the usual definition.
2. E: Frailty.
3. A: In particular it ignores age variation in the risk of dying within the year.
4. A: Often life expectancy at birth is lower than the life expectancy at the first birthday anniversary. This is because the former is heavily influenced by the infant mortality rate while the latter is not.

### *4.6.11. Answers*

5. E: The borrowing of death-control know-how from the developed countries was a major factor that made this possible.
6. E: All except low infant mortality rate are characteristics of less-developed countries of Africa.

7. E: India's life expectancy at birth was 57 years in 1994, while all the other countries mentioned had life expectancy at birth exceeding 70 years in that year: Singapore, 74; Malaysia, 71; Hong Kong, 78; Taiwan, 74.

8. C: All except Eastern Europe have life expectancy at birth exceeding 75, while that of Eastern Europe is lower than 70 years.

9. E: India. The 1995 life expectancy at birth in India was 60 years, according to Population Reference Bureau's *1995 World Population Data Sheet.* The corresponding figures for the other countries were: Sri Lanka, 73; the Philippines, 65; Malaysia, 71; Thailand, 70.

10. A: In all regions other than Northern Africa, the 1994 infant mortality rate was higher than 95, whereas, in Northern Africa it was only 65.

11. C: The infant mortality rate in 1994 was 102 infant deaths per 1000 live births in Middle Africa, while the corresponding figures for the other regions were: Northern Africa, 65, Southern Africa, 52, Southern Asia, 58, and Eastern Asia 29. Population Reference Bureau's *1994 World Population Data Sheet.*

### *4.6.12. Answers*

12. D: Advances in medical technology became a major factor only after the turn of the 20th century.

13. A: Public health and medical services.

### *4.6.13. Answers*

14. E: Suicide was the ninth leading cause of death in 1992, for all races and both sexes combined. The ten leading causes of death (for all races and both sexes combined) in the United States during 1992 were, in order from high to low of the percentage deaths claimed, diseases of heart, cancer, stroke, chronic obstructive pulmonary diseases, unintentional injuries, pneumonia and influenza, diabetes mellitus, HIV infection, suicide, homicide and legal intervention. (NCHS, 1995, p. 101.)

15. D.

16. B: Older white males.

17. B: Heart disease. See Question 14 in this section.

18. E: All except alligators are carriers of disease causing agents.

### 4.6.14. Answers

19. A: Social and economic factors affecting lifestyle and access to medical care.
20. E: Mortality rates are now lower in urban than in rural areas. However, it was not always so.

### 4.6.15. Answers

1. False. The reference is to the weekly summaries of information on deaths that occurred in European cities prepared for use by city authorities, a practice that started in the 15th century and became increasingly more complete and more detailed over time. Thus the London's "bills of mortality" included in the 17th century a classification of deaths by cause (Wilson, 1985).
2. True. Coronary heart disease and stroke are the major ones. The former affects the coronary arteries that supply blood to the tissues of the heart itself and stroke affects the brain.
3. False. It is calculated by relating the number of deaths from the disease to the number of persons contracting the disease. It is interpreted as the probability of dying following contraction of the disease in question, and hence is a measure of the virulence of the disease.
4. False. The cohort life table describes the mortality experience of a real cohort born at the same time (e.g., in the same calendar year). It is contrasted with the period life table, which is the more usual life table, that describes the mortality information contained in the age-specific death rates for a calendar year or a period of that type.
5. False. The complete life table is contrasted with the abridged life table. The former gives information for each individual age and the intervals between them, while the abridged life table gives information for age groups (e.g., 0–1, 1–5, 5–10, ...) and the beginning point of each.
6. True. Famines, epidemics, and the like cause such crises. An example is the Black Death that ravaged Europe in the middle of the 14th century, which killed about 25 million people, almost a quarter of the population.
7. True. Two populations with identical age-specific death rates may have different crude death rates, the one with a greater proportion in the elderly age groups showing the higher crude death rate.
8. True. According to the definition of death adopted by the World Health Organization, death occurs only after birth. Stillbirth is regarded as fetal death,

involving loss of all signs of life before the expulsion or extraction of the product of conception from the mother.

9. True. Abortion and stillbirth are both classified as fetal death.

10. False. The term refers to mortality differences among subgroups of a population. Examples include mortality differences among social classes, among women of different marital status groups, and among people by residence (e.g., rural, urban).

11. True. The directly standardized death rate is a weighted average of the age-specific death rates of a particular population, using for weights the age-composition of a standard population.

12. True. In the U.S. National Health Interview Survey, a disability is defined as any short- or long-term reduction in a person's activity because of an acute or chronic condition. A "condition" is understood as a departure from a state of physical or mental well-being. An acute condition is one lasting less than 3 months. A chronic condition is one lasting 3 months or more.

13. False. On the contrary, it is the term "exogenous mortality" that refers to mortality attributable to environmental forces and factors. Mortality due to genetic factors and conditions prevailing just before, during, or just after the delivery is called endogenous mortality.

14. False. Epidemics are mass outbreaks of a disease in a locality. Endemics on the other hand are diseases that continue in a locality for so long that it is regarded as a permanent feature of the locality. Among these, it is epidemics that attract the attention of the people, even though in many instances endemics are greater killers.

15. False. Epidemiology deals with the incidence, prevalence, spread, and control of diseases in a population.

16. True. This happens when the arteries that carry blood to the heart tissues get constricted or obstructed.

17. False. The incidence rate in epidemiology stands for the number of new cases of a disease per $K$ (usually 1000) persons, using the mid-year population in the denominator. The prevalence rate is the number of cases, new or old, during a given interval, per $K$ (usually 1000) persons, using the mid-year population for the denominator. Incidence is the number of cases of disease having their onset during a specified time period. Prevalence is the number of cases of a disease present during a particular period of time.

18. True. The infant death rate is conventionally defined as the number of infant deaths (i.e., deaths below one year of age) in a population during a given year per $K$ (usually 1000) live births. The term infant mortality rate is often used as a

synonym. But it is preferable to reserve the latter term for the probability of dying before reaching the first birthday anniversary, a statistic available in the life table.

19. True. Infection means the establishment of a pathogen in its host after invasion. Infectious means caused by or capable of being communicated by infection.

20. False. Instantaneous death rate is the limiting value of duration-specific death rate (e.g., age-specific death rate), when the duration in question becomes infinitesimally small. Think of calculating age specific death rates for progressively smaller age intervals: 5-year age groups, 2-year age groups, individual ages, ½-year age groups, and so on. Soon you will be thinking of age intervals as small a minute, a second, a micro-second. The age-specific death rate calculated for such small age intervals are instantaneous death rates. Another term for the same is the force of mortality. Demographers use this concept in the investigation of factors associated with the chance of experiencing an event (e.g., death).

21. False. Life expectancy at a given age is the average remaining lifetime for those who have survived to the given age under conditions of mortality specified by given age-specific death rates. The last column a life table gives the life expectancies at various ages. The life expectancy at birth is the most frequently used figures among these.

22. False. The reference is to the various statistics presented in the life table. Among these are $l_x$ the number of persons surviving to the $x$th birthday anniversary, out of a hypothetical number at birth, usually a multiple of 1,000, called the radix of the life table; ${}_nq_x$ the probability of dying within the next $n$ years for those alive on their $x$th birthday anniversary, ${}_nd_x$ the number of deaths occurring between the $x$th and $(x + n)$th birthday anniversaries, ${}_nL_x$ the total number of years lived between the $x$th and $(x + n)$th birthday anniversaries, $T_x$ the total number of years lived beyond the $x$th birthday anniversary, and $e_x^0$ the average remaining lifetime for those alive on their $x$th birthday anniversary.

23. True. Neonatal deaths are deaths to infants during the first 4 weeks of life. The major causes of such deaths are congenital defects and conditions prevailing just before, during, or just after the birth. The causes of neonatal deaths are more difficult to control than the causes of postneonatal deaths.

24. False. Pandemic is an epidemic affecting an exceptionally high proportion of a population spread over a wide area.

25. True. To illustrate, diarrheal diseases lead to reduction in body's capacity to absorb nutrients, which, in turn, leads to a reduction in body's ability to withstand further attack of disease.

# CHAPTER 5

# *Fertility*

In the 1960s and 1970s, of the three components of population change, fertility, mortality, and mobility, fertility was the primary focus of demographic research. This was prompted by the belief that fertility is the most problematic component of population change, in regard to both understanding why it changes when it does and identifying ways to influence its changing pace. Also, it was recognized that the consequences of fertility trends are far more serious than those of the most likely trends in mortality or migration. For example, fertility has more serious consequences to the age structure of national populations than mortality or migration.

When thinking about human reproduction, one is reminded of fertilization, which begins with the contact between spermatozoon and ovum, leading to their fusion. Ordinarily, sexual intercourse is a necessary step for fertilization, although artificial insemination and other methods of external and internal fertilization are currently available. The fertilized ovum develops into a full-grown fetus over a period of about 9 months in the mother's womb. This phase is called gestation or pregnancy. The pregnancy terminates with the expulsion or extraction of the product of fertilization from the mother. The act of giving birth to a child is called parturition. It is thus clear that gestation presumes fertilization, and parturition presumes gestation.

In order to understand fertility as a component of population change, one needs to become familiar with various concepts, measures, and correlates of fertility. Also needed is a familiarity with the various explanatory schemes developed in the literature regarding fertility.

## *5.1. CONCEPTS*

Birth is the complete expulsion or extraction from the mother of a product of conception, irrespective of the duration of pregnancy, which, after such separation, breathes or shows any other evidence of life, such as beating of the heart, pulsation of the umbilical cord, or definite movement of any voluntary muscle. Often the term "live birth" is used for birth as just defined, to distinguish it from what is called stillbirth, the event in which the product of conception fails to breathe or show any other evidence of life after expulsion or extraction from the mother.

Fertility is the process by which a population's membership is replenished through births. The term, however, is commonly used to mean the childbearing performance of individuals, couples, groups of people, or whole populations (Wilson, 1985, p. 81). Sometimes the term "natality" is used as a synonym for fertility. Demographic analysis of fertility is ordinarily confined to the study of live births, rather than all pregnancies. Births are most commonly related to women when measuring fertility. Marital fertility refers to fertility of married persons. Fertility is contrasted with fecundity, the biological capacity to reproduce. A man and woman may be fecund as individuals but as a couple they may not be; hence it makes sense to focus on the fecundity of the couple when discussing reproduction. Fecundity is only a necessary condition for producing a live birth. Fecund couples can prevent pregnancies by means of contraception and can use abortion to terminate pregnancies before reaching full term.

Natural fertility is usually defined as fertility where the reproduction is not influenced by the number of children already born. In practice, this has been taken to mean fertility performance in the absence of the use of contraception or induced abortion. The concept was introduced by Louis Henry, a French demographer, in 1961. Natural fertility varies widely among populations. Breast-feeding practices, sexual taboos, physiological sterility, and fetal mortality all affect natural fertility.

The term "intermediate variables" (introduced by Davis and Blake in 1956) refers to such factors as age of entry into sexual union, permanent celibacy, separation, divorce, widowhood, coital frequency, contraception, abortion, abstinence, infecundity, and fetal mortality. The term "proximate determinants" is a currently used synonym. As the name indicates, the intermediate variables (proximate determinants) are a block of variables located between fertility and the block of social and economic factors in the causal nexus:

(social and economic factors) → (intermediate variables → (fertility)

The term "birth cohort" is used for persons born in a given period (e.g., a calendar year). The term marriage cohort, similarly, is applied to persons who entered matrimony in a given period. In general, a cohort is a group of persons experiencing an event such as birth, marriage, or graduation from school, during the same time interval.

Cohabitation refers to people of opposite sex living together without getting married legally or according to religious marriage rites. The terms consensual union and common-law marriage are often used instead, especially in the literature on fertility of Latin American countries and the Caribbean. Cohabitation has been very common in Latin America. It has become quite common recently in developed countries and is a context for bearing and rearing children.

Typically, the age pattern of fertility (the curve of age-specific fertility rates, defined below, plotted against the age of women) rises with age, reaches a peak in the twenties, and then declines. The pattern varies across populations and, with social and economic changes, within a population. The variation may be with respect to the steepness of the climb, the age at which the peak occurs, or the slowness of the fall afterwards. The age pattern of cumulative fertility (see below for definition) for cohorts has an elongated S-shape. (Fig. 5.1).

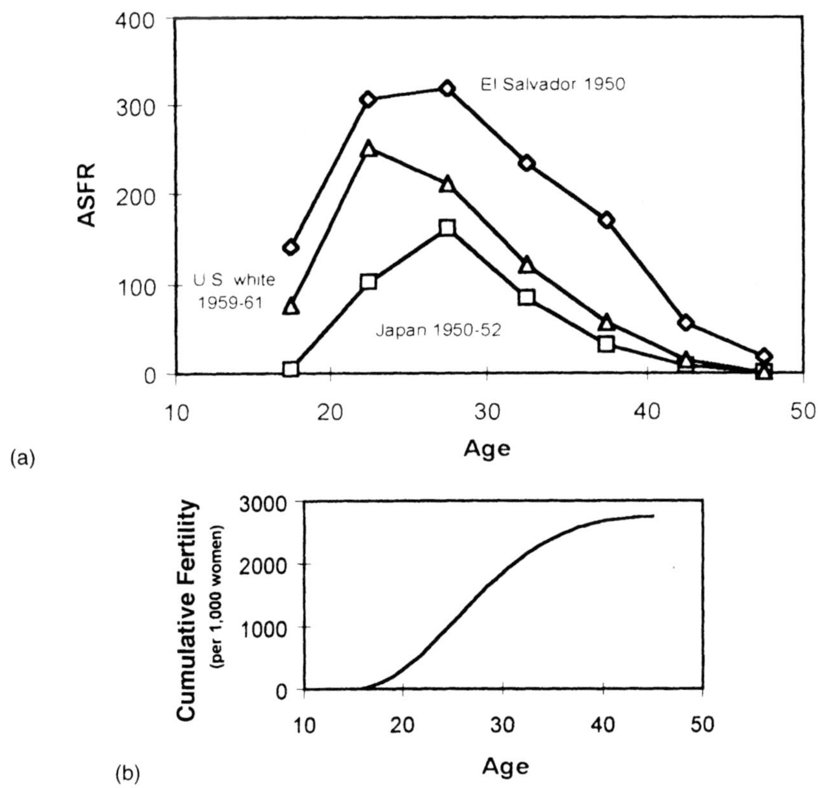


*Figure 5.1* (a) Age pattern of fertility: ASFR by age (Source: Bogue, 1969, Table 18.4). (b) Birth cumulated to successive ages: U.S. women born in 1920–1924 (Source: U.S. Department of Commerce, 1984).

## 5.2. MEASURES

The crude birth rate (CBR), a widely used period measure of fertility, is defined as the annual number of births in a population per 1000 persons, using the mid-year population in the denominator. It is a period measure because it refers to the flow of births during a specific period (time interval), standardized for population size. The calculation of the CBR ignores the fact that the chance of producing a live birth during a given period varies considerably by characteristics such as age.

The general fertility rate (GFR), sometimes referred to simply as the fertility rate, is another period measure of fertility; it differs from the CBR only in that its denominator is the number of women of childbearing age, whereas that of the CBR is for the total population. It is a slightly more refined measure of fertility than the CBR because it relates births to a relatively more homogeneous at-risk population (women of childbearing age as opposed to the total population). It is not sophisticated enough, however, because it does not take into account the age pattern of fertility.

The child/woman ratio, defined as the number of children under 5 years of age per 1000 women of childbearing age, is used as a rough indicator of fertility when other, better measures are not available. It reflects a combined result of fertility as well as the mortality levels of children and adult women. Among its weaknesses is its sensitivity to underenumeration of infants and young children. One advantage of the measure is that it can be calculated exclusively from census age-sex distribution.

The age-specific fertility rate is defined the same way as the general fertility rate is, but with the numerator (births) and denominator (at-risk population) restricted to women of a specific age group. Thus the annual number of births per 1000 women in the age group 20–24 years gives the age-specific fertility rate for that age group. Usually age-specific fertility rates are calculated for 5-year age groups: 10–14, 15–19, 20–24, 25–29, 30–34, 35–39, ... years (See Table 5.1.).

*Table 5.1.* Calculation of Age-specific Fertility rates

| Age of woman | Number of women | Number of births | Age-specific fertility rate |
|---|---|---|---|
| 15–19 | 8,890,000 | 488,941 | 0.055 |
| 20–24 | 9,574,000 | 1,067,472 | 0.111 |
| 25–29 | 10,928,000 | 1,239,256 | 0.113 |
| 30–34 | 10,903,000 | 803,547 | 0.074 |
| 35–39 | 9,660,000 | 269,518 | 0.028 |
| 40–44 | 8,155,000 | 40,776 | 0.005 |

The total fertility rate (TFR), a widely used period measure of fertility, is interpreted as the number of births a group of women would have on average if they survive to the end of the reproductive period and have births at each age in accordance with the age-specific fertility rates of the given period. If the age-specific fertility rates are given for 5-year age groups, then the corresponding total fertility rate is equal to five times the sum of the age-specific fertility rates (see Table 5.1 for an illustration, where U.S. data for 1988 are used.)

From Table 5.1, the total fertility rate is equal to 5(0.055 + 0.111 + 0.113 + 0.074 + 0.028 + 0.005) or 1.93 children per woman. Notice that the figures in the last column of the table are the age-specific fertility rates. Usually, these are expressed per 1000 women rather than per woman. But the TFR is frequently expressed on a per woman basis.

The gross reproduction rate (GRR), calculated on a per-woman basis, is the same as the TFR except that the GRR is based exclusively on female children. If sex ratio at birth is unrelated to the age of mother, then the GRR = the TFR × the proportion females at birth. Thus if the TFR is 1.93 children per woman and the sex ratio at birth is 105 males per 100 females, then the GRR = 1.93 times (100/205) = 0.94 daughters per woman.

The net reproduction rate (NRR), calculated on a per-woman basis, differs from the GRR only in that it (NRR) takes into account the mortality of women below age 45 (or 50) years, whereas the GRR does not. As illustrated in Table 5.2, the 1989 NRR for the United States was 0.956, the sum of the figures in the last column. Note that the figures in column 3 are from an appropriate life table for females. They give, for each age group, the effective number of years women in that age group are expected to be reproducing at the rate characteristic of that age group. Obviously if no woman dies during any age interval, then the effective number of years of reproduction during each interval equals the length of the interval in years. The figures in column 3 of Table 5.2 are less than the length of the intervals involved, 5 years in the present case, because of mortality.

The NRR is interpreted as the average number of daughters a group of women

*Table 5.2.* Calculation of the Net Reproduction Rate

| Age of women | Daughters per woman per year | Years lived in the age interval | Column 2 × column 3 |
|---|---|---|---|
| 15–19 | 0.028 | 4.93 | 0.138 |
| 20–24 | 0.056 | 4.92 | 0.276 |
| 25–29 | 0.057 | 4.90 | 0.279 |
| 30–34 | 0.037 | 4.89 | 0.181 |
| 35–39 | 0.014 | 4.86 | 0.068 |
| 40–44 | 0.003 | 4.83 | 0.014 |

would bear during their lifetimes if they reproduce in accordance with a given schedule of age-specific fertility rates and die in accordance with a given schedule of age-specific death rates. It is viewed as a measure of the degree to which women replace themselves by their counterparts in the next generation, if they were subjected to the prevailing age-specific fertility and age-specific mortality rates.

The sum of the age-specific fertility rates for a cohort, up to a given age, is called the cumulative fertility rate for that age. The cumulative fertility rate for the end of the childbearing period is called the terminal cumulative fertility rate, completed fertility, or life-time fertility. Cumulative fertility rates can be calculated for birth cohorts or marriage cohorts. (See Fig. 5.1b.)

*Fertility orientations*: It is common to collect, in fertility interviews of women, details regarding their fertility orientations (ideal and desired family sizes, intended and expected family sizes). The wordings of interview questions on fertility orientations are typically: "How many children do you consider IDEAL for an average (American) family?" "If you could start all over again and could have exactly the number of children you WANT, how many would that be?" "How many children do you EXPECT to have altogether by the time you reach the end of the childbearing period?" "How many more children do you INTEND to have?"

*Pregnancy history*: Fertility surveys usually collect information on each pregnancy (e.g., date of termination and outcome.) Such data shed light on fetal deaths in addition to live births.

*Intermediate variables*: It is common for fertility surveys to collect information on the age at menarche, age of entry into sexual union, knowledge and use of contraception, and abortion. Less frequently, data on coital frequency and abstinence are collected. From pregnancy history it is possible to estimate the monthly probability of conception, i.e., fecundability, for women of given characteristics (e.g., age). Data on breast-feeding are used in allowing for reduction in the monthly probability of conception because of lactation amenorrhea (absence of menses).

## 5.3. FERTILITY CONTROL THROUGH THE PROXIMATE DETERMINANTS

Commonly, the higher the mean age at marriage for women in a population the lower the marital fertility. If, however, the average age at marriage is very low, such as in the early teens, then a small increase in the average age at marriage will have virtually no effect on marital fertility. Also, the connection between marriage and childbearing changes in a society over time. For example, in the United States before 1960, age at marriage and age of entry into sexual union were essentially the same. Since then, however, as in other industrialized Western countries, premarital and extramarital sexual unions have become common. In the late 1980s, about one in four of U.S. births occurred to women outside marriage.

Diseases such as gonorrhea make women infecund (unable to become pregnant or to carry a pregnancy to full term). Diseases in general affect fecundity through inability to engage in coitus, failure to become pregnant, or loss of pregnancy. (See, however, question 26 in section 5.7.4. Poor nutrition also reduces women's fecundity. The onset of puberty may be delayed in undernourished girls. Breast-feeding produces in most women temporary infecundity (Weeks, 1994, p. 99; Frank, 1983; McFalls and McFalls, 1984).

There are many methods of birth control. The IUD, diaphragm, foam tablets, jellies, creams, the sponge, the douche, and the male and female condoms are among the so-called barrier methods of contraception and birth control pills, implants, injectables, the vaginal ring, and the morning-after pill are among the chemical contraceptives. Withdrawal (or *coitus interruptus*) was a commonly used method before the introduction of any of the modem barrier or chemical methods. Abortion was, and is, also widely used for birth control. Sterilization is a popular method for preventing pregnancies. Among the intermediate variables, coital frequency tends to have a positive effect on fertility, whereas most others have a negative effect. Also, the effect of each vary from population to population. Fertility differences between populations can be, to a large extent, accounted for in terms of marriage, contraception, induced abortion, and lactational infecundity (Bongaarts, 1982).

## 5.4. LEVELS AND TRENDS

How high can fertility be? A group known for its very high fertility level (an average of 10 or more children per woman, among those who marry at age of 20) in the 1920s and 1930s is the Hutterites, a small religious sect concentrated in the North-central United States and the neighboring regions of Canada.

In the early period of American history, crude birth rates of about 55 births per 1000 persons (roughly equivalent to eight children on average per woman) were common. The American fertility level at that time far surpassed the then-prevailing European fertility levels.

Table 5.3 shows the trends in the CBR in the United States, 1800–1980. Sustained decline in fertility started in the early 1800s and continued through the years of the Great Depression in the 1930s. Then followed a post-World War 11 "baby boom" and a subsequent "baby bust" (Fig. 5.2).

Within Europe, sustained fertility decline started first in Northern and Western Europe; only later did it start in Southern and Eastern Europe. Currently almost all of the more-developed countries are characterized by very low fertility. Period fertility rates have been below replacement level (the total fertility rate of 2.1) for a long time now in most of the industrialized countries (see Fig. 5.3).

Childlessness and small family patterns are two components of low fertility.

*Table 5.3.* Trends in the CBR in the United States

| Year | CBR | Year | CBR | Year | CBR |
|---|---|---|---|---|---|
| 1800 | 55.2 | 1925 | 25.1 | 1951–1955 | 25.1 |
| 1840 | 51.8 | 1930 | 21.3 | 1956–1960 | 24.5 |
| 1860 | 44.3 | 1935 | 18.7 | 1961–1965 | 21.6 |
| 1880 | 39.8 | 1940 | 19.4 | 1966–1970 | 18.0 |
| 1900 | 32.3 | 1941–1945 | 21.4 | 1971–1975 | 15.4 |
| 1920 | 27.7 | 1946–1950 | 24.8 | 1976–1980 | 15.2 |

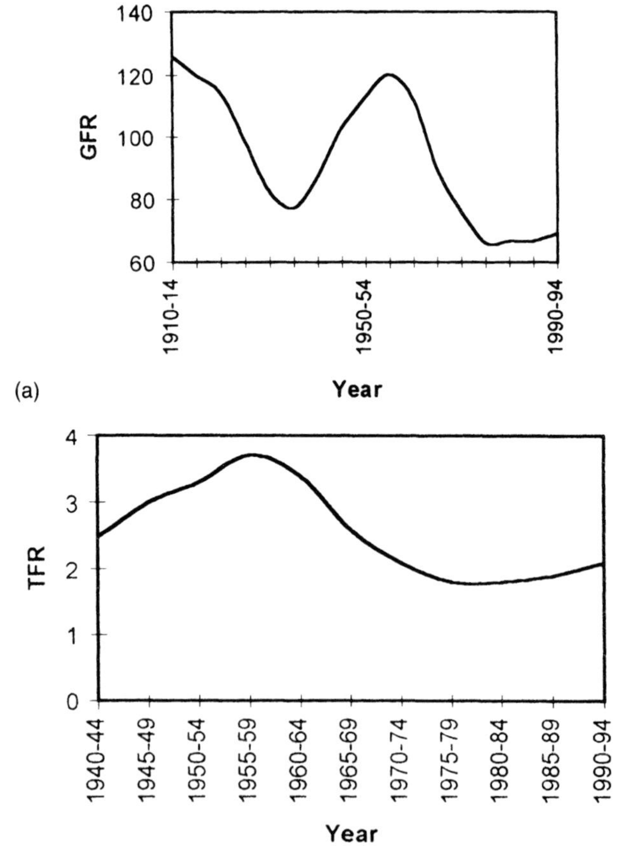

(b)

*Figure 5.2* (a) General fertility rates: U.S. 1910–1992, (b) Total fertility rates: U.S. 1940–1995 (Source: U.S. Bureau of the Census, 1975, p. 49; NCHS, 1995, Table 4).

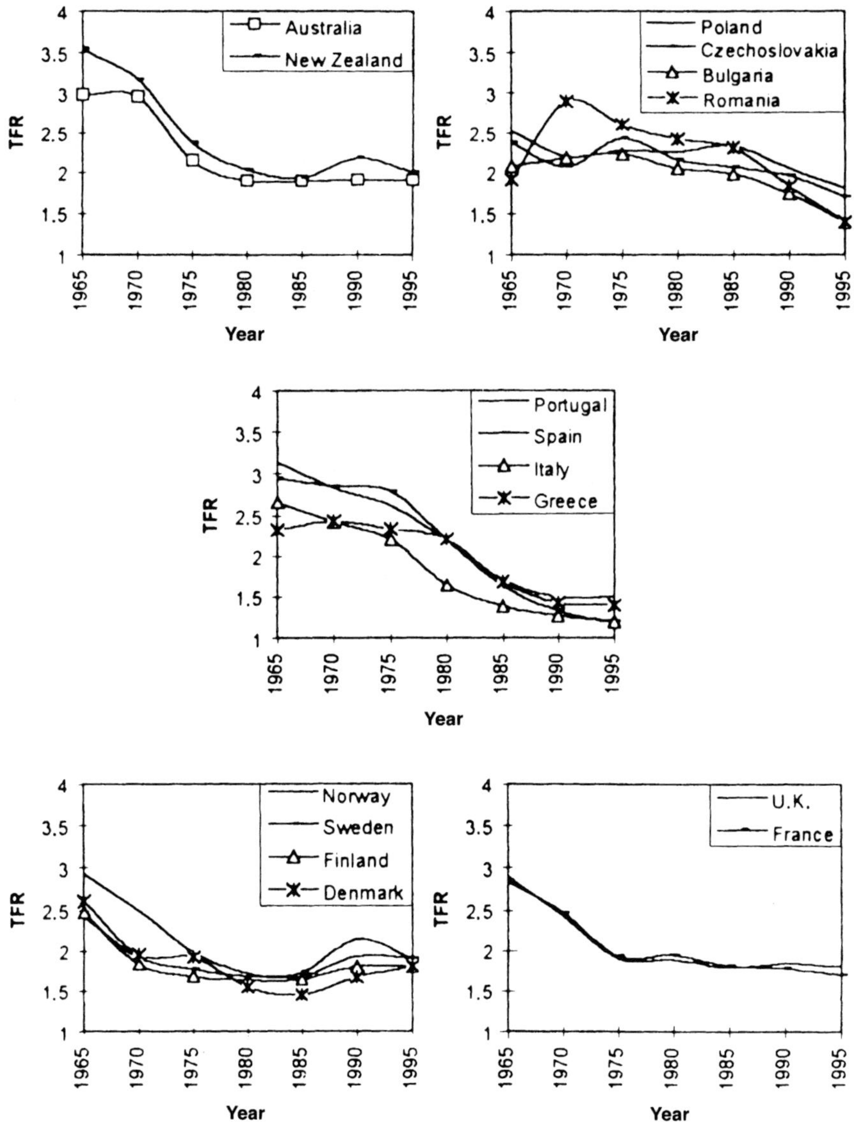


*Figure 5.3.* Total fertility rate 1965–1995, selected countries (Source: Monnior and Guibert-Lantoine, 1994; Population Reference Bureau, 1995).

Sixteen percent of U.S. women who reached the end of childbearing period in 1992 had not borne a child. The corresponding figure in 1976 was only 10%. In the 1980s, experts were convinced that close to 50% of young U.S. women were likely to complete their childbearing years bearing, at most, one child (Westoff, 1987, p. 164).

In many localities of Europe, fertility started declining before 1800. This happened first through delay and/or curtailment of marriage. Later, birth control within marriage became common. It should be emphasized that there was a time when marriage was nearly universal and age at marriage was relatively low in Europe. Departure from this traditional pattern took hold before the onset of the Industrial Revolution. Marital fertility, however, varied from place to place in Europe, even when marriage was almost universal. The factors responsible for this variation included frequency and duration of breast-feeding, periods of separation of spouses resulting from work-related temporary migration, frequency of sexual intercourse, and the level of nutrition (van de Walle and Knodel, 1980, p. 12). Marital fertility began to decline at different times in different parts of Europe. France led the way, with sustained decline in marital fertility beginning in the early 1800s, much before the beginning of intense urbanization and industrialization. Ireland was one of the latest to join (early in the 20th century). Generally speaking, however, Western and Northern European countries started sustained marital fertility decline earlier than Eastern and Southern Europe.

When thinking about current fertility levels and trends in the more-developed countries, teenage fertility and unwed motherhood demand attention. Teenage fertility, usually defined as births to women under 20 years of age, is markedly lower in the more-developed countries than in the less-developed countries, partly because of the differences in age at marriage and in the use of contraception. In the United States, the age-specific fertility rates for younger teens (15–17 years) decreased from 38.8 per 1000 girls in 1970 to 31.0 per 1000 girls by 1985 and then steadily increased to 38.7 per 1000 by 1991. Similarly, the age-specific fertility rate for older teens (18–19 years) decreased from 114.7 per 1,000 in 1970 to 79.6 by 1985 and then steadily increased to 94.4 by 1991. A shift toward nonmarital fertility has occurred among U.S. teenagers: In 1970 there were 22 births per 1000 unmarried teenage girls; in 1989 the corresponding figure was 41. (NCHS, 1995, Tables 4 and 15.)

A significant proportion of all births occur to unwed mothers in many industrialized countries. Five percent of all U.S. births in 1960 were to unmarried mothers; the corresponding figure in 1989 was 27%; the level has been twice as high in Sweden (11.3% in 1960 and 51.8% in 1989). Fertility surveys between 1973 and 1988 in the United States showed that about one in three unwed childbearing was planned (Ahlburg and De Vita, 1992, p. 23). There has been an increase in the deliberate choice of single-motherhood among U.S. women 25 years of age or older. But the practice does not seem to have won widespread approval (Ahlburg and De Vita, 1992).

The Japanese story of fertility decline is different from that of the other more-developed countries. When a baby boom was occurring in the United States (1946–1964), Japan was experiencing a rapid decline in fertility. The total fertility rate was 4.42 during 1945–1949. It dropped to 2.04 by 1959, and remained between 1.95 and 2.05 during 1960–1964, between 1.58 and 2.14 during 1965–1969, between 2.05 and 2.16 during 1970–1974, and below 2.0 since 1975 (see Preston, 1987, p. 27). In 1994 Japan's TFR was 1.5.

Fertility levels continue to be high in most of the less-developed countries. As of 1994. African countries had on average a total fertility rate of 5.9 children per woman, while the Asian average was 3.1 and the Latin American average was 3.2. Fertility levels vary greatly among the less-developed countries, much more than among the industrialized countries. In Asia, for example, the TFR was only 2.0 in China in 1994 and 2.2 in Thailand, but 3.6 in India, 6.1 in Pakistan, 6.3 in Laos, and 6.9 in Syria. Countries of Southern and Northern Africa had an average TFR of 4.5 in 1994, while the remaining African regions had an average TFR of 6.5 (Population Reference Bureau's *1994 World Population Data Sheet*). There are several countries in Asia with below-replacement fertility levels (approximately a TFR of 2.1 per woman). Examples include China. Japan, Hong Kong, South Korea, and Taiwan.

Fertility was high (the TFR exceeding 5.00 children per woman) in China during the 1940s and 1950s. During 1959–1961 there was a sharp drop in the TFR in that country, but it bounced back immediately thereafter. Sustained fertility decline started in China in the 1960s. Between 1970 and 1979 Chinese fertility plummeted nearly 50% (Tien et al., 1992). The TFR dropped below the replacement level by the early 1990s. As mentioned, the 1994 TFR was 2.0.

In India, the crude birth rate, which had averaged about 45 births per 1000 persons during 1941–1961, had dropped to 30 by the early 1990s. Parts of South India (e.g., Kerala State and Goa) have already reached below-replacement fertility levels (Nam, 1994, p. 207; Weeks, 1994, pp. 129–132). Bangladesh is an anomaly in that, despite high mortality and illiteracy, a substantial fertility decline has occurred there, from a TFR of 6.9 in the late 1960s to about 3.4 by the early 1990s.

In a recent assessment of fertility decline in Asia, Freedman (1995) found that between the late 1960s and the late 1980s, Asian fertility fell by 39%. By the 1990s, nearly two-thirds of Asian countries had experienced declines of at least 25%. This substantial decline in fertility in Asia's poor and populous countries came as a surprise to many demographers.

## 5.5. FERTILITY DIFFERENTIALS

Fertility levels differ between population subgroups defined in terms of one or more demographic, economic, or social variables (e.g., educational attainment of women, rural versus urban residence, occupational status of the husband, and religious background of the couple).

During fertility transition, fertility differentials usually increase: Urban fertility drops before rural fertility does; the middle- and upper-class people start restricting fertility before the lower-class people do; the better-educated and those in nonagricultural occupations lower their fertility before those with lower levels of education and agricultural occupations do.

In the United States, the fertility of nonwhites has followed the same trends as that of whites, but the former has consistently remained higher than the latter. For both groups, fertility declined until the mid-1930s, remained at a low level for several years, rose dramatically reaching a peak in 1957, and then started a downward course. Racial/ethnic group differences in fertility are to a considerable degree due to the corresponding differences in socio-economic status (education, occupation, income) and the associated differences in fertility orientations, access to family planning, and use of contraception.

The U.S. Catholics used to have significantly higher fertility than their non-Catholic counterparts. The gap has, however, almost vanished over the years (Mosher et al., 1992) (see Fig. 5.4).

In industrialized countries, women who work tend to have fewer children. The causal relationship runs in both ways. Work participation tends to lower fertility; and lower fertility tends to increase the likelihood of women's work participation.

In populations that have completed fertility transition (from high to low levels) most traditional fertility differentials have become very small. When the fertility level is low, variation in fertility is also likely to be low, in general. Furthermore, in post-transition societies most people are likely to be exposed to the same set of influences that affect their reproductive behavior.

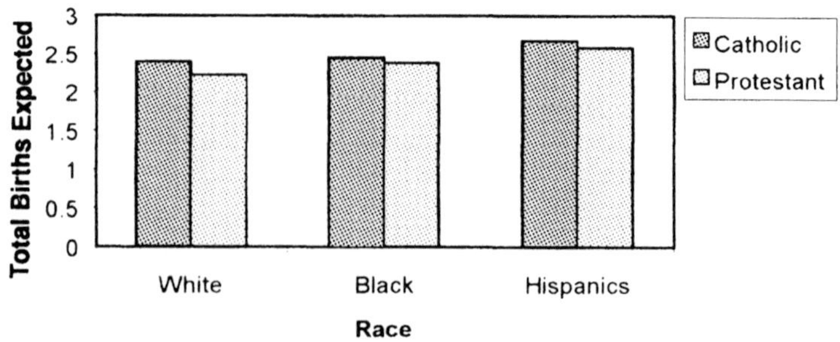


*Figure 5.4.* Total births expected: Catholic and Protestant differences among hispanics, blacks, and whites, U.S. 1980s (Source: Mosher *et al.*, 1992, p. 203).

## 5.6. EXPLANATORY SCHEMES

Explanatory analyses of fertility fall into two major categories: one in which the emphasis is on the combination of the intermediate variables that account for the differences or trends; the other in which the emphasis is on social and economic determinants.

As mentioned, in the United States fertility had been consistently higher for blacks than for whites. Part of this pattern can be explained in terms of black–white differences in one or more of the following: fertility orientation, tendency to have unwanted births, and age at which childbearing starts. Socio-economic status is a correlate of these, as is residence (rural/urban).

The early part of the post-World War II baby boom has been attributed (see, e.g., Campbell, 1969) to a combination of factors: (i) a "catching up" behavior (in terms of marriage and marital fertility) of people who had postponed marriage and/or births because of the economic depression of the 1930s or because of combat duty in the armed forces during the war; (ii) a "true" increase in the propensity to get married and a "true" decrease in voluntary childlessness; (iii) "extra" births prompted by the post-war prosperity; (iv) a decrease in birth intervals; and (v) a marked increase in the proportion of women in childbearing ages. Why the baby boom lasted a relatively long time (1946–1964), however, has not yet been satisfactorily understood.

The current unpopularity of childbearing in the industrialized countries has been attributed (see, e.g., Westoff, 1987) to (i) the radical alteration of the economic value of children, making children a liability rather than an asset under current conditions, (ii) increased participation of women in the labor force, and the incompatibility between non-home-centered and home-centered activities, (iii) redefinition of women's role, de-emphasizing the wife–mother role, in particular, (iv) increased individualism, materialism and priority attached to actions and choices that help win in the competition for economic advantage, status, power, and privilege.

The commonly observed negative relationship between literacy and fertility in the less-developed countries has been attributed to literate women being more knowledgeable regarding family planning, having greater interest in extra-familial activities, and being more concerned with the quality of children rather than quantity.

The tendency for some women to have fewer children than they desire, has been attributed to physiological impairment of the reproductive system, disagreement with the spouse regarding family size preferences, and deliberate birth control prompted by considerations of costs of a large family.

The "new home economics" of fertility likens children to refrigerators, cars, washing machines, and other consumer-durable items. People are seen as rational planners and optimizers of their overall satisfaction when choosing between

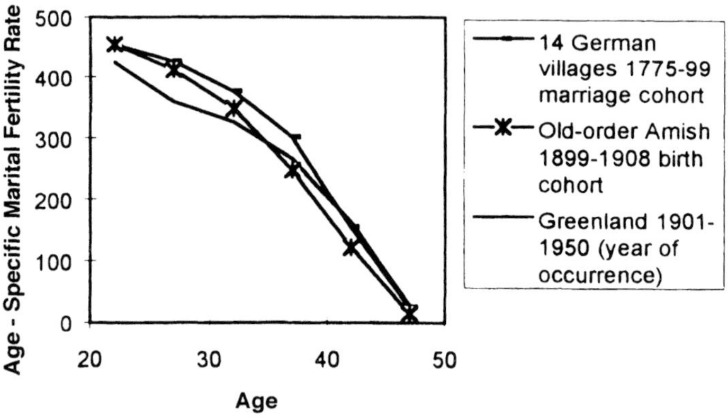


*Figure 5.5.* Age pattern of natural (marital) fertility rates (Source: Knodel, 1983, p. 88).

"consumption baskets." With respect to children in the "consumption basket," as with other items, quality is distinguished from quantity. Quality of children is regarded as a function of the resource expenditure on children. Time at one's disposal is treated as a scarce resource. All items of final consumption are produced and enjoyed by the consumer using his or her own time and other inputs. When considering costs of children, opportunities that are foregone in order to have children of the desired quality are given due consideration. Opportunity costs of children are believed to be positively associated with socioeconomic status. The main attractive feature of the "new home economic" approach to fertility analysis is that it places fertility analysis within a very general theoretical framework, supposedly capable of handling such widely varying phenomena as consumer choice, marriage and divorce, sex and race discrimination, charitable behavior, love and concern, and envy and hatred. Another attractive feature is its elegance, particularly its mathematical foundation. The main problem with it is that it is too narrow. A strong case can be made for viewing this approach as little more than a prescriptive approach, one that says, in effect, "If you are making fertility decisions rationally, then this is one way to do it" rather than a descriptive model, one that tries to capture the reality of fertility decision-making (see Namboodiri, 1975 for an elaboration of these points).

Having children can be approached from decision-making perspectives developed in social psychology. For an exposition of a particular version of this approach, see DeJong and Fawcett, 1981. In general, the decision-maker is confronted with making choices between alternative courses of action (e.g., whether to have the first child this year, whether to abort this pregnancy, and so on). Each action has one or more possible consequences. Some consequences are more certain to occur than are others. (One can perhaps be more certain about the survival chances of an infant than about whether it will become a genius.)

Associated with each possible consequence are also short-run as well as long-run costs and benefits. (Having a child now would make your in-laws very happy, but it may mean taking time out of work.) Everything considered (probability, costs, and benefits of each consequence; reactions of significant others to each course of action; and weights attached to those reactions), the various courses of action can be ordered in terms of increasing overall attractiveness. The decision maker chooses the course of action that ranks best in this ordered set. A serious drawback of the approach is that to apply it one has to measure a large number of variables, many of which are difficult to measure through the usual survey-interview method.

According to the relative income hypothesis of Richard Easterlin (1973), fertility varies with relative income, which is often operationally defined as the income (or resources) of the younger generation at peak reproductive ages, relative to that of the older generation at comparable ages. The underlying idea is that each generation cultivates certain tastes and preferences while growing up, and when that generation reaches reproductive age, fertility choices are made in accordance with the resources available and the costs of children and other things in life, given the tastes and preferences acquired at younger ages. Smaller birth cohorts are likely to have higher fertility than larger cohorts because "good times" are in store for the former resulting from the lighter competition they run into at successive age levels (school-going age, working age, old age).

Another framework, also first proposed by Easterlin (1975), views the number of children surviving as a function of natural fertility, child survival. desired fertility, and costs of fertility control. The first two factors together determine what is called the supply of children and the third may be called the demand for children. As for the fourth factor, a distinction is made between the cost of access to, and the cost of actual use of, fertility regulation. It is postulated that people resort to fertility control only if supply of children exceeds demand and even then only if cost considerations permit it. One could use this framework as a point of departure to develop theories regarding why natural fertility varies among populations, why different population segments differ in desired fertility, and so on. Serious efforts in these directions remain to be undertaken.

## 5.7. QUESTIONS AND ANSWERS*

**FOR EACH OF THE QUESTIONS IN SECTIONS 5.7.1. TO 5.7.5., STATE TRUE OR FALSE AND EXPLAIN.**

### 5.7.1. Concepts

1. The marital fertility of a population, when no one uses contraception or induced abortion, is called maximum fertility.

*Answers start on page 122.

2. Abortion and miscarriage are synonyms.
3. Annual induced abortions per 1000 mid-year population is called the crude abortion rate.
4. Amenorrhea and anovulation are synonyms.
5. Age-specific fertility rates are incidence rates.
6. The Hutterite fertility is the maximum possible fertility level.
7. Natural fertility varies considerably from one population to another.

### 5.7.2. Measures

8. Age-specific marital fertility rates are more appropriate to measure the extent of birth control.
9. The total fertility rate is interpreted using a cohort perspective.
10. The crude birth rate is crude because in its calculation one relies exclusively on data from census sources.
11. The number of children ever born is a fertility measure available from fertility surveys.

### 5.7.3. Levels and Trends

12. Pre-transition societies all have fertility at the biologically maximum level.
13. In earliest America. the fertility levels were as high as in many of the less-developed countries in the 20th century.
14. In East Asia the TFR had fallen below the replacement level by the early 1990s.
15. Western Asia lags behind other Asian sub-regions in fertility decline.
16. With respect to the total fertility rate, the gap between Asia and Latin America has significantly widened over the last three decades.
17. With respect to the total fertility rate, the gap between Asia and Africa has widened over the last three decades.
18. Bangladesh is an example of a society in which fertility decline occurred in the absence of marked social or economic development.
19. In Sri Lanka fertility declined substantially in spite of its economic "backwardness."

20. In Indonesia fertility decline occurred as a joint result of an effective family planning program and social and economic development.

### *5.7.4. Differentials*

21. Fecundity varies with the age.
22. Fertility shows a characteristic pattern by age.
23. Fertility is negatively associated with age at marriage.
24. Fecundity is a necessary condition for parenthood.
25. Adolescents are commonly subfecund.
26. Diseases reduce fecundity.
27. Demographers attach considerable importance to breast-feeding in connection with the study of fertility trends and differentials.

### *5.7.5. Fertility Control*

28. Abortion laws have been liberalized worldwide.
29. Neo-Malthusians are pronatalists.
30. Margaret Sanger is credited with the first popularization of birth control in the United States.

**IN EACH OF QUESTIONS IN SECTIONS 5.7.6. TO 5.7.9. FOUR POSSIBLE ANSWERS ARE SUGGESTED, AT LEAST ONE OF WHICH IS CORRECT. IDENTIFY THE CORRECT ANSWER(S) AND EXPLAIN**

### *5.7.6. Concepts*

1. Fertility as used in demography:
   A. Refers to the physiological capacity to reproduce
   B. Stands for the actual performance of child-bearing
   C. Applies only to women
   D. Is often measured in terms of the annual number of births per 1000 mid-year population
2. Natural fertility:
   A. Refers to the level of reproduction in a population in which birth control linked to parity is absent
   B. Is synonymous to fecundity

C. Varies between populations
D. Is equal to the biologically possible maximum fertility level in a population

3. Which of the following statements apply to the effect of intermediate variables on fertility?
   A. The effect of each remains more or less constant from one population to another
   B. Between-population variation in fertility can be largely accounted for in terms of marriage, contraception, abortion, and involuntary infecundity
   C. Each intermediate variable has a negative effect on fertility
   D. The transition from high to low fertility is accompanied by a combination of decline in breast-feeding (and the resulting decline in postpartum infecundity) and increases in age at marriage, contraceptive use, and abortion

4. Amenorrhea (the absence of menstruation) results from:
   A. Sexual immaturity
   B. Advanced age
   C. Pregnancy
   D. Breast-feeding

5. Anovulation (the absence of the rupture of a mature ovarian follicle and the release of an ovum)
   A. May be total (life-long) for some women
   B. Is of two long periods for most women, one before the beginning, and the other after the end, of the reproductive period
   C. Can be induced by medication
   D. Lasts through each pregnancy and continues for durations up to 18 months or more after childbirth

6. Fetal mortality covers:
   A. Stillbirths
   B. Miscarriages
   C. Abortions
   D. Neonatal deaths

### 5.7.7. *Measures*

7. The general fertility rate (GFR)
   A. Is never less than the CBR (crude birth rate)
   B. Is a slightly more refined fertility measure than the CBR
   C. Is less commonly reported than the CBR
   D. Has the same numerator as the CBR.

8. The child/woman ratio:
   A. Is sensitive to the underenumeration of infants and young children
   B. Can be calculated exclusively from age-sex counts in a census
   C. Is affected by the mortality levels of young children and women in childbearing ages
   D. Shares the same denominator with the general fertility rate

9. The GRR:
   A. Is the same as the TFR, except that the GRR is calculated using female births only, whereas the TFR is calculated using all births
   B. Never falls below one
   C. Does not take into account the mortality of women
   D. Contains more information about fertility than the TFR does

10. The NRR:
    A. Is the same as the GRR, except that the NRR takes into account the mortality of women below the end of the childbearing ages
    B. Is less than or equal to GRR
    C. Is a period measure
    D. When it is less than one it indicates that the population is declining

### 5.7.8. *Levels and Trends*

11. The Hutterites:
    A. Are a religious group living in the southwestern United States
    B. Are well known for their high fertility in the 1920s and 1930s
    C. Had, in the early decades of the twentieth century, fertility levels almost as high as the biological maximum possible
    D. Have reduced their fertility level over the past several decades

12. The U.S. CBR:
    A. Was as high as 55 per 1000 persons at the turn of the 19th century
    B. Declined to about 30 per 1000 persons by the turn of the 20th century
    C. Reached a low during the Great Depression of the 1930s
    D. Embarked on a dramatic upturn in the early 1990s

13. The U.S. teenage fertility:
    A. Is lower than many LDC teenage fertility levels
    B. Was lower in the early 1980s than in the 1970s
    C. Shifted toward non-marital fertility during the early 1980s
    D. Showed a sharp upturn in the late 1980s

14. In most of the MDCs:
    A. The TFR has been remaining below the replacement level for some time now

B. The proportion of people who ever marry has been dropping
C. Childlessness has become common
D. The family form of married couple with two children has ceased to be the mode

15. In comparison with the rest of the MDCs:
A. The U.S. fertility level is in the lower range
B. The U.S. teenage fertility is extremely high
C. The U.S. teenage fertility has been consistently rising for the past two decades, when in other MDCs the trend was the reverse
D. The teenage abortion rate has risen in the United States, when in many other countries it has fallen

16. In the opinion of many analysts, the low fertility levels are likely to continue in the United States because the historical forces for the long-term fertility decline have been joined by:
A. Changes in women's status
B. Increased popularity of cohabitation
C. High divorce rate
D. Development in birth control techniques

17. The early declines in fertility in Europe were due to:
A. Late marriage
B. Curtailment of marriage (a significant proportion of the people remaining never married)
C. Limiting sexual contact for young never-married women
D. Contraception within marriage

18. The factors affecting fertility during the early phase of fertility transition in Europe included:
A. Prevention of additional births after bearing the desired number of children
B. Improved fecundity through improved health and nutrition
C. Decline in the duration of breast-feeding
D. Ignoring customs regarding when to resume regular sexual relations after a pregnancy termination

19. In the 1960s, demographers used to emphasize as the main factors accounting for the cross-national variation in fertility:
A. Mortality decline
B. Level of social and economic development
C. Nature and intensity of family planning programs
D. Independence from colonial rule

20. The current writings emphasize which of the following factors as influencing fertility decline?
    A. Family planning programs
    B. Improved health, education of women, and advances in women's status
    C. Ideas about family planning and lifestyles in general
    D. Linguistic and ethnic commonalities and other cultural factors not usually covered by conventional indicators of development

### *5.7.9. Differentials*

21. In less-developed countries, literate women compared to their non-literate counterparts:
    A. Have lower fertility
    B. Know more about family planning
    C. Have more interest in extra-familial activities
    D. Emphasize quality of children more

22. With respect to religious differentials in fertility, which of the following statements are true?
    A. The minority religious groups have lower fertility than the majority
    B. The official tenets of the majority religious group in a country determine the reproductive practices of the people of that country
    C. In Muslim countries, there are very little differences in fertility between different Muslim groups
    D. Higher fertility for Muslims than for Christians has been reported in a number of less-developed countries

**FOR EACH OF THE QUESTIONS IN SECTIONS 5.7.10. TO 5.7.13., FIVE POSSIBLE ANSWERS ARE SUGGESTED, ONLY ONE OF WHICH IS CORRECT. IDENTIFY THE CORRECT ANSWER AND EXPLAIN**

### *5.7.10. Concepts*

1. Which of the following is not an "intermediate variable" (Davis and Blake, 1956)?
    A. Exposure to intercourse within sexual unions
    B. Age of entry into sexual unions
    C. Exposure to conception
    D. Exposure to sexual education
    E. Gestation and successful parturition

### 5.7.11. Measures

2. The fertility measure that can be calculated exclusively from age-sex counts in a census is:
   A. The CBR
   B. The TFR
   C. The child/woman ratio
   D. The GFR
   E. The United Nations' sex-age adjusted birth rate

### 5.7.12. Levels and Trends

3. Which of the following has been frequently mentioned in the literature in connection with the discussion of why fertility has not declined dramatically in India, despite decades of family planning efforts.
   A. Lack of strong commitment on the part of the government to the family planning efforts
   B. Inadequate training given to the family planning workers
   C. Low investment in the infrastructure
   D. Poor implementation of the program in the field
   E. Religious fundamentalists' opposition

4. Fertility has never been known to be anywhere near the biological maximum in northern India because of which of the following factors?
   A. Late marriage
   B. Non-marriage
   C. Contraception and/or abortion
   D. High cost of children
   E. Social factors affecting duration and intensity of breast-feeding and coital frequency

5. Which of the following factors has been emphasized in attempting to explain the rapid change in fertility in Bangladesh?
   A. Dramatic economic development
   B. A strong family planning effort
   C. Rapid improvement in the educational level of women
   D. A marked increase in the status of women relative to that of men
   E. A low mortality level uncharacteristic of low income countries

6. American fertility levels in the early 1800s were:
   A. As high as or higher than the early 1990s levels of fertility in some of the high fertility countries of Africa
   B. Not different from the 1980 level of Japanese fertility
   C. Equal to the 1990s level of U.S.fertility

D. Greater than the 1920s level of Hutterite fertility
E. Lower than the then current level of fertility in Europe

7. Historically, which group was in the lead with respect to fertility decline at the beginning of demographic transition in England?
   A. Farmers
   B. Unskilled laborers
   C. Aborigines
   D. Poor people
   E. Aristocrats

8. Among the following Asian countries, which had the highest fertility level as of the early 1990s?
   A. China
   B. Indonesia
   C. Sri Lanka
   D. India
   E. Pakistan

9. Which of the following major regions had the lowest fertility level as of the early 1990s?
   A. Africa
   B. Asia
   C. Middle America
   D. South America
   E. North America

### *5.7.13. Differentials and Determinants*

10. Which of the following has a positive effect on the fertility level of a population?
    A. Longer breast-feeding period
    B. Legalization of abortion
    C. Higher divorce rate
    D. Lowered age at marriage
    E. Increase in the prevalence of nonmarriage

11. Which of the following is NOT an economic reason for wanting children?
    A. Children as a source of labor
    B. Children for old age security
    C. Children as an insurance against economic risk
    D. Children to continue ancestor worship
    E. Children as a consumption item

12. Which of the following is NOT usually mentioned in connection with the discussion of the physiological mechanism through which breast-feeding inhibits ovulation?
    A. Suckling by the infant
    B. Stimulation of receptors in the nipple
    C. Initiating a signal to the hypothalamus (a nerve center in the brain)
    D. Increased production of prolactin
    E. Mother's weight loss

13. Which of the following is NOT among the most important proximate determinants of fertility identified by Bongaarts?
    A. Marriage
    B. The lost time between marriages
    C. Contraception
    D. Abortion
    E. Breast-feeding

14. Some demographers who have analyzed fertility dynamics in India have compared North India with South India. Which of the following features is NOT emphasized in this comparison?
    A. Fertility level
    B. Status of women
    C. Age at marriage
    D. Infant and child mortality
    E. Language

15. It is NOT true that post-transitional societies are characterized by:
    A. High levels of labor-force participation rates for women
    B. High age at marriage
    C. Widespread use of effective contraception
    D. Decreasing male–female gap with respect to educational attainment
    E. Increasing fecundity

16. It is NOT true that fertility in pre-transition societies is significantly affected by:
    A. Breast-feeding practices
    B. Subfecundity
    C. Contraceptive use
    D. Fetal mortality
    E. Age of entry into sexual union

17. In the United States in 1991, which racial/ethnic group had the highest incidence of unwed motherhood?
    A. Chinese

B. Japanese
C. Filipino
D. black
E. white

18. Which of the following factors is likely to be least associated with fertility?
    A. Economic factors
    B. Social factors
    C. Psychological factors
    D. Climatic factors
    E. Biological factors

19. Compared to the respective opposite group, which of the following groups has lower fertility?
    A. Working women
    B. Rural residents
    C. Catholics among U.S. Hispanics
    D. U.S. nonwhites
    E. Indian Muslims

20. Of the world religions, which has been most doctrinally hostile to family limitation?
    A. Roman Catholicism
    B. Hinduism
    C. Buddhism
    D. Islam
    E. Judaism

**FOR EACH OF THE QUESTIONS IN SECTIONS 5.7.14. TO 5.7.16., STATE TRUE OR FALSE AND EXPLAIN. (THESE QUESTIONS MAY BE MORE DIFFICULT THAN THOSE INCLUDED IN SECTION 5.7.1.)**

### 5.7.14. Concepts

1. Abortion refers to the termination of pregnancy while the fetus is non-viable.
2. The term neo-Malthusianism and anti-natalism are interchangeable.
3. The term "birth interval" is used for the interval between entry into sexual union and the first birth, in addition to interbirth intervals.
4. The terms "parity" and "birth order" are synonyms.
5. The term "supply of children" in fertility analysis stands for natural fertility.
6. The so-called Easterlin cycles refer to fertility dynamics.

7. The term "illegitimate births" has been replaced by "live births to unmarried mothers."

### 5.7.15. Measures

8. The total fertility rate can be expressed as a fraction of the hypothetical maximum fertility, the fraction being the product of deflating multipliers (all between 0 and 1), attributable to marriage, contraception, abortion, and post-partum non-susceptibility.
9. Children-ever-born as used in fertility studies refer to the total number of live human births ever occurring on this planet.
10. When reproduction outside marriage is negligible, fertility can be thought of as the product of a Malthusian component and a neo-Malthusian component.
11. Cohort fertility is the same as the total fertility rate.
12. The general marital fertility rate is greater than or equal to the corresponding general fertility rate.
13. The mean length of generation varies very little from one population to another.
14. The gross reproduction rate is equal to 0.488 $\times$ the total fertility rate.
15. The gap between the actual and desired family size is a valid indicator of the unmet need for family planning services and facilities.

### 5.7.16. Determinants and Differentials

16. The curve of age-specific marital fertility rates (age on the horizontal axis) is convex for natural fertility populations and concave for controlled fertility populations.

❖ ❖ ❖ ❖

### 5.7.1. Answers

1. False. The term "natural fertility" is applied to the marital fertility in the absence of contraception or abortion.
2. False. Abortion may be spontaneous or induced. The former is called miscarriage. Induced abortion carried out in accordance with the laws of the country is called legal abortion. Laws specify a duration of pregnancy (commonly 12 weeks) within which abortion is permissible.

3. True. The measure is analogous to the crude birth rate. Note, however, that the label is less popular than the crude birth rate. Moreover, sometimes the ratio of the annual number of abortions to the corresponding number of live births is called the abortion rate. although it should more appropriately be called an abortion ratio.

4. False. Amenorrhea (the absence of menstruation) is not the same as anovulation (the absence of ovulation—discharging the egg from the ovary). However, demographers do use amenorrhea as an indicator of anovulation because data on the former are easier to collect than that on the latter.

5. True. In epidemiology, incidence is the number of cases of a disease having their onset during a given period (e.g., a calendar year). When the age-specific fertility rate is viewed as an incidence rate, one draws an analogy between the cases of a disease having their onset during a calendar year and the number of births to women of a given age group during the year.

6. False. With a reproductive span of 30 years (say from age 15 until 45) and an average birth interval of one to two years, under ideal conditions a woman may produce 15 or more live births (including twins, triplets, etc.). The Hutterite fertility has remained below this level because of relatively late marriage and long periods of infecundity induced by breast-feeding. Another factor involved may have been a moderate coital frequency (Robinson, 1986).

7. True. Leridon (1977) observed a range of 3.7 to 9.5 in the total fertility rate in 23 natural fertility populations. In addition to being highly variable, natural fertility remains below the biological maximum. Four factors explain why. (i) The total infecundable period following termination of pregnancy. (This is often lengthened beyond the first postpartum ovulation if abstinence is observed, as in a number of societies). (ii) The waiting time to conception, once the woman starts ovulating regularly and engages in sexual intercourse. (iii) Fetal mortality. (iv) The onset of permanent sterility, which becomes increasingly certain with age. These four factors are, in turn, influenced by factors such as breast-feeding, frequency of intercourse, and the length of the fertile period within a woman's menstrual cycle. The first (breast-feeding) is the principal determinant of postpartum amenorrhea; the second and the third are determinants of the waiting time to conceive.

### 5.7.2. Answers

8. True, in so far as childbearing occurs almost exclusively within the context of marriage. The shifts in the age-specific fertility rates in such situations reflect changes in marriage pattern as well as changes in childbearing within marriage.

9. True. In interpreting the total fertility rate, we imagine a follow up of a hypothetical group of women who share a common starting point for their reproductive career (usually, age 15).

10. False. The adjective "crude" signifies that the at-risk population (the denominator) used in its calculation is not homogeneous enough. For example, the age variation in fertility is ignored, when the total population is used as the at-risk population.

11. True. In fertility surveys it is common to ascertain the number of children borne to date by each woman in the sample. This includes the surviving children as well as those who died before the date of the survey.

### 5.7.3. Answers

12. False. The fertility level in pre-transition societies are kept far below the biological maximum possible by factors such as malnutrition, disease, and high rates of fetal mortality. See also question (7) above.

13. True. The crude birth rate in earliest America is estimated to have been as high as 55 births per 1000 persons.

14. True. According to the estimates prepared by the United Nations (1993), the total fertility rate in East Asia during 1965–1970 was 5.4 per woman. By 1994, it had fallen to 1.9 (Population Reference Bureau's *1994 World Population Data Sheet.*)

15. True. Between the late 1960s and 1994, the TFR declined from 5.4 to 1.9 in Eastern Asia, from 5.8 to 3.4 in Southeast Asia, from 6.0 to 4.2 in Southern (South-Central) Asia, and from 6.3 to 4.6 in Western Asia.

16. False. In the late 1960s, the Latin American TFR was 5.5 when the Asian TFR was 5.7. In 1994 the corresponding figures were Latin America 3.2 and Asia 3.1 (United Nations, 1993; Population Reference Bureau's *1994 World Population Data Sheet*).

17. True. Between the late 1960s and 1994, the Asian TFR declined from 5.7 to 3.1 while the African TFR declined from 6.7 to only 5.9.

18. True. Between 1970 and the early 1990s the total fertility rate fell from 7.0 to 3.4 per woman. "The Bangladesh case is particularly important because this is a country in which most of the factors favorable to fertility decline—improving socioeconomic development and improving status of women—are hardly visible" (Freedman, 1995, pp. 13–14).

19. True. Sri Lanka has long been known as a poor country, but one that has accomplished substantial fertility decline, from 4.7 in the late 1960s to 2.5 by

1994 (United Nations, 1993, and Population Reference Bureau, 1994). This accomplishment has been commonly attributed to the combined influence of a well-organized, noncoercive family planning program, low mortality, and high female literacy (Freedman, 1995, p. 14). In this respect Sri Lanka resembles Kerala and Tamil Nadu, two of the southern states in India, with 1991 TFRs of 1.8 and 2.2, respectively.

20. True. In Indonesia between the late 1960s and 1994, the TFR declined from 5.6 to 3.0. Indonesia has an administrative structure that reaches to the grass-root level. This has facilitated effective implementation of development activities and family planning programs (World Bank, 1992; Freedman, 1995, p. 10).

### 5.7.4. Answers

21. True. The age pattern of fecundity is more clear for women. Fecundity is zero before menarche and after menopause. In a population the percentage of women capable of procreation peaks by the late teens or early twenties and then gradually declines until about age 40, after which, the decline becomes rapid (United Nations, 1963, p. 101).
22. True. The age-specific fertility rate rises from low levels, reaches a peak (usually in the 20s), and then declines. The pattern varies depending upon the age of entry into sexual union, the degree to which fertility is deliberately controlled, and so on.
23. True. However, at very low levels of age at marriage (e.g., below 15) a small increase in the age at marriage has virtually no effect on fertility. Also, the relationship between age at marriage and fertility in a population depends upon the prevalence of reproduction outside marriage.
24. True. Fecundity, being the biological capacity to reproduce, is a necessary but not a sufficient condition for parenthood. It is not a sufficient condition because contraception can prevent pregnancies and abortion can be used to terminate a pregnancy.
25. True. Irregular ovulation during the years immediately following menarche cause subfecundity among females, and sub-normal production of sperm is responsible for subfecundity among young males.
26. True. Theoretically speaking, that is. Diseases affect fecundity through their effect on the ability to have coitus, on the probability that coitus results in conception, and on the ability to carry the pregnancy to full term (McFalls and McFalls, 1984). Malnourishment and ill health frequently occur together and interact. There is evidence that well-nourished girls reach menarche 2 or 3 years earlier than those with a poor diet, chronic malnourishment may also

affect postpartum amenorrhea. But there is no evidence of a significant increase in the waiting time for conception or in the frequency of spontaneous abortion among malnourished women (Gray, 1983).

27. True. Breast-feeding tends to lengthen intervals between births by lengthening the duration of the period of nonsusceptibility to conception following a birth. In addition, breast-feeding reduces infant mortality, which, in turn, influences the number of births. Some couples may have a tendency to replace lost infants as soon as possible.

### 5.7.5. Answers

28. True. Forty percent of the world's population live in countries where induced abortion is permitted on request and an additional 25% live in countries where abortion is permissible if the woman's life is endangered by a pregnancy (Henshaw, 1990).

29. False. Neo-Malthusians are anti-natalists: They advocate policies and programs that are explicitly pro-birth control.

30. True. The first birth control clinic in the United States was opened in New York in 1916 by Margaret Sanger. She printed thousands of handbills in English, Italian, and Yiddish, which began thus: "Do you want any more children? If not, why do you have them? DO NOT KILL, DO NOT TAKE LIFE, BUT PREVENT." Arrest, trial, incarceration, release, and reopening of the clinic were repeated in that sequence several times before she established the first permanent clinic in 1923 (Thomlinson, 1976, p. 253).

### 5.7.6. Answers

1. B and D. Fertility is contrasted with fecundity, the biological capacity to reproduce. Fertility analysis is usually confined to live births and most of the measures of fertility relate births to women. But that does not mean that fertility applies only to women.

2. A and C. Natural marital fertility is far below the biological maximum. Typical birth intervals are 2–3 years, much longer than the minimum possible spacing of about 1 year. Natural fertility varies between populations (Leridon, 1977). These features of natural fertility can be accounted for in terms of the postpartum infecundable period, the waiting time to conception, intrauterine mortality, and permanent sterility (Bongaarts, 1982, pp. 103–104).

3. B and D. The opposite of choice A is true. As for choice C, note that coital frequency has a positive effect on fertility while age at marriage has a negative effect.

4. A, B, C, and D. Frequent and intense breast-feeding inhibits menstruation. Other factors inhibiting menstruation include conditions of extreme malnutrition, endocrine disorders, and medication.

5. A, B, C, and D. Variability in the post-partum anovulation and in the contraception-induced anovulation are known to be major factors accounting for fertility variation (Bongaarts 1982).

6. A, B, and C: Neonatal deaths are deaths to live-born infants during the first four weeks of life.

### 5.7.7. Answers

7. A, B, C, and D. Since choice D is true, the truth of choice A follows from the fact that the GFR uses in the denominator the number of women in the reproductive ages, which is less than the total population used in the denominator of the CBR.

8. A, B, C, and D. The child/woman ratio is a rough indicator of fertility used when other, better measures are not available. Its weaknesses are those stated in choices A and C and its chief merit is the one stated in choice B.

9. A and C. If the sex ratio at birth is unrelated to the age of the mother, and if the sex ratio at birth is 105 males to 100 females, then GRR = TFR × (100/205). If the sex ratio at birth is $f$ then GRR = TFR/$(1 + f)$. Hence the GRR contains scarcely any more information than the TFR does.

10. A, B, and C. The NRR is viewed as a measure of the degree to which women replace themselves with their counterparts in the next generation, if they experience a given age schedule of mortality and one of fertility rates. It indicates the long-run (not the short-run) tendency of a population to grow or decline, in the absence of migration, given time-invariant fertility and mortality schedules.

### 5.7.8. Answers

11. B and D. The Hutterites live in North and South Dakota and the neighboring regions of Canada. Their fertility levels, as far as we know, have never been as high as the biologically possible maximum. The overall fertility level of the Hutterites in 1980 was only half of what it was fifty years earlier (Peter, 1987).

12. A, B, and C. There is no indication of any dramatic upturn in the U.S. CBR as of now. All indications are that the U.S. fertility level will remain low for many years to come. The average CBR for the years 1971–1975 in the United States was 15.4, the corresponding figure for 1976–1980 was 15.2, and for 1981–

1985, it was 15.8. During the latter half of the 1980s, it went up slightly reaching 16.7 by 1990. The 1994 figure was 16.0.

13. A, B, C, and D. In many LDCs, teenage fertility is high because of early age at marriage and the absence of contraceptive practice at the beginning of the reproductive career. Regarding choice C see Nathanson and Kim (1989) and regarding choice D see Ahlburg and De Vita (1992, pp. 22–24).

14. A, B, C, and D. As one demographer put it "childbearing is becoming less popular" in the MDCs (Westoff, 1987, p. 161).

15. B and D. The U.S. TFR was 2.1 in 1994, while most other MDCs had a much lower TFR (Canada, 1.8; Northern Europe, 1.8; Western Europe, 1.5; Eastern Europe, 1.6; Southern Europe, 1.4; Australia, 1.9; New Zealand, 2.1). As for choice C, the U.S. teenage fertility was in fact declining as in several other Western countries until the late 1980s, when a dramatic reversal occurred in the U.S. (Ahlburg and De Vita, 1992, pp. 19–25; Westoff, 1987, p. 168.)

16. A, B, C, and D. As Westoff (1987) put it "enough radical changes have occurred in recent decades—including changes in women's status, cohabitation, high marital dissolution rates, developments in contraceptive technology, and legal abortion—which, when combined with historical forces that have been driving birth rate down for a century or more, strongly suggest a future of low rates of reproduction in the Western world."

17. A, B, and C. It is known that what has come to be known as the European marriage pattern involving late marriage and non-marriage was widespread in Europe before the Industrial Revolution got underway (Hajnal, 1965). Effective contraception came into use only toward the end of 1800s. So the relatively low level of fertility that prevailed in pre-transition Europe must have been due to the factors mentioned in choices A–C.

18. A, B, C, and D. Note that the last three factors tended to push fertility upward (Yaukey, 1990. p. 194; Nag, 1980).

19. A, B, and C. As Freedman put it, "While insufficient to explain everything that has happened since then, they (the first three factors mentioned) proved to be, and remain, powerful determinants" (Freedman, 1995, p. 3). Demographic discussion of fertility dynamics does not pay the political structure of a country the attention it deserves. It is recognized, however, that political structure influences population dynamics directly (through population policies) and indirectly (through such things as economic and social development strategies).

20. A, B, C, and D. Broad-based macrolevel development is no longer believed to be necessary for major fertility decline; specific changes such as the ones

mentioned in choice B are regarded as sufficient (Freedman, 1995). The so-called ideational hypothesis maintains that ideas about family planning and lifestyles in general are highly influential in triggering and sustaining fertility declines (Cleland and Wilson, 1987). From the *Princeton Study of European Fertility* (Coale and Watkins, 1986), it has been concluded that the factors mentioned in choice D are important in explaining fertility declines.

### 5.7.9. Answers

21. A, B, C, and D. See Nam (1994, p. 200). Sharma and Retherford (1990) comparing Indian states found a negative association between literacy level and fertility. Literacy can affect fertility indirectly through its influence on infant and child mortality, as well as on the age at marriage.

22. D. See Nam (1994, p. 203). As for choice A, note that in India, Muslims are in a minority, but they have higher fertility than the majority group (Hindus). Regarding choice B, note that France, mostly a Catholic country, led the way in fertility transition. As for choice C, it is known that in Lebanon, Shia Muslims have higher fertility than Sunni Muslims.

### 5.7.10. Answers

1. D. Exposure to sexual education.

### 5.7.11. Answers

2. C. The United Nations' sex-age adjusted birth rate is the ratio of the annual number of births to a weighted sum of the numbers of women in the age groups 15–19, 20–24, ..., 40–44, the weights being 1, 7, 7, 6, 4, and 1, respectively. (See United Nations, 1956, p.45).

### 5.7.12. Answers

3. D. Poor implementation (See Freedman, 1995, pp. 12–13).

4. E. That births are spaced at longer intervals (e.g., 3 to 4 years) in India is often stressed in the literature (Mandelbaum, 1974) as also are social pressures against a grandmother becoming pregnant (Caldwell *et al.*, 1988). But the main point is that practices reducing the frequency of coitus after each birth or avoiding it altogether after attaining certain life-course stages (e.g., grandparenthood) have been adopted by people, as a matter of routine, resulting in a reduced natural fertility level.

5. B. (Freedman, 1995, pp. 13–14). In Bangladesh none of the factors such as socio-economic development or an increase in the status of women is visible, and yet the total fertility rate has come down from 7.0 to 3.4 children per woman between 1970 and the early 1990s. This accomplishment has been credited to the strong family planning program in that country. In the 1970s it was fashionable to predict that fertility reduction of any appreciable magnitude would not occur in Bangladesh any time soon (Demeny, 1975).
6. A. As high as or higher than the early-1990s levels of fertility in some of the high fertility countries of Africa.
7. E. Aristocrats.
8. E. Pakistan. The 1994 TFRs for these countries according to the Population Reference Bureau's *1994 World Population Data Sheet* were China, 2.0; Indonesia, 3.0; Sri Lanka, 2.5; India, 3.6; and Pakistan, 6.1.
9. E. North America.

### 5.7.13. *Answers*

10. D: Lowered age at marriage.
11. D: All the others are mentioned in the literature as economic reasons for having children. See Leibenstein (1957) regarding choices A and B, Cain (1981) regarding choice C, and Willis (1973) regarding choice E.
12. E. The general idea is that frequent nipple stimulation is the critical factor, which causes, through a chain of physiological mechanisms, an increase in the production of the hormone prolactin, which, in turn, inhibits ovulation, either by reducing the release of gonadotropic hormones needed for ovulation or by directly affecting the ovaries (see Wood, 1994, p. 337).
13. B. The lost time between marriages.
14. E. The languages of south India are non-Indo-European, whereas the languages of north are Indo-European. No one has regarded this difference relevant for explaining fertility differences of the two regions. "In contrast to states in the north, southern states are characterized by lower marital fertility, later age at marriage, lower infant and child mortality ... The division between the two regimes broadly coincides with the division between areas of northern kinship/low female autonomy and southern kinship/high female autonomy" (Dyson and Moore, 1983, p. 195). Several writers have emphasized the point that the higher and more autonomous status of women in the south is the major factor accounting for the corresponding lower fertility. One study, however, reported findings inconsistent with the afore-mentioned hypothesis. Visaria

(1993) found that women in Kerala in the south were not significantly different from Gujarati women (in the north) with respect to direct indicators of "the ability to make one's own decisions about what to do" (e.g., with one's own earnings) (see Freedman, 1995).

15. E. It is fair to say that in such societies fecundity level of the population remains more or less time invariant.
16. C. Contraceptive use.
17. D. Among blacks, 68% of mothers of live-born infants were unmarried; the corresponding figures for the other groups were: white (22%); Chinese (6%); Japanese (10%); Filipino (17%) (NCHS, 1994, p. 15).
18. D. Climate factors.
19. A. Note: working women are to be compared to non-working women; rural residents to urban residents, Muslims to non-Muslims, and so on.
20. A. Roman Catholicism (see Thomlinson, 1975, pp. 136–151).

### 5.7.14. Answers

1. True. Non-viability is usually defined in terms of the duration of pregnancy. A fetus is assumed to be viable (capable of sustaining life outside the womb) after 28 weeks of gestation.
2. True. Neo-Malthusians regard fertility control within marriage essential. They strongly support the use of contraception and abortion as means of birth control, contrary to the position held by Malthus. Anti-natalists, as the term indicates, are explicit advocates of birth control. For this reason often the two terms are used as synonyms.
3. True. The interval from marriage or entry into sexual union and the first birth is conventionally called the first birth interval. The terms closed and open intervals are used in this connection. For example, if a couple have not yet (as of the date of survey or inquiry) had their first birth, for them the first birth interval is "open," whereas for those who had theirs, it is "closed." Birth interval analysis, using life table techniques, has received considerable attention in demography (see, e.g., Namboodiri and Suchindran, 1987; Smith, 1992; Wood, 1994).
4. False. Birth order applies to the infant. Parity, on the other hand, refers to the classification of a woman (or couple) in terms of the number of live births to date. Thus a zero-parity woman had no live births to date, a two-parity woman had two, and so on. The proportion of $n$-parity women (couples) who go on to have at least one more live birth is called the parity progression ratio.

5. False. The supply of children is the number of surviving children a couple would have if fertility were not deliberately limited (Easterlin, 1975). Natural fertility is greater than or equal to the supply of children thus defined.

6. True. The fertility of a birth cohort is inversely related to the size of the cohort relative to that of the parental birth cohort. This leads to cycles in fertility two generations long (see Easterlin, 1980).

7. True. Out-of-wedlock births used to be classified as illegitimate births. But nowadays the term illegitimate births is less frequently used. The term "live births to unmarried mothers" has taken its place (NCHS, 1994, pp. 11–15.) The name illegitimacy ratio used to be applied to the number of illegitimate births as a proportion of all births. The current practice is to call this "live births to unmarried mothers as a proportion of all births" (NCHS, 1994, p. 15).

### 5.7.15. *Answers*

8. True. This was suggested by Bongaarts (1978): TFR = $C$ times TF, where TF stands for the hypothetical maximum fertility, TFR is the observed total fertility rate, and $C$ is the deflating multiplier, which is equal to the product of $C_m$, $C_a$, $C_c$, and $C_i$, the multipliers for marriage effect, abortion effect, contraception effect, and postpartum non-susceptibility effect respectively. For example, for Bangladesh the marriage effect in 1975 was estimated as 0.853 whereas for the Dominican Republic it was estimated as 0.601 in the same year. The corresponding figures for the postpartum non-susceptibility effect were 0.539 and 0.860, respectively (Bongaarts and Potter, 1983).

9. False. The reference is to the number of live births to a woman (or couple) until the date of inquiry or recording. This, together with the number of children surviving, are commonly collected in fertility surveys and censuses.

10. True. This was suggested by Coale (1967) using the formula $I_f = I_g I_m$, where the symbol on the left hand side stands for an index of overall fertility, the first factor on the right-hand side stands for an index of marital fertility (neo-Malthusian component), and the second factor on the right-hand side stands for an index of the proportion of women married (the Malthusian component). $I_f = \Sigma f_i w_i / \Sigma F_i w_i$ [the ratio of a weighted average of age-specific fertility rates ($f$) of the focal population to the corresponding weighted average of the age-specific marital fertility rates ($F$) of the Hutterites, using the age composition ($w$) of women in the focal population as the weights]; $I_g = \Sigma g_i m_i / \Sigma F_i m_i$ [the ratio of a weighted average of the age-specific marital fertility rates ($g$) of the focal population to the corresponding weighted average of the age-specific marital fertility of the Hutterites, using the age composition ($m$) of married women in the focal population as the weights]; $I_m = \Sigma F_i m_i / \Sigma F_i w_i$ (which is the

number of births to married women in the focal population expressed as a ratio of the number of births to all women, if the respective segments were to adopt the age-specific marital fertility rates of the Hutterites.) Note that when there is no reproduction outside marriage, $\Sigma g_i m_i = \Sigma f_i w_i$ = the total number of births in the focal population. Coale (1967) suggested these components as a way of making full use of the wealth of information in European censuses and registration data for the 19th and early 20th centuries.

11. False. Cohort fertility refers to the reproductive performance of a particular birth or marriage cohort. It is contrasted with period fertility, which refers to an exhaustive collection of the fertility performance of different cohort in a given period, e.g., the age-specific fertility rates for a given calendar year. A commonly calculated measure of cohort fertility is the cumulative fertility, which is the sum of the age-specific fertility rates of a real birth (marriage) cohort up to a given age (duration). The cumulative fertility at the end of the reproductive period is called the completed fertility, terminal cumulative fertility, or life-time fertility.

12. True. The denominator of the former is married females in the reproductive age groups, which is fewer than all females in the same age group, the denominator of the general fertility rate. The numerator of both is the same, the annual number of births. Hence the result.

13. True. It (the average age of mothers at the birth of their daughters) remains within a small range, around 29 years (Wilson, 1985, p. 87).

14. True. Assuming that the sex ratio at birth is 105 males per 100 females, and that it remains invariant to the age of the mother, the GRR is equal to (100/205) × the corresponding TFR.

15. False. Survey after survey conducted in the 1950s and 1960s sought data on contraceptive "knowledge, attitude, and practice" (KAP), believing that such information revealed the extent of the unmet need for family planning services and facilities. In particular, the discrepancy between the actual number of children couples have and their desired or ideal family sizes as stated in KAP surveys was interpreted as indicative of the latent demand for family planning. By the 1970s such surveys became the basis for the intervention of rich countries and international agencies on the population affairs of poor countries. Among demographers there were many who questioned the casual interpretation given to the gap between the actual and desired or ideal family sizes. In some societies the very idea of individual control over reproduction may be foreign, in which case the numerical responses to the desired-family size question "If you could have exactly the number of children you want, how many would that be?" may not make much sense. Even in the Western

countries such data are difficult to interpret. For example, a child may be "unwanted" initially but "wanted" later on. Some demographers have also argued that the responses to the desired family size question often reflect what the respondent thinks a "proper" response should be.

### 5.7.16. Answers

16. True. The convex pattern looks like ∩ (an inverted U) with its left leg broken off, whereas the concave pattern looks like ∪ with its right arm broken off (see Fig. 5.5; Wilson, 1985, p. 157; Wood, 1994, pp. 54–56; Pressat, 1972, p. 181).

CHAPTER 6

# *Migration*

The human population has always been mobile. During the hunting-and-gathering stage of societal evolution, frequent shifting of camp was necessary because within a few weeks of stay at a camp all fruits and roots nearby would have been gathered and the game would have been either hunted or frightened away to distant places. During the early stages of sedentary agriculture too, frequent moves were necessitated by the exhaustion of soil fertility resulting from repeated cultivation of the same area, requiring people to move in search of more fertile lands. Geographic mobility has of course accelerated with economic development and technological progress.

Geographic mobility began to receive demographers' attention much later than mortality and fertility did. Also, geographic mobility is the least understood of the three components of population change (fertility, mortality, and mobility), largely because of inadequate data and underdeveloped analytical frameworks.

Migration is a special type of geographic mobility, involving a more or less permanent shift in residence, a change in the physical and/or social environment, i.e., severing ties with people and things in one place (locality, community) and establishing ties with those in another. It is one thing to conceptualize migration in this way, but it is an entirely different matter to ascertain whether in each instance of a residential shift all the features mentioned have been associated with the move. To facilitate data collection and analysis, demographers have defined migration as a residential move involving the crossing of a political boundary (e.g., the county line in the United States). Moves across political boundaries are regarded as migration as opposed to moves within political boundaries, which are called local moves.

Geographic mobility has played a major role in the distribution and redistribution of humans on the surface of this planet. Moreover, in the case of some populations (e.g. Ireland), geographic mobility had a significant impact on fertility transition.

In the study of geographic mobility, issues such as the following demand attention: Which trait combination (involving, for example, age, education, marital status, etc.) is associated with higher propensities of residential mobility? Which features of a community (e.g., economically expanding, politically unstable, climatically mild) attract or repel migrants? Under what conditions do people move from one area to another (e.g., when the former is going through a depression while the other is in an expanding phase)? To address such questions, a number of basic concepts and measurements have been introduced and data have been assembled to reveal major trends and differentials in migration. Also a number of theories and perspectives on population distribution and redistribution have been given close attention.

## 6.1. CONCEPTS, DATA, AND MEASUREMENTS

The following definitions are standard in the United States. Local movers are those who move residence within a county; they are "in-movers" to the destination and "out-movers" from the origin. Those who move from one county to another are internal migrants, contrasted with international migrants, who are movers from one country to another. International migrants are immigrants to their destination and emigrants from their origin.

Migrations can be distinguished in terms of migration-defining boundaries or origin-destination categories. Inter-regional, inter-state, and inter-community migrations illustrate the former and rural–urban migration illustrate the latter. Insofar as the units of interest, e.g., states or regions, are aggregations of basic units such as counties, it is possible, from migration data tabulated using the basic units, to obtain the needed tabulations for more inclusive units. Notice, however, the arbitrariness of the basic unit itself.

Moves of seasonal workers between primary residence and a temporary place of residence at the work place, as well as moves back and forth between one's primary residence and a vacation home, are examples of circulatory moves.

The concept of one's usual place of residence enters the definition of migration. Yet there is no universal agreement regarding how long one should be at an address before that becomes deemed as his or her usual place of residence. In Indonesia (Nam, 1994, p. 222) a minimum of 6 months of continuous residence at a place is required before that becomes one's usual place of residence. In the United States, on the other hand, moving in is all that seems to be required.

Migratory moves from A to B during a given time interval form a migration stream, and moves in the opposite direction during the same period form a counterstream.

Petersen (1958) suggested distinguishing between different types of migration (mainly between, in his terminology, primitive, group, free-individual, and forced migration). Primitive migration results from the inability of a group to cope with natural forces in their physical environment (e.g., a cataclysm such as drought, a sudden attack by locusts, or the gradually increasing pressure of growing numbers on land of limited area or fertility). Group migration involves the movement of groups such as a clan, a tribe, or any other group larger than a family. Most of the major movements of people in the pre-modern periods consisted of this type of migration. Free-individual migration involves the movement of individuals acting on their own initiative, without government support or compulsion. A great deal of international migration in the modern period has been of this type. Forced migration involves the movement of people activated by the state or some other political or social institution. The Jewish emigration from Germany between 1933 and 1938 prompted by anti-Semitic laws and acts was a type of forced migration—impelled migration in Petersen's (1958) terminology. The enslavement and transport of Africans to the New World was another type of forced migration.

Immigrants to the United States are persons who have been admitted to the country with visas that permit them to acquire permanent resident status. At present (early 1990s), the following categories of persons qualify for entry on an immigrant visa: (i) immediate relatives (e.g., spouse, children, parents) of adult citizens; (ii) not-so-immediate relatives of adult citizens; (iii) spouses and unmarried children of permanent adult residents; (iv) needed workers or persons in the arts or professions, or in occupations with a short supply of workers; (v) refugees and asylees.

Migration has little in common with death (migration) but has some features in common with having children (fertility) (Nam, 1994, p. 221; Goldscheider 1971). Births and deaths have obvious biological aspects to them, whereas migration has none. Births and deaths affect only one population, whereas migration affects two, the origin and the destination. Death occurs once and only once, whereas migratory moves and the number of children a woman bears may range from none to many. Having children and moving residence both have a sequential nature—both can be ordered: first, second, third, and so on. This feature demands special attention when one tries to build explanatory frameworks for fertility or migration (Namboodiri, 1972).

As for migration measure, if $O$ is the number of out-migrants from an area, $I$ the number of in-migrants to the area, $P$ the mid-year population in the area, and $k$ a constant (usually 1000), then $k \times (O/P)$, is called out-migration rate, $k \times (I/P)$ is called in-migration rate, $k \times$ the difference, $(I/P) - (O/P)$, is called the net-migration rate, and $k \times$ the sum $(I/P) + (O/P)$, is called the gross migration rate. Each of these can be calculated for subpopulations specified in terms of age, occupation, income, race, sex, or any other trait. In specific rates, the numerator and denominator refer to the same particular subgroup of the population.

## 6.2. MIGRATION STREAMS, LEVELS, AND TRENDS

The main streams of intercontinental migration during 1500–1950 included those from all parts of Europe to North America, and from Latin countries of Europe to Middle and South America; from Great Britain to Africa and Australia; from Africa to the New World; and from China and India to different parts of the world (Woytinsky and Woytinsky, 1953; Weeks, 1994, pp. 208–209).

Between the two World Wars massive free migration from Europe subsided due to the Great Depression and the immigration-restricting legislation in the major receiving countries such as the United States, and millions of Jews left Germany in the 1930s as political refugees.

In the post-World War II period there was a huge volume of movement of people in Eastern and Central Europe, involving exchanges, expulsions, and transfers; about 3 million Japanese who had moved to different parts of the empire returned to Japan (Weller and Bouvier, 1981, p. 211; Bouvier, et al, 1977); the movement of displaced persons between India and Pakistan involved about 15 million people; and the creation of the new state of Israel produced 700,000 Palestinian out-migrants from, and a large number of Jewish immigrants to, the new state (Yaukey, 1990, p. 267; United Nations, 1979). Other major movements in the same period included the movement of Cubans to Florida and other destinations following the establishment of the Castro regime, and the movement of people from mainland China to Taiwan and other Asian countries following Communist victory.

Also in the post-World War II period, international migration of the old-type (from Europe to such overseas destinations as North and South America and Australia) continued, although at a much-reduced volume, but "... the main currents [were] now to the industrialized countries from the less developed countries" (United Nations, 1979, p. 2).

During the 1960s Europe switched from a net exporter to a net importer of migrants, an increasing number of immigrants coming from the LDCs. During the same period, within Europe short-distance and temporary migration (e.g., from Southern Europe to Northern and Western Europe) grew in volume. During the 1960s and 1970s Latin America switched from a net importer to a net exporter of migrants, accompanied by a strong return movement to Europe and an increasing volume of outflow to North America (United Nations, 1979) and as a source of migration to the MDCs, Asia rose to a par with Latin America.

During this period the refugee movements increased in volume (United Nations, 1979, p. 4). In the 1970s millions of Southeast Asians and Africans were uprooted because of political or economic upheavals, resulting in a huge refugee problem (Weller and Bouvier, 1981, p. 212).

Obviously, internal migration takes different forms for different countries. In the United States, one major inter-regional migration has been, and continues to be, that from east to west; another one, prominent for a long time until the 1960s had been the flow from the South to the Northeast and North-central regions, which, during its peak period, had a heavy component of blacks and poor whites seeking opportunities in the industrializing North. By the 1960s, the flow from the South had reversed and the reversed stream gained strength in the 1970s. Overall, the flow to the South became dominant compared to the flow to the West.

Rural–urban migration has played a major part in the population redistribution in less-developed countries. It used to be a major factor in the currently more-developed countries also, but not anymore, because the rural component of the total population has become in the MDCs too small to serve as a major source of migration to any urban area.

With respect to the level of migration, it is important to note that some populations, such as Americans, are characteristically more mobile than others. In a 12-month-period, one in five of the U.S. population changes residence, less than 50% of the moves being migration. Of course, mobility tendency changes over time. There was, for example, a decline in the American mobility tendencies over the period from the late 1960s to the early 1980s (Long, 1988).

## 6.3. MIGRATION IN DIFFERENT HISTORICAL PERIODS

Hunters and gatherers moved from place to place in search of food, short distances in any particular day, but long distances in the long-run; the early agriculturalists moved in search of land and water for them to settle down; also, wandering was common in early periods of human history, in order to escape from tyrants who held people in slavery (Nam, 1994, p. 242).

In early modern England, children were commonly hired as servants in villages other than their own; mobility linked to marriage and inheritance of property was common; and in many instances the elderly would change residence in order to be closer to their relatives (Nam, 1994, p. 242).

When the populations were growing rapidly, Europeans emigrated to distant lands to establish colonies, as well as to nearby countries to take advantage of opportunities that emerged with social and economic changes. During the same period the slave trade from Africa flourished (Nam, 1994, pp. 244–246).

Currently, there is considerable migration from the Third World countries to the more-developed countries (Nam, 1994, p. 255). The volume of illegal migration has increased with that of legal migration from the less-developed countries. Many of the more-developed countries started to depend on the use of guest-workers.

The United States has been always a country of immigration. For a long time immigration was more or less unrestricted, but gradually the situation changed. (i) Most of the immigrants who came during the colonial period were of British ancestry, although there were among them people from other countries of Europe.

(ii) The period of "old immigrants" (1800–1880) involved a considerable increase in the volume of immigration, Northern and Western Europe being the major source (accounting for 95% of the flow). (iii) The period of "new immigration" (1880–1920) was marked by a shift in the source of immigrants from Northern and Western Europe to Eastern and Southern Europe. (iv) The volume of immigration reached a peak at the turn of the 20th century: in 6 of the 11 years from 1905 through 1915, there were more than one million immigrants. (iv) Since 1921, immigration to the United States has no longer been free. (v) At most points in the U.S. history, net immigration accounted for a small portion of total population increases, although at some points, the relative contribution was substantial (about two-fifths during 1880–1890 and 1900–1910). (See Bouvier, et al., 1977, for a detailed discussion of the changing patterns of immigration to the United States.) (vi) The 1990 U.S. census counted nearly 9 million foreign-born persons as having entered the United States since the 1980 census. This is consistent with the estimate of about one million net immigration per year—880,000 legal immigrants, 150,000 to 200,000 emigrants, and 300,000 net illegal immigrants. (vii) The volume of immigration increased markedly in the late 1980s and early 1990s, peaking at 1.8 million in 1991. Most of this increase in immigration resulted from granting legal resident status (under the provisions of the 1986 Immigration Reform and Control Act) to illegal immigrants who had been living in the country.

The migration of Europeans during the early period of demographic transition (between the 17th and 20th centuries) involved about 60 million people. This mass mobility started with a number of pioneering individuals making the journey. Their major destinations were the United States, Argentina, Canada, and Brazil. Other destinations included Australia, New Zealand, South Africa, and the British West Indies.

Intercontinental migration between the mid-17th century and late 19th century from Africa formed a class by itself in that it was involuntary, involving the transportation of an estimated 10 million slaves to the New World over several centuries, ending with the abolition of slavery at various dates in the 19th century. It constituted in that period the only form of international migration of any appreciable magnitude involving Africans (Davis, 1974; Weller and Bouvier, 1981).

When slavery was abolished it was substituted with indentured labor, particularly to recruit plantation workers and coolies for naval duty. Most of the recruits came from densely settled areas such as southern China, Java, and India. Historically, the indentured labor migration was brief, but it was much greater in volume than the slave trade (Davis, 1974).

## 6.4. DIFFERENTIALS

When migration rates are plotted by age, one notices the following universal regularities: The rates are relatively high among children under 5 years of age and

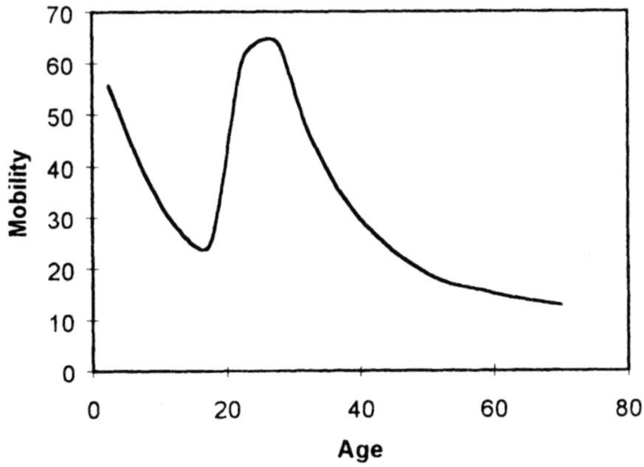


*Figure 6.1.* General mobility U.S. March 1975 to March 1978. (Source: U.S. Bureau of the Census, 1978, p. 17).

low for slightly older children. The rate is highest for those in the early 20s (Fig. 6.1). The decline beyond mid-twenties is rapid at first and gradual afterwards. The patterns just described reflect dependent children accompanying parents who move and the peak mobility associated with going to college, taking a job, and marriage.

In the United States, the net migration of blacks was still out of the South through the 1960s, whereas that of whites already had reversed its direction by the 1960s; it was not until the latter half of 1970s that a strong net in-migration to the South had become established for blacks (Yaukey, 1990, p. 273).

With respect to migration selectivity, generally speaking, when migration is prompted mostly by pull factors at the destination, those who have the qualities to take advantage of those factors are more likely to migrate, but when the push factors at the origin are the major determinants of migration, out-migration is likely to be less selective. Also, distance between origin and destination, legal barriers to migration, threats to safety, and other such obstacles tend to make migration more selective (Yaukey, 1990, pp. 273–274). In terms of migration differentials, unemployed persons are more likely to move than employed persons, farmers are less likely to move than nonfarmers, the more educated are more mobile, and historically, males tended to predominate among long-distance migrants and females tended to predominate among short-distance migrants (Zopf, 1984, pp. 246–249; Weeks, 1994, pp. 197–201). In Europe in the 19th century the usual pattern had been for males to move internationally and for females to move locally to accept service positions (Petersen, 1975; Yaukey, 1990, p. 275). Since World War II, however, the number of female immigrants has exceeded the number of male immigrants to the United States (Yaukey, 1990, p. 275; United

Nations, 1979, p. 4). At present, guest-worker migration in Europe is predominantly male. Women's propensity to migrate is influenced by labor-force participation status. The married-versus-never married difference in migration rate is pronounced only under age 25 (Weeks, 1995, p. 218). The divorced, separated, and widowed tend to have higher migration rate than those who are currently married or single. In follow-up studies, it has been observed that people who change marital status between two consecutive interviews report a higher migration rate than those whose marital status remain intact (Weeks, 1994, p. 199). The U.S. data show that there is a positive association between migration propensity and income and occupational prestige (Weeks, 1994, pp. 200–201). Among couples with the householder spouse in the age group 45–54 years, in 1985, the presence of children

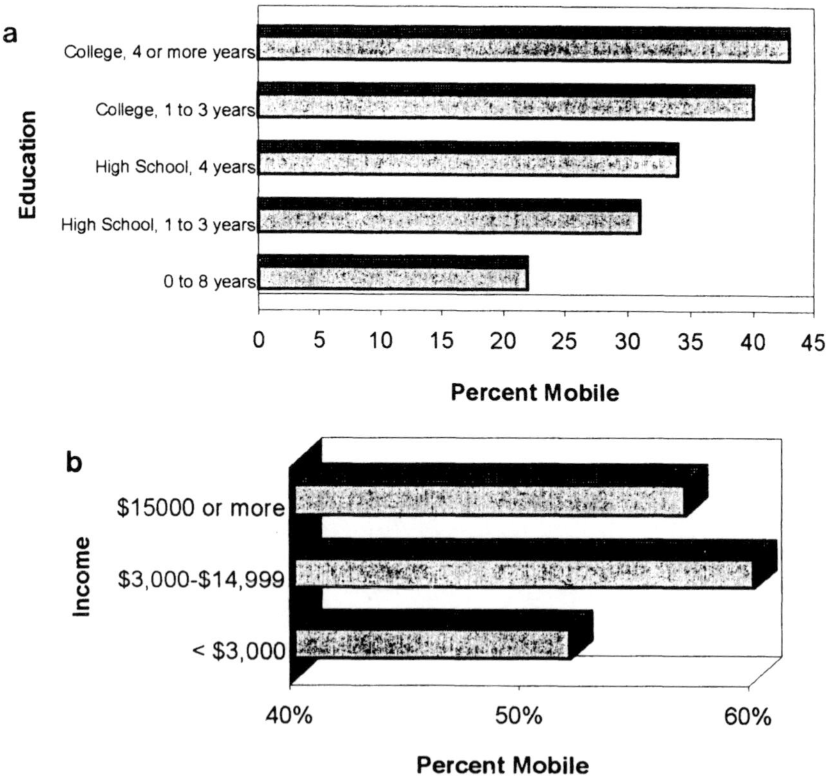


*Figure 6.2.* (a) Percent of U.S. population 18 years and older classified as movers between 1975 and 1978: educational differential; (b) percent males, age 25–34 years in U.S. metropolitan areas classified as movers between 1975 and 1978 (Source: U.S. Bureau of the Census, 1978, p. 41 and p. 70).

under 18 years of age did not make any difference with respect to migration rate (Weeks, 1994, p. 200, citing U.S. census sources).

## 6.5. CAUSES AND CONSEQUENCES

At the macro level, net in-migration is a cause and a consequence of economic growth and net out-migration could be a cause, and often a consequence of, economic slump. At the micro-level, migration is a cause of stress. Ordinarily, migration has greater impact on society in the short-run than mortality and fertility. "Brain drain" (the emigration of highly-skilled individuals such as physicians and engineers to countries offering better career opportunities) from developing countries, if voluminous, could be a problem for the sending countries. The impact of migration on the population size and growth rate depends upon the volume of net migration relative to the size of the resident population. There is also an indirect impact of migration on size and growth rate. This depends upon the composition of the net migration stream. For example, Mexican migrants to the United States tend to be concentrated in the age range 15–35 years. This age selectivity tends to make those who are left behind relatively older and, consequently, the crude death rate of those left behind would be higher, the crude birth rate lower, and the dependency ratio (the ratio of the number of people outside the usual working age range 15–64 to those within that age range) higher. The opposite may be expected in the receiving country, but the magnitude of the effects may be negligible if the size of the base population is very large relative to the volume of the migration stream. If the immigrants collect in enclaves, however, the impact on the local population may be dramatic (Yaukey, 1990, p. 289).

In the sending country, the vacancies created by the departure of people might help increase the labor-force participation rate of women and income inequality might increase as a result of remittance flow from emigrants.

A certain degree of labor displacement is to be expected in the receiving country as the immigrants increase the supply of willing workers. Usually it is the reluctant workers who are replaced by eager immigrant workers. Employers and native workers whose jobs are made possible by the availability of such workers benefit from this displacement; those who are marginal to the workforce are, however, likely to be adversely affected by it (Keely, 1979; Teitelbaum, 1980; Yaukey, 1990, p. 294).

## 6.6. EXPLANATIONS

It is taken axiomatic that "... human beings will tend to gravitate from places having fewer advantages (however they are defined) to those having more"

(Zelinsky, 1983; Nam, 1994, p. 233). Asking people why they moved has been a popular research strategy in migration studies. Opinions differ as to the effectiveness of this strategy in identifying sound explanations for migration.

Demographers agree (more or less) that any sound explanatory framework for mobility is bound to be more complex than those for mortality or fertility (Nam, 1994, p. 238) and that to understand mobility one has to understand the conditions in which mobility occurs and those in which mobility does not occur (Hawley, 1950, p. 328–330). There are, of course, those who subscribe to the view that once motivations of movers and nonmovers are identified, one has full explanations for migration. Similarly, there are those who believe that psychological factors provide adequate explanations of all human behavior.

Lee (1966) emphasized factors associated with current place of residence (origin), those associated with potential destinations for those who contemplate moving, personal factors, and intervening obstacles, which may be thought of as hindrances that a potential migrant has to overcome before the contemplated migration could become a reality. The basic assumption is that a potential migrant compares each possible destination with the origin in terms of the attractive and repelling features and intervening obstacles before choosing whether to move, and, if so, to where.

A simple macroeconomic theory of migration would assume that migration is the mechanism by which human resources move to their highest valued use, that migrants move from low-wage areas to high-wage areas, and that migration would serve as an equilibrating mechanism. The ideal setting assumed is that of perfect market mechanism, which is indeed a rare situation.

Microeconomic theories assume that people decide to move when the benefits from moving are perceived to outweigh the costs. More specifically, it is assumed that the potential migrant calculates for each potential area of residence the discounted present value of expected return if he or she were to take residence there as well as the corresponding discounted value of the expected costs (monetary as well as psychic), and then selects to live in that area for which the expected return less the expected cost is the highest (Molho, 1986, pp. 398–399).

According to the push–pull theory of migration, there are factors that prompt (push) a person to move out of a place and those that prompt (pull) a person to move into an area (see, e.g., Bogue 1969, pp. 753–754). One could think of factors that keep a person from moving out of an area as pull factors and, similarly, factors that discourage a person to move into a potential destination can be viewed as push factors. The idea of the push–pull theory is that the migration from one area to another is a result of the balance between these push and pull factors.

A decision-making model of migration can be outlined as follows (see, e.g., DeJong and Gardner, 1981): Consider each possible course of action (i.e., move; not move). For each of them enumerate the consequences (among the possible consequences of moving to a new place may be, for example, income increase, a higher-prestige job, improved living conditions). For each consequence, attach a likelihood score (indicating the strength of your conviction that the consequences would follow) and a desirability score (indicating how strongly you desire it). Sum the product of the two scores for the different possible consequences of each course of action. Next obtain the product of each significant other person's (e.g., parent, friend) approval rating of each course of action with a weight indicating the importance you attach to that person's approval of your action. Add the products over all significant others. You have now two scores, each a sum of products. They can be combined into a composite, attractiveness score, for each possible course of action, which can be the basis for choosing between the options considered. One would assume that the option with the highest attractiveness score will be the choice. In practice the attractiveness scores of alternatives are likely to be influenced by background factors (e.g. socio-economic status, family characteristics), prevailing social norms regarding behaviors under consideration, and personal characteristics (e.g., whether the decision-maker is habitually a risk-taker).

## 6.7. POLICIES

Some countries have no emigration policies; some (e.g. China) have policies that discourage; and some (e.g., Morocco) have policies that encourage emigration. Emigration is sometimes seen as a temporary solution to the unemployment problem facing a country (Yaukey, 1990, p. 295).

Migration policies change. When the United States was formed and for a short time thereafter, immigration was free of restrictions of any kind (Nam, 1994, p. 230). In 1798 an Alien Act was passed authorizing the President to deport aliens suspected to be dangerous to the country. The Chinese Exclusion Act of 1882 banned further Chinese immigration. This act remained in force until 1943. The Quota Act of 1921 established national-origin quotas, and was replaced three years later by The National Origins Act of 1924, which made some changes in the way quotas were determined. The policy remained in force, in one form or another, until the Immigration Reform Act of 1965.

Western Europe had a liberal immigration policy from 1943 until 1973, a period in which those countries had labor shortages. That policy was replaced by restrictive policies in the 1970s, when the countries began experiencing labor surplus. This illustrates the tendency to tailor immigration policies to suit the prevailing or emerging economic conditions.

Because the predominant tendency is to be restrictive rather than liberal with respect to immigration policy, it is unlikely that global redistribution of population of any appreciable magnitude would result from international migration in the future.

## 6.8. QUESTIONS AND ANSWERS*

**FOR EACH OF THE QUESTIONS IN SECTIONS 6.9.1. TO 6.9.3., STATE TRUE OR FALSE AND EXPLAIN.**

### 6.8.1. Concepts

1. The terms "migrants" and "movers" are synonyms in demographic usage.
2. If you live in Chapel Hill, Orange county, and work in an adjoining county, you are a migrant, according to the U.S. Census Bureau's definition.
3. All migrations are residential moves, but not vice versa.
4. In the United States naturalized citizens are called aliens.

### 6.8.2. Levels and Trends

5. In the United States, during a 12-month-period, about 20% of the people move from one address to another.
6. The United States has higher rates of residential mobility than many of the industrialized countries.
7. Residents of the United States average 25 changes of residence over their lifetime.
8. The U.S. immigration rate peaked early in the 20th century.
9. European migration overseas was greater in volume during 1840–1930 than before or after that period.
10. Western Europe now experiences net emigration.
11. The transportation of slaves from Africa continued for a long time.
12. International migration to industrialized countries has become increasingly restricted.
13. A substantial number of people cross national boundaries illegally.
14. Net international migration in the U.S. affects some states much more than others.
15. In the United States, California attracts more immigrants than any other state.
16. Over nine-tenths of the immigrants who enter the United States currently (the early 1990s) are from non-European countries.

*Answers start on page 156.

### 6.8.3. Differentials, Determinants, and Consequences

17. Migration, no doubt, is selective.
18. There is considerable overlap between the "push–pull" theory of migration and the "cost-benefit analysis" of migration behavior.
19. Migration rate is higher for the better educated.
20. Geographic mobility rate is higher for toddlers than for young teens.
21. Migration rate peaks at young adulthood.
22. Ireland is a classic example of a country that experienced substantial population loss due to net emigration.
23. Most studies have shown that undocumented workers take away jobs from legal residents.
24. At the current rate, international migration makes no substantial difference in the size of the U.S. population.
25. Crude birth rates as high as 65 per 1000 were common among immigrants in French Canada.
26. In general, the European countries with higher rate of emigration during the 18th century were the ones where substantial fertility decline started later.

**FOR EACH OF THE QUESTIONS IN SECTIONS 6.9.4. TO 6.9.8., FOUR ANSWERS ARE SUGGESTED, AT LEAST ONE OF WHICH IS CORRECT. IDENTIFY THE CORRECT ANSWER(S) AND EXPLAIN.**

### 6.8.4. Concepts

1. Which of the following are consistent with the definitions used by the U.S. Bureau of the Census?
   A. A change of residence may involve breaking prior social affiliations and starting new ones, and yet may not constitute a migratory move.
   B. A change of residence involving a short distance and very few changes in social affiliations may constitute a migratory move.
   C. Migration need not necessarily produce a substantial change in the migrant's environment.
   D. A local move may involve a substantial change of environment.
2. Noncitizens enter the United States legally:
   A. As immigrants
   B. As refugees

C. As nonimmigrants
D. As asylees

3. International mobility includes:
   A. Durable changes in societal affiliation
   B. Temporary migration
   C. Refugee migration
   D. Illegal migration

### *6.8.5. Data and Measures*

4. In the United States, which of the following types of migration data are available?
   A. Comparison of birthplace with current residence
   B. Data showing the number of moves between successive pairs of fixed time points
   C. Comparison of residence $x$ years earlier with current residence
   D. Data on each move until the date of inquiry

5. What are the advantages of place-of-prior-residence (POPR) data over place-of-birth (POB) data as a source of information on migration?
   A. POPR has a fixed, while the other has a varying, reference period
   B. POPR has flexibility in fixing the reference period, while the other does not
   C. The place of birth may not necessarily reflect a place to which one is socially affiliated
   D. POB data are costlier to collect than the other

6. Which of the following are among the criticisms of the usefulness of interview data on reasons for moving?
   A. Retrospective identification of the reasons for moving may have little to do with the actual reasons
   B. Respondents are likely to express only those reasons that they regard as socially and culturally acceptable
   C. Persons other than the respondent may have made the decision to move, in which case the respondent may not be aware of the real reasons for the move
   D. What an individual thinks as the reasons for moving are irrelevant for migration studies

7. Which of the following statements apply to migration data in the United States?
   A. The census and survey data are the principal sources of information on U.S. migration and local moves within the national boundaries
   B. The data are confined to moves involving primary residence

C. The available data underestimates the frequency of moves
D. Neither in the census nor in any of the surveys migration histories have been routinely collected

### 6.8.6. Levels and Trends

8. Which of the following statements apply to international migrations during the period between the two World Wars?
   A. Massive free migration from Europe subsided
   B. A large number of Japanese who had moved to different parts of the world returned to Japan
   C. Millions of Jews fled Germany as political refugees
   D. Millions of Eastern and Central Europeans were uprooted

9. During the post-World War II period:
   A. Emigration from Europe declined to insignificance
   B. The dominant character of international migration changed
   C. The days of free migration became a thing of the past
   D. The industrialized countries became gainers in net migration

10. Which of the following statements apply to Asia as of the 1960s and early 1970s?
    A. The number of emigrants from Asia during this period was large
    B. The emigration rate was not large
    C. As a source of migration to Europe, Oceania, and North America, Asia rose to a par with Latin America
    D. Refugee movement was large

11. Within the United States:
    A. The east to west flow of migration has been, and continues to be, a major inter-regional population movement
    B. The South to Northeast and the South to North-Central flows have been strong for most of the past century
    C. These latter flows had a heavy component of blacks during their heyday
    D. These latter flows each had reversed itself (on a net basis) by the 1960s.

12. When the U.S. inter-regional net migration during 1975–1980 is compared to that during 1965–1970, one notices:
    A. That the net flow from the Northeast to the South as well as to the West doubled
    B. That the net flow from the North Central to the South more than doubled, while the increase in the corresponding net flow to the West was less dramatic
    C. That the South-to-West net flow reversed itself
    D. That there was a significant net flow from the North Central to the Northeast during both the periods

### 6.8.7 Differentials, Determinants, and Consequences

13. Which of the following are among the consequences of massive international migration between 1750 and 1930?
    A. The main areas of destination of the European immigrants multiplied their population several fold
    B. These areas increased their share of the world's population dramatically
    C. Europe's share of all whites diminished to two-thirds
    D. Africa's share of all blacks diminished more than one-fifth.

14. Which of the following arguments are made by those who advocate a reduction in immigration flow to the United States?
    A. Immigration adds to the U.S. population growth and thereby adversely affects the quality of life in the country
    B. Immigrant workers are partly responsible for keeping wage rates down and working conditions poor
    C. Immigrants put a heavy load on the welfare program
    D. Hispanic and Asian immigrants contribute toward the creation and perpetuation of a segmented society.

15. Many economic theories of migration:
    A. Focus on the individual
    B. View the individual as making cost-now-benefit-later reasoning
    C. Give attention to uncertainties regarding the consequences of actions
    D. Are rational choice models

### 6.8.8. U.S. Immigration Laws

16. Which of the following statements apply to some of the early U.S. immigration laws?
    A. When the United States was formed and for a short time thereafter, immigration was free of restrictions of any kind
    B. In 1798 an Alien Act was passed authorizing the President to deport aliens regarded as dangerous to the country
    C. The Chinese Exclusion Act of 1882 banned further Chinese immigration
    D. The Quota Act of 1921 established national origin quotas

17. Which of the following are among the U.S. legislations passed during the 1980s and the early 1990s concerning international migration?
    A. The Refugee Act of 1980
    B. The Immigration Reform and Control Act of 1986
    C. The Immigration Act of 1990
    D. The Immigration Reform Act of 1994

**IN EACH OF THE QUESTIONS IN SECTIONS 6.9.9. TO 6.9.10., FIVE POSSIBLE ANSWERS ARE GIVEN, ONLY ONE OF WHICH IS CORRECT. IDENTIFY THE CORRECT ANSWER AND EXPLAIN.**

## *6.8.9. Concepts*

1. In determining a person's migrant status, the U.S. Census Bureau examines whether the person has changed during the migration-defining interval his or her:
   A. De facto address
   B. Usual place of residence
   C. Voting registration area
   D. Work place
   E. County to which tax is owed
2. Moving back and forth between a primary and a secondary residence is called:
   A. Migration
   B. Local move
   C. Circulatory mobility
   D. Social mobility
   E. Mover-stayer cycle
3. Which of the following certainly is a migratory move according to the definition adopted by the U.S. Bureau of the Census?
   A. Moving from an apartment to a rented house
   B. Spending summer in the Bahamas
   C. Moving residence from Chicago to New York in connection with a job change
   D. Living in one county and working in another county
   E. Shifting residence within a county
4. According to the U.S. Census Bureau's definition, migration differs from local move in which of the following respects?
   A. Distance moved
   B. Job change
   C. Severing old connections
   D. Establishing new connections
   E. Crossing county line
5. In the history of immigration to the United States, the term "old migration" is associated with which of the following regions as the source?
   A. Northern and Western Europe
   B. Eastern and Southern Europe
   C. Africa

D. Asia
E. Latin America

6. When East Pakistan became a new country called Bangladesh, the movement of people between what used to be the two wings of Pakistan changed from —— to ———
A. Internal migration, international migration
B. International migration, internal migration
C. Circulatory move, local move
D. Migratory move, local move
E. Local move, migratory move

7. According to the conventional definitions, internal migration definitely differs from international migration in which of the following respects?
A. Distance moved
B. Separation from one's family
C. Remittance to relatives
D. Shifting residence across the boundary of an administrative unit
E. Shifting residence across a national boundary

8. The concept of geographic mobility encompasses ALL BUT which of the following?
A. Internal migration
B. Immigration
C. Emigration
D. Local move
E. Taking a vacation trip to another country

9. In the United States the term "alien" applies to ALL BUT which of the following?
A. Non-immigrant
B. Refugee
C. Unauthorized worker
D. Illegal migrant
E. Naturalized citizen

10. Which of the following is NOT included in the demographic study of geographic mobility?
A. Daily move between home and the place of work
B. Circulatory mobility between primary residence and a secondary residence
C. Relocation of residence within a territorial community
D. Relocation of residence from one community to another within a nation
E. Residential move from one nation to another

11. Which of the following DOES NOT belong to the cluster that includes all the rest?
    A. Sending of Jews to concentration camps during World War II
    B. Confining American Indians to reservations
    C. Incarceration of convicted criminals
    D. Elimination of an urban neighborhood under an urban renewal program
    E. Dispatching an army to free a country from the occupying forces of another country

### *6.8.10. Differentials, Determinants, and Consequences*

12. The age curve of mobility rate is shaped like:
    A. An inverted U
    B. A J
    C. An m
    D. A v
    E. The top portion of the silhouette of a brontosaurus raising its head shoulder-high and stretching its tail

13. The propensity to migrate is highest:
    A. At infancy
    B. At young adulthood
    C. At middle age
    D. Just before retirement
    E. Just after retirement

14. In the United States a number of factors contributed to the changeover of the South from a net loser to a net gainer with respect to migration. Which of the following is NOT among these?
    A. Depressed natural increase in the South
    B. Increased return migration of Southerners from elsewhere
    C. Reduced out-migration of native Southerners
    D. Increased migration of non-Southerners to the South
    E. Increased opportunities in the South

15. The population pressure that increases the emigration potential of countries like India can be described in terms of pressures to provide jobs for the large number of:
    A. Young people entering the work force
    B. Rural-to-urban migrants who are seeking non-farm work
    C. Women entering the labor force
    D. The unemployed and underemployed
    E. All of the above

16. One of the well-known theories of migration is:
    A. The demographic transition theory
    B. The theory of change and response
    C. The push–pull theory
    D. The wealth-flow hypothesis
    E. Theory of relative income

17. In the literature on migration theories, the concepts of "intervening obstacles" was popularized by:
    A. E. G. Ravenstein
    B. Everett S. Lee
    C. Kingsley Davis
    D. Richard Easterlin
    E. Sidney Goldstein

18. A direct approach to determining the reasons for moving is to ask movers the reason for their mobility and stayers the reason for their non-mobility. Which of the following is the most common response to the question: "Why did you move?"
    A. Work-related reason
    B. Family-related reason
    C. Education-related reason
    D. Weather-related reason
    E. Housing-related reason

19. Which of the following statements DOES NOT belong to the cluster that includes all the others, considering the determinants and covariates of mobility of married couples in the United States as the criteria?
    A. Unemployment or dissatisfaction with a job is a push factor.
    B. Wife's working status strongly influences the decision regarding whether to move or not.
    C. Destination choice tends to be influenced by husbands' and wives' employment prospects and interests.
    D. A significant fraction of repeat migrants consists of those who return to the original location.
    E. Irrespective of the reason for moving to a place, nonavailability of employment would serve as a strong push factor.

20. Which of the following statements does not belong to the cluster that includes all the others, considering the developing countries as the setting and the influence of the family on the actual or potential migrant as the criterion?
    A. The extended family has a strong influence on the decision regarding migration of its members.

B. The migrant from the destination keeps in communication with his or her family.
C. The migrant sends money from the work place to his or her family left behind.
D. The migrant considers it as his (her) obligation to assist financially his (her) family.
E. The migrant is concerned only with the welfare of his or her nuclear family members.

**FOR EACH OF THE QUESTIONS IN SECTIONS 6.9.11. TO 6.9.14. STATE TRUE OR FALSE AND EXPLAIN. (THESE QUESTIONS MAY BE MORE DIFFICULT THAN THOSE IN SECTION 6.9.1.)**

### *6.8.11. Concepts*

1. Doctors migrating from less-developed countries to an industrialized country is an example of the so-called brain drain.
2. Commuting and seasonal migrations are examples of what is called circulation.
3. Switzerland provides a good example of the so-called rotation system or guestworker policy.
4. Migration field can be small or large.
5. The concept of intervening opportunities was introduced to the migration literature by Davis and Blake (1956).

### *6.8.12. Data and Measures*

6. Migration data can be presented in the form of a two-way table classifying migrants by place of origin and place of destination.
7. The number of people who are classified as migrants and the proportion they form of the total population are influenced by the size and shape of the areas used in defining migration.
8. When reliable statistics on births and deaths are available it is possible to use that data and the population counts in two successive censuses to estimate migration, using a balancing equation.
9. The number of migrants among those of age 10–14 years at the 1990 census is equal to the 1990 census count of people of that age group − the number of persons of that age group expected to be present at the time of the 1990 census if there had been no migration, in or out.

### 6.8.13. Levels and Trends

10. In the late 1940s and early 1950s, extensive labor migration began from Southern Europe to Northwestern Europe.
11. Labor migration in Europe reached massive proportions during 1955–1973.
12. Labor migration to Northwestern Europe was drastically reduced after 1973 following the oil crisis, but immigration continued.
13. There are clear signs that illegal immigration will decrease in the future.
14. Western Europe is likely to experience in the near future a sharp increase in immigration.

### 6.8.14. Differentials, Determinants, and Consequences

15. One of the migration models popularized by human geographers holds that the gross migration between two places is equal to the product of origin-specific factors, destination-specific factors, and a function of the distance between the two places.
16. The push–pull hypothesis regarding migration between two places can be understood in terms of demand and supply notions.
17. Ravenstein's "laws" of migration are not immutable laws.
18. Migration has a direct impact on the population composition of the sending and receiving areas.
19. Migration may have a direct impact on savings and wealth in the sending and receiving populations.
20. The role migration plays in the socio-economic development varies from one context to another.

❖ ❖ ❖ ❖

### 6.8.1. Answers

1. False. In some countries (e.g., the United States) a clear distinction is made between migrants and local movers. Those who move from one county to another are migrants and those who move within a county are local movers. Such distinctions as between migration and local move are not universal, however. When such a distinction exists, the term mover may be thought of as inclusive, covering migrants and local movers.

2. False. Separation of home and work-place is not a criterion for defining migrants.
3. True, insofar as a distinction is made between migration and local move, as the U. S. Census Bureau does.
4. False. Aliens are non-citizen residents.

### 6.8.2. Answers

5. True. Data on residential mobility, using a 12-month mobility defining interval collected by the U.S. Bureau of the Census through the Current Population Survey annually since 1947, indicate that about 20% of persons report having moved residence during the reference period (see, e.g. U.S. Bureau of the Census, 1969, cover chart.)
6. True. For example, the mobility rate was higher in the United States than in Great Britain, Japan, Ireland, and New Zealand at each age for 1970–1971 (Long, 1988).
7. False. Estimates arrived at by Long (1988) indicate that the data for 1982–1983 implied 10–11 moves over a lifetime, whereas earlier data (for 1966–1971) implied about 13 moves over a lifetime.
8. True. The annual immigration rate per 1000 population peaked at 10.4 (arrivals per 1000 population) in the decade 1901–1910. There were intervals during the 19th century when the corresponding figures came close: 9.3 during 1851–1860 and 9.2 during 1881–1890. But from the peak reached during 1901–1910, the rate declined rather steadily until it reached a low (of 0.4) during 1931–1940, and then started inching up. The 1990 amendments to immigration laws gave a boost to the immigration volume by raising the number of legal immigrants per year from 540,000 to 700,000 temporarily, and to 650,000 permanently (starting 1995). (See *Statistical Abstract of the United States* for statistics on immigration.)
9. True. It is estimated that at least 52 million people emigrated from Europe during that period (Davis, 1974, p. 98; Weller and Bouvier, 1981, p. 210).
10. False. On the contrary the nations of Western Europe have become countries of net immigration. In fact, voluntary international migration has been for some time now flowing in the direction of industrialized countries from less-developed countries (Weller and Bouvier, 1981, p. 212).
11. True. It is estimated that about 9.6 million slaves from Africa reached the New World from 1651 until the abolition of slavery in the 19th century. About 25% of the enslaved died en route. (Curtin, 1969; Weller and Bouvier, 1981, p. 211).

12. True. Controlling immigration is apparently a top priority in the European Union. This is true of other countries too. Hong Kong, South Korea, Taiwan, and Singapore are initiating or expanding guestworker programs, partly aimed at managing the growing influx of illegal migrant workers. Guestworker programs have been in operation in many of the European countries for some time now. The United States also has a policy of issuing temporary work visas to a limited number of applicants. In 1993, 165,000 such visas were issued. All countries are pursuing policies aimed at controlling the types and numbers of people who enter. (Martin and Midgley, 1994, p. 41).

13. True. The term "unauthorized migrants" is applied to foreigners of two categories: one consisting of those who enter a country illegally, and the other of those who enter legally but then violate the terms of the visa (e.g., enter as a tourist and then stay beyond the duration permitted). The number of unauthorized migrants is difficult to estimate. In the United States, according to one estimate (Warren, 1994), there were 3.4 million unauthorized migrants in 1992 and the number increases by 300,000 annually.

14. True. According to the 1990 U.S. Census figures, six states (California, New York, Florida, Texas, New Jersey, and Illinois) account for nearly three-fourths of the foreign-born residents.

15. True. California was the intended destination of over one-third of the immigrants who entered the country in 1992. (*1992 Statistical Yearbook of the Immigration and Naturalization Service*).

16. True. One consequence of this is that immigration tends to alter the racial/ethnic makeup of the population, particularly in subregions where immigrants are concentrated. (Martin and Midgley 1994, p. 6).

### 6.8.3. Answers

17. True. Young adults (of age 20–24 years) are more likely to migrate than are people of other age groups. Among the married, migration propensity is associated with the number and ages of children—the smaller the family and the younger the children, the greater the migration propensity. Migration propensity usually goes up with educational level. These are just a few examples of migration selectivity. (See Fig. 6.2)

18. True. The central idea of the push–pull theory is that there are certain features of a place that prompt the residents to move elsewhere and that places with certain features tend to attract people to move there. An implicit assumption is that people tend to gravitate themselves from places with fewer advantages to places having more (Zelinsky, 1983). If one defines advantages in terms of the

excess of benefits over costs, then one can see the overlap between the push–pull theory and the cost-benefit framework for migration analysis. If the excess of benefits over the costs of staying where one resides is more than that associated with moving elsewhere, then the tendency will be not to move.

19. True. In general, migration rate is higher for those with higher education, other things being equal. For example, college-educated people tend to have higher migration rates that their counterparts with less than college education. When educational attainment is represented on a finer scale, however, exceptions are likely to occur. For example, postgraduates had a lower migration rate than college graduates in the United States during 1986–1987; similarly, females who were high school graduates had a lower migration rate than their counterparts with "some high school" (U.S. Bureau of the Census, 1991d, Table 24).

20. True. The age pattern of geographic mobility rate shows that the rate is higher for children of age 1–4 years than for older children of age 5–9, and 10–14. (See, e.g., Long, 1988. This is true in most countries.) See Fig. 6.1.

21. True. Migration rate peaks in the age group 20–24 years. The same is also true of local moves. See Fig. 6.1.

22. True. The population of Ireland in 1781 was 4.0 million. By 1841 it had more than doubled to 8.1 million. This growth is said to have stimulated a large emigration, which became a massive exodus after the failure of the potato crops and the famine that followed. By 1956 the population was only 4.3 million, almost the same as it was in 1781. This population decline was only in part due to emigration. Higher age at marriage and nonmarriage had kept overall fertility level down (Petersen, 1975, pp. 542–543).

23. False. Some people believe that the unauthorized workers take away jobs from the native population. Others believe that the unauthorized workers fill jobs the native population would not want anyway. The immigrant workers, because they add to the supply of labor, cause wage rate to go down in the immediately affected market. Thus the native-born workers who compete with immigrants for jobs may experience reduced earnings or reduced employment. But even then, the economy as a whole often stands to benefit, especially if the availability of immigrant workers (e.g., for unskilled construction jobs) increases opportunities for, and raises the wage rates of, complementary workers (e.g., carpenters, electricians, and the like in the construction industry). A study of the effect of unskilled immigrant workers on similar Americans came to the following conclusion: "as a general rule, increases in output, brought about by ... [immigration], outweigh reductions that may occur in the wages of workers who compete with immigrants" (U.S. Council of Economic Advisors, 1986; also see Martin and Midgley, 1994, p. 30).

24. False. According to the U.S. Census Bureau's population projections, if the net immigration were to remain at the current level, the U.S. population would be 383 million by the year 2050 whereas a no immigration scenario from now on would result in a population of only 310 million by that date.

25. True. At the area of destination, immigrants in the 17th century tended to have very high fertility. (Sabagh, 1942; Weller and Bouvier, 1981, p. 211).

26. True. France had very low emigration rates and their fertility rates started much earlier than most other countries in Europe. Ireland had high rates of emigration. Their fertility decline started much later than in most other countries.

### 6.8.4. Answers

1. A, B, C, and D. With respect to choice A, imagine (see question 7 in section 6.8.12) moving from one corner of a large county to the opposite corner. This may involve a long-distance move, a change of job, affiliation to a new friendship group, and so on. Yet the move is not a migratory move, since it is within the same county. With respect to choice B, note that a very short distance move may in fact involve crossing a county line and hence constitute a migratory move. For choice C imagine moving from an upper-middle-class neighborhood of Washington, D.C., to a similar neighborhood of New York. In this case no substantial change in the type of environment is likely to occur. For choice D, imagine a move from a central city to the fringe area. This may not be a migratory move, if it is within the same county, and yet may involve a substantial change in the environment.

2. A, B, C, and D. A majority of immigrants are granted entry because they are relatives of U.S. citizens. Nonimmigrants are those who come to the United States for a specific period of time to visit, to work, or to study. Over three-fourths of nonimmigrants enter as tourists. Temporary work permits are given to a substantial number (about 165,000 in 1993) of people each year. When those who enter as nonimmigrants stay beyond the time specified in their visa, they become unauthorized aliens, among whom are also those who enter without proper papers (visas). (See question 13, section 6.8.2.)

3. A, B, C, and D. Notice that the term "mobility" is broader in scope than the term "migration." Kritz and Keely (1981) observed that international mobility has been increasing more rapidly than international migration. See Keely (1981) for a discussion of the definition of the term refugee. Also see Petersen (1975) for a more relaxed definition of refugees compared to the one given in the UN Protocol on Refugees. According to the UN definition, a refugee is anyone "who, owing to well-founded fear of being persecuted for reasons of

race, religion, nationality, membership of a particular group or political opinion, is outside the country of his nationality and is unable or, owing to such fear, is unwilling to avail himself of the protection of that country." Petersen's (1975) broader definition would include as refugees those who live in their own countries under "refugee conditions."

### 6.8.5. Answers

4. A and C: Asking place of birth in the census is a widespread practice. By comparing the state of birth with current residence, it is possible to classify people into (i) "nonmigrants" or those enumerated in the same state where they were born and (ii) others ("lifetime migrants"). The comparison of the current residence with the residence $x$ years earlier provides a classification of people into (i) "nonmovers," (ii) local movers, and (iii) migrants. Data or migration of the kind described in choices B and D are not available on a routine basis in the United States. Countries that maintain Population Registers have a complete account of residential histories.
5. A, B, and C. With respect to choice C, note that the place of birth may be the home of a relative, a town where there is a hospital, or any such place which does not qualify to be regarded as a place of residence for the infant's parents. With respect to choice D, it should be emphasized that there is no cost difference for the two types of data.
6. A, B, C, and D. See in this connection Goldstein and Goldstein (1981); Hawley (1950); Pryor (1975); Fawcett and DeJong (1982). As for choice A, the tendency to rationalize the action already taken may color the reasons that people give retrospectively. The criticism of choice B applies not only to the reasons for moving but other decisions as well. For example the same criticism applies to the responses one gets from a 30-year-old woman when she is asked why she postponed her first birth $x$ years after marriage. For choice C, note that when a respondent is asked to enumerate the reason for an action, it is assumed that the respondent was the decision maker and the decision-making process involved a deliberate examination of all the factors that deserved consideration. But in reality, many of the actions are impelled by circumstances that are not well understood by the actors.
7. The answer is A, B, C, D. With respect to C, note that the place of residence $x$ years ago does not reveal multiple moves, if any, during the previous $x$ years.

### 6.8.6. Answers

8. A and C. Massive free migration from Europe subsided because of the Great Depression of the 1930s and restrictive legislation on migration in countries

such as the United States; however, during Hitler's rise to power millions of Jews and political refugees left Germany (Weller and Bouvier, 1981, p. 211). The developments mentioned in choices B and D occurred after World War II. About 3 million Japanese who had moved to different parts of the empire were forced to return to Japan and about 20 million people in Eastern and Central Europe were uprooted because of exchanges, expulsions, and transfers of people following the Second World War (Rystad, 1992; Weller and Bouvier, 1981, p. 211).

9. B and D. Emigration from Europe continued during the period, although at a much reduced scale compared to what was the pattern previously. The main current was, however, from the less-developed countries to the more-developed ones (See United Nations, 1979).

10. A, B, C, and D. In 1960, there were less than 1 million Asian immigrants residing in North America, Oceania, and Western and Northern Europe combined. This number grew to 3.725 million by 1974, almost equal to the Latin American figure of 3.8 million. But with the Asian base population being very large, the rate of emigration remained very small throughout the period. Individual countries, of course, had their own stories to tell. For example, emigration rate from Turkey and Cyprus increased substantially. As for choice D, note that globally, the estimated number of refugees increased from 9.8 million in 1965 to 17.6 million by 1970 and then declined to 15.7 million by 1972 (U.S. Committee on Refugees, 1973). According to one demographer, "The implication of the data can be better grasped when we recall that the usual estimate of the total migration from all of Europe between 1800 and 1950 is 60 million, or only about eight times the increase in the number of refugees over 5 years" (Petersen, 1975, p. 314). Petersen's (1975, Table 8-6) compilation shows that in 1970, there were 2 million Chinese refugees in Hong Kong, 4.45 million East Pakistan (now Bangladesh) refugees in India, 260,000 Indian refugees in West Pakistan, and a large number of South Vietnam refugees in various parts of Asia.

11. A, B, C, and D. The "center of [gravity of the spatially spread] population" (see Glossary for definition) had been steadily shifting due westward from 1790 until 1960 and from then on toward the southwest, the main reason for this shift being the redistribution of the population by internal migration. Of course, the center could shift if regional differences in natural increase or in net international migration were to change the regional shares of the total population. But regional differences in natural increase have not been appreciable in recent decades, and the volume of international migration being small, regional differences in the absorption of international migrants also have had relatively little impact on regional shares of the total population.

Hence the shift in the center of population, especially, during the recent decades, has to be attributed primarily to internal migration.

The following net flows for 1965–1970, 1970–1975, and 1975–1980 bring out the post-1960 story of inter-regional migration: The Northeast region had a net loss of 715,000, 1,342,000, and 1,486,000 respectively, during the three periods. The corresponding figures for the North Central region were 637,000, 1,195,000 and 1,173,000, respectively. The South on the other hand, had a net gain of 656,000, 1,829,000 and 1,764,000, respectively, during the three periods, while the corresponding net gains for the West were 696,000, 708,000, and 893,000, respectively.

Notice that the net loss to the Northeast more than doubled between 1965–1970 and 1975–1980 and the story of the North Central region was not much different. The net gain of the South increased 2.7 fold during the period, while the net gain of the West was not as dramatic.

12. A, B, and C. The net flow from the Northeast to the South during the periods were 438,000 and 863,000, respectively. The corresponding net flow to the West were 224,000 and 478,000, respectively. Notice the doubling of the figures in both cases. The net flow from the North Central to the South increased from 275,000 in 1965-70 to 738,000 in 1975–1980. The corresponding net flow to the West increased from 415,000 to only 579,000. The net flow was 56,000 from the South to the West in 1965–1970 but was 163,000 in the reverse direction in 1975–1980. As for choice D, note that in both periods the net flow was from the Northeast to the North Central (53,000 during 1965–1970 and 144,000 during 1975–1980).

### 6.8.7. Answers

13. A, B, C, and D. Between 1750 and 1930, the population of the main areas of destination of European emigrants increased 14 fold (compared to 2.5 fold elsewhere) and their share of the world's population increased from 3 percent in 1750 to 16 percent by 1930 (see Davis, 1974, p. 99).

14. A, B, C, and D. The argument in choice A is not exclusively aimed at immigrants but at population growth in general. The argument in choice B is based on the fact that wage rates for immigrants in many jobs are low. The point is that the availability of such workers makes it possible for employers to get away with poor working conditions and low wage rate, instead of making the capital investment necessary to improve the working conditions and to increase efficiency of production using modern technology. The point of choice C is that the low level of education of the newcomers, such as the Mexican farm workers, makes them more likely than the native-born people to depend upon public assistance. The point of choice D is that Hispanics and

Asian immigrants are slow in joining the American mainstream, and that they and the native born people remain "worlds apart." Such arguments have been dismissed by many politicians and immigration experts by pointing out that the always-popular view in the United States has been against immigration and that the dire predictions made by restrictionists have repeatedly turned out wrong (Weintraub, 1989, p. 185; Martin and Midgley, 1994, p. 10).

15. A, B, C, and D. Imagine a young man employed as an electronic engineer in India thinking about migrating to the United States. He considers the cost of foregoing the steady income from his current job, cost of travel to the United States, that of getting additional training, as necessary, in the United States, and the cost of job search. He also considers the future benefit in terms of, for example, increased income. The future of course is full of uncertainties and the young man can think in terms of probabilities and expectations only. Consideringthetwoalternatives,stayinginthecurrentjobversusseeking opportunities in the United States, the young man has to evaluate all the consequences of each alternative and the overall attractiveness of each in terms of expected costs and benefits. If his calculation shows that the migrating to the United States is more attractive, then he chooses to migrate; otherwise, he stays put. This is the essence of rational choice models.

### 6.8.8. Answers

16. A, B, C, and D. The Chinese Exclusion Act of 1882 initially imposed a two-year embargo, but it was extended in one form or another until 1943, when it was repealed. The 1921 Quota Act set limits on the number of persons from each country to be admitted. The limit was 3% of the corresponding population segment as of the 1910 U.S. population census. The National Origins Act of 1924 replaced the 1921 Act, reducing the 3% to 2%, but changing the base year from 1910 to 1890. The policy remained in force, in one form or another, until the Immigration Reform Act of 1965.

17. A, B, and C. There is no act of the name mentioned in choice D. The 1980 act brought the definition of refugee status consistent with the U.N. standard definition. Prior to this, attention was focused primarily on persons leaving Communist countries. The Immigration Reform and Control Act of 1986 was aimed at controlling illegal immigration. The act imposed penalties for knowingly hiring unauthorized workers. The act provided for granting legal immigrant status for the illegal aliens who had established roots in the United States. According to some investigators, in spite of the 1986 act, illegal immigration has continued through the use of fraudulent documents (Martin and Midgley, 1994, p. 13). The Immigration Act of 1990 substantially increased the number of immigrants permitted to enter as employment-

preference workers. This was in response to the view that the previous immigration laws had been severely limiting U.S. firms' capability to compete successfully in the global market.

### 6.8.9. Answers

1. B. Usual place of residence
2. C. Circulatory mobility
3. C. Moving residence from Chicago to New York in connection with job change.
4. E. Crossing county line
5. A. Northern and Western Europe
6. A. Internal migration, international migration
7. E. Shifting residence across a national boundary
8. E. Taking a vacation trip to another country
9. E. Naturalized citizen
10. A. Journey to work. Circulatory mobility is a topic of study in many less-developed countries (Skeldon, 1985; 1990; Nam, 1994, p. 247). Circulation often is a temporary phenomenon. As Nam puts it, rising cities first draw workers from nearby villages. These workers keep their ties with their villages intact; later as the city expands the same workers may start commuting from their villages; eventually they may reduce their connections with their villages and decide to shift residence to the city (Nam, 1994, p. 247).
11. E. All the others are instances in which the moves are instigated by external agencies.

### 6.8.10. Answers

12. E: The rate declines, then rises, and after reaching a peak, declines slowly.
13. B. At young adulthood
14. A. Depressed natural increase in the South
15. E. All of the above
16. C. The push–pull theory
17. B. Everett S. Lee. In every area there are factors that hold people to that area or attract people to it, and there are others that repel people from it. Also, there

may be factors that are inconsequential, as far as the migration-contemplating individual is concerned. Lee represented these by pluses, minuses, and zeros respectively. Both the origin and the destination have these. An abundance of pluses would serve as a "pull" and an abundance of minuses as a "push." An abundance of intervening obstacles, e.g., costs of moving and institutional obstacles to migration embodied in official migration policy, tends to reduce the weight of the "pull" and "push" factors. For a discussion of institutional obstacles to migration see Tomasi (1981, pp. 321–322); and Petersen (1978).

18. A. Work-related reason; see Nam, 1994, p. 235; Long, 1988; Kols and Lewison, 1983.

19. B. DaVanzo (1976) observed in an investigation using a set of national longitudinal data that families with working wives are as likely to move as are those with non-working wives. The other four statements represents some of the other findings of the same study.

20. E. All the others form a cluster. In developing countries the migrant is, more often than not, concerned with the welfare of his extended family too (see Nam, 1994, p. 236; Root and DeJong, 1991).

### 6.8.11. Answers

1. True. The term refers to the migration or skilled workers from poor countries to rich countries. In most cases the actual number of persons involved may not be large. But the point usually made is that a poor country's loss of its doctors, engineers, and other professional workers means that the country trained them in vain and that their departure significantly diminishes the country's ability to render essential services to its people. The other side of the coin is that such emigrants send remittance which in many cases more than compensates for the investment in their training.

2. True. Broadly defined, circulation involves a geographic mobility of a short-term, cyclic type, requiring no permanent change of residence. Circulation in the low-income countries is believed to be associated with socio-economic disequilibrium. Circular migration is regarded as one form of circulation. Apprentices in towns in historic Europe returning home after training are an example of circular migration (Wilson, 1985, p. 31).

3. True. Switzerland has a long tradition of having a large number of guest-workers. In 1974, for example, there were over one million such persons in that country. Having guest-workers is viewed as an economic expedient. The number of such workers present at any time is closely regulated by the requirement that each such person must renew residence permit regularly.

This allows reduction of guest-workers when such an action becomes necessary (Rystad, 1992).

4. True. Migration field represents an area of well-established migration paths, or an area that serves as the source of migrants to a particular country. For example, a village-town association may take the form in which the town provides apprenticeships to young people of the village. Commonly this operates on a small-scale, but it could operate on a large scale, too. A whole country may serve as the source of guest-workers to another country, for example.

5. False. The concept was introduced by Samuel A. Stouffer in 1960. He proposed an extension of the simple gravity model by hypothesizing that the number of migrants moving a given distance is directly proportional to the opportunities (broadly defined) at that distance and inversely proportional to the opportunities in between.

### 6.8.12. Answers

6. True. The diagonal cells of the table represent non-migrants, the other cells represent migrants, the rows and columns represent the origins and destinations respectively. Other forms of the table include (i) a classification of people by current residence and the birth place, (ii) a classification of people by current residence and residence $x$ years earlier, and (iii) a classification of people by current residence and the last place of residence. Such tables can be constructed separately for each age group, and for that matter for any population subgroups.

7. True. In the accompanying figure, in which the interior lines represent migration-defining boundaries, a move from A to B is a local move, whereas a move from C to D is migration. Suppose the density of the area in which A and B are located is low while it is high in the other areas. A preponderance of mi-

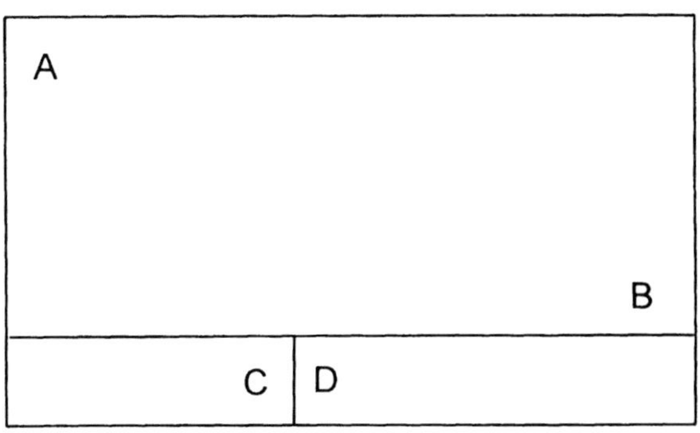

gration (most of which being of the short-distance type) can be expected under the circumstances, if residential shifts were primarily a matter of distance.

8. True. Population change = natural increase + change due to migration. Therefore, change due to migration = total population change − natural increase. This is an indirect way of estimating migration. Note, however, that the estimate thus obtained is of the increase or decrease in the size of the population in question, attributable to migration, which may not necessarily be the same as the number of migratory moves. Also note that the estimate obtained in this fashion combines net international migration and net internal migration.

9. True. The expected number of persons of age 10–14 years at the given census, in the absence of migration, in or out, can be calculated by multiplying the number of persons of age 0–4 years at the census 10 years earlier with a survival fraction representing the proportion expected to survive 10 years among those of age 0–4 at the earlier census. This survival fraction can be obtained from an appropriate life table. This is also an indirect way of estimating migration.

### 6.8.13. Answers

10. True. Switzerland and Sweden were initially the main receiving countries, although France and England were also involved. Italy was the main source. By late 1940s, France began recruiting workers from Turkey (see Rystad, 1992).

11. True. The post-war reconstruction and industrial expansion of Northwestern Europe required more workers than the countries within the regions could supply. West Germany began recruiting "guest-workers" by the late 1950s. New sources from the Mediterranean region emerged during this period, including Yugoslavia, Portugal, Greece, Morocco, and Tunisia. France started recruiting workers from Spain and Algeria. By the end of 1960s, there were about 2.5 million foreign workers in France and as many in West Germany.

12. True. The members of the families of the already-in workers were permitted to enter during this period. This accounted for the continuation of immigration even after labor migration was drastically reduced (Rystad, 1992).

13. False. Illegal entry is difficult to control if (i) two countries have long borders, (ii) one is poor and the other is rich, and (iii) collusion exists between illegal immigrants and special interest groups (e.g., employers who stand to benefit from employing illegal immigrants at low wage rates and under poor working conditions.)

14. True. The sources might be Eastern Europe as well as other continents. The economic discrepancy between Western Europe and its neighbors is a major factor promoting this development. The demographic discrepancy is another factor. Europe's population is shrinking and aging while countries south and east of Mediterranean are growing and remaining young, creating an enormous emigration potential. If even a fraction of this potential were matched with an immigration potential in Europe, migration flow to Europe will become a reality.

### 6.8.14. Answers

15. True. Human geographers refer to this as the gravity model. A very simple version of this model is the following: the gross migration between two places is proportional to the product of the population sizes of the two places and inversely proportional to the geographic distance between the places. This simple form was popularized by Zipf (Wilson, 1985). A thorough review of the gravity model and its extensions is available in Molho (1986), which is reproduced in Bogue *et al.* (1993, Vol. 4).

16. True. The push–pull hypothesis assumes that given the current place of residence and a potential destination, there are factors promoting and inhibiting migration at both ends. For example, if place A is in an economic depression while place B is in an expansion period, B has a preponderance of pull factors while A has a preponderance of push factors. Also A has a surplus of labor and hence is in a position to supply labor to other places while B may be in need of more workers than is available there and could use some of the surplus labor in A.

17. True. E. G. Ravenstein arrived at a number of generalizations which he termed "laws," based on his analysis of data for England and several other nations. His generalizations included the following: (i) The volume of migration from a given place diminishes with distance from that place. (ii) Persons living near large cities migrate when economic expansion occurs; the positions they vacate are filled by migrants from more remote places; thus the expanding city exerts an impact step by step on distant places. (iii) To every migration stream there is a counterstream. (iv) Urban populations are less migratory than rural populations. (v) Females predominate in short-distance migrations. (vi) Migration rate increases with technological development. (vii) Although a variety of forces can produce migration, the desire of people to improve their economic condition is by far the most potent force. Grigg (1977) concluded that the applicability of these generalizations to 19th-century England was confirmed by subsequent research. But it should be emphasized that Ravenstein's empirical generalizations are not immutable "laws." In fact, in an

important study, Dorothy S. Thomas (1938) concluded that almost no generalizations of this type could be supported by empirical research. To explain exceptions to the generalizations, researchers have tended to introduce situational factors such as those invoked in "push–pull-obstacles" models (Bogue, 1969, p. 756).

18. True. This is so particularly with respect to age, sex, and occupational composition. Of course, the impact depends on the relative magnitudes of the migration, in and out, and the extent to which the movement is selective with respect to the traits in focus. The demographic impact on the age, sex, and occupational compositions has been widely examined and documented.

19. True. Migrants often take with them funds for their travel and installation at the destination. In the case of a single worker moving temporarily for seasonal work, the amount involved may be negligible. But not so if a whole family moves to a distant place. Migrants frequently remit to their households significant fractions of their earnings. In many cases migrants return home after a period, bringing with them sizable savings and material possessions. Also migrants take with them and returning migrants bring with them labor force capacity and human capital (technical/productive knowledge and experience).

20. True. The contrast between the historical experience of the industrialized nations and the current experience of the less-developed countries illustrates the point. The historical economic development of Western and Northern Europe and North America has been often interpreted in terms of the central role played by migration and urbanization. When industrial growth is sufficiently rapid and labor intensive, farm workers are drawn into more productive manufacturing, while farming itself is mechanized. Thus productivity rises in both rural and urban areas, the latter somewhat faster than the former. Rural–urban migration in this scenario is permanent and its economic impact is rising productivity and incomes at the national level. In many of the currently developing countries mechanization of farming is confined to large farms, urban-industrial growth is not labor intensive, and population growth is much more rapid than was the case in the West at comparable level of urban-industrial growth. The combined result of all these features in the less-developed countries is high levels of unemployment and underemployment in both rural and urban areas. Migrants generally move to urban areas, but not necessarily to jobs with higher productivity. Many work in the informal sector, e.g., as sidewalk vendors. Under the circumstances, the economic impact of rural–urban migration is less clear. There may be some truth to the saying that rural–urban migration under such circumstances is aimed at keeping the migrant's income from falling below what it would have been had he (she) stayed put.

CHAPTER 7

# *Population Composition*

Social change is influenced not only by the number and growth rate of the people involved but by the dynamics of their makeup (composition) as well. A population with an older age structure may be spending more on health care, other things being equal, than one with a younger age structure. If among the young immigrants to a country males predominate, some of those men are likely to marry women of a different nationality. When the elderly's share of the total population increases, businesses begin to change their practices accordingly, for example, they may use older people in advertisements, or make and market materials that are of particular interest and use to the elderly. If the opportunity structure in a community is not consistent with the makeup of the opportunity seekers, the imbalance is likely to trigger out-migration. When the absolute and relative numbers of people on welfare increase, some begin to shout that the social welfare system is destroying the work ethic and prompting the poor to prefer welfare to other ways of life. Talks about scrapping the U.S. Social Security system increase in frequency and intensity as the day draws near when the "elderly boom" is expected to descend on it, causing severe financial strain.

Differences between men and women in occupational composition and similarly male–female differences in income distribution within occupations prompt the search for explanations of such differences and the plea for corrective actions. Identification of employer-level discrimination in allocating men and women to jobs as one of the causes of such disparities leads to legislation aimed at preventing such practices (e.g., the U.S. Equal Pay Act of 1963, Title VII of the Civil Rights Act of 1964).

A population with an older age structure is likely to have more deaths annually per 1000 persons than one with a relatively younger age structure, other things being equal. Also, a younger population (closed to migration) has an inherent tendency to increase at a higher rate than an older population, other things (age-specific death rates and age-specific fertility rates) being equal.

No wonder therefore that the study of population composition receives considerable attention from demographers, social scientists, business people, political leaders, and others.

## 7.1. CONCEPTS AND MEASUREMENTS

It is useful to make a distinction between a characteristic and composition. The former is an attribute of an individual: a person may be a male Caucasian, Hindu by religious affiliation, a college professor by occupation, and so forth. Composition, on the other hand, is a property of a population, describing its makeup: 52% female, 45% below age 15 years and 5% 65 years and older, etc. Notice that the same term may appear in descriptive phrases referring to a trait of an individual (a person is a female), a property of a population (females form 52% of a population), or the definition of a sub-population (U.S. females).

Characteristics (traits) of individuals are of two kinds: ascribed and achieved. The former refers to assigned traits (sex, age, race/ethnicity) whereas the latter refers to traits supposedly open to the choice of individuals (education, income, occupation).

Age-sex structure of a population stands for the classification of a people by age and sex. A pictorial representation of the age-sex structure, called the age-sex pyramid or population pyramid, uses a double histogram, one for males and the other for females, the two placed on either side of a central, vertical axis, the bars for males oriented to the left and those for females to the right of the vertical line, and age represented vertically with the youngest at the bottom. Fast growing populations with each birth cohort larger than the previous one have strictly pyramidal (▲), Christmas tree-like age-sex profiles. This was characteristic of almost all populations of the world before 1700 and is still so of many of today's less-developed countries where fertility levels are high. A population with a history of low (near-replacement) fertility and low mortality has an age-sex profile in the shape of a '■' with a '▲' on top of it, the former representing ages up to 70 years or so and the latter representing the ages older than tat. A striking deviation from the Christmas tree shapes is found in populations devoid of women and/or children (e.g., "skid row").

The age-sex structure reveals a population's history in some detail. "Baby boom," "baby bust," losses due to war, and the like, leave clearly discernible marks on the age-sex profile (Fig. 7.1). In general, countries with fluctuating fertility have age-sex profiles that are irregular in shape.

Age-specific sex ratio is the ratio of the number of males to the number of females in a given age group; at birth the sex ratio is approximately 105 males per

100 females. Between ages 5 and 15, the sex ratio starts declining, reaching parity (100 males per 100 females) in the 20s; it continues to decline progressively with age, reaching close to one male per three females by the late 90s. Age pattern of sex ratio is affected by sex differentials in mortality and sex selectivity in migration.

Sex in demographic parlance refers to the biological division of people into males and females, whereas gender, as used by social scientists, refers to the social meanings attached to being regarded as a male or female.

The age-dependency ratio is the ratio of the number of persons who are either too young (e.g., under 15 years of age) or too old (e.g., 65 years of age or older) to be economically productive to the number of persons who are economically active (those in the age range 15–64). Opinions differ regarding the validity of the assumptions that all children under 15 years of age are too young and all people of age 65 and older are too old to be economically productive.

A stable population is one in which the age-sex structure and the growth rate remain unchanged over time. Any population, closed to migration, can evolve into a stable population if is age-specific fertility rates and age-specific mortality rates were to remain unchanged for a sufficiently long period of time. Populations, closed to migration, in which fertility changes have been insignificant for a long time and mortality has not been fluctuating widely could be treated as approximately stable. A stationary population is a stable population with zero population growth; hypothetical examples can be found in each life table (the ${}_nL_x$ column labeled the life table population or person years lived in each interval).

The perspective of age stratification (see, e.g., Foner, 1975) is based on the notion that age is a basis of social status and that aging is analogous to the process of social mobility (change of status), with the power and privileges attached to each age stratum varying among societies. Transition from one age class to another, of course, is inevitable and unidirectional.

Three age categories are generally recognized as important in all societies: child, adult, and old. The passage from childhood to adulthood is not necessarily based on physiological changes. In many societies a child becomes an adult only when society formally recognizes the transition. Rituals marking this transition are commonly performed. Most modern societies, however, define the transition to adulthood in terms of chronological age. The transition to the elderly state also varies from one society to another. Most Western societies regard age 65 years as the boundary between adults and "senior citizens" (as old people are euphemistically called). This practice is consistent with the use of 65 years as the mandatory retirement age and the time when a person becomes eligible for Social Security benefits and the like. Even after the removal of 65 years as the mandatory retirement age in the United States, the practice of regarding that age as the great divide between adults and the elderly continues. Note, however, that in some societies the retirement age is lower than 65 years. For example, in India it is 60 years for university professors, 55 years for employees in certain states, 58 years

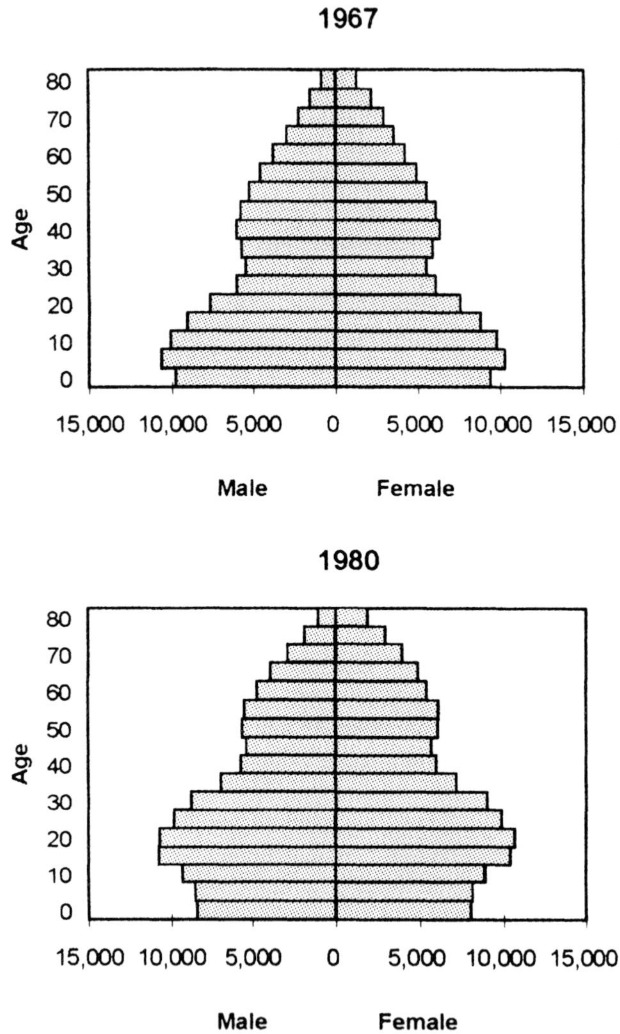


*Figure 7.1.* Age-sex pyramid, U.S. selected years.

for some other category of employees, and so on. Demographers emphasize chronological age in distinguishing children from adults and adults from the elderly because it is easy to measure and it facilitates cross-cultural comparisons.

A commonly-used summary measure of the age distribution is the median age, i.e., the age that divides a population, arranged in order of age, into two halves,

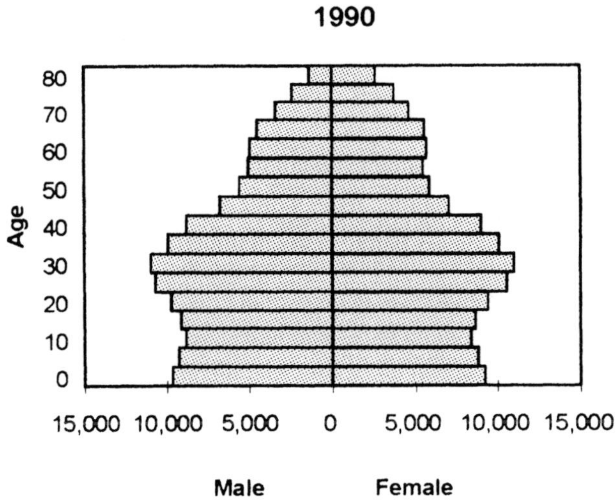


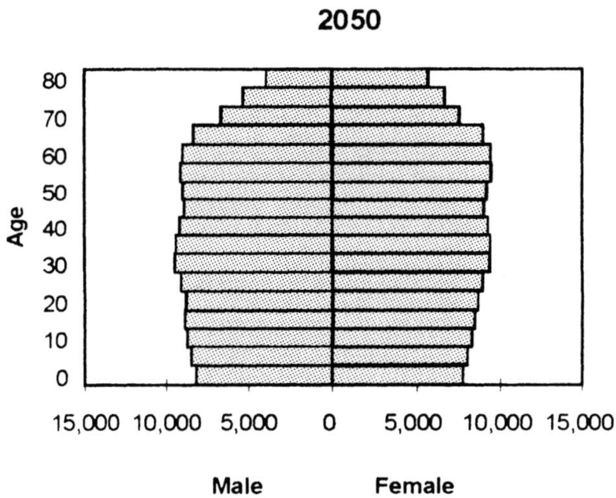


*Figure 7.1 (continued).*

one below the median and the other above it. The U.S. population's median age was 22.9 years in 1900; it steadily increased to 30.2 by 1950, then declined to 27.9 by 1970 and has been increasing since then.

Another summary measure of age composition is the number of elderly of age 65 years and older as a percentage of the number of children under 15 years of age.

In the United States at the turn of the 20th century there was only one elderly person per 10 children; by the mid-1990s, the number had increased to five times as many. This measure is sometimes called an index of aging.

## 7.2. AGE-SEX STRUCTURE

Comparison of the average population pyramid of the current LDCs (excluding China) with the corresponding one for the MDCs (Population Reference Bureau's *1994 World Population Data Sheet,*) shows that in the former the proportion of population under age 15 years is 39%, almost twice as high as the corresponding figure in the MDCs (20%), whereas the proportion of population in the age group 65 years and older is 13% in the MDCs, more than three times as high as in the LDCs (4%). Despite such differences, about 35% of the population fall in the age interval 20–44 years (Bogue, 1969, p. 149).

In both groups of countries males outnumber females at the very young ages (e.g., below 10). The age-sex pyramid typical of LDCs is almost symmetrical, but the one typical of MDCs is progressively more tilted to the right (the female side) at advanced ages, primarily because of the male-female differences with respect to mortality. The degree to which females tend to outnumber males at advanced ages differs significantly between LDCs and MDCs.

Data on age-sex structure are usually presented in two forms: (1) as a classification of the population by age and sex, using, more often than not, five-year age groups or (2) the same tabulation in percentage form, with the total (both sexes combined) as the base.

Where age data are known to be accurate, sometimes the age-sex structure is presented using individual ages. In most LDCs, however, this is seldom done because of the pronounced age-heaping tendencies. To illustrate, notice the "heaping" at age 55 and deficit at ages 54 and 56 in the 1960 age data for the Philippines (U.N., 1962, Table 6):

age 54: 95,715 age 55: 165,093 age 56: 87,754

and similarly the preference for age 70 over 69 and 71 in the same data:

age 69: 20,921 age 70: 136,093 age 71: 13,000

When age data are grouped (e.g., into five-year age classes), the errors from digital preferences are reduced to a considerable degree.

## 7.3. THE U.S. AGE-SEX STRUCTURE

The long-term trend in the U.S. age distribution has been toward growing older. The median age has increased from 18 years in 1800 to 33 years by 1990. The proportion of the population 65 years of age or older increased from 4% in 1900 to 13% by 1994. The most influential factor in the aging of the population has been the secular decline in fertility.

The 1980 U.S. age-sex structure had two constrictions, each revealing significant past experiences of the population. By 1980, the 1930–1939, "Depression cohorts" had moved into the 40–49 age range, and the "baby bust" that followed the post-World War II "baby boom" had created slimmer birth cohorts reaching 0–9 in 1980. In 1990, 22% of the population was under age 15 years, and more than 12% was 65 years of age or older; the age-sex pyramid had a slightly wider base compared to the 1980 profile, reflecting the rebound of the birth rate in the 1980s.

Comparison of the 1970 and 1980 U.S. population pyramids shows that the 1980 pyramid has a narrower base (under age 15), a fatter waist (15–39 years), and a narrower chest (40–49 years) than the 1970 pyramid:

| Year | <15 years | 15–39 years | 40–49 years |
|---|---|---|---|
| 1970 | 28.3% | 35.6% | 11.7% |
| 1980 | 22.4% | 41.5% | 10.1% |

The "baby bust" of the 1970s, the post-World War II "baby boom," and the Great Depression of the 1930s explain these figures.

## 7.4. DETERMINANTS

The decline in mortality of the kind that occurred in the Western-type demographic transition favored younger age groups, making the age-sex structure slightly "younger." The impact of fertility changes on age structure is more pronounced than that of mortality changes, however. Thus, as noted, the historical aging of the population of the U.S. population was much more due to fertility decline than to mortality decline. The median age of the U.S. population was 20 in 1870, 23 in 1900, 30 in 1950, 29 in 1960, 28 in 1970, 30 in 1980 and 33 in 1990. Notice the decrease in the median age from 30 in 1950 to 28 in 1970 and the subsequent increase to 30 in 1980 and 35 in 1990, reflecting the "baby boom" and the subsequent "baby bust."

Future mortality reductions in MDCs are likely to affect disproportionately older ages; hence the effect of such changes would be to make the age structure older.

The potential impact of migration on age-sex structure varies with the size of the population in question. A college town with a small base population (other than the student population) would experience massive alterations in age-sex structure every fall and the following summer as students arrive in the fall and go away in the summer. However, for large populations, the impact may be insignificant because the volume of migration is dwarfed by the size of the base population. If it is noticeable, the effect of in-migration would be to make the population younger because of the usual age-selectivity of migrants.

Many people believe that reduction in mortality increases the median age of a population, other things (fertility and migration) remaining the same. It is true that reductions in mortality causes the median length of life to increase, but the median age of a population is the median of ages at a point in time of those who are alive at that time. Reduction in mortality typical of the past has increased the number of young persons alive at any given time point more than it has increased older people alive at that time point. The effect of mortality on age composition is dependent on what ages are most affected and the initial age composition. Thus mortality changes can make the population older or younger.

## 7.5. CONSEQUENCES

When thinking about the consequences of age composition, it is useful to think in terms a summary measure such as the young-age dependency ratio or relative sizes of birth cohorts. An example of the use of the first type of measure can be found in the thesis that young-age dependency has a negative impact on savings and investment, and hence, on economic development. An example of the use of the second type of measure is provided by the Easterlin hypothesis, which holds that young people in a relatively large cohort generally grow up in affluence, but face stiff competition at each successive stage in life and, consequently, find it difficult to keep up with the standard of living they are accustomed to and at the same time have large families. Postponement of marriage, delayed childbearing, and reduction in family size are to be expected among members of a large cohort.

To continue the focus on the relative size of birth cohorts, note that during the early years of the "baby boom" new schools had to be built and more teachers had to be trained and as a result during the "baby bust" period that followed there was an oversupply of school space and teachers. As the U.S. "baby boomers" grew up and hit the labor market, the economy's ability to provide jobs for all applicants came under severe strain, and as a result unemployment rates went up. The U.S. "baby boomers" prompted a rise in the construction of retirement communities. It is feared that when the "baby boomers" begin drawing Social Security benefits, the U.S. Social Security system will be under severe strain.

Still, on the implications of relative sizes of cohorts, note that one of the factors accounting for the post-World War II "baby boom" was the greater relative number of women in the childbearing years, resulting from the relatively high fertility of the 1920s. The increase in the number of women in the childbearing years during the 1970s and 1980s resulting from the "baby boom" could have produced another "baby boom" if it had not been for the postponement of marriage and the substantial reduction in marital fertility.

## 7.6. THE ELDERLY

Aging can be viewed as a population phenomena or as an individual matter. Individuals inexorably become older as years go by. Populations may grow older or younger, depending upon what happens to the components of population change, particularly fertility. When fertility increases (falls), the population grows younger (older), if other things such as migration and mortality remain the same. Migration being age-selective, net in-migration, if large enough, can make a population younger (as happens in a college town when students arrive in the fall). Mortality declines that disproportionately favor people in the older (younger) ages make the population grow older (become younger).

At the individual level, aging occurs with gradual changes that take place over time in the structure of human body. Such changes are not the result of disease, accidents, or the like, but they eventually lead to the increased probability of death as the individual grows older. The term "senescence" is applied to this process. Aging in the sense just defined brings with it a diminished ability to resist disease. It is important to note that individuals differ in the rate at which they "age" and that different tissues and systems within the body seem to "age" at different rates.

Using the criterion of 65 years of age to separate the elderly from the rest of the population, the size of the elderly segment of the world's population was about 336 million in 1994, or about 6% of the total population. The elderly formed 13% of the total population in the more-developed regions of the world in 1994, but only 4% in the less-developed regions. The elderly segment of the population is growing at a faster rate in the less-developed regions than in the rest of the world. In 1950, there were almost the same number of elderly persons in the less-developed and more-developed regions (64 million and 66 million, respectively); but by the year 2010, according to U.N. projections (United Nations, 1990b), it is expected that there will be 1.7 times as many elderly persons in the less-developed as in the more-developed regions (330 million versus 194 million).

In the United States, the elderly segment of the population has been increasing much more rapidly than the rest of the population for most of the 20th century. In the last two decades the percentage increase of the elderly (65 and older) was three times that of the non-elderly (under 65 years of age). When the "baby boom" generation begins to collect Social Security benefits in the early part of the 21st century, it will swell the ranks of the elderly, at least one in five of the total population will be 65 years or older. The median age of the population is projected to increase to 36 years by the year 2000 and to 42 years by the year 2040, when the total U.S. population is likely to grow to about 309 million, of whom 67 million (or 21.7%) are likely to be 65 years or older. By that time the percentage of children under 18 years of age would be about the same as the percentage of elderly. This is a dramatic change from the 40% children versus 4% elderly pattern that prevailed at the turn of the 20th century.

Another feature worth emphasizing is that the elderly segment of the population itself is aging: the old-old (85 years and older) are increasing at a much faster rate than the rest of the elderly. Between 1990 and 2040, the old-old are expected to almost triple their number whereas the rest of the elderly are expected to increase by only 55%. Put differently, whereas in 1990, 57% of the elderly belonged to the "young-old" age category (those of age 65 to 74 years) and 10% to the "old-old" category (those of age 85 years and older), by the year 2040 these numbers are likely to change to 43% and 19%, respectively.

Since women live longer than men, the sex ratio increasingly favors females with age. Thus in 1990 there were in the United States about 80 men per 100 women in the age group 65–69 years, whereas only half as many in the age group 85 years and older. Elderly women are more likely to live alone longer and average a longer period of retirement than elderly men.

## 7.7. SOCIOECONOMIC COMPOSITION

### 7.7.1. Education

Educational attainment is a covariate of a number of demographic behaviors and traits. The better-educated population segments have lower fertility, higher chances of securing high-prestige occupations, and higher median income than lower educated segments. Education affects demographic behavior through (i) higher-paying jobs and hence higher income, (ii) higher probability of marital stability, (iii) greater knowledge of opportunities that exist, and (iv) higher levels of skills that enable one to take advantage of opportunities that present themselves.

Several explanations have been suggested for the commonly observed racial/ethnic group differences in educational attainment. Among these are the following: (i) racial-group differences in cultural emphasis on the value of education; (ii) discrimination against minority groups, creating unequal opportunities for educational attainment for different groups of people; (iii) racial/ethnic-group differences in innate intelligence, an explanation that seems to be held only by a small minority.

In many of the LDCs, the male-female gap in literacy and educational attainment is pronounced. For example, in South Asia (except in Sri Lanka), female illiteracy is very high and the male-female gap is large (Mason, 1995, p. 4). In the MDCs, the male-female gap in educational attainment has been narrowing. For a long time now there has been no male-female gap in the probability of graduating from high school in the United States. The prognosis is that the corresponding gap in the probability of graduating from college and in other indicators of educational attainment will also vanish soon. These observations apply to many other industrialized countries.

### 7.7.2. Occupation

In examining occupational composition, demographers often use broad categories such as the following: Executive, managerial, and professional specialty; Technical, sales, and administrative support; Service; Precision production, craft, and repair; Operators, fabricators, and laborers; and Farming, forestry, and fishing.

The U.S. census data show that population segments differ with respect to the occupational category in which they are more likely to be employed: white males in the "executive, managerial, or professional" category, black males in the "operators, fabricators, and laborers" category, females (whites and blacks) in the "technical, sales, and administrative support" category.

The same data also show a higher proportion of females than males in the broad category "executive, managerial, and professional specialty," largely because it includes elementary school teachers and nurses.

Since 1900, the proportion of the labor force engaged in white collar occupations (professional, managerial, administrative, clerical, and sales workers) has been steadily increasing (e.g., from 18% in 1900 to 52% in 1980); farm workers (farmers, farm managers, farm laborers and supervisors) have become progressively a small fraction of the total labor force (37% in 1900 versus 3% in 1980); the share of total labor force accruing to private household workers has dramatically declined (e.g., from 5% in 1900 to 1% in 1980), while that of other service workers (dental technicians, hairdressers, police workers, etc.) has increased (from 4% in 1900 to 12% in 1980).

### 7.7.3. Industrial Composition

Industry refers to the answer one expects from an employed person to the question "what kind of business or industry is your employer engaged in?" A three-part industrial classification is commonly used in presenting data: primary (e.g., farming, fishing, forestry work, mining); secondary (e.g., manufacturing); and tertiary (e.g., all kinds of services such as those provided by educational institutions, governments, banks, and court systems). In the industrialized countries of the world, the primary sector employs only a small fraction of the work force, whereas in the LDCs it is the major source of employment, as the following figures for 1980 illustrate (World Bank, 1986, Table 30): Bangladesh (75% primary, 19% tertiary), Indonesia (57% primary, 30% tertiary), Mexico (37% primary, 34% tertiary), Spain (17% primary, 46% tertiary), United States (4% primary, 66% tertiary.)

Frequently the proportion of workers employed in the primary sector has been used as an indicator of economic development. A problem with this practice is that the primary sector's share of the labor force may be reduced by the inflation of the tertiary sector's share due to people engaging themselves in service activities (e.g., as street vendors, household servants in most LDCs) that have little to do with economic development.

### 7.7.4. Labor-Force Participation

The labor force includes employed as well as unemployed persons (those who are out of work, but are seeking work). In the United States, at all ages, there were higher proportions of women participating in the labor force in 1990 than in 1940, while the opposite was true for men. The age pattern of labor force participation of men is ∩-shaped. The female pattern used to be somewhat different from this, having two humps as a result of a reduction in the rate during peak childbearing ages, but this dissimilarity has diminished over time. Still, the female curve is nested within the male curve, that is, at almost all ages the rate for females is lower than that for males. Considerable variation exists among the MDCs with respect to the male-female differences in the age curve of labor force participation rate and changes in it over time.

In the LDCs, women have increased their labor force participation rate but have not yet reached the current levels for MDC women. The so-called informal sector absorbs a large fraction of working women in the LDCs, and LDC women are more likely to be self-employed than are MDC women.

Unemployed persons are, as mentioned above, those who are out of work but are looking for work. The overall unemployment rate is a weighted average of age-specific unemployment rates, the weights being the age-composition of the labor force. The unemployment rates are usually higher at younger ages than at older ages. A swelling of the job seekers at young ages could make the overall unemployment rate rise, even if all age-specific unemployment rates fall. Also, aging of the labor force could make the overall unemployment rate go down even if the age-specific unemployment rates remain unchanged.

### 7.7.5. Indicators of Level of Living

The income inequality (see question 9 in Section 7.8.6 for a measure of income inequality) of employed persons in the United States in 1990 was much lower than it was 200 years earlier. But this does not mean that income inequality has been progressively declining through the last 200 years. In fact, the income inequality of the U.S. population increased during the 1980s (Nam, 1994, pp. 359–366). In 1990 there was marked racial/ethnic group differences in income inequality.

The prevalence of poverty is a macro-level indicator of the standard of living. Three times the cost of obtaining a minimally adequate diet has been used in the United States as a criterion (poverty line) to classify families into "poor" and "not poor." During the 1960s and early 1970s, the number of poor and the poverty rate declined, but they consistently increased during the late 1970s and 1980s. In 1991,

14% of all persons were below the poverty line (O'Hare, 1985; Nam, 1994, p. 362). The chances of falling below the poverty line vary by family type, race/ethnicity, and residence (central city, suburbs, rural farm). For example, in the United States in 1991, about 6% of married persons of age 35 to 44 years with children under 18 were below the poverty line, while 33% of females living without a spouse and having children under 18 were so classified (almost 50% for black and Hispanic women but only 25% of white women) (see Nam, 1994, p. 364; O'Hare, 1985). Shifts in age composition affect the overall prevalence of poverty.

The persistence of poverty has been attributed by some writers (e.g. Murray, 1984) to antipoverty programs, the argument being that such programs have undermined work ethics. Others (e.g., O'Hare, 1989, p. 37), however, have held that there is little evidence to support this contention.

Savings, insurance, and Social Security are, other than income, among the indicators of economic security. The proportion of the U.S. population having life insurance has increased over time. Saving rates fluctuate over time; the U.S. rates dropped during the 1970s and 1980s, but the future aging of the population is expected to increase savings during the first few decades of the 21st century. The long-run solvency of the U.S. Social Security System has been questioned by many of those who have looked into the matter. Demographic factors are partly to blame for the difficulties the U.S. Social Security System is running into: The more than anticipated improvement in life expectancy at the older ages and the post-World War II baby boom, creating an "elderly boom" in the 21st century, are among these factors (Nam, 1994, pp. 363–366; Longman, 1989).

### 7.7.6. Racial/Ethnic Minorities

The racial/ethnic composition varies from population to population and also within populations over time. The situation in each population has to be studied in its own terms. Here the focus is on the U.S. scene.

Race and ethnic categories used in U.S. censuses have changed. The 1860 Census used the following categories: white, black, mulatto. Currently, the government uses many more categories and publishes statistics for the following four main minority groups: blacks, Asian and Pacific Islanders, American Indians, and Hispanics (of all races).

The U.S. population's racial/ethnic composition is undergoing dramatic changes. For a long time the population was mostly white. By the middle of the 21st century it is expected that the minorities' share of the U.S. population will approach close to 50%.

The composition of the minorities itself is changing markedly. By the year 2010, Hispanics are expected to outnumber blacks, and hence become the largest minority group (O'Hare, 1992).

Racial/ethnic groups in the U.S. population differ significantly in their age-sex distribution. The ratio of men to women is unusually high among Hispanics, reflecting sex-selectivity in migration; all minority groups have a younger age structure than whites, as the following figures for 1992 show, using broad age groups—under 18, 18–44, 45–64, and 65 and over (O'Hare, 1992, p. 17–18)—white: 24, 41, 20, 15; black: 32, 44, 15, 8; Hispanic: 35, 47, 13, 5; Asian: 29, 48, 17, 7; American Indian: 35, 43, 15, 6. In the early 1990s, minority children accounted for almost one-third of all children under 18 years of age.

The minority share of the working age population is expected to rise steadily over the next 50 years (O'Hare, 1992, p. 18). The ratio of younger (18–44 years) to older (45–64 years) working-age minority adults as of the early 1990s was about 3 to 1. Disproportionately fewer minority workers are occupying managerial positions as of the early 1990s.

Family-type composition differs among racial/ethnic minorities in the United States (O'Hare, 1992, p. 19). Asians are more likely than any of the other major racial/ethnic groups to be living in married-couple families with children (53% as opposed to 38% among whites, 29% among blacks, 41% among American Indians and 47% among Hispanics). Single-parent families are most common among blacks (37% of black families are of this type, as opposed to 10% among whites and Asians, 27% among American Indians, and 22% among Hispanics). Asian households have a higher probability of being extended family units. Young Hispanics, especially women, have a higher probability of living with parents until marriage.

Educational attainment has increased in all racial/ethnic groups, but pronounced heterogeneity still prevails: The percent compositions in terms of highest level of educational attainment (less than high school, high school graduate, some college, college graduate) were as follows for persons of age 25–44 in 1992 (see O'Hare, 1992, p. 29): whites: 9, 36, 27, 28; blacks: 19, 41, 26, 14; Hispanics: 40, 30, 20, 10; Asians: 8, 25, 20, 47; and American Indians: 22, 37, 30, 11. Hispanics lag behind all the other groups with respect to completion of high school and completion of college. Asians are ahead of the others with respect to graduation from college.

Occupational status of minorities has been improving over the years (O'Hare, 1992), but marked differences in occupational composition persist (O'Hare, 1992, p. 33). The proportion of employed persons holding white collar jobs was higher in 1990 among Asians than among any other major racial/ethnic group (63% as compared to 60% among whites, 46% among blacks, 43% among American Indians, and 39% among Hispanics). The proportion of workers engaged in farming, fishing, and forestry was higher among American Indians (4%) and Hispanics (5%) than among the other groups (2% or less).

Pronounced income differences exist between racial/ethnic groups in the United States (O'Hare, 1992, p. 34). The rankings from lowest to highest median income in 1979 and 1989 were the same: in increasing order of 1989 income, blacks

($19,800), American Indians ($20,000), Hispanics ($24,200), whites ($31,400) and Asians ($36,800).

Poverty level varies among the racial/ethnic groups (O'Hare, 1992, p. 38). In 1991, 9% of whites were in poverty; the corresponding figures for the other groups were: blacks, 33%; Asians, 14%; Hispanics, 29%; and American Indians, 32%. Similar variation exists in the prevalence of deep poverty (falling below 50% of the poverty line): whites, 3%; blacks, 16%; Asians, 7%; Hispanics, 10%; and American Indians, 14%. Those who were receiving welfare benefits among the poor were whites, 61%; blacks, 85%; Asians, 62%; Hispanics, 79%; and American Indians, 87%.

It was mentioned earlier that the racial/ethnic makeup of the U.S. population is changing dramatically and that immigration, fertility, and mortality all play their part in this development. A few details are worth adding. The Caribbean serves as a major source of black immigrants. Other sources include Ethiopia, Ghana, Nigeria, and Kenya. The immigrant component, however, constitutes a much smaller component of growth of the U.S. black population than is true for Hispanics or Asians. Fertility differentials account for a major part of the growth differentials among U.S. racial/ethnic groups. As of 1992, the total fertility rates for whites, blacks, Asians, American Indians, and Hispanics, were 1.9, 2.5, 2.3, 2.9, and 2.7, respectively. Teenagers contributed 23% of births among blacks in 1989, 20% among American Indians, 17% among Hispanics, and 6% among Asians. Mortality differentials also play a role in producing growth differentials among racial/ethnic groups in the United States. During 1985–1987, infant mortality rate (number of deaths per 1000 live births) was 8.5 among whites, 18.2 among blacks, 13.3 among American Indians, 7.6 among Asians, and 8.5 among Hispanics (NCHS, 1994, p. 80). Minority groups have higher mortality rates than whites from several causes of death. For example, death rates from infectious diseases are higher among minority women than among white women. The reverse is true with respect to some other causes of death. For example, some minority groups have lower death rates from heart diseases than whites (the age-adjusted death rates from heart diseases for age 45 years and over was 726 per 100,000 during 1989–1991 for whites while the corresponding figures were 373 for Asians, 523 for American Indians, and 485 for Hispanics (NCHS, 1994, p. 103). Those not covered by private insurance, Medicaid, Medicare, or military plans in 1992 constituted 16.1% for whites, 22.3% for blacks, and 34.0% for Hispanics (NCHS, 1994, p. 240).

### 7.7.7. More on the Elderly

The age-sex composition of the elderly has already been discussed. One related point worth adding is that the elderly is made up of survivors of a number of successive birth cohorts. Thus the elderly of 1990 were all born in 1925 or earlier.

Many of them survived World War I and the flu pandemic of 1919–1920. All of the 1990 elderly lived through the Great Depression of the 1930s, World War II, the "baby boom," and so on. However, the survivors of each birth cohort among the U.S. 1990 elders have had their own unique experiences. Thus those who were at the peak of their reproductive period during the 1930s, that is, roughly those born between 1900 and 1910, have exclusive experiences to report regarding how they ended up with small families on average. Of course, life experiences are bound not only with cohort identification but with many other characteristics as well, e.g., race/ethnicity. Hence the composition of the elderly with respect to those characteristics are of interest.

Minority elders have been increasing in numbers at a faster rate than their white counterparts in recent years and this pattern is expected to continue well into the next century. In 1985, only 10% of the U.S. elderly were non-white, but by the year 2025, the non-white's share of the elderly is expected to increase to 15%. Many among the minority elderly carry with them scars of social and economic discrimination experienced earlier in life. Per capita dependence on services such as income maintenance, housing, meals, transportation, and health care is greater among the minority elders than among white elders.

As educational levels have increased over time, the elderly of today are better educated than the elderly of yesterday, but less educated than the elderly of tomorrow, i.e., the non-elderly of today.

Those of age 65 years and older as a group have, on average, lower income than younger people, mainly because of retirement (leaving the labor force), which, on average, cuts income drastically. But averages are misleading in this context: A very high proportion of the elderly have incomes and other economic resources below or just above the poverty line, while a few have substantial resources and many have practically none (U.S. Senate Special Committee on Aging, 1987). The old-old (age 85 and older) tend to have significantly lower median income than the young-old (age 65–74 years) and those in-between (age 75–84 years):

| Type of unit | Age 65–74 years | Age 75–84 years | Age 85 years and older |
|---|---|---|---|
| Families | $20,354 | $16,412 | $15,111 |
| Unrelated individuals | $8,160 | $7,186 | $6,400 |

Source: U.S. Senate Special Committee on Aging, 1987, p. 45.

Most older men are married, but most older women are widowed. Among the reasons for this pattern are that men, because they have lower life expectancy than women, predecease their wives; men tend to marry women younger than themselves; men when widowed or divorced are more likely than women to remarry.

One of the striking differences by race/ethnicity in the living arrangements of the elderly is the tendency for widowed minority women to live with other family members, while most widowed white females maintain separate households (U.S. Senate Special Committee on Aging, p. 140, based on Mach 1986 Current Population Survey data.)

The propensity to vote in national elections is high among the elderly. The percentage of persons who report voting in national elections increase consistently with age until it drops for the age groups 75 and older (U.S. Senate Special Committee on Aging, p. 147, based on U.S. Census Bureau Current Population Reports Series P-20, Voting and Registration in the Elections of November of various years).

## 7.8. QUESTIONS AND ANSWERS*

**FOR EACH OF THE QUESTIONS IN SECTIONS 7.8.1. to 7.8.4., STATE TRUE OR FALSE AND EXPLAIN.**

### 7.8.1. Concepts

1. Individuals grow older as time passes but populations grow older or get younger over time.
2. All stable populations are stationary populations.
3. Gainful workers are self-employed persons whose income is higher than expenses, annually.
4. All persons except those who are very young or very old, and those who are unable to work because of disability, form the potential labor force.
5. In the United States children under 16 years of age are not included in work statistics.

### 7.8.2. Measures

6. The number of years of schooling completed (as indicated by graduation certificates, college degrees, and the like) is a reliable indicator of intellectual capabilities.

### 7.8.3. Levels and Trends

7. In the future, the populations of the more-developed and the less-developed regions are expected to continue to age demographically.

*Answers start page 196.

8. The countries in the more-developed regions are homogeneous with respect to age structure.
9. The countries in the less-developed regions are heterogeneous with respect to age structure.
10. In the less-developed regions, the number of children under 15 years of age has been increasing steadily since 1970.
11. Since 1980, the population of age 60 years and older has been increasing at a faster rate in the less-developed regions than in the more-developed regions.
12. For the world as a whole, the dependency ratio increased gradually from 66 to 75 between 1950 and 1965 and has been declining ever since.
13. The projected trends for the young age and old age components of the total dependency ratio are the same.
14. Africa has the highest total dependency ratio as of now.
15. The total dependency ratio is expected to decline over the next three decades in the less- and more-developed regions.
16. The sex ratio at birth is typically 105 boys per 100 girls.
17. The number of older people (age 65 years and older) is higher in the less-developed regions than in the more-developed regions.
18. In the United States, the elderly (older than 64 years) increased in number faster than the total population did from 1900 to 1994.
19. The rise in educational attainment in the United States bypassed minority group members.
20. Africa lags behind Asia and Latin America in school enrollment ratio for children of ages 6–11 years.
21. Illiteracy rates have fallen markedly since 1970 in the world.
22. It took several centuries in Western Europe to reduce illiteracy from near maximum level to a near minimum level.
23. In the Western societies, folkways concerning working women have changed since the 19th century.
24. In the United States, income inequality had a declining long-term trend.
25. In the United States in April 1992, the unemployment rate was very low among white males of age 75 years and older.

### 7.8.4. Differentials, Determinants, and Consequences

26. Declines in mortality that disproportionately favor infant and childhood ages have the same effect on age structure as an increase in fertility.
27. If a population with a long history of low fertility and low mortality were to experience a "baby boom," the population pyramid takes the shape of a bell-jar.
28. Two countries that have similar mortality levels but different fertility levels and no migration have different age-sex structures.
29. The illiteracy rate is higher among women of age 15 years and older than among men of that age group.
30. Unemployment rates are negatively associated with educational level.

**FOR EACH OF THE QUESTIONS IN SECTIONS 7.8.5. TO 7.8.8., FOUR ANSWERS ARE GIVEN, AT LEAST ONE OF WHICH IS CORRECT. IDENTIFY THE CORRECT ANSWER(S) AND EXPLAIN.**

### 7.8.5. Concepts

1. The perspective of age stratification:
   A. Implies a set of inequalities
   B. Assumes mobility between strata
   C. Differs from the perspective of social stratification in some ways
   D. Applies only to the developed regions of the world
2. Age strata:
   A. In most societies are identifiable
   B. Were three in number in Europe a few hundred years ago
   C. Are seven in number in contemporary Western societies
   D. Are not the same in all countries at present
3. A stable population is:
   A. One in which the age-structure and growth rate remain unchanging over time
   B. Little more than a figment of the demographer's imagination
   C. Called a stationary population when the growth rate is zero
   D. Is an idea that has virtually no application in demographic analysis
4. A stationary population:
   A. Has zero population growth
   B. Can be found in each life table

C. Has during each year the same number of births as deaths
D. Has one-half of its members above age 64 years

5. Which of the following statements apply to the momentum of population growth and/or its manifestations?
A. The concept of momentum of a population refers to the growth potential exclusively attributable to the age structure of the population
B. The concept of momentum of a population refers to the growth potential of the current fertility-mortality patterns, ignoring the age structure
C. In typical MDCs, a sequence of relatively larger successive cohorts could produce a large cohort of babies, even at a smaller reproduction rate
D. The concept of momentum of a population and the concept of intrinsic rate of natural increase are interchangeable

6. Which of the following receive attention in the study of industrial and/or occupational composition of the labor force?
A. The occupational classification of a person, referring to the type of job he or she holds
B. The industrial classification of a person, referring to the type of organization, firm or industry for which he or she works
C. The fact that the same occupation can be found in different industries
D. The marked difference between developed and less developed countries in their industrial composition

### 7.8.6. Measures

7. Popular ways of summarizing age-sex structure use:
A. Median age
B. Total dependency ratio
C. Young age dependency ratio
D. Old age dependency ratio

8. To measure sex structure, one calculates:
A. Sex ratio
B. Sex ratio at birth
C. Sex ratio at each age
D. Dependency ratio

9. The Gini coefficient:
A. Is linked to the Lorenz curve
B. Gives the area between the observed Lorenz curve and the line of absolute equality as a proportion of the total area under the latter
C. Has a maximum of unity
D. Has a minimum of zero ("absolute equality")

### *7.8.7. Levels and Trends*

10. Which of the following major regions have a sex ratio (males per 100 females in the population as a whole) of more than 100:
    A. Africa
    B. Latin America
    C. North America
    D. Asia

11. Which of the following is NOT true, with reference to the likely trend in the dependency ratio or in one of its components over the next 25 years?
    A. Young age dependency ratio in the world as a whole is expected to decline
    B. The same is true of the less-developed regions of the world
    C. Total dependency ratio is expected to decline in the world as a whole
    D. The old age dependency ratio is expected to remain rather steady in the less-developed regions of the world

12. Which of the following statements apply to the income inequality in the United States?
    A. The U.S. income inequality, as measured by the Gini coefficient, increased during the 1970s and 1980s
    B. Income inequality varied among race/ethnic groups during the 1970s and 1980s
    C. Demographic factors affect income inequality
    D. The recent trends in income inequality sets the United States apart from most of the more-developed countries

13. Comparison of income distribution in the MDCs with that of the LDCs indicates:
    A. That the shares of the total income accruing to upper-income groups in the LDCs are larger than the corresponding figures in the MDCs
    B. That the shares of the total income accruing to the lower income groups are lower in the LDCs than in the MDCs
    C. That the inequality in income distribution is higher in the LDCs than in the MDCs
    D. That the pattern of greater income inequality characteristic of the LDCs prevailed in the MDCs decades ago

14. The age pattern of labor force participation rate for women has changed in the United States in which of the following ways since World War II?
    A. The labor force participation rate in each age group increased steadily over the years
    B. The age pattern for women has become more similar to that of men over the years

C. Women have become more likely to be year-round, full-time workers, in contrast to the earlier pattern of part-time participation.
D. The labor force participation of women with preschool children increased markedly over time.

### 7.8.8. *Differentials, Determinants, and Consequences*

15. Assuming that sex selection is widely practiced (through sex-selective abortions, for example), the sex ratio at birth:
    A. Would not significantly change
    B. Would change at least temporarily
    C. Would change worldwide into a new permanent level different from what is common now
    D. Is unlikely to converge to a level heavily favoring boys or girls
16. Change in relative cohort size may affect:
    A. The distribution of marriage by age at marriage
    B. Timing of births
    C. Socio-economic mobility
    D. Suicidal propensity
17. A careful examination of the 1990 U.S. age-sex pyramid would reveal telltale evidence of:
    A. The Great Depression
    B. The post-World War II "baby boom"
    C. The "baby bust" following the "baby boom"
    D. The "elderly boom"
18. Which of the following statements apply to the relationship between ascribed and achieved characteristics on the one hand and fertility on the other?
    A. At the individual level, ascribed and achieved characteristics affect fertility
    B. Fertility affects one or more achieved characteristics
    C. At the population level, racial/ethnic/religious/socio-economic groups differ in fertility
    D. Such fertility differentials affect the population composition by race/ethnicity, religion, and socio-economic status
19. Which of the following statements apply to the U.S. male-female gap in educational attainment?
    A. In general, the gap has been narrowing over time and could disappear before long
    B. Virtually no male-female gap exists with respect to the probability of graduating from high school
    C. There is still some gap between males and females with respect to the probability of graduating from college

D. With respect to the median school years completed, the male-female gap is 1.5 years wider for Hispanics than for whites

20. Which of the following statements apply to the role education plays in population dynamics?
    A. Fertility is negatively associated with education
    B. Infant survival is positively associated with education
    C. Childlessness is positively associated with education
    D. Women's education attainment tends to delay childbearing

21. Economists have argued that economic development brings with it certain predictable changes in the industrial composition of the labor force. These changes include:
    A. A steady decline in the primary sector's share
    B. A decline followed by an increase in the secondary sector's share
    C. A steady increase in the tertiary sector's share
    D. A floor above which all shares remain always

22. Which of the following factors affect the size of the labor force?
    A. A rise and then a fall of fertility level
    B. Improvement in mortality levels
    C. Shifting family structure
    D. Changes in retirement ages

**FOR EACH OF THE QUESTIONS IN SECTIONS 7.8.9. TO 7.8.11., FIVE ANSWERS ARE SUGGESTED, ONLY ONE OF WHICH IS CORRECT. IDENTIFY THE CORRECT ANSWER AND EXPLAIN.**

### *7.8.9. Concepts*

1. Which of the following is NOT a feature of age-sex (population) pyramids?
    A. It is a double histogram
    B. The area of each rectangle in it is proportional to the number of persons in the corresponding age-sex group
    C. It is broad-based and tapers to the top in all large populations with a history of high fertility
    D. It is shaped more like a barrel with a narrow top for the Western populations
    E. It is symmetrical

2. All stable populations:
    A. Are stationary populations
    B. Have a time-invariant age structure
    C. Have invariably high dependency ratio
    D. Are figments of demographer's imagination
    E. Have a steadily increasing growth rate

3. Which of the following is NOT an ascribed characteristic?
   A. Race
   B. Nationality
   C. Male-female distinction
   D. Ethnicity
   E. Age

4. The idea of social class is most closely linked to which of the following, in most peoples' minds in the United States?
   A. Occupation
   B. Income
   C. Education
   D. Health
   E. Race

### *7.8.10. Levels and Trends*

5. The sex ratio at older ages in Western industrialized countries:
   A. Is age-invariant
   B. Highly favors males (many more males than females)
   C. Highly favors females (many more females than males)
   D. Has no consistent age pattern characteristic of a majority of countries
   E. Is a constant after age 50 years

6. The rise in educational attainment in the United States over the past has:
   A. Bypassed Hispanics
   B. Resulted in widening the male-female gap in educational attainment
   C. Been primarily confined to the increase in the probability of high school graduation
   D. Been shared virtually by all population subgroups
   E. Led to the abolition of mandatory school enrollment until a certain age

7. In the United States currently, working women constitute about ______ percent of the total civilian labor force:
   A. 12
   B. 22
   C. 42
   D. 62
   E. 72

8. During the past few decades, the labor force participation rates in the United States have been ______ for males and ______ for females:
   A. Increasing, increasing
   B. Increasing, decreasing
   C. Decreasing, decreasing

D. Decreasing, increasing
E. Decreasing, remaining unchanged

9. During the past few decades the labor force participation rates in the United States among persons of age 65 years and older have been ______for males and ______ for females.
A. Increasing, decreasing
B. Increasing, decreasing
C. Decreasing, increasing
D. Decreasing, decreasing
E. Decreasing, not changing

### 7.8.11. *Differentials, Determinants, and Consequences*

10. The sex ratio of a population is affected by ALL BUT which of the following?
A. Sex-selected abortion
B. Sex-selectivity in migration
C. Sex ratio at birth
D. Sex differences in mortality
E. Sex differences in disability

11. In general, the sex ratio is highest in which age group?
A. Under 4 years
B. 20–29 years
C. 40–49 years
D. 70–79 years
E. 90–99 years

12. Since the 1960s, the U.S. population has aged as a result of:
A. Increase in immigration
B. Increase in emigration
C. Reduction in fertility
D. Reduction in maternal mortality
E. Stress associated with modern urban living conditions

13. The unemployment rate is highest in which age group?
A. 16–19 years
B. 20–24 years
C. 25–34 years
D. 35–64 years
E. 65 years and older

14. Which of the following statements is NOT true with respect to the age pattern of marital status in the United States?
A. Percent single steadily decreases with age

B. Percent married increases and then decreases with age
C. Percent widowed steadily increases with age
D. Percent divorced increases and then decreases with age
E. The percent widowed among females is lower at each age than for males at that age

15. Mean income for households is highest in which group in terms of the age of the householder (formerly called the head of the household) in the United States?
A. 15–24 years
B. 25–34 years
C. 35–44 years
D. 45–54 years
E. 55–64 years

16. Which of the following DOES NOT apply to the U.S. black-white comparison of family income distribution, the U.S. white-black family income gap, or changes in these during 1969–1989?
A. The median income for whites remained higher than that for blacks throughout the period
B. The median income for blacks increased at a higher percentage point between 1969 and 1989 than the median income for whites did
C. The dollar gap between whites and blacks widened during the period
D. The income inequality among blacks was higher than that among whites throughout the period
E. The black-white gap in income inequality narrowed during the period

17. In comparing the median family income for blacks with that of whites, one should give attention to which of the following?
A. Black families have on the average fewer earners
B. A substantial proportion of black families are headed by females, more than three times as many than among whites
C. Females, in general, earn less, other things being equal
D. The rate of deaths due to HIV infection among blacks tends to be more than three times that among whites
E. Choice A, B, and C

### 7.8.1. Answers

1. True. As long as chronological age is the basis for determining how old an individual is, there is no choice for an individual but to get older as time passes. A population on the other hand can grow older (indicated, for example, by an increase in the median age) or get younger. In 1950 the median age of the

world's population was 23.4 years. It dropped to 21.6 by 1970 and then increased to 23.4 by 1985, and is expected to increase continuously in the future. The population of the more-developed regions of the world, however, grew continuously older since 1950 and is expected to do so in the future. The population of the less developed regions, on the other hand, became younger over the period 1950–1970 and then began to grow older continuously. The aging of the more-developed regions was caused by a combined action of fertility decline and mortality decline. The factor responsible for the population of the less-developed regions getting younger demographically between 1950 and 1970 was the significant reduction in mortality (mostly concentrated in the infant and childhood ages) when fertility remained virtually unchanged. Reductions in infant and child mortality have the same effect as that of an increase in fertility, resulting in a relatively larger population of young people. The aging of the population of the less-developed region beginning in 1970 was due to a significant reduction in fertility coupled with the fact that the post-1970 mortality reductions were less concentrated in the infant and childhood ages, the mortality levels for those ages having already fallen to moderate levels by 1970. (See U.N., 1990b.)

2. False. All stationary populations are stable populations, but not vice versa. Recall that stable populations may or may not be growing in size, whereas stationary populations always have zero population growth.

3. False. The term stands for persons who work for wages or salaries. This was the basic concept before the introduction of the labor force concept.

4. True. In some countries the term "manpower" is used instead. All those who have the potential for working under some circumstances or other constitute this class. They can be classified into those who are employed, those who are not employed but are actively seeking work, and others (not employed and are not actively looking for work); the first two together form the labor force.

5. True. The cutoff varies from one country to another, ranging from 10 to 16 years of age.

### 7.8.2. Answers

6. False. it is known that many high school graduates are functionally illiterate, that is, they do not have the ability to read, write, and do arithmetic at a level necessary to function effectively at work. The data from U.S. Department of Education's 1985 *Young Adults Literacy Assessment* study have shown that "many high school graduates, and even college graduates, did not have the basic literacy skills that might be expected of them" (Pendleton, 1988, p. 24,

quoted in Nam, 1994). Also, inadequate school systems may fail to develop the intellectual capabilities of students enrolled.

### 7.8.3. Answers

7. True. In the more-developed regions, the pace will become faster on account of persistence of low fertility levels and the likely future gains in mortality (mostly confined to the advanced ages). The U.N. projections indicate that the median age in the more developed countries is expected to increase to 40.7 years by 2025. In the less-developed countries also the pace is expected to accelerate and the median is expected to increase to 29.7 years by 2025, on account of the likely declines in fertility and mortality. (See U.N., 1990b).
8. False. There are considerable variations in this respect among the countries in the more-developed regions. For decades Europe had been the oldest, demographically. The 1985 median age in Europe was 33.9 years. This is expected to reach 42.9 years by 2025. North America's 1985 median age was 31.5 years and it is expected to increase to 40.8 years by 2025. The former Soviet Union had a median age of 30.0 years in 1985 and the projected 2025 median age there is 36.4 years. (See U.N., 1990b.)
9. True. Between 1950 and 1970 Africa, Asia, and Latin America all became younger demographically. In 1970 Africa was the youngest (with the median age of 17.6 years), Asia the oldest (with the median age of 19.7), and Latin America in-between (with the median age of 18.6 years). In Africa, because of the persistent high fertility and declining mortality, the age structure became younger still and by 1985, the median age had dropped to 17.3 years. Asia and Latin America started growing older after 1970 and their median ages in 1985 were 22.2 years and 20.9 years, respectively. This trend is expected to continue in both of these regions. The projected 2025 median age in these regions are 32.5 years and 30.2 years, respectively. Africa is expected to start growing older towards the end of the 20th century and attain a median age of 22.6 years by 2025. (See U.N., 1990b.)
10. True. In 1970 there were 1.107 billion children under age 15 years in the less-developed regions, accounting for 42% of the total population of the regions. In 1992 there were about 1.510 billion children under age 15, accounting for 36% of the total population. Notice the decline in the relative size of the young segment of the population. With the expected fertility decline in these regions this proportion is projected to decline to 34.2 years by the year 2000 and to 25.6 years by the year 2025. (See U.N., 1990b.)
11. True. In the 1980s the population of age 60 years and older in the less-developed countries grew at an average annual rate of 3.0% while the corre-

sponding rate of growth in the more developed regions was only 1.7 percent. (Calculations based on data in U.N. 1990b.)

12. True. Recall that the dependency ratio is the number of "dependents" (those outside the age range 15–64 years) per 100 persons of working ages (those in the age range 15–64 years). This ratio is sometimes referred to as the total dependency ratio, to distinguish it from its young age and old age components. The total dependency ratio of 75 in 1965 was the highest ever recorded for the world as a whole. The U.N. projections indicate that the total dependency ratio will decline steadily to 52 per 100 persons of working age by 2025. (See U.N., 1990b.)

13. False. In the coming decades, the young age component is expected to decline while the old age component is expected to increase, as a consequence of the likely declines in fertility and mortality, the latter, contrary to the past patterns, not primarily confined to young age groups. (See U.N., 1990b.)

14. True. Between 1990 and 2000, the total dependency ratio is expected to decline from 93.5 to 90.1 in Africa, from 68.7 to 61.6 in Latin America, from 60.8 to 59.2 in Asia, from 51.3 to 49.2 in North America, from 56.0 to 54.7 in Oceania, and to increase from 49.3 to 50.3 in Europe. (See U.N., 1990b.)

15. False. In the more-developed regions the total dependency ratio is expected to increase from 50 to 58 over the next three decades, whereas during that time the ratio is expected to decline from 65 to 51 in the less-developed regions. (See U.N., 1990b.)

16. True. This assumes that sex-selective abortions do not occur. Exceptions do exist. In Africa, for example, the sex ratio at birth is lower (103 boys per 100 girls).

17. True. The less-developed regions have more people of age 65 years and older than in the more-developed regions (178 million versus 151 million in 1994). But the elderly account for a larger fraction of the total population in the more-developed regions than in the less-developed regions (13% versus 4%). (The explanation lies in the much higher LDC population. The 1994 total population of the more-developed regions was 1.164 billion and that of the less-developed regions was 4.443 billion. With a larger base, even small multipliers produce large numbers.)

18. True. In 1900 there were only 3 million people older than 64 years of age in a total population of 76 million in the United States. The corresponding numbers in 1994 were 34 million and 261 million, respectively. Thus the total population grew 3.4 times while the elderly grew 11.3 times. Note that the world over the elderly is growing faster than the overall population.

19. False. The rise in educational attainment in the United States over the past several decades has been shared by almost all population segments, including minority groups. Note, however, that the disparity between different (e.g., racial/ethnic) groups continues.

20. True. School enrollment ratio is the percentage of persons of a given age group enrolled in school. UNESCO's (1989) *Statistical Yearbook* shows that in 1987 only 59.1% of children of ages 6–11 in Africa were enrolled in school, contrasted with 79.7% in Asia and 78.8% in Latin America. (Note that school enrollment represents registering in a school system and getting assigned to a class, grade or program. It is not to be confused with school attendance.)

21. True. Among persons of age 15 years and older, 38.5% were illiterate (could not with understanding read and write a short simple statement) in the world as a whole in 1970. The corresponding figure in 1990 was 26.5%. In the less-developed regions the 1970 figure was 54.7% and the 1990 figure 34.9% and in the more-developed regions 6.2% and 3.3%, respectively. The illiteracy rate continues to be high in Sub-Saharan Africa (52.7% in 1990), and Southern Asia (53.9% in 1990). (See Nam, 1994, p. 345, based on UNESCO, 1990.)

22. True. See Maynes (1985) and Nam (1994, p. 344). At the turn of the 16th century nearly all women and nine out of ten men in England were illiterate. By 1900, the illiteracy rate and dropped below 5% for women and the same thing had happened to men somewhat earlier. The story of France was nearly the same. Most of the developed countries today have an illiteracy rate below 5% for persons of age 15 years and older (U.N., 1990b).

23. True. Husbands in the Western societies used to be afraid that they would be viewed as "poor providers" if their wives worked. So it was common for husbands to disapprove of their wives working for wages. Current folkways are just the opposite. Participation in the labor force is viewed as the normal way of life for women. Remaining at home as full-time homemakers, especially if there are no young children to attend to at home, is considered a waste of time and talent. Social pressures to enter the labor force are strong and non-working women are under pressure to participate in community activities and the like.

24. True. Soltow's (1989) calculations showed that in the United States around 1798, the Gini coefficient, a measure of income inequality, was in the range 0.63 to 0.71, as contrasted with 0.43 in the late 1980s. (Gini coefficient ranges from 0 to 1, the latter representing maximum inequality). However, the short run picture has often been different. For example, the Gini coefficient increased from 0.394 in 1970 to 0.403 by 1980 and to 0.428 in 1990 (Nam, 1994, p. 361, based on U.S. Census Bureau, 1991b).

25. True. The unemployment rate in April 1992 for this group was only 1.4%. Note that many persons in this category were not employed and were not seeking work. But most of those who were looking for work found it. The unemployment rate varies by age, sex, race, and other characteristics. In April 1992, the unemployment rate was highest for black males of age 16 and 17, many of them were high school dropouts who could not find work.

### 7.8.4. Answers

26. True. Such declines in mortality have the same effect as producing more children per adult. This makes the age structure younger.
27. True. The base will broaden, the trunk will remain more like a barrel, the head tapering off to the top.
28. True. One expects a younger age structure for the country with higher fertility.
29. True. For the world as a whole the gap in 1990 was 19.4% for males versus 33.6% for females. The corresponding figures for the less-developed regions were 25.1% and 45.0%, respectively and for the more-developed regions, 2.6% and 3.9%, respectively (See Nam, 1994, p. 345.)
30. True. In general, unemployment rates are lower for the better-educated. For the civilian, noninstitutional population of age 25–64 years in the United States, the unemployment rates in March 1986 were 9.6% for people with 1–3 years of high school, whereas the corresponding figures for high school graduates, those with some college education, and college graduates were 5.4%, 3.7% and 1.7%, respectively (U.S. Bureau of the Census, 1989).

### 7.8.5. Answers

1. A, B, and C: The perspective of age stratification implies that societies distribute resources unequally to persons of different age groups. It also assumes that people move from one age stratum to another; the move is inevitable, universal, and unidirectional, unlike movements from one stratum to another when strata are defined in terms of income, occupational class, and the like, where movement in and out of a stratum is possible. The perspective applies to all societies.
2. A, B, C, and D: In Europe a few hundred years ago the following three age strata were distinguished: infancy, adulthood, old age. In contemporary Western societies, the commonly recognized age strata are infancy, childhood, adolescence, young adulthood, middle age, young old, and old old. Age strata are not the same in all countries.

3. A and C: A population closed to migration and experiencing unchanging fertility and mortality schedules will eventually become stable. A stable population may grow in size or may not; if the growth rate is zero, it is called a stationary population. The idea of stable population is not just the figment of demographer's imagination. Approximately stable populations can be found in the real world. The concept of stable population has been widely used in demographic analysis, particularly in estimating demographic parameters when data are inadequate or defective.

4. A, B, and C: The ${}_nL_x$ column of the life table represents a stationary population. It has the same number of births as deaths each year and hence its annual growth rate is zero. None of the life tables constructed so far satisfy choice D.

5. A and C: The concept of momentum of a population refers to the change in the population growth rate expected if the net reproduction rate suddenly becomes 1 and stays at that level indefinitely, and migration is ruled out. Keyfitz (1977) has shown that in Ecuador in 1965, with a crude birth rate of 45 births per 1000 persons, and a life expectancy at birth of 60 years, if the age-specific fertility rates had dropped suddenly so as to make the net reproduction rate equal to 1, and if NRR had continued to be 1 thereafter, the Ecuador population would have increased by about 50% before it attained the state of zero-growth rate. This is because Ecuador was a rapidly increasing population, i.e., one with a young age structure, at that time, and any such population has a built-in growth potential in its age structure. Keyfitz used mathematical reasoning for his demonstration. But the basic notion that a population with a young age structure grows faster than one with a not-so-young age structure, other things being equal, can be illustrated by a simple numerical exercise.

   Compare two populations, each with a life span of 4 years. Suppose in population A, the numbers in the four age groups (youngest to oldest, in that sequence) at the initial time point are 6, 6, 3, and 1, respectively. Suppose the corresponding figures in population B are 3, 3, 3, 1. Clearly population A has a younger age structure than population B. Now imagine that these two populations share the same age-specific fertility rates and the same survival probabilities. For example, suppose the survival probabilities are 1, 1, 0.3, 0, respectively, for the four age groups. That is, no one dies until the second birthday anniversary is reached; only 30% survive from the second to the third birthday anniversary, and for those who survive to the third birthday anniversary, death is certain to occur within the year. Assume that reproduction is confined to the second and third age groups.

   For simplicity, assume that each person in the second and third age groups produces one offspring each year. Under such circumstances, it is easy to see that in the third year the two populations distributed by age would be A: 12, 9, 6, 2 and B: 6, 6, 3, 1, or in total population size 29 and 16, respectively.

The point to note is that a population with a younger age structure will retain the younger age structure, relatively speaking, for some time into the future and consequently will have relatively more people to produce children in comparison with the population with an older age structure. The intrinsic rate of natural increase, on the other hand, represents the growth potential of a population reflected in the current age-specific fertility rates and age-specific death rates, ignoring age structure.

Large birth cohorts when they reach reproductive ages can produce a "baby boom," even if they reproduce at relatively low rates.

6. A, B, C and D: Most censuses and demographic surveys ask respondents questions about their occupation, i.e., the "kind of work" they do. Of course, some of the activities have to be pooled to make the data manageable. There is no consensus as to how many and what specific categories are to be used in tabulating the data. The International Labor Organization (ILO) has attempted to bring cross-national comparability in this respect by recommending a system of classification. Many countries have adopted the ILO recommendations, but many have not.

### 7.8.6. Answers

7. A, B, C, and D: Note, however, that summary measures do not exhaust the information in the age-sex distribution.
8. A, B, and C: Dependency ratio is a measure of the age structure. Of course, it can be calculated separately for each sex or for both sexes combined.
9. A, B, C, and D: The Lorenz curve for the income distribution is obtained by plotting the "less-than" cumulative percentages of total income received against cumulative percentage of income recipients (the percentage of income recipients in the income class "less than \$Y" and the percentage of total income accruing to them). A point on the Lorenz curve gives the percentage of the income recipients that account for a given percentage of the total income. If $p$ % of income recipients account for $p$ % of the total income, for each value of $p$ (10% of income recipients accounting for 10% of the total income, 20% for 20% of the total income, and so on), then the Lorenz curve will be the line of "absolute equality" (a line bisecting the right angle between the positive side of the horizontal axis and the positive side of the vertical axis). The extent to which the "observed" Lorenz curve deviates from this line of absolute equality is a measure of income inequality. If income data are available for each individual recipient, then the Gini coefficient can be calculated using the following formula:

$$G = 1 = (1/n) - 2(y_1 + 2y_2 + \dots + ny_n)/(n^2 \cdot \text{mean } y)$$

where $y_1, \ldots, y_n$ represent individual incomes in decreasing order of size and $n$ is the number of individuals.

### 7.8.7. Answers

10. D: Asia has a sex ratio of about 104 males per 100 females. The corresponding figures for Africa, Latin America, and North America are 99.3, 99.5 and 95.7, respectively. The comparatively low sex ratio in Africa is due to a relatively low sex ratio at birth (about 103) and a high level of mortality. It is expected that in due course the sex ratio differences between regions will diminish. (See United Nations, 1990b.)

11. D: In the less-developed regions as well as the more-developed regions of the world the old age dependency ratio is expected to increase over the coming 25 years, about 50% in both regions. (See United Nations, 1990b, p. 48.)

12. A, B, and C: For the total population the Gini coefficient was 0.394 in 1970, 0.403 in 1980, and 0.428 in 1990. In both 1980 and 1990, the Gini coefficient was higher for blacks than for Hispanics and higher for Hispanics than for whites. As for choice C, note that changes such as an increase in the proportion of households that include broken families, the aging of the population, changing racial/ethnic composition of the population could affect income inequality. As for choice D, income inequality is present in all developed countries and has increased recently in many of them. (For U.S. data on income see U.S. Bureau of the Census, 1991b. For a brief discussion of income inequality, see Nam, 1994, p. 360).

13. A, B, C, and D: A classical study that came to these conclusions is that of Kuznets (1973). For a brief discussion of the points see Bogue (1969, pp. 401–402).

14. A, B, C, and D: The earlier age pattern of labor force participation of women had two humps, owing to the withdrawal from the labor force during peak childbearing periods. Fertility reduction and changes in attitude toward working when children are young have been responsible for virtually wiping out the reduction in participation rate during the peak period of childbearing. (See Shank, 1988; Nam, 1994, p. 357.)

### 7.8.8. Answers

15. B and D: The widespread preference of sons as first children is likely to result in a short-run rise in the sex ratio at birth. But the imbalance would eventually be controlled by a shift to the other side (Westoff and Rindfuss, 1974).

16. A, B, C, and D: Members of large cohorts are likely to face stiffer competition

at each stage in life, in contrast with members of relatively small cohorts. This leads to postponement of marriage, nonmarriage, delayed childbearing within marriage, slower socio-economic mobility, and higher suicide rates. (See Ahlburg and Schapiro, 1984.)

17. A, B, and C: The evidence to look for are the small cohort size representing the low fertility level that prevailed in the 1930s; the bulge representing the "baby boom" (1940s and 1950s); a constriction, representing the "baby bust" (late 1960s and 1970s). It should be possible to see in the slightly broader base of the pyramid indication of the small increase in the birth rate in the 1980s. To read such indicators, it would be convenient to use for the vertical axis the birth cohort identification rather than age ranges. The so-called "elderly boom" is expected to occur in the early part of the 21st century when the "baby boom" cohorts reach retirement ages (those born in 1946 reaching 65 years in 2011, and so on.)

18. A, B, C, and D: Survey data have shown, for example, that people with higher education tend to have lower fertility, those in lower socio-economic levels tend to have higher fertility, and those with larger family size find it more difficult than those with smaller families to rise in social status. Similarly, racial/ethnic/religious differences in fertility have been in existence in many countries and fertility differentials produce, other things remaining the same, growth rate differentials by racial/ethnic/religious and socio-economic categories. All such relationships are subject to change over time. Thus religious differentials in fertility have narrowed considerably in the United States. Race differentials in fertility are likely to vanish when the corresponding differentials by socio-economic status and rural/urban residence progressively diminish.

19. A, B, and C: Among high-school graduates, age 25–34 years in 1990, 29% of males and 27% of females were college graduates. The corresponding figures in 1970 were 26% for males and 17% for females. For the same age group in 1990, 85% of males and 87% of females were high school graduates. The corresponding figures for 1970 were 72% for males and 71% for females. (See U.S. Bureau of the Census, 1992.) As for choice D, note, for example, that the male–female gap in the median years of schooling completed has been rather small for all racial/ethnic groups. Thus the median school years completed, as of 1987, was 12.8 for men and 12.6 for women among whites, and 12.1 for men and 12.0 for women among Hispanics (U.S. Bureau of the Census, 1989).

20. A, B, C, and D: Education opens up many options in life. This tends to delay childbearing, increase the propensity to remain childless, and reduce family size. Children born to the better-educated women have a greater chance of survival. (See Weeks, 1994, pp. 265–266 and references cited therein.)

21. A and C: As for choice B, note that the argument has been that the secondary (manufacturing) sector's share rises at first with economic development and then declines. No one has specified a floor above which all of the three shares remain. In fact by 1970, the primary (agriculture) sector's share had gone below 5% in the United States and below 2% in the United Kingdom. In the latter, the primary (agriculture) sector's share was 13.4% in 1901 and it steadily declined to 1.4% by 1981; the secondary (manufacturing) sector's share was 45.4% in 1901, which increased to 53.9% by 1921 and then declined to 32.5% by 1981; and the tertiary (service) sector's share increased more or less steadily from 41.2% in 1901 to 66.1% by 1981. The corresponding patterns in the United States were: a steady decline in the primary (agriculture) sector's share from 44.2% in 1900 to 4.4% by 1980, a steady increase in the tertiary (service) sector's share from 31.5% in 1900 to 67.9% by 1980, and a fluctuating pattern for the secondary sector's share during the period. (See Liesner, 1985.)

22. A, B,C, and D: Fluctuations in fertility levels affect the size of cohorts entering and proceeding through the labor force ages. Improvement in mortality levels reduces the probability of exits from the labor force because of death. Changes in retirement age also affect the age pattern of exits from the labor force. Shifting family structure affects the orientation to enter the labor force. (See Brinkmann, 1987; Nam, 1994, p. 357.)

### *7.8.9. Answers*

1. E: The age-sex pyramid is not symmetrical. There are more infant boys than infant girls, but there are more older women than older men, in most developed countries. With declines in maternal mortality, the asymmetry at the top of the pyramid increases.

2. B: A stable population has a time-invariant age structure, growth rate, and age-schedules of fertility and mortality rates. Whether the dependency ratio is high is primarily determined by the fertility level.

3. B: Recall that ascribed characteristics are those on which the individual has no choice whereas achieved characteristics are those on which the individual is presumed to have a choice.

4. B: A social class is a category of people sharing similar economic positions or relatively similar amounts of property, income, or wealth, with resulting similarity in life-style. In a 1978 study Coleman and Rainwater found that in Boston and Kansas City, "money, far more than anything else, is what [people] associate with the idea of social class."

### 7.8.10. Answers

5. C: At older ages there are many more women than men, an imbalance that increases with age. The main reason for this pattern is the sex-differences in mortality—males having higher levels of mortality at all ages than females.

6. D: The male–female gap has been narrowing in respect to educational attainment. There is virtually no difference with respect to the probability of completing high school. There is still some male–female difference with respect to the probability of college attendance and of completing college education among high school graduates, but these differences have been narrowing.

7. C: In 1995 there were about 110 million males and 80 million females in the civilian labor force in the United States. Thus, women constituted about 42% of the civilian labor force.

8. D: The labor force participation rate for U.S. males in 1970 was 79.7% and the rate rather consistently declined to about 75% by 1995. For females the rate was 43.3% in 1970 and increased to about 60% by 1995. (See Statistical Abstracts of the United States, U.S. Bureau of the Census, various years).

9. D: In 1970 for elderly (65 years and older) females, the labor force participation rate was about 10% and the rate declined to about 6% by 1995; the corresponding figures for males were 27% and 12%. (See Statistical Abstract of the United States, U.S. Bureau of the Census, various years.)

### 7.8.11. Answers

10. E: Sex-selected abortion would affect the sex ratio at birth, which in turn would affect the overall sex ratio. The effect of sex-selectivity in migration would depend upon the volume of migration relative to the size of the population.

11. A: The sex ratio at birth is approximately 105 males to 100 females and starts to decline between 10 and 15 years in most countries as a result of sex selectivity in mortality.

12. C: The volume of migration has not been large enough to make a major impact on the age structure. In any case, given the usual age-selectivity of immigration, an increase in the volume of immigration makes the population younger, not older. The pattern of emigration from the United States had been, and continues to be, concentrated at the older ages, e.g., retirees returning to their country of origin. This also has the effect of making the population younger.

By 1970, maternal mortality had already declined to low levels and hence the changes in it since then were not dramatic enough to affect the overall age structure. As for choice E, the popular notion of stress making a person "older" (in appearance or in mental state) is not applicable to the population as a whole. The main reason for the aging of the U.S. population since the 1960s has been the significant decline in fertility. Recall that decline in fertility makes the base of the population pyramid narrower, implying fewer children per adult.

13. A: In general, the unemployment rate is highest for young people. It more or less steadily declines with age, as the following figures for U.S. males, 1987, illustrate: 17.8% for age 16–19 years; 9.9% for 20–24 years, 5.9% for 25–34 years, 4.4% for 35–64 years, and 2.5% for 65 years and older. When examining the age pattern of unemployment rate, remember that a person is considered as unemployed if and only if he or she has been looking for work and could not find any. Among the elderly, the low unemployment rate does not mean that most of them were employed; it simply means that those who were looking for work could find it. For data on the unemployment rate see, e.g., Statistical Abstract of the United States 1989, U.S. Bureau of the Census, Table 625, p. 379.

14. E: In fact the percent widowed is higher for females than for males at each age. For males the percent married reaches a peak during 45–64 years of age; for females it does so during 35–54 years of age. The percent divorced is maximum during 35–44 years for males and females. (See Statistical Abstract of the United States, U.S. Bureau of the Census, various years.)

15. D: In 1987, the mean household income was $43,796 for households with the householder in the age group 45–54 years. The corresponding figures for the other groups were: $19,504 for 15–24 years, $30,200 for 25–34 years, $39,529 for 35–44 years, $34,818 for 55–64 years, and $20,333 for 65 years and older. (See U.S. Bureau of the Census, 1989, Table 714, p. 442).

16. E: In fact the opposite of choice E occurred. At first thought, choices B and C may seem inconsistent, but reflection reveals that they are not. To make the point in terms of a simple example, suppose the initial income for white was $10,000 and that for blacks was $5,000. If the former were to increase 35% during a certain period, while the latter increased 40%, the income at the end of the period would be for whites $13,500 and for blacks $7,000. The gap between the two thus increased from $5,000 to $6,500. A relatively smaller increase for a larger base could add a relatively large absolute amount to the base. As for choices D and E, note that the Gini coefficient measuring income inequality increased from 0.422 to 0.464 over the period 1969–1989 for blacks

when the corresponding figure of whites increased from 0.387 to 0.419. The black–white gap in income inequality, as measured by the corresponding gap in the Gini coefficient, increased from 0.035 to 0.045 during the period.

17. E: The differential in mortality due to HIV infection has no marked effect on the black-white differences in the median family income.

# CHAPTER 8

# *Population Distribution*

A view from an airplane on a clear day tells us that human settlements are clustered. In modern societies, these clusters are called villages, towns, cities, suburbs, and so on. Charles H. Cooley (1930) held that population and wealth tend to collect at breaks or interruptions in transportation routes. "Both the integration of local activities and the inclusion of the local population in an interregional division of labor are favored by a site at a route intersection" (Hawley, 1950, p. 242). Transportation and communication technologies greatly influence the clustering patterns of human settlements. Also influential, especially in less complex societies, are physical factors such as landform, soils, precipitation, temperature, and natural resources.

## *8.1. UNITS OF ANALYSIS*

In demographic parlance, the term "population distribution" refers to the spatial or geographical distribution of a population, a topic studied using political or administrative areas or statistically defined areas as units of analysis. A hierarchy of political areas exists in most countries. In the United States, for example, the nation is divided into 50 states and the District of Columbia, and each state is divided into counties or county equivalents. Cities, towns, and villages are also political units used in the study of population distribution. In addition to such political units, various types of statistical areas have been defined in some countries. In the United States, examples include metropolitan area and urbanized area. The former consists of a county with large population (e.g., 50,000 or more) as the nucleus of the adjoining counties that are integrated economically and socially with the nucleus. An urbanized area consists of a city of 50,000 or more people and the densely settled territory surrounding it. All groupings mentioned so far are contiguous pieces of territory. Groupings that are not of this kind are also used in the study of population distribution. Examples are rural/urban, farm/nonfarm, and places (locality, town, metropolitan area, etc.) grouped by population size class.

## 8.2. CONCEPTS

An urban place is a spatial concentration of people engaged primarily in non-agricultural activities. Typically, however, an urban place is defined in terms of population size alone. All places with a population exceeding a fixed number (which varies from one country to another) are considered urban.

Urbanization is a process by which the proportion urban in a population, i.e., the fraction, urban population/total population, increases. Urbanization occurs as a result of natural increase, net rural-to-urban migration, net immigration to urban areas, annexation, and/or reclassification of places from rural to urban. The last occurs when a rural place exceeds the minimum-size criterion used to distinguish a rural place from an urban place.

Size of place refers to the population size of an urban place. The 1960 U.S. census, for example, used 15 size classes (under 200, 200–499, 500–999, 1,000–1,999, ..., 250,000–499,999, and 500,000 or more) to tabulate data by size of place.

A suburban community is an organized community outside the political boundaries of a city; usually it is residential in character, and culturally and economically dependent on the central city.

A primate city is a leading city overwhelmingly large in population size compared with all other cities in the country. Most primate cities were developed by European colonizers. Cities such as Saigon, Singapore, Nairobi, and Hanoi were created by colonial powers as bases from which to wield administrative and commercial control of the colonies. In general, the primate city of a country dominates the rest of the country economically, socially, and politically. The population of the largest city relative to that of a second largest city has been termed the primacy rate, most MDCs have low primacy rate. "Countries with high primacy rate tend to be characterized by a low percent urban, low income, and recent political or economic dependency on another country" (Thomlinson, 1976, p. 422).

Overurbanization refers to a premature concentration of population in cities—a higher proportion of a country's population residing in urban areas than is consistent with the country's level of economic development. Evidence of overurbanization can be found in the slums surrounding major cities.

Residential segregation refers to the tendency of the residential clusters of various racial and ethnic groups to be segregated (set apart) from each other in cities and metropolitan areas.

Succession refers to the tendency of an existing land use pattern in the cities to succumb to the invasion by another. The term is frequently applied to the racial changes taking place in central cities. It is also applied to the flow of limited number of affluent young whites to sections of central city in a state of decline to rehabilitate them. Another term for this latter type of succession is "gentrification." The "baby boom" generation has been disproportionately involved in this. A few neighborhoods in New York City, Chicago, Baltimore, and Washington, D.C., have been radically transformed through the process (Blum, 1982; Frey, 1990; Weeks, 1994, p. 364).

## 8.3. MEASURES

The density of population, usually computed as population per square kilometer or per square mile (1 square kilometer = 0.386103 square mile), is a frequently used measure in the study of population distribution. For some purposes, it is more meaningful to use population per unit land area. Another density measure sometimes used is population per square mile of agricultural land. For "city-states" such as Singapore and Hong Kong, this last measure is not of much relevance, most of their food supplies being imported.

Percentage distribution of population by political divisions (e.g., states) or statistical areas of a given class is a simple way of depicting the geographic distribution of the population. Sometimes geographic units of a given class (e.g., states) are arranged in rank order of population size.

The center of population of a territory is the point upon which the territory would balance if it were a rigid, weightless plane with the population distributed on it, all individuals assumed to be of equal weight and each assumed to exert an influence on the central point proportional to his or her distance from it. It is analogous to the concept of center of gravity.

## 8.4. DYNAMICS OF POPULATION DISTRIBUTION

Consider a division of a country into two regions, say, North and South. Suppose according to one census the population was distributed 40% in the North and 60% in the South. Suppose at a subsequent census the distribution was 60% in the North and 40% in the South. For a demographic accounting of this change, one examines the North–South differences in fertility, mortality, and net-international migration in the interim, and also looks at movements of people between the two regions during the period. Note that the population distribution may change because of the difference between the regions in any one of the components of change just mentioned, or it may be due to a combination of two or more components. For example, the change described above may be exclusively due to movement of people between the two regions, or it may have been brought about by the regional differences in mortality and fertility. The study of population distribution is not just a study of geographic mobility.

## 8.5. CURRENT PATTERNS; PAST AND FUTURE TRENDS

Population distribution can be discussed at different levels, e.g., global, national, or subnational. It can be discussed also in terms of residence, e.g., rural-urban; size of place. To illustrate this point, a few characteristic features of the population distribution at the global level are highlighted below, followed by a brief discussion of the spatial distribution of racial/ethnic groups within the United States. We will then turn our attention to urbanization.

### 8.5.1. A Global Picture

Approximately 90% of the people live on just 10% of earth's land area. Eighty percent of the total land area is located in the Northern Hemisphere, which houses 90% of the world's population. Two out of three people live within 500 kilometers of the sea and only one in five lives more than 500 meters above the sea level (see Clarke, 1972).

Europe and Asia are more densely settled than other continents. The following examples give an idea of the variation in population density (population per square mile) as of 1994: Bangladesh, 2320; Belgium, 863; Canada, 8; China, 331; Denmark, 319; Egypt, 153; Finland, 43; France, 273; Greece, 205; Hong Kong, 15,297; India, 794; Mexico, 125; New Zealand, 34; Singapore, 12,440; United States, 74 (Population Reference Bureau, 1994).

### 8.5.2. Distribution of Racial/Ethnic Groups in the United States

Turning to population distribution within a nation, consider the distribution of racial/ethnic groups within the United States. Slightly over half of all U.S. blacks live in the South and close to 60% live in central cities of metropolitan areas. U.S. Hispanics are primarily concentrated in the West, Southwest, New York, and Florida. Over half (56%) of U.S. Asians live in the West; 10% in New York, and 9% in Hawaii. Nearly half (48%) of American Indians live in the West (O'Hare, 1992).

Three out of every five Chinese Americans live in California or New York. Two-thirds of Filipino-Americans and Japanese-Americans live in California or Hawaii. Asian-Indian-Americans and Korean-Americans are somewhat less concentrated geographically (O'Hare, 1992).

Three-fourths of Mexican-Americans live in Texas or California; over two-thirds of Puerto Ricans are in the Northeast; about two-thirds of Cuban-Americans live in Florida. Some of the Hispanics in the Southwest are, of course, descendants of early Mexican and Spanish settlers in that region; but a majority are newcomers (O'Hare, 1992).

### 8.5.3. Urbanization

As mentioned, urbanization refers to the process that results in an increasing concentration of the population in urban areas. The history of cities is at least 5500 years long. Most of the ancient urban places were relatively small in population size. The development of settled agriculture was a necessary step in the urbanization process. Concomitant with the development of settled agriculture was the development of agricultural technology including wheeled cart, ox-drawn plow, art of metallurgy, and new irrigation techniques. Such developments directly or indirectly contributed to urbanization.

During the Middle Ages (AD 500 to 1500), thousands of new towns were formed. Whereas earlier cities were large, self-sufficient agricultural settlements, the medieval cities were economically specialized units dependent on other areas. The two-class system (a few aristocratic landlords and a huge lower class) characteristic of rural communities was not compatible with city life and urban occupations in the medieval times. As a consequence, an urban middle-class emerged (Thomlinson, 1976, p. 405). The total urban population fluctuated around 5% of the total population until about 1850 (Grauman, 1976).

In the modern era in the West, urbanization and industrialization have been proceeding hand in hand. Shifting industrial composition of the labor force and advances in transportation and communication technologies were concomitants of urbanization.

In the West, urbanization proceeded faster in countries that became industrialized later. "The change from a population with 10 percent of its members in cities of 100,000 or larger to one in which 30 percent lived in such cities took about 79 years in England and Wales, 66 years in the United States, 48 in Germany, 36 in Japan, and 26 in Australia" (Davis, 1965, p. 43).

In 1800, the United States was only 6% urbanized; in 1900 the corresponding figure was 40%; by the mid-1990s, the urban share of the total population had surpassed 75%. Urban centers were first located on the eastern seaboard and in the peripheral areas. During the 18th century more cities were formed on the eastern seaboard and also many were founded in the river valleys (e.g., Mississippi and Ohio River valleys). During the same period several cities were founded on the western seaboard. Urban growth in the United States (as in other developed countries) is now mostly a product of natural increase and immigration.

The world's major regions are at different stages of urbanization. As of 1994, the more-developed regions of the world were 74% urbanized whereas the less-developed regions were less than half as much urbanized (35%). Africa and Asia are the least urbanized (31 and and 32%, respectively); the level of urbanization in Latin America is 71%, that of Europe 73%, North America 75%, and Oceania 70% (see Population Reference Bureau, 1994).

Among the major features of urbanization and urban growth in the LDCs are the following: (i) the unemployment rate is high and slums grow in size and numbers in urban areas; (ii) the growth rate of urban population is nearly twice that of the population as a whole; (iii) by the year 2000, it is expected that the LDC urban population would be 39% of the LDC population and about two-thirds of the world's urban population; (iv) higher rates of natural increase within their urban areas are combining with large net migration to urban areas causing severe strains to the social and economic fabric of the LDC cities; (v) in the LDCs, "pull" from the urban areas, "push" from the rural areas, and the low level of "intervening obstacles" (particularly low transportation costs) promote urbanization; (vi) unlike the case in the MDCs when they were going through accelerated urbanization, migration to foreign countries is not a major option for LDCs populations; (vii) new LDC urbanites are predominantly unskilled laborers with very little educational attainments.

*8.5.3.1. Distribution within Urban Areas* Railroads and steam power did much to produce the 19th century American city. Since 1920, the automobile has permitted a form of population dispersal that was previously impossible. Technological change in transportation and communication has drastically reduced the attractiveness of the central city as a place of residence for the elite (Palen, 1987, pp. 180–181). The upper-class shifted to suburbs and the lower-class took their place in the central area (Schnore, 1965, pp. 373–374).

The metropolitan areas in the United States changed their shape drastically over time. Concentration was characteristic of population distribution in the United States in the 19th century and early 20th century. Since then urban deconcentration and dispersal have increasingly become the American pattern. As of the mid-1990s, the growth cities are service-based and the importance of propinquity has declined drastically (Palen, 1987, pp. 116–122).

Metropolitan versus nonmetropolitan growth differentials changed in the United States over time: (i) From 1900 to 1970, metropolitan areas gained population at a rate far in excess of the rate of nonmetropolitan areas; (ii) Within metropolitan areas, the population of the outer "suburban" areas grew faster than that of central city; (iii) During the 1970s, rural counties not only stopped declining, but increased in population; (iv) In the early 1980s there were signs that the pattern of the 1970s was reversed, but by the late 1980s, the pattern started to reverse again.

Black–white differentials in suburbanization changed over time in the United States. Since 1970, black suburbanization has been on the increase and blacks living in the central cities as a fraction of total black population has been declining.

"In the future, white suburbanization maybe at a less hectic pace. Most upper- and middle-class whites who want to move to suburbs have already done so" (Palen, 1987, p. 201).

The spatial segregation of blacks in cities in the United States has been associated with urbanization of blacks during the 20th century, the relatively higher rate of natural increase for urban blacks, and the relatively higher rates of suburbanization of whites (Weeks, 1994, pp. 365–366). Spatial segregation was still evident in 1990, 22 years after the passing of the Fair Housing Act of 1968 (Denton and Massey, 1991).

Black–white spatial segregation has been attributed to the use by whites of spatial segregation facilitated by suburbanization as a means of keeping social distance from blacks, as other ways (e.g., separate facilities) for doing so were all removed (Weeks, 1994, p. 366) and to the tendency for blacks to prefer to live in neighborhoods with a high proportion of blacks (Lieberson and Carter, 1982).

## 8.6. QUESTIONS AND ANSWERS*

**FOR EACH OF THE QUESTIONS IN SECTIONS 8.6.1. TO 8.6.4., STATE TRUE OR FALSE AND EXPLAIN.**

### 8.6.1. Concepts

1. Urbanization and urban growth are synonyms.
2. A large number of definitions of "urban population" are currently in use.
3. "Urbanization" and "urbanism" are interchangeable terms.
4. The so-called rural renaissance in the United States means a renaissance of the family farm and a return to agricultural pursuits.

### 8.6.2. Structure

5. Twentieth century metropolitan areas reflect dispersion rather than concentration.
6. The history of American city is a story of succession of one type of land use by another.
7. During the first half of the 20th century, the influence of the central city expanded in the United States.

*Answers start on page 220.

8. The population movement within metropolitan areas has always been inward, i.e., in the direction of the center.
9. Japan's urban residents live in congested living quarters.

### 8.6.3. Levels and Trends

10. More than two persons in five of the world's population live in urban places.
11. Urban population grows faster than the rural populations in most of the major regions.
12. The rural segment of a population tends to have higher fertility than the urban segment of the same population.
13. Seven of the ten largest urban agglomerations are located in the less-developed countries, as of the early 1990s.
14. By the turn of the 19th century, the world's population had already become 25% urban.
15. The urban America started with five communities.
16. The first U.S. population census showed that only 5% of the new nation's 4 million people lived in urban places.
17. A century after its founding, the United States had become almost 40% urban.
18. In the United States during the 1970s, rural counties not only stopped declining in population size, but actually increased.
19. The population net gains in the south since 1960 resulted from the abandoning of the industrial heartland by smokestack industries in favor of the low-wage, nonunion locations in the south.
20. Cities are doomed.

### 8.6.4. Determinants and Consequences

21. The creation of agriculture surplus was a necessary condition for the emergence of non-agricultural occupations.
22. Unhealthful conditions in early industrial cities meant that they were not able to increase their size, nor even maintain it, without in-migration from rural areas.
23. In the early American cities, the well-to-do tended to live in the suburbs and the poor in the central city.
24. Only one in seven of the national governments is satisfied with the prevailing patterns of population distribution.

**FOR EACH OF THE QUESTIONS IN SECTIONS 8.6.5. TO 8.6.8., FOUR ANSWERS ARE GIVEN, AT LEAST ONE OF WHICH IS CORRECT. IDENTIFY THE CORRECT ANSWER(S) AND EXPLAIN.**

### 8.6.5. *Concepts*

1. Examples of succession include:
   A. The transition within neighborhoods from single-family to multiple-family dwelling units
   B. Change from residential to commercial land use
   C. "Gentrification"
   D. Change of political party in power

### 8.6.6. *Levels and Trends*

2. Which of the following statements apply to the growing level of urbanization of the world's population?
   A. The more-developed regions have three-fourths of the population living in urban areas.
   B. In the less-developed regions the corresponding figure is less than two-fifths.
   C. By the year 2025, the level of urbanization in the less-developed areas is expected to reach the same level as the mid-1950 level of urbanization in the currently more-developed regions.
   D. Population in the larger urban agglomerations of the less-developed regions is expected to continue to grow at relatively high rates for some more time.

3. Which of the following statements apply to the number of large urban agglomerations of 15 million persons or more in the world and changes in that number over time?
   A. In 1970 there was only one such large urban agglomeration.
   B. In 1985 there were four.
   C. In the year 2000, there will be six.
   D. Two-thirds of the large urban agglomerations with more than 15 million persons, in the year 2000, are expected to be in just two less-developed countries.

4. Which of the following statements apply to Asian urbanization?
   A. Asia is urbanizing rapidly.
   B. There are extremely large individual cities in Asia, although overall level of urbanization is relatively low.
   C. Japan is by far the most urbanized of the large nations of Asia.
   D. India's large cities come close to the old "teeming masses of Asia" stereotype.

5. Which of the following statements apply to Singapore?
   A. Officially Singapore is 100% urban.
   B. It is the most densely crowded country as of the early 1990s.
   C. Singapore is transforming itself into an ultramodern urban area.
   D. Squatter settlements are common in Singapore too.

6. Which of the following statements apply to Japanese urbanization?
   A. Japan had large cities as early as the beginning of the 18th century.
   B. Before World War II, the poor lived outside the municipal boundaries.
   C. Middle-class and upper-class suburbanization has occurred heavily since World War II.
   D. Public housing is built for the middle-class rather than for the poor.

### 8.6.7. Determinants and Consequences

7. Which of the following statements apply to the relationship between population density and economic development?
   A. There is no clear relationship between the two variables.
   B. High agricultural density is usually a sign of underdevelopment.
   C. High density can be beneficial for a highly organized and industrial economy.
   D. The requirement of contemporary urban life and those of industrialization complement each other.

### 8.6.8. Policy

8. Among the strategies adopted by governments to influence population distribution (and migration) are:
   A. Slow primate city growth
   B. Relocate national capital city
   C. Establish new growth centers and/or towns
   D. Colonize sparsely occupied territory

❖ ❖ ❖ ❖

### 8.6.1. Answers

1. False. Urbanization refers to the increase during a given time interval in the proportion that urban population bears to the total population. Urban growth refers to the growth of the population residing in urban areas. If urban growth rate is the same as rural growth rate, the urban share of the total population will remain unaffected. For example, suppose initially the urban-rural split of a population was 40 million urban versus 60 million rural. A 10% growth rate

applied to these would result in 44 million in urban areas and 66 million in rural areas. The proportion urban remains unaffected (= 40% at both time points).

2. True. (See Macura, 1961; see also United Nations Secretariat, 1974). Only 250 persons are necessary to qualify an area as urban in Denmark, while 10,000 are needed in Greece. This is a major problem when making international comparisons. Also, some countries change definitions, thus creating problems for comparison over time. The results of cross-national comparative studies of urbanization, whether on a cross-sectional basis or time-series basis, should be viewed with caution.

3. False. Urbanization refers to the increase during a given time interval in the proportion that urban population bears to the total population. Urbanism, on the other hand, refers to the conditions of life associated with living in urban areas—conditions that affect the attitudes, values, mores, customs, and behaviors of people.

4. False. There is no evidence of such a change. Then what explains the so-called rural renaissance? Full explanations are not yet available, but several factors have been identified. There was some growth in rural manufacturing. For example, Nissan built its new Datsun plant in a semi-rural area in Tennessee. More important than rural manufacturing, however, was the expansion of service industry to rural areas: Two-thirds of non-metropolitan workers are employed in such industries, including those linked to recreation and retirement (see Palen, 1987, p. 122).

### 8.6.2. Answers

5. True. The telephone, the electric streetcar, and later the automobile made this possible. The electric streetcar was perfected in 1888. The replacement of horse-drawn car by the electric streetcar led to the rapid development of outer areas of the city and the proliferation of middle-class streetcar suburbs. The cities came to have a star-shaped configuration, a shape that prevailed until the era of the automobile.

6. True. As the cities have grown, areas that were once occupied by single-family houses have been converted into apartments or to some other (e.g., commercial or industrial) use. This is an example of the so-called succession. Today, the most talked-about instance of succession is found in the racial changes taking place in central-city residents. The inaccurate belief that the coming of blacks was the cause of the deterioration of a neighborhood persists. The real causes of the process are, however, age and condition of the housing and the incomes of residents, be they white or black (see Palen, 1987, p. 87).

7. True. Outlying towns, villages, and cross-roads markets found themselves part of an urban network. The local, independent bank became, or was replaced by, a branch of a large city bank; local papers were replaced by metropolitan dailies; and so on. Put differently, self-sufficiency gave way to interdependence and independent communities became satellite towns.

8. False. Throughout the 20th century in the United States, the population of outer "suburban" areas has grown faster than that of the central cities (Zimmer, 1975, cited in Palen, 1987, p. 111). This is referred to by the term "suburbanization." The automobile increased the commuting distance for people. After World War II, retail trade, service establishments, and manufacturing all increasingly moved to the suburbs. Trucks and the building of expressways in the 1950s, 1960s, and 1970s provided industries with alternatives to central-city locations. No longer was it necessary for the factory to be near the rail line. The inter-state highway system extended the trucks' long-haul advantage. And what the motor vehicle did for transportation, the telephone did for communication.

9. True. Seventy-seven percent of urban residents in Japan live in homes or apartments with less than 60 square yards of floor space (Palen, 1987, p. 373). Central-city housing in Tokyo is so expensive that most people commute between their offices in Tokyo and the city's satellite towns, where residence is cheaper. Standard of housing in Japan is not commensurate with Japan's wealth. Almost all residential units have color television, but many have no flush toilets (Hall, 1977; Palen, 1987, p. 373).

### 8.6.3. Answers

10. True. About 45% of the world's population live in urban areas. In the more-developed regions three out of four people are urban dwellers. The corresponding fraction in the less-developed regions is about one in three. By the year 2025, the world's population is likely to be 60% urban. The more-developed regions of today are expected to be by that date about 80% urban.

11. True. During 1970–1975, urban population of the more-developed regions grew at the average annual rate of 1.5%, while the total population grew at the rate of 0.9%. The corresponding figures for the less-developed regions were 3.8% and 2.4%, respectively. During 1990–1995, the corresponding rates were 0.8% versus 0.5% for the MDCs and 3.6% versus 2.1% for the LDCs. For Africa the 1990–1995 average annual growth rates were 5.0% for urban and 3.1% for the total. The corresponding figures for other major regions were: Latin America (2.7 versus 2.0%), North America (0.8 versus 0.7%), Asia (3.3

versus 1.8%), Europe (0.6 versus 0.2%), and Oceania (1.3 versus 1.3%). (See United Nations, *World Population Monitoring*, various years.)

12. True. It is important that the comparison is between the rural and urban segments of the SAME population. It is possible that the rural fertility in a country is lower than the urban fertility of another country. The total fertility rates around 1990 in Botswana (urban, 4.0 and rural, 5.3) and Uganda (urban, 5.6 and rural, 7.5) illustrate the point.

13. True. This is a dramatic change from the situation in 1950 when New York, London, Paris, Chicago, Moscow, and Los Angeles were in that class.

14. False. As of 1800, the world's population was over 90% rural (Hauser and Schnore, 1965).

15. True. The northernmost was Boston and the southernmost Charles Town (which became later Charleston of South Carolina). In between were Newport, New Amsterdam (which became New York in 1664) and Philadelphia. All were port cities except Philadelphia, which had access to the sea through Delaware River. Politically, economically, and socially these five towns dominated early colonial life.

16. True. But the urban population influenced government, finance, and society as a whole far out of proportion to its relative size.

17. True. By that time the proportion of employed persons engaged in agriculture had dropped below 50%. The last quarter of the 19th century was a period of economic expansion. Capital-intensive industrialism was transforming what was a rural country to an urban one. By the turn of the 20th century, 50 cities had entered the size class of 100,000 or more. Between 1790 and 1890, the total population grew from 4 million to 63 million, while the urban population grew from 0.2 million to 22 million.

18. True. This became known as the rural renaissance. To appreciate the significance of this development, note that historically, metropolitan areas in the United States have been growing faster than nonmetropolitan areas. The 20th century witnessed the massive population implosion, i.e., the gathering of people into urban concentrations. So the development in the 1970s mentioned above came as a surprise. In the early part of the 1980s, the pattern reverted to the historical one. But during the latter part of the 1980s, the pattern reversed again. Perhaps such frequent changes in patterns are to be expected in mature urban populations.

19. False. (See Perry and Watkins, 1977; Sawers and Tabb, 1984.) Rather than attracting smokestack industries, the sunbelt states have been attracting service and technological (e.g., real estate, tourism, electronic, aircraft) indus-

tries. There are those who see the industrial growth in the south as a transitory phenomenon (see Palen, 1987, pp. 131–132, and citation therein).

20. False. In any case, not true entirely. Note that during the 1970s it was fashionable to predict that large cities are doomed. This was followed within a few years by writers proclaiming that the crisis was over. Pessimists pointed to the weakening of the central business district (CBD) as a center of retail trade, the grave financial crisis—growing expenditures and declining tax base, heavy dependence on federal and state aid to balance the budget, and infrastructure deterioration (bursting water mains, collapsing streets, aging building, etc.). The optimists emphasized that the downtown continued to be a major white-collar employment center, the choice location for insurance firms, financial services, government, headquarters of many enterprises, improvement in the financial situation over time, and so on. What is likely to happen is that some cities will have a more difficult time than others. For example, Boston and Baltimore have undergone an urban renaissance. In some cities middle- and upper-income whites, and to a certain degree blacks too, are buying and restoring old homes and new houses. In some cities, structures used for commercial purposes, e.g., warehouses, are transformed into homes. This sort of urban regeneration has been funded by private sector.

### 8.6.4. Answers

21. True. It is generally believed that before urban places could emerge an agricultural revolution was necessary (see Palen, 1987, p. 23 and the references cited therein for contrary views). With some surplus, it was no longer necessary for everyone to be engaged in agriculture. In other words, specialization became possible under the circumstances. Archeological records indicate that the earliest public buildings were probably temples, indicating that specialized priests were the first to be released from direct subsistence production duties. Kingship and dynastic political regimes developed later.

22. True. Eighteenth century London was characteristically filthy, crowded and disease-ridden. When rural mortality was declining, urban mortality continued to be high, mainly because of poor sanitation. Cholera and other epidemics were common. Until the latter part of the 19th century, the city was in a sense "the graveyard" of country people.

23. False. In fact the opposite was the case. In an era of slow, uncomfortable, and inadequate transportation, the poor were out in the periphery and the wealthy near the city center.

24. True. A source of information on this score is the "Population Inquiry" that the United Nations conducts periodically. Returns to such inquiries indicate that

only 14% of governments of countries (out of about 170) considered their patterns of population distribution as satisfactory (United Nations, 1990, pp. 191–192).

### 8.6.5. Answers

1. A, B, and C. The term succession in the literature on urbanization refers to changing land use. Hence choice D does not apply. "Gentrification" refers to the in-migration of affluent younger people, mostly whites, to older neighborhoods in a state of decline. Instances of choices A and B can be seen in residential areas abutting colleges and universities.

### 8.6.6. Answers

2. A, B, C, and D. The 1994 level of urbanization in the more-developed regions was 74%, and in the less-developed regions 35%. The United Nations's projections indicate that by the year 2025, the level of urbanization in the currently less-developed regions is expected to reach 57%, which was the mid-1950s level of urbanization in the currently more-developed regions. With respect to choice D note, however, that the rate of growth of the large agglomerations in the less-developed countries is expected to slow down somewhat because of the decelerating growth rates of the total population and the diminishing rate of urbanization. The number of large urban agglomerations with more than 5 million people is nonetheless expected to increase for some more time.
3. A, B, C, and D. In 1970 New York was the only large urban agglomeration with a population size of 15 million or more. In 1985 three others joined New York: Mexico City, São Paulo, and Tokyo/Yokohama. Calcutta and Great Bombay are expected to join the group before the year 2000.
4. A, B, C, and D. Tokyo/Yokohama urban agglomeration is expected to have a population of over 21 million by the year 2000, almost a 50% increase from the size as of 1970. Shanghai, China, is expected to have a population size of 14.7 million by the year 2000, up from 11.4 million in 1970 and 12.1 million in 1985. Both Calcutta and Great Bombay are expected to join the 15 million plus group by the year 2000.
5. A and C. Although officially Singapore is 100% urban, there are some semirural areas on the island. Hong Kong is more densely settled than Singapore (15,297 versus 12,440 persons per square mile in 1994). Since independence in 1965, the government of Singapore has been involved in an ambitious program to replace the island's previous housing with high-rise apartment buildings. Slums and squatter settlements have been eradicated. More residents own than rent apartments.

6. A, B, and C. Japan's urban history goes back at least to the 15th century (Palen, 1987, p. 369). At the beginning of the 18th century, Edo, as Tokyo was then called, was already in the one million plus class. At that time, Osaka and Kyoto (the ancient capital) both had several hundred thousands inhabitants. Suburbanization became significant in Japan in the early 1920s, especially after the massive earthquake of 1923, which encouraged decentralization. The poor, because they could not afford the high housing costs in the city, had little choice but to live outside the city limits. After World War II, high land costs drove many middle-class and upper-class people also to suburbs. The Japan Housing Corporation and the Metropolitan Housing Supply Corporation build public housing. Those built by the former go primarily to the middle-class, because the poor cannot afford the high rent charged; the latter builds low-rent public housing (Palen, 1987, p. 375).

### 8.6.7. Answers

7. A, B, C, and D. High population density in rural labor, particularly in agriculture, usually is a sign of underemployment and underemployment. In countries where the primary sector accounts for 70% or more of the total labor force, high population density usually means very low average land holdings. Outmigration from the rural areas under such circumstances is to be expected. In industrialized regions, on the other hand, high density is likely to be less problematic and in many instances even beneficial. The Netherlands, the Rhine River urban complex in Germany, and Hong Kong are examples of areas where high population density seems to have helped, rather than hindered, rise in per capita income. Population concentration in the industrialized setting provides economies of scale and other advantages. It also brings problems such as a high crime rate.

### 8.6.8. Answers

8. A, B, C, and D. (See United Nations, 1990, pp. 195–196). Nigeria in West Africa and Argentina, in Latin America, are just two examples of countries considering moving their national capitals to new locations with a view to influencing population distribution. The government of Colombia is considering policies aimed at promoting medium-sized urban centers. Indonesia, Malaysia, Thailand, Vietnam, and Sri Lanka all have, or have had, land colonization schemes.

CHAPTER 9

# *Family and Household*

The centrality of the familial institution in pre-industrial societies is taken for granted by demographers, and the variation in kinship structure has often been suggested as a key to explaining the variation in natural fertility between and within pre-industrial populations (Freedman, 1961/62, p. 50). Particular attention has been given to the influence of kinship structure on the proximate (intermediate) variables.

An often-noted general proposition is that the more inclusive the kinship structure the higher the fertility level (Lorimer, 1954). In increasing order of fertility level are the nuclear family system, the joint family system (consisting of two or more nuclear units), and the corporate system involving an immortal clan.

It has been noted that young people are judged ready to get married early in life under the extended family system (a nuclear unit plus other relatives) and that they can expect support in terms of time and resources from the extended family. Under the circumstances there is little to prevent young people from marrying early and starting reproduction as soon as possible (Petersen, 1975, p. 202). The evidence for the proposition that nuclear family system leads to lower fertility in preindustrial societies comes mainly from pre-industrial Europe, where the relationship has been linked to economic arrangements such as inheritance rules (e.g., primogeniture) that promoted late marriage or non-marriage (Freedman, 1961/62, p. 50). Empirical studies of fertility comparing women in different family-living arrangements in contemporary societies, however, have not produced consistent findings (Freedman, 1961/62, pp. 50–51).

Turning to the intermediate variables, in theory it seems reasonable to speculate that young people living in extended families are likely to adhere more strictly to traditional practices regarding sexual abstinence, thereby causing fertility to remain lower than it would be otherwise. Petersen (1975, p. 204), for example, estimated that if all the traditional rules are observed in China, only about a hundred days per year are recommended for intercourse.

The role of extended family members and their dominance on the younger generation in the household may, of course, change with modernization. "Traditionally, the young bride ... did the hard housework and cooking, and had a subordinate position in the household for many years. Now she is likely to be well educated and to work outside the household, while her mother-in-law does much of the child care and housework" (Freedman, 1995).

In all societies, the family is heavily involved in the socialization of the young. The family is also a major source of economic and emotional support for its members. To elaborate this latter point, note that those of us who work in a factory, school, office, or the like, go home at the end of work and get "recharged," as it were, through rest, relaxation, and refueling for another day's work. It is at home where we make things for our exclusive consumption, to borrow an idea from the "new home economics." An example is physical and mental well-being, which each of us produce at home using our own time and other goods and services, some of which, such as jogging outfit or physician's services are bought in the market. Of course, not all forms of family/households are equally suitable for the production of various consumption items, e.g., children (again borrowing an idea from the "new home economics"). How many different forms of families and households are there? What are their distinguishing characteristics?

## 9.1. CONCEPTS

The standard demographic definition of a family is "two or more persons related by birth, marriage, or adoption, who live together." Notice the emphasis on (i) two or more persons, (ii) relationship by birth, marriage, or adoption, and (iii) co-residence, i.e., sharing common housing. This definition excludes non-resident kin, irrespective of the frequency of interaction with them and their proximity.

A household consists of one or more persons occupying a housing unit, i.e., living quarters with separate entrance and cooking facilities. Two types of households are commonly distinguished: family and non-family, the latter standing for a man or woman living alone or with persons unrelated by birth, marriage, or adoption.

In modern times, families are typically formed when two persons get married and establish a separate residence. Single-parent families consisting of a man or woman with one or more children, their own or adopted, are formed, for example, when a woman living alone bears or adopts a child, or when the death of a spouse transforms a two-parent family with children into a one-parent family. A family dissolves when loss of membership due to death, divorce, or geographic mobility, transforms it into a non-family unit. Households are formed when one or more persons (relatives or non-relatives) establish a common residence. A household dissolves when the last resident dies or moves on. There are those who consider that these definitions are all arbitrary (see Burch, 1979 for a discussion.)

The term "cohabitation" is applied to the living together of persons of opposite sex without going through marriage rites, religious or civil. Cohabiting couples with coresident children, own or adopted, form a family; it is similar in structure to a single-parent family living together with a non-relative. In some instances, cohabitation may be a prelude to marriage; in others it may not be.

## 9.2. TYPES OF HOUSEHOLDS

In many MDCs, among households, the so-called family households have become less common, and among family households, those of married-couple have become less common while those headed by single females have become more common. In the United States, for example, family-households accounted for 81% of all households in 1970, but only 71% in 1990; married-couple families accounted for 87% of all family households in 1970, but only 79% in 1990; female-headed households (without spouse present) accounted for only 10.7% of all family households in 1970, but 16.5 percent in 1990 (U.S. Bureau of the Census, 1990).

A systematic way of defining types of households is to start with a list of elementary households, which when combined in various ways generate the wide variety of households one finds in reality (Namboodiri, 1994, p. 240). Four elementary types of households invite consideration in this connection: (1) individual person without any dependents; (2) individual person with one or more dependents; (3) couple without any dependents; (4) couple with one or more dependents. Here a dependent person is one who is incapable of forming a household by himself or herself (e.g., infants and people with severe mental or physical disability). The term couple is to be understood broadly, so as to include married couple as well as cohabiting homosexual and heterosexual pairs. Of course, one could think of subtypes for type 3 and type 4 elementary households mentioned above, with a view to distinguishing between married couples, cohabiting heterosexual pairs, and cohabiting homosexual pairs. In terms of the given simple typology, two college students sharing an apartment is a combination of two type 1 elementary households, an elderly woman living with her son and daughter-in-law, with no dependents, is a combination of type 1 and type 3 elementary households.

## 9.3. TEENAGE CHILDBEARING

Teenage parenting has been a topic of serious discussion in many MDCs, partly because teen parents and their children are very likely to be socially and economically disadvantaged (Ahlburg and De Vita, 1992, pp. 19–20) for reasons such as the following: (i) Teenage mothers foreclose many opportunities to improve their lot in life. (ii) They do not get exposed to the influences that potentially shape the tastes and preferences for extrafamilial activities, economic independence, and upward mobility. (iii) They tend to have high fertility and become trapped in the welfare morass (Weeks, 1994, p. 310). Of course, a very important conditioning factor in all this is the support the teenage mother receives from others, especially from her own family.

Throughout the 1970s and early 1980s, the number of births as well as the birth rates to U.S. women of age below 20 years fell steadily, but then the trend was reversed. Many MDCs experienced similar scenarios. But teenage birth rate has been higher in the United States than in many other MDCs.

## 9.4. UNMARRIED MOTHERHOOD

Unwed motherhood also has a bearing on the future of the women and the children involved. Between 1970 and 1991 the proportion of live births to unmarried U.S. mothers increased nearly threefold, to 30%. About 50% of all births to never-married mothers are to women less than 25 years of age. Some women deliberately choose to have children outside wedlock; but a majority of the out-of-wedlock births are unintentional (Ahlburg and De Vita, 1992, p. 23).

## 9.5. MARRIAGE AND COHABITATION

For the first half of the 20th century the median age at first marriage fell for both males and females in the United States, reaching a low by about the late 1950s, and then reversed direction. At the turn of the century, the median age at marriage was 26 years for males and 22 years for females. By the mid 1950s, these medians had declined to 22.6 and 20.2, respectively. In 1991 the corresponding figures were 26.3 and 24.1, respectively (see U.S. Bureau of the Census, 1991c).

The tendency to delay marriage can be explained in terms of the opportunities for women to be economically independent, the availability of acceptable alternatives to marriage and childbearing, men's reluctance to make long-term marital and parental commitments, and the permissibility of sexual relations outside marriage (Weeks, 1994, pp. 313–314).

It should be emphasized that a rise in age at marriage does not necessarily mean that people wait longer to start being sexually active. The post-World War II birth cohorts in the United States and Europe, unlike their predecessors, had been increasingly turning to cohabitation before marriage. Data from the 1987–1988 U.S. National Survey of Families and Households showed that almost 50% of the persons in their early thirties had cohabited for some time, and that cohabitation rates are negatively associated with socioeconomic status (Bumpass and Sweet, 1989). Cohabitation has been typically viewed as an alternative or a prelude to marriage. But Rindfuss and Vanden Heuvel (1990) have suggested, based on their analysis of data from the National Longitudinal Study of the High School Class of 1972, that cohabitors tend to be more like single persons than like married persons and on that ground they recommend viewing cohabitation as an alternative to being single.

## 9.6. DIVORCES AND REMARRIAGES

Dissolving a marriage by divorce has become quite common in the more-developed countries. In the United States divorce rates remained relatively low and stable throughout the 1950s and 1960s and then began to rise. Among white and Hispanic women of age 15–44 years in 1988, over a third had experienced the dissolution of their first marriage; the corresponding figure for blacks was nearly one-half (Ahlburg and De Vita, 1992, p. 14; London, 1991). *U.S. Statistical Abstracts*, 1991, shows divorce rates for many MDCs. In Canada, France, Japan, Sweden, and U.K., to give a few examples, divorce rates (divorces per 1000 married women) have been increasing since the 1960s. But the rates are, and always have been, higher in the United States than in other MDCs.

Most Americans who divorce remarry; for those who do, the average length of time between divorce and remarriage is relatively brief, although it changes over time. (In 1988 the median length of time between divorce and remarriage was 2.5 years for women and 2.3 years for men. In 1970 the corresponding figures were closer to one year). Remarriage rates are lower for Hispanics than for whites and lower for blacks than for Hispanics. For women remarriage rates vary with age and the presence of children. Younger women remarry sooner after divorce than older women do. The presence of children lowers the probability of remarriage for women (Ahlburg and De Vita, 1992, p. 17).

## 9.7. FUTURE OF THE FAMILY

There was a time when family sociologists believed that societies all over the world are converging on a single family type—the nuclear family. Today the consensus is that the diversity of family living arrangements that has emerged over the recent decades is here to stay (Weeks, 1994, pp. 317–318; Ahlburg and De Vita, 1992, pp. 38–39). The composition of families with children (in terms of whether intact-nuclear, single-parent, blended, or multigenerational) might shift over time. The current speculation is that future shifts in family structure would not be as dramatic as they have been in the fourth quarter of the twentieth century.

## 9.8. QUESTIONS AND ANSWERS*

**FOR EACH OF THE QUESTIONS IN SECTIONS 9.8.1. TO 9.8.5., STATE TRUE OR FALSE AND EXPLAIN**

### 9.8.1. Concepts

1. One person living alone in a house does not form a family unit.
2. A household may have one or more members.
3. Dissolution of a marriage may or may not necessarily mean the dissolution of the family unit.
4. All families are households, but all households are not families.

### 9.8.2. Levels and Trends

5. People in less-developed countries tend to have early marriages.
6. If family units can be classified into married couple without children, married couple with children, single parent-family with children headed by a female, single-parent family with children headed by a male, and other families, then the first two categories together form the majority of family units.
7. If married-couple families are classified into biological families and blended families (those with stepchildren or adopted children), then those in the first category form the vast majority.
8. Single parent families have become more common in the United States over time.
9. Interracial marriages have become more common in the United States over time.
10. The median age at marriage was lower in the United States in the 19th century and increased steadily during the 20th century.
11. There has been a long-term trend to later age at marriage for females across Asia.
12. The incidence of marital dissolution by separation or divorce has increased markedly over time in the United States.
13. An increasing proportion of teenage women are sexually active in the United States.
14. The level of teenage childbearing in the United States at present is much higher than those of many European countries.

*Answers start on page 238.

### 9.8.3. Women's Status: Differentials, Determinants, and Consequences

15. Labor force participation rate among mothers of pre-school children has been increasing in the United States.
16. Women's labor force participation rate is positively associated with the demand for service workers.
17. Parenthood tends to reduce the extent of maternal employment and increase the extent of paternal employment.
18. "Today's father is at least as adept at changing diapers as changing tires."
19. In all less-developed societies, both men and women will benefit equally from economic growth.
20. Women are the main bread-winners in a large fraction of households in the less-developed countries.
21. In almost all countries among the poor, household resources are distributed without regard to male–female distinction.

### 9.8.4. Family Type: Differentials, Determinants, and Consequences

22. Family types and the social structure associated with each exert a significant influence on the level of fertility of the population involved.
23. Teenage childbearing in the United States is primarily confined to minority groups.

### 9.8.5. Policy

24. Some governments have enacted legislation to provide equal opportunities for women and men and to protect women from discrimination.

**FOR EACH OF THE QUESTIONS IN SECTIONS 9.8.6. to 9.8.7., FOUR ANSWERS ARE GIVEN, AT LEAST ONE OF WHICH IS CORRECT. IDENTIFY THE CORRECT ANSWER(S) AND EXPLAIN.**

### 9.8.6. Family Structure: Differentials, Determinants, and Consequences

1. The explanations for the dramatic changes in the U.S. marriage patterns include:
   A. Change in social norms concerning marriage and childbearing

B. Change in attitude toward cohabitation
C. Marriage squeeze
D. The trends in women's and men's wages in the 1970s and 1980s

2. Among the explanations for the high divorce rates in contemporary MDCs are:
   A. The replacement of the "provider-husband, homemaker-wife" model with the two-earner couple model
   B. The breaking down of the traditional husband dominance structure within the family
   C. Increasing centrality given to emotional gratification within marriage
   D. Increasing emphasis on "successful" marriage

3. When one tries to explain why teenage childbearing is higher in the United States than in many of the European countries one must give due attention to the differences between the United States and the European countries in the social context of marriage. But focusing primarily on knowledge and practice of contraception, the explanations might include which of the following?
   A. Non-use of family planning clinics
   B. Non-use of contraception
   C. Lower use of effective contraception
   D. Greater non-availability of contraceptives in the United States than in many of the European countries.

### *9.8.7. Women's Status: Differentials, Determinants, and Consequences*

4. Which of the following statements apply to women's status or factors affecting it?
   A. Women tend to have lower status and lower salary levels than men in the formal work force
   B. In many developing countries a large proportion of women work in the informal sector of the economy
   C. Female-headed households have been increasing their share of all households
   D. Women are under-represented in national governments

5. The relatively high sex ratio in India has been attributed to:
   A. Discrimination against females
   B. Underenumeration of females in the censuses
   C. Relatively higher female infant and adult mortality
   D. An intrinsic physiological feature of Indians

6. Which of the following statements apply to women's contribution to the economy and society?
   A. With few exceptions, women work, on average, longer hours than men

B. Women throughout the world have been almost exclusively responsible for child care and housework
C. In subsistence economies, women usually contribute as much as, or more than, men to family welfare
D. A substantial part of women's work in less-developed countries is in nonwage economy

7. Why is there a male-female gap in wages and salaries? Because of:
A. Job segregation
B. Male-female differences in average years of job experience
C. "Comparable worth" discrimination
D. Lack of relevant laws aimed at improving women's status.

8. Between 1950 and 1991, female labor force participation increased from 34% to 57% in the United States. What factors caused this increase?
A. Economic necessity among the increasing number of female-headed households
B. Economic necessity prompting a number of wives to join the labor force
C. Greater demand in jobs that had been sex-typed as female
D. The upward shift in the wage rate available for women

9. What is the nature of the relationship between labor force participation of the women and fertility?
A. The relationship runs in both directions
B. The more of one, the less of the other
C. Opportunity costs play a significant part in the relationship
D. Quality/quantity trade-off plays a part

**FOR EACH OF THE QUESTIONS IN SECTIONS 9.5.8. TO 9.5.10. FIVE ANSWERS ARE GIVEN, ONLY ONE OF WHICH IS CORRECT. IDENTIFY THE CORRECT ANSWER AND EXPLAIN.**

### *9.8.8. Family and Household Types*

1. Divorce can generate a variety of households. Which of the following are possible?
A. The family becomes a non-family household
B. The family splits into two non-family households
C. The family splits into two units, one of which is a family household while the other is not
D. Each member becomes a member of a relative's family.
E. All of the above

2. In the United States, the prevalence of female-headed households (measured by that type of households as a fraction of all households):
   A. Has been a topic of public debate
   B. Differs significantly among racial/ethnic groups
   C. Was higher among African-Americans in 1970 than among whites or Hispanics in the early 1990s
   D. Is higher in the early 1990s among African-Americans than among whites and Hispanics
   E. All of the above

3. The nuclear family (husband, wife, and unmarried children) has been:
   A. The predominant family form since the Agricultural Revolution
   B. Is the most viable family form under high mortality conditions
   C. Is the family form of the future
   D. All of the above
   E. None of the above

4. A non-family household is transformed into a family household when:
   A. A woman living alone gives birth to a child and decides to keep it
   B. A woman living alone adopts a child
   C. A cohabiting couple adopt a child
   D. A cohabiting couple undergo formal marriage rites
   E. All of the above

### 9.8.9. Status of Women: Determinants and Consequences

5. The status of women is of special interest in demography because it affects, among other things:
   A. Fertility
   B. Mortality
   C. Morbidity
   D. Social and geographic mobility
   E. All of the above

6. In urbanized-industrialized countries, women who work outside the home, compared to their counterparts who do not work, tend to have:
   A. Lower fertility
   B. Higher mortality
   C. Lower status
   D. Smarter children
   E. Healthier children

7. Regarding the underlying causes of women's status, it is known:
   A. That in South Korea, despite rapid economic development, son preference

persists, illustrating that economic development by itself does not eliminate all signs of lower status for women
B. That in Sri Lanka, women's status relative to men is higher than that of their counterparts in other south Asian countries, illustrating that economic development is not a necessary condition for improvement in women's status
C. In general, the sociocultural traditions of a country tend to exert enduring influence on women's status in that country
D. That economic development improves women's status in certain, though not in all, respects
E. All of the above

### 9.5.10. *Marriage and Sexual Unions*

8. What factors led to the disconnecting of marriage and sexual intercourse?
   A. The invention of effective devices of contraception
   B. Legalization of abortion
   C. Permissive society
   D. All of the above
   E. None of the above

9. Cohabitation:
   A. Has increased in frequency in the United States and Europe
   B. Has in the United States been higher in its prevalence rate among the college educated than among those with less than a high school education
   C. Has shown a negative association in prevalence with education attainment in all European countries
   D. Has been a contributory cause of a substantial decline in the proportion of Americans, in all socio-economic classes, who ever marry
   E. As a prelude to marriage has the effect of reducing the probability of the marriage ending in divorce

10. Remarriage rate has fallen in the United States because of:
   A. The growing acceptance of cohabitation
   B. The increased prevalence of non-marital sexual relations
   C. Legal and social acceptance of single-parent families
   D. Economic viability of female-headed households
   E. All of the above

11. The marriage-divorce-remarriage patterns in the United States during the 1970s and 1980s have shown that:
   A. The probability of ever getting married for those surviving to age 15 years decreased somewhat

B. The average age at first marriage increased
C. The probability of remarriage for a divorcee decreased
D. The average duration of first marriage decreased
E. All of the above

❖ ❖ ❖ ❖

### 9.8.1. Answers

1. True. Recall the standard demographic definition of a family: "two or more persons related by birth, marriage, or adoption and residing together."

2. True. Recall that the standard demographic definition of a household includes one-person households as well as multi-person households (two or more persons residing together in a housing unit). Units in residential hotels are, but occupied dormitory rooms and prison cells are not, housing units.

3. True. A married-couple family unit with their own or adopted children remains a family unit upon the death of a spouse. After the event it becomes a single-parent family unit.

4. True, under the definitions used by the U.S. Census Bureau. The growth of non-family households (persons living alone or with unrelated individuals) has been one of the dramatic developments in many MDCs during the post-1960 period. In the United States, such households formed 30% of all households in 1991, a doubling of the corresponding figure (15%) in 1960.

### 9.8.2. Answers

5. True. This is usually explained in part by the history of high mortality. To match high mortality with high fertility, it is highly desirable to start the reproductive period as early as possible. One could stretch the same argument as an explanation of infant betrothal. When fertility decline starts, one finds in most societies age at marriage rising. Concomitant changes such as increasing education of women are also observed. Structural conditions that promote late marriage include limiting land inheritance to a single heir.

6. True. In the United States, for example, these two forms of families accounted for 87% of all families in 1970 and are likely to account for 77% of all families in the year 2000.

7. True. In the United States in 1985, 77% of married couple families were biological families and about one-fifth had stepchildren.

8. True. In the early 1990s in the United States, about one in eight of all family units was a single-parent family, double the corresponding figure (6.4%) in 1970. Five out of six single-parent families were headed by women. (Ahlburg and De Vita, 1992, p. 7).

9. True. About 2% of all married couples in 1991 were inter-racial, double the figure as of 1970 (Ahlburg and De Vita, 1992, p. 13, citing figures from a U.S. Census Bureau publication).

10. False. In fact, the median age at marriage for women declined from about 22 years in 1890 to about 20 years by the post World War II years and remained low for a while, following which it began to increase rather steadily (since the early 1960s) (see U.S. Bureau of the Census, 1975, p. 19).

11. True. (See Xenos and Gultiano, 1992). To give some examples, the mean age at marriage was about 13 years in 1891 in India; it rose to about 18 years by 1980. In Sri Lanka, it was about 18 years at the turn of the 20th century, by 1981 it had increased to 24.4 years. In Singapore it increased during the period 1957–1980 from 20 to 26 years; in Thailand during 1947–1980 from 20.6 to 22.8 years; and in Malaysia during 1947–1980 from 18.5 to 23.5 years. In Japan, it increased during 1920–1985 from 21 to 25.7 years, rather steadily, except for a minor decline and reversal thereof during 1960–1975. In Taiwan it increased from 19.1 to 24.7 years during 1915–1985. In China it increased from 19.1 to 22.8 years during 1955–1980, and then declined, reaching 22.0 years by 1987.

12. True. (See, e.g., Espenshade 1987). For the 1905–1909 birth cohort of white females the rate of dissolution of marriage by separation or divorce was 12%. The corresponding figure was 47% for the 1940–1944 birth cohort. For black females the figure for the 1905–1909 birth cohort was 27% and for the 1940–1944 birth cohort it was 63%. Note that the incidence of marital dissolution can be measured either using a period perspective or a cohort perspective. A commonly used period measure is the number of dissolutions per 1000 existing marriages. In terms of such a measure too, it can be seen that the rate of marital dissolution due to separation or divorce has been increasing in the United States (Weeks, 1994, p. 278).

13. True. One-quarter of 15-year-old women and one-half of 17-year-old women were sexually active in 1988, a 40–50% increase from the corresponding figures for 1980, according to estimates prepared from the National Survey of Family Growth (Ahlburg and De Vita, 1992, p. 19).

14. True. The U.S. rate is about five times those of many European countries. In 1989 the age-specific fertility rates for the age group 15–19 years was 58 per

1000 women, the corresponding figures for some of the European countries being 9 for Denmark and France, 6 for the Netherlands, 11 for the former West Germany, and 32 for the United Kingdom. Interestingly, the rates systematically dropped since 1970 in the European countries mentioned while in the United States, it declined until the mid-1980s and then reversed itself. See Ahlburg and De Vita (1992, p. 20).

### 9.8.3. Answers

15. True. In 1960 only one in five mothers of pre-school children worked outside home. In 1991 the corresponding figure was 58% (Ahlburg and De Vita, 1992, p. 25, citing Bureau of Labor Statistics sources.)

16. True. The growth of the service sector is considered to be a major factor that has increased the demand for women's labor force participation, because "female occupations" constitute a high proportion of the service sector. The relationship runs in the other way too: (i) The decline in full-time homemaking has contributed to an increase in the demand for homemaking services, (ii) increase in daytime labor force participation has increased the demand for non-daytime services, (iii) increased family income of dual-earner couples has increased demand for recreation and entertainment during evenings, nights, and weekends (Presser, 1989, p. 525).

17. True. Mothers with children under age 14 years living at home are working fewer hours and fewer days than other women, whereas fathers with children under 14 years of age living at home are working more hours and slightly more days than other men (Presser, 1989, p. 525).

18. True, in the sense that fathers are becoming increasingly involved in child-care activities. The quotation is from Furstenberg (1988). According to one estimate, in the United States the father is the primary child-care provider in 15% of families with children under 5 years of age whose mothers are employed; grandparents and other relatives provide primary child care in 25% of such families (O'Connel and Bachu, 1990).

19. False. As economic growth takes place, initially at least, the existing male-female inequality in income, wealth, and access to resources persists and often gets worse (United Nations, 1991d).

20. True, in the sense that many women do have earnings and they contribute a larger fraction of their earnings to family expenses than their male counterparts do. (See Jacobson, 1993, p. 64.)

21. False. In many cultures men and boys fare far better than women and girls.

### 9.8.4. Answers

22. True, theoretically speaking. Thus it has been argued that fertility is likely to be higher for couples living in extended family setting than for those who live in nuclear family setting. One would expect that in the extended family setting the median age at marriage would be lower and fertility higher. But empirical findings have not been altogether consistent with this theory. For example, in two Indian studies (Pakrasi and Malakar, 1967), the family size was smaller in extended than in nuclear families, though the difference was not statistically significant. Whether the pattern expected on theoretical grounds once prevailed, but was reversed as a result of modernization, is not clear. There are scholars who argue that under the extended family setting, traditionally, even though age at marriage was low, rules regarding sleeping arrangements, abstention, and the like would have kept natural fertility relatively low and that these rules became ineffective over time with a consequent rise in natural fertility. Again hard empirical evidence to shed light on such hypotheses is scanty.

    Another type of family structure worth noting in this connection is one in which the entire property goes to a single heir, whose brothers and sisters either move away or remain unmarried. This pattern was aimed at preventing the partition and repartition of family plots. The typical family unit under this system consisted of a farmer, his wife and minor children, his unmarried brothers and sisters, and probably his father and/or mother. Almost all farmhands were family members. For the farmer mentioned above, his marriage was timed according to when he inherited the property. For others there was no social pressure at all to marry (see Petersen, 1975, p. 415). In the population group with this system as a predominant pattern, fertility must have been low because many members remained unmarried.

23. False. Black teenagers tend to be at greater risk of teenage parenthood: The age-specific fertility rate for ages under 20 years was 115 per 1000 women for blacks and 47 for whites, and 58 for Hispanics.

### 9.8.5. Answers

24. True. In Brazil, for example, as a result of pressure from women's groups, their rights have been incorporated into the national constitution (Ashford, 1995, p. 19, citing U.N. sources). On September 30, 1983, the Minneapolis City Council unanimously declared its intention to develop a new comparable worth wage policy in response to labor and feminist pressures for wage justice in public employment. In April 1984, the state of Minnesota passed a law

requiring all political subdivisions within the state to adopt a similar policy (see Evans and Nelson, 1989). By August 1987, 20 states and 166 localities outside Minnesota had implemented comparable-worth policies, and 26 additional states were in the earlier stages of action (Evans and Nelson, 1989, p. 173).

### 9.8.6. Answers

1. A, B, C, and D: In the 1950s, young people were expected to marry and have at least two children as soon as economic circumstances permitted. These norms were not as strong in 1970s and 1980s as they seemed to be in the 1950s. Cohabitation became more acceptable beginning in the 1960s, thus providing an alternative to marriage. As for choice C, note that the term "marriage squeeze" refers to the situation when eligible partners (in terms of age) are in short supply for prospective brides or grooms. For women born during the first half of the post-World War II "baby boom" there were not enough eligible (somewhat older) men. (To appreciate this situation, note that for any birth cohort of women the eligible men are the survivors of earlier cohorts and, when birth rates were increasing, earlier cohorts were smaller in size than later ones.) As for choice D, note that rise in women's wages during the 1970s and 1980s relative to those of men may have diluted women's economic incentive to marry. Similarly, the fall in men's wages during the 1970s and 1980s probably made marriage and the long-term commitment of resources implied by it less affordable to them. (See Ahlburg and De Vita 1992, p. 13–14.)

2. A, B, C, and D: With the entry of women into the labor force, the traditional "provider-husband, homemaker-wife" model was replaced with the two-earner couple model. Also, working wives gained economic independence and found less time available for investment in home-centered activities, with the consequence that many husbands saw a reduction in domestic support and less deference in decision-making than was true under the "provider-husband, homemaker-wife" model. Also, both men and women probably began to assess the benefit of marriage increasingly in terms of emotional satisfaction. Furthermore, for many couples the choice was between successful marriage and divorce. (See Furstenberg and Cherlin, 1991; Ahlburg and De Vita, 1992, p. 15.)

3. A, B, and C: In the United States teenage women do not use family planning clinics, apparently because of the widely held perception that the clinics are for disadvantaged persons. Many teenagers do not use contraception because of lack of knowledge about sexuality and contraception and among the users only a small fraction use effective methods. (See Ahlburg and De Vita, 1992, p. 21.)

### *9.8.7. Answers*

4. A, B, C, and D: The United Nation's (1994) *Report of the International Conference on Population and Development* (Cairo, 5–13, September 1994) emphasizes that "in all parts of the world, women are facing threats to their lives, health and well-being as a result of being overburdened with work and of their lack of power and influence" (Section 4.1). In many developing countries women hold less than a quarter of all formal-sector jobs. Instead they are engaged in the informal sector of the economy (e.g., in cottage industries, or as street vendors). At the global level, the proportion of household headed by women has been rising (Ashford, 1995, p. 19). As for choice D, note the following data on women's share of national legislatures in selected countries in 1992: Norway, 30%; China, 21%; United States, 10%; Bangladesh, 10%; India, 7%; Mexico, 7%; Egypt, 2% (see Ashford 1995, p. 18).

5. A, B, and C: According to the 1991 Census of India there were 108 men per 100 women in the Indian Population as of 1991. Contrast this with 95 men per 100 women in the United States. Some analysts have assumed that the subordinate position of women resulted in their omission from the census counts (Coale and Hoover, 1958, p. 351). Another group has assumed that the factor responsible was especially high mortality rates among female children and also high maternal mortality. According to a World Bank study (Chatterjee, 1990), at ages 0–9 and 15–34, Indian females die from preventable causes at higher rates than males. According to a Census of India publication "... there is a traditional fondness for male issues in most parts of the country and a corresponding dislike for female children.... In the circumstances, it is to be expected that the slight advantage of female infants shown in a lower infant mortality rate shall soon wear itself out and that female mortality in the very young ages should be heavier than the male mortality" (Census of India, 1954, p. 26).

6. A, B, C, and D: A compilation published by the United Nations (1991d) indicates that choice A is true of all countries except Australia, Canada, and the United States. Choice A is partly explained by choice B. Women, in addition to working for wages or for subsistence production, put in long hours as homemakers. Measuring work in terms of the value of goods produced and time spent shows that choice C is true (Jacobson, 1993, p. 66). As for choice D, note that the reference is to activities such as producing food crops in gardens, collecting firewood, gathering fodder, and so on. Such activities are not counted in statistics on work in most countries.

7. A, B, and C: In the United States in 1990, the average female wage earner, working year-round, full-time, earned only 66% of the wage/salary income

that a corresponding male earner obtained. Job segregation refers to the fact that there are "male" jobs and "female" jobs: There are very few female construction workers, very few male nurses, and so on. "Comparable worth" discrimination occurs when employers set wages lower in "female" than in "male" jobs involving different tasks, but making comparable contribution to the firm's product. [see England and Farkas, 1986, pp. 147–148; see the same source, pp. 172–176, for a list of the most significant laws regulating sex discrimination in employment (Equal Pay Act of 1963; Title VII of the Civil Rights Act of 1964; and Executive Order 11246 of 1965).]

8. A, B, C, and D: Note that the reference is to the labor force participation rates of women of age 16 years and older. As pointed out earlier, about 10% of families were headed by single women with children in 1990, a jump from 5.7% in 1970. Changing patterns of marriage, divorce, and remarriage, and the rise in births to unmarried women, all contributed to the growth of single-parent families. And among these, those resulting from divorce probably had the toughest time economically. Many fathers fail to provide child support after divorce. Never-married women are one-third as likely as divorced women to be awarded child support, and only a fraction of those who have been awarded child support actually receive it in full. (Ahlburg and De Vita, 1992, citing Census sources). Thus it is not difficult to see the point of choice A. As for choice B, it is an empirical fact that women whose husbands had relatively lower incomes are likely to join the labor force because of economic necessity. Regarding choice C, see Oppenheimer (1970), who pointed out that during the post-war period, jobs that had been sex-typed as female (waitresses, sales clerks, nurses, secretaries, etc.) increased in numbers because of the expansion of the service sector. As for choice D, a number of studies have shown that the increase in the labor force participation of women was partly due to the wage rate increase for women (see, e.g., Devaney, 1983; Butz and Ward, 1979a,b).

9. A, B, C, and D: With respect to choice A note that women with lower fertility have more time to devote to extra-familial activities, and labor force participation is a commonly chosen activity of that type. With respect to choices B and C, note that women who participate in the labor force have higher opportunity costs for children, particularly when wage rates are increasing, and this, other things remaining the same, militates against high fertility. As for choice D, note that the type of education and training one wants to give one's children is an important consideration when deciding how many children one wants to have. Given resource constraints, one is forced to make quality/quantity trade offs.

### 9.8.8. Answers

1. E: If the divorce was resorted to simply as a matter of convenience (e.g., to reduce tax burden), the partners may continue to live together, in which case what was a family before the divorce becomes a non-family unit after the divorce. If children are not involved, and if both partners decide to live alone, then the result would be choice B. If children are involved, they, together with the partner who gets their custody, form a family unit, while the other, if he or she chooses to live alone, forms a non-family unit. If children are not involved, and if both partners choose to move in with their respective parents, for example, then the result is choice D.
2. E: All of the above (Weeks, 1995, pp. 331–332).
3. E: The nuclear family form is a relatively new phenomenon historically. Under high mortality conditions, this family form has low viability. There was a time when sociologists believed that in all societies family forms will converge to the nuclear family type. But this view is no longer seriously entertained by analysts of family structure and dynamics.
4. E: All of the above.

### 9.8.9. Answers

5. E: Literacy, educational level, employment status, and occupation are among the means to influence women's status. But women's status also has effects on literacy, educational level, etc. Furthermore, it is known that fertility, mortality, morbidity, migration, and chances of social mobility are all linked to literacy, educational level, and the like.
6. A: The concept of opportunity costs is used in connection with the discussion of the relationship between women's labor-force participation and fertility. The question is whether, by having children, women forego opportunities to work. In those situations, modern urban setting being one of them, having children is believed to make it harder for women to work and build a career. In agrarian societies, however, women's work and child-centered activities are not as incompatible with each other as they are in modern, urban setting.
7. E: (Mason, 1995) (i) Economic development tends to improve the educational status of women, both in absolute terms and in relation to men in the same country. (ii) Also, age at marriage tends to increase, and the between-spouse difference in age tends to narrow with economic development. (Age at marriage and the interspouse difference in age are indicators of the resources

with which women enter marriage.) (iii) Economic development, in general, tends to transfer women from unpaid family work to regular, remunerative employment.

### 9.8.10. Answers

8. D: In traditional societies, marriage coincided with the beginning of sexual intercourse. Contraceptive revolution contributed to disconnecting this linkage. Legalization of abortion also made a similar contribution. In a less permissive society, marriage tends to be the only widely acceptable context of regular sexual activity.

9. A: Data from the 1992–1994 National Surveys of Family Growth show, according to Bumpass and Sweet (1995) that cohabitation is more common among less-than-high-school educated than among the college educated. In some of the European countries, however, the prevalence rate of cohabitation seems to increase with education level (Weeks, 1995). Cohabitation has the effect of delaying marriage, but a great majority in the United States get married. Thus in 1990, 95% of women and 94% of men of age 45–54 had been married at least once. The corresponding figures are lower in other MDCs (see Ahlburg and De Vita, 1992, p. 12). Cohabitation before marriage does not seem to reduce the probability of the marriage ending in divorce (Axinn and Thornton, 1992).

10. E: All of the above (Weeks, 1995, p. 339).

11. E: Schoen and Weinick (1993) constructed marital status life tables using the U.S. age-specific marriage, divorce, death, and widowhood rates of 1970 and 1988. They found that between 1970 and 1988, the percentage ever marrying among those surviving to age 15, decreased from 96.0 to 83.5 for males and 96.5 to 87.9 for females; the average at marriage increased from 23.4 years to 27.5 years for males and from 21.8 to 25.1 years for females; the probability of remarriage for a widowed person decreased from 0.27 to 0.173 for males and from .103 to .063 for females; average duration of a marriage decreased from 26.5 years to 24.5 years for males and 26.8 years to 24.8 years for females.

# CHAPTER 10

# *Population, Food, and the Environment*

Is the earth's capacity to produce food high enough to keep food production in step with population growth? Is feeding the growing population of the world just a matter of producing enough food? Which countries continue to be the major exporters of food? What does the future hold in respect to feeding those who come to dinner? Is mass starvation a thing of the past? In a not too distant future can we all expect to get enough food to satisfy our hunger before going to bed each night?

## *10.1. FOOD PRODUCTION*

In his *An Essay on the Principle of Population*, Malthus argued that population tends to oscillate around its means of subsistence. "When population has increased nearly to the utmost limits of the food, all the preventive and positive checks will naturally operate with increased force ... till the population is sunk below the level of the food; and then the return of comparative plenty will again produce an increase, and, after a certain period, its further progress will again be checked by the same cause." To many experts, the most obvious limitation to population growth is food supply (Petersen, 1975, p. 168). Regarding the question of whether the food production will keep ahead of population, there are, however, optimists as well as pessimists. Opinions also may change over time. The Food and Agricultural Organization (FAO), for example, after a year of stagnation in food output during 1965–1966, issued a report saying that the "outlook is alarming....

The world food situation is now more precarious than at any time since the period of acute shortage immediately after the Second World War" (quoted in Petersen, 1975, p. 170). Yet the very next year's FAO report asserted optimism. By 1970 the mood had definitely become optimistic. Since the 1970s, the world's food production has been increasing faster than the world's population. But the overall picture is deceiving. There are regions where the amount of hungry people are increasing in absolute and in relative numbers, sub-Saharan Africa being a prime example (Tarrant, 1990).

In 1987 the FAO estimated that to meet the food production requirements at the end of this century, the arable land should be increased about 11%. Most of the new lands that could be brought under cultivation, however, are of poor quality: Soils are marginal and/or rainfall is unreliable. The prospects of increasing farmland are dim, for various other reasons too, among which are the following: (i) the amount of good farmland is actually shrinking because of soil erosion, desert encroachment, conversion to urban use or to highways and the like, (ii) in many LDCs farmland once used for producing food has been converted into gardens for growing nonfood cash crops, and (iii) transforming deserts, swamps, and other such lands into farmland is technically possible, but tremendously costly.

The upshot is that increase in food output has to be accomplished mostly from increasing land productivity. Crop yields, of course, can be raised through the use of chemical fertilizers, pesticides and herbicides, irrigation, and improvement of plants. Fertilizers help plants grow healthier and more productive. Pesticides and herbicides reduce losses. Irrigation helps to ensure adequate water supply. Genetic engineering produces high yield varieties of plants and develops strains that are capable of surviving in harsh environments.

*Irrigation*: First developed in the Middle East, irrigation plays a major role in food production all over the world today. The irrigated land area grew at an annual rate of 4% between 1950 and 1980. In the first half of 1980s, however, the annual growth rate declined to about 1% (see Brown, 1989).

Only about 12% of the earth's cultivated land is currently being irrigated. However, half of the world's food output comes from irrigated land. Expansion of irrigated land is constrained by distribution of water and capital cost considerations. In India 30% of cultivated land is under irrigation; in Pakistan and China the corresponding figures are 65% and 50%, respectively. In some countries the amount of irrigated land is actually declining.

Improper use of irrigation can cause harm. In coastal Gujarat in India, massive withdrawals of water using irrigation pumps led to a steep drop in the water table, allowing sea water to seep in. Overpumping of ground water is pervasive in many regions, including the western United States (Postel, 1993). The World Health Organization, commenting on the harmful effects of African irrigation projects, referred to bilharzia (schistosomiasis) as a "man-made-sickness" (cited in Petersen, 1975, p. 172). [Bilharzia affects about 200 million people in 74 countries. It is produced by a water-borne flatworm. Between 9 and 13 million people are estimated to be affected by genital lesions, which are among the common symptoms of bilharzia. Such symptoms are easily confused with those of sexually transmitted diseases (see United Nations, 1995, p. 5).]

*Genetic engineering*: The increase in the world's food production during recent decades owes a great deal to the so-called Green Revolution, a name coined by the U.S. Agency for International Development (Brown, 1973). It refers to improvements in agricultural production, beginning in the 1940s, resulting from the cultivation of genetically-engineered high yield varieties (HYV) in modern ways using chemical fertilizers, pesticides, herbicides, and irrigation.

The high-yield varieties are being used in only about one-third of grain-growing land in the LDCs (Darlymple, 1986). Most of the subsistence farmers who grow food for their families on marginal lands have been bypassed by the Green Revolution. The adoption rate has been lowest in Africa (1% of grain area) and highest in Asia and the Middle East (over 33% of grain area), with Latin America falling in between (less than 25% of grain area).

*Fertilizers*: There was a time when fertilizers were provided by the "night-soil" (human feces) collector, who was in charge of returning nutrients to the farm (Petersen, 1975, p. 172). In preindustrial Europe and in many of the currently less-developed countries, livestock used to provide the manure for increasing the fertility of the soil. Today, modern farming methods require the use of artificial, i.e., chemical, fertilizers. Chemical fertilizer can improve yields dramatically, although the rate of increase in yield declines after the level of use reaches a certain point. Put another way, the response curve of fertilizer use goes up sharply and then levels off. Two-thirds of the chemical fertilizers produced are used in MDCs. In some LDCs government subsidies keep the price of chemical fertilizers down, and when the subsidies are withdrawn the use of fertilizers goes down. From 1950 until 1989 fertilizer use in the world as a whole has steadily increased, after which time it has been dropping. The 1993 level was about 124 million tons as compared to the 1989 level of 146 tons. The decline in fertilizer use in many parts of the world is largely due to withdrawal of government subsidy (e.g., in India and in the former Soviet Union). In some regions, however, fertilizer use continued to increase in the 1990s as in the 1980s (Latin America and Africa, for example).

*Reducing waste*: One way to maximize the "effective supply" of food is to reduce waste. As it is, a considerable amount of food is being wasted: People eat more than they need; food distributors throw away or allow a large amount to be spoiled; a significant portion of food is eaten by pests (Weeks, 1994, p. 419). Also it is believed that meat consumption is an inefficient way of getting what one needs, because several pounds of grain are needed to produce one pound of meat and the protein, the amino acids, and other such things one gets from meat can be obtained in more efficient ways. But experts agree that food habits are unlikely to change drastically in the near future.

## 10.2. FOOD EXPORTING COUNTRIES

The major exporters of food in the world market today are North America, Argentina, and Western Europe. William and Paul Paddock suggested that America's surplus food can be best allocated using the "triage" approach, which involves classifying countries into a number of categories and giving priority to those who could be best helped with maximum result. (The term triage has been mainly used in military medicine, referring to a method of assigning treatment priority to the wounded who will survive if and only if they receive prompt medical attention.) Not many people take such suggestions seriously of course (Simon, 1975).

## 10.3. ENVIRONMENTAL IMPACT

Modern methods of food production adversely affects the environment through soil erosion caused by improper use of irrigation, toxicity built through the food chain caused by the use of pesticides and herbicides, and the depletion of the earth's ozone layer caused by the use of artificial fertilizers (Weeks, 1994:424–427). There is a growing body of literature documenting the environmental and health hazards arising from agricultural use of chemical fertilizers.

## 10.4. QUESTIONS AND ANSWERS*

**FOR EACH OF THE QUESTIONS IN SECTIONS 10.4.1. TO 10.4.3., STATE TRUE OR FALSE AND EXPLAIN.**

### 10.4.1. Food Production in Different Parts of the World

1. North America has always been, and continues to be, a net exporter of food.
2. Western Europe ended its 200 years of dependence on grain import early in the 1980s.
3. During the mid-1980s, grain production plateaued in some of the world's most populous countries.
4. Australia has been, and continues to be, a net importer of grain.

*Answers start page 256.

5. At the mid-20th century, most of the grain in international trade flowed from North America to Western Europe; the rest of the world was essentially self-sufficient.
6. Latin America switched from a net exporter to a net importer early in the 1970s.
7. During 1984–1993, the world's grain output per person fell 11%.
8. Countries that have doubled or tripled grain yields during the last several decades cannot expect to match that record during the coming decades.

### 10.4.2. Different Ways to Increase Food Production

9. From the beginning of agriculture until the mid-20th century, most of the increase in the world's food output came from expanding the cultivated area.
10. By increasing fertilizer use, yield per acre can be increased indefinitely.
11. Irrigation has been expanding constantly for the past several decades.
12. There are no large jumps in output in prospect comparable to those that followed expanded fertilizer use and/or hybridization of corn.

### 10.4.3. Environmental and Health Impacts

13. Large areas of tropical forest are lost each year through the combined action of land clearing for crop production, fuel-wood gathering, and cattle ranching.
14. Absence of secure land tenure can lead to degradation of land.
15. In 1990 the U.S. government endorsed the message urging Americans to limit their fat intake to no more than 30% of their calories.

**FOR EACH OF THE QUESTIONS IN SECTIONS 10.4.4. TO 10.4.6., FOUR ANSWERS ARE SUGGESTED, AT LEAST ONE OF WHICH IS CORRECT. IDENTIFY THE CORRECT ANSWER(S) AND EXPLAIN.**

### 10.4.4. Food Habits

1. Which of the following apply to the MDC–LDC diet-pattern differences?
   A. Per capita meat consumption is far greater in MDCs than in LDCs
   B. The U.S. per capita cereal consumption is many times that of India's
   C. In most MDCs, most of the cereal consumption is indirect—through meat
   D. Increasing affluence tends to increase demand for food

### 10.4.5. *Food Production*

2. The record of human history is sufficiently clear to allow the general statement that human evolution, focusing on socio-cultural aspect of it, may be divided into at least three stages: a very long food-gathering and collecting stage, a relatively recent food producing stage, and the present-day industrial stage. The second of these stages:
   A. Started with the domestication of plants and animals or primarily plant elements
   B. Probably took place many thousands of years ago
   C. May have occurred independently in different parts of the world
   D. May have diffused from diverse centers of its birth to outlying regions still inhabited by food collectors

3. Which of the following have been suggested as possible actions to enhance supply of food, world over?
   A. Increase of fertilizer use in countries like India where current use is below the level prevailing in other major grain-producing countries
   B. Investments in the efficiency of water use
   C. Development of varieties that are more drought-resistant, salt-tolerant, and early-maturing
   D. Safeguard cropland from conversion to nonfarm use

4. Which of the following apply to the issues of producing enough food?
   A. From an economist's point of view there may be a distribution problem in the world food economy, but not a production problem
   B. From an ecologist's point of view the prospect of growth in output does not seem promising
   C. Many countries have reached the point where using additional fertilizer does little to boost food output
   D. Ecologists are encouraged by recent population trends

5. The carrying capacity of a given land depends on:
   A. Climate
   B. The land's inherent productivity
   C. The purpose for which the land is used
   D. Methods used to increase the productivity of the land.

6. Which of the following statements apply to the so-called Green Revolution?
   A. It refers to improvements in agricultural production resulting from the use of genetically-engineered high-yield varieties of grain and modern methods of farming

B. The name was coined by the Rockefeller Foundation's International Maize and Wheat Improvement Center, where the research on high-yield varieties of wheat started
C. Now high-yield varieties of wheat, rice, corn, and soybeans are available for use
D. Almost all farmers now use high-yield varieties

7. Which of the following apply to wasting food?
   A. People eat more than they need
   B. A large quantity of food is thrown away or allowed to be spoiled
   C. A significant portion of food produced is eaten by pests
   D. Food habits are often suboptimal

### 10.4.6. Environmental Impact

8. The principal causes of land degradation are:
   A. Overgrazing of rangelands
   B. Overcultivation of croplands
   C. Waterlogging and salinization of irrigated lands
   D. Deforestation

9. What is good/bad about chemical fertilizer use in agriculture?
   A. Chemical fertilizer can improve yields dramatically
   B. Chemical fertilizers are costly and many farmers in less-developed countries cannot afford them
   C. There is a growing body of literature on the environmental hazards arising from the use of chemical fertilizers in agriculture
   D. Chemical fertilizers are not of much help, unless other aspects of modern methods of cultivation are given equal attention

**FOR EACH OF THE QUESTIONS IN SECTIONS 10.4.7. TO 10.4.10., FIVE ANSWERS ARE SUGGESTED, ONLY ONE OF WHICH IS CORRECT. IDENTIFY THE CORRECT ANSWER AND EXPLAIN.**

### 10.4.7. Food Production

1. The Green Revolution:
   A. Affected only the more developed areas of the world
   B. Popularized multicrop practices for the first time
   C. Involved the adoption of modern methods of farming
   D. Bypassed no significant groups of farmers

E. Marked the first demonstration that Malthus was wrong in his thesis regarding the race between food production and population growth

2. The world's farmers now face which of the following?
   A. Ample opportunity to expand cultivated area
   B. Few advanced technologies for those who have already adopted modern methods of farming.
   C. Poor market for their products.
   D. Substantial returns of additional yield for each increment in fertilizer use.
   E. Freedom from the vagaries of weather.

3. How many pounds of grain it would take to produce one pound of beef?
   A. One
   B. Three
   C. Five to seven
   D. Eight to ten
   E. More than ten

4. One of the ways in which effective supply of food can be "increased" is to reduce waste. People in the more-developed regions of the world throw away as much as ____________ of the food they buy.
   A. 1%
   B. 5%
   C. one-tenth
   D. one-fourth
   E. three-fourths

5. The Green Revolution resulted in ____________ in the use of chemical fertilizer in agriculture.
   A. A substantial increase
   B. A mild increase
   C. No change
   D. A mild decrease
   E. A substantial decrease

### *10.4.8. Environmental Impact*

6. Among the major food-producing countries, ____________ is the only one attempting to systematically reduce excessive soil erosion.
   A. China
   B. India
   C. The United States
   D. Brazil
   E. Argentina

7. Chemical pesticides affect human health ___________.
   A. Negligibly
   B. Appreciably, with immediate effect after exposure
   C. Perhaps appreciably, but with delayed effect after exposure
   D. Too much to warrant discontinuance of their use in agriculture
   E. Enough to outweigh the benefits of their use

### 10.4.9. Food as a Political Tool

8. The so-called "triage" orientation as applied to food distribution implies:
   A. Cutting off food export to all less-developed countries with a population growth rate of over 2.0% per year
   B. Giving food aid only to famine-stricken countries
   C. Leaving the market system to work itself out without interference from governments
   D. Holding the more-developed countries fully responsible for helping to eradicate hunger and malnutrition from the face of the earth
   E. Giving good aid only to those countries that are most likely to bring population growth under control and develop economically

### 10.4.10. Food Habits

9. Suppose people are classified into the following three groups: the poorest, the "meat eaters," and others. The poorest are unable to provide themselves with a healthy diet. The "meat eaters" on average consume more than what they need and they obtain 40% of their caloric intake from fat. The "meat eaters" constitute approximately what percentage of the world's population?
   A. 10%
   B. 25%
   C. 40%
   D. 50%
   E. 67%

10. The meat-eating fraction of the world's population mentioned in Question 9, account for the direct or indirect consumption of _____ percent of world's grain.
    A. 10
    B. 15
    C. 20
    D. 30
    E. 40

11. Which of the following best captures the resource cost of the affluent diet?
    A. Disproportionately more grain is used in the production of the affluent diet.
    B. Food items for the affluent diet are transported over long distance.
    C. Processing and packaging add to the cost.
    D. Health care costs are augmented.
    E. All of the above.

12. Per capita consumption of soft drinks in the United States is ____ times the global average.
    A. two
    B. three
    C. five
    D. six
    E. seven

❖ ❖ ❖ ❖

### 10.4.1. Answers

1. True. North America's net export of grain was 23 million metric tons in 1950; by 1980 it had increased to 131 million metric tons (Brown, 1989, p. 45).

2. True. The region's dependence on imported grain started with the Industrial Revolution. The region began exporting manufactured goods and importing raw materials and food. The factors responsible for the shift include: (i) steadily-advancing farm technologies, (ii) farm support prices above the world level, and (iii) low population growth rate (Brown, 1989, pp. 45–46).

3. True. This was true of India, Indonesia, and Mexico, to give a few examples. India tripled its wheat harvest between 1965 and 1983 and then entered a plateau (Brown, 1989, p. 43, citing U.S. Department of Agriculture, Economic Research Service, sources). Indonesia doubled its grain harvest between 1970 and 1984, and then the output levelled off. In Mexico, where the Green Revolution originated, grain harvest grew four-fold during 1950–1984 and then started to level off.

4. False. Australia has been, and continues to be, a net exporter of grain. The prognosis is that Western Europe is likely to emerge as a larger net exporter of grain than Australia and New Zealand combined (Brown, 1989).

5. True. In 1950, North America exported 23 million metric tons of grain. Western Europe imported 22 million metric tons of grain during that year. Other major regions were more or less self-sufficient in grain production, major exceptions were Latin America (net exporter of about 1 million metric

tons), Australia and New Zealand (net exporter of 3 million metric tons), and Asia (net importer of about 6 million metric tons.)

6. True. Despite a vast land area, Brazil now regularly imports both wheat and feed-grains. Argentina is the only major country that continues to be a net exporter. Food deficit is increasing in Mexico. Many smaller countries in the region also have growing food deficits.

7. True. The year 1984 is likely to be known as a watershed year, one marking the transition from an era of rapid growth in food production to one of much slower growth. Between 1950 and 1984, world's grain production expanded 2.6-fold; after 1984, the growth of grain production slowed abruptly. (Brown, 1994, p. 177).

8. True. Many of the farmers are already using advanced yield-raising technologies. Obviously, this rapid rise in food output cannot continue unabated. To give an example, wheat production in U.K. remained remarkably stable from 1884–1940. From 1940 until 1984, the output more than tripled. Since 1984, however, there has been no evidence of a continuing rapid rise. To give another example, yields of corn were essentially unchanged in the United States for several decades, until 1940. Between 1940 and 1985 there was a more than four-fold increase occurred in the corn output. Since 1985, however, the rise in output slowed to a near standstill. After increasing for nearly a century, the rise in rice output in Japan came to a halt in 1984; since then the outputs have fallen slightly. (Brown, 1994).

### 10.4.2. Answers

9. True. Since 1950 the emphasis began to shift to increasing land productivity. "Even in those countries where a choice was permitted by unutilized land resources, intensification was chosen as the main component of increases in agricultural production ... [for] in general the returns ... are higher than those accruing to development of new land and water resources" (FAO 1970, quoted in Petersen, 1975, p. 171).

10. False. After a point, additional fertilizer use would not be effective. 1984 was the last year in which a large increase in fertilizer use led to a comparable increase in grain output. During the next five years farmers continued to use more fertilizer, but the response of their crops was disappointing. Between 1989 and 1993 fertilizer use declined by about 12%. (See Brown, 1994, p. 194).

11. False. From 1950 to 1978 irrigation expanded at record rate. After that its annual rate of expansion has dipped to below 1% (Brown, 1994, p. 184).

12. True. When the 1950s began there were a great deal of technology waiting to be used. These included chemical fertilizer, irrigation, and hybrid varieties. As these technologies have been exploited during the last four decades, no new technologies that could match them have taken their place. Consequently, the 1990s began with little prospects for expecting quantum leaps in agricultural outputs (see Brown, 1994, pp. 186–187).

### 10.4.3. Answers

13. True. The Food and Agricultural Organization estimates that each year 11.3 million hectares of tropical forest are lost this way. According to some observers, this may be a gross underestimate (Postel, 1989, p. 26).
14. True. Since land is often needed as collateral, farmers without titles to the property have difficulty getting loans they need if they were to try to maintain the productivity of the land. Moreover farmers, in such conditions, may not be sufficiently motivated to invest the necessary funds to maintain or enhance the productivity of the land they cultivate. This is said to be a major problem in many of the less-developed countries (Postel, 1989, pp. 28–29).
15. True. The medical profession has been suggesting this step for a long time. On May 8, 1990 *The New York Times* carried an article "Huge Study of Diet Indicts Fat and Meat," in which the findings of a largest-ever study of diet and health in China was reported to have shown that the healthiest diet for humans is nearly vegetarian, containing 10–15% of calories from fat (cited in Durning, 1991, p. 159).

### 10.4.4. Answers

1. A, B, C, and D: The world's population can be categorized into three groups in terms of food consumption: at the bottom are the poorest 12% of the world's population, deprived of a healthy diet; in the middle are 64% of the people, who eat plenty of plant-based food and get enough calories from the food they consume; and at the other end are the remaining 24%, who are the meat eaters. Those in the middle category receive less than 20% of their calories from fat, whereas those in the last category receive 40% of their calories from fat. Also a typical person in the last category consumes three times as much fat as a typical person in the other two categories combined. The meat eating 24% of the world's population consume nearly 40% of the world's grain, through meat. [According to one estimate, in the case of American beef, producing 1 kilogram of steak requires 5 kilograms of grain and the energy equivalent of 9 liters of gasoline (Durning, 1991, p. 159).]

   Per capita red meat consumption (in kilograms) of selected countries (as of

1989): U.S. 76; Argentina 73; France 66; Japan 27; China 21; Egypt 12; India 1 (U.S. Department of Agriculture, Foreign Agricultural Service, 1990, World Livestock Situation, quoted in Durning 1991, p. 159). Regarding Choice A note that annual meat consumption per person ranges from 112 kilograms in the United States to 2 kilograms in India. In the United States annual per capita cereal consumption is five times that of India's, most of the U.S. consumption being for feeding animals.

### 10.4.5. Answers

2. A, B, C, and D: To some authors the transition from the food-collecting stage to the food-producing stage deserves the name the Agricultural Revolution. Many authors believe that this occurred 10,000 years ago. But information is scantly about the beginning of the food-producing stage. There is consensus on the point that it occurred independently in different places. Two instances for which scholars have gained some idea were centered in southwestern Asia and Mesoamerica (see *Encyclopedia for Social Sciences*, article on domestication). Neither of these is believed to have emerged before 10,000 BC. It is also known that from the southwest Asian and Mesoamerican centers the idea diffused to outlying areas inhabited by food collectors.

3. A, B, C, and D: India's grain yield per acre is much less than China's. One of the reasons seems to be the lower use of chemical fertilizers. Investment in irrigation and measures to encourage the use of more fertilizers might raise food output considerably in such instances. As for choices B and C, in a world where water is becoming scarce, the future of agriculture would depend upon the more efficient use of water. Measures to stop leakage from canals and ditches, use of such techniques as underground drip system, which is put to good use in Israel, for example, and the development of varieties of the kind mentioned in choice C have been suggested. One of the keys to raising agricultural output on a sustainable basis is keeping cropland from being converted to nonfarm use. Japan, for example, has made it illegal to build on cropland. As for choice D, it has been estimated that worldwide, about 25 billion tons of topsoil is being lost from cropland each year (Brown, 1989, p. 49). Efforts to conserve topsoil are being made in some countries. The United States, for example, has a Conservation Reserve Program under which conversion of highly erodible cropland to grassland or woodland is encouraged and farmers who manage their farmland poorly are penalized by denying them the benefits from farm programs (Brown *et al.* 1989, p. 186).

4. A, B, and C: An economist might point out that by conventional measures the world's agriculture seems to be doing well. Western Europe is worried about

surpluses, particularly dairy products. The United States still idles cropland to control production. Grain-exporting countries use subsidies to compete for markets that never seem large enough. Ecologists look at the world's agricultural situation differently. They emphasize that currently the world's food output is kept high because a great deal of highly erodible land is being cultivated—land that will soon be abandoned. Also, ground-water is currently being overpumped, and this cannot continue indefinitely. There is the conversion of land to nonfarm use, and this, together with the abandoning of degraded land, threatens to shrink the cropland base. As for choice C, note that in countries such as the United States growth in fertilizer use has stopped. There are of course some countries, such as India—now a distant fourth among the four major grain producers—where there is potential for profitable increase in fertilizer use. But on a worldwide basis, the opportunities for doing so seem to be diminishing. As for choice D, ecologists are not encouraged by the current population growth pattern. They see the natural resource base diminishing because of increasing pressures exerted on it by population growth and rising affluence. They worry about the projected shrinkage of per capita availability of key resources such as land, water, and forest products (e.g., firewood). See Brown (1991) for an elaboration of these points.

5. A, B, C, and D: Carrying capacity means the number of people a given land area can support. It is difficult to measure the carrying capacity of any given land area. As for choices C and D, note that, as mentioned, a fertile piece of land can become degraded depending on how and for what purpose the land is used. Thus clearing forests for fuel-wood can lead to deforestation. According to one estimate, in India 1.3 million hectares of forest land are lost in this fashion per year (Postel, 1989, p. 28).

6. A and C: The name was coined by the U.S. Agency for International Development (Brown, 1973). The high yield varieties are being cultivated only on about a third of the grain-growing land in less-developed countries (Darlymple, 1986). The adoption rate has been lowest in Africa.

7. A, B, C, and D: People in developed countries are notorious for overeating. In the United States about a third of males of age 20–74 were overweight as of 1988–1991 (NCHS, 1994, Table 80). As for choice B, according to one estimate (*Newsweek*, cited in Weeks, 1994, p. 419), people in MDCs throw away up to 25% of the food they buy. In addition, food distributors throw away large quantities of food each week. As for choice C, estimates are scanty, but it is known that a substantial portion of food is eaten by pests each season (Weeks, 1994, p. 419). As for choice D, it is now recognized that eating red meat is not a good habit, yet people continue to do so; meat eating in general is an inefficient way of getting the nutrients one wants.

### 10.4.6. Answers

8. A, B, C, and D: (i) Overgrazing and trampling tend to leave the land exposed to the ravages of wind and water. Concentration of livestock around the watering points leads to severe localized overgrazing, which gradually spreads outward from the central area. Agricultural land left without vegetative cover or situated on steeply sloping hillsides is subject to erosion caused by wind and water. (ii) Seepage from irrigation canals and excessive watering of fields cause the underlying water table to rise. In the absence of proper drainage, water eventually enters the root zone, damaging the crops. The name "wet deserts" is applied to such once-fertile fields in India. In dry regions, salinization usually accompanies waterlogging: When the moisture near the surface evaporates, a layer of salt, toxic to plants, is left behind. India and Pakistan account for about half of such lands. Deforestation and cultivation of the Himalayan slopes in India have accelerated the erosion of the top soil, resulting in millions of tons of silts being washed out to the ocean. (See Postel, 1989, for elaboration of these points).

9. A, B, C, and D: While it is true that chemical fertilizers when used in conjunction with irrigation, pesticides, and herbicides, increase yield, it should be noted that the response curve levels off. In other words, beyond a certain level, additional use is unlikely to increase yield. Some of the pesticides in use are known to cause cancer. DDT use has been discontinued in most developed countries, but not in all less-developed countries. The substitutes in use are also believed to be unsafe (Weeks, 1994, p. 425). Chemical fertilizers seem to produce a kind of gas that could deplete earth's ozone layer, thus reducing protection from ultraviolet rays. Food preservatives have also become under attack as possible causes of cancer. Of course, some writers react to such points by saying that this is overreaction based on flimsy evidence.

### 10.4.7. Answers

1. C.: The major impact was on the less-developed countries. It bypassed the traditional small farmers. The Malthusian thesis regarding the race between food production and population growth was proved wrong long time before the occurrence of the Green Revolution.

2. B.: There seems to very few prospects for increasing cultivated area. And, although irrigated area is increasing slowly in some countries, it is diminishing in many areas. Fertilizer use has reached in many countries a level at which the response curve has levelled off. Weather is a problem in many areas, especially where people cultivate on rain-fed lands. For many countries in Africa,

for example, local rainfall is too low and irrigation water too scarce to permit extensive use of fertilizer.

3. C.: (Brown *et al.*, 1989, p. 187). The relative efficiency of converting grain to various types of animal protein affects the effective supply-demand balance of world grain. Shifts from beef to poultry help stretch the world supply of grain. The production of broiler chickens requires only two pounds of grain per pound of meat.
4. D.: One-fourth (Weeks, 1994, p. 419, citing a *Newsweek* article).
5. A. In some countries, such as India, fertilizer use is still lower than in other countries. It is believed that an increase in fertilizer use in India would result in a boost of agricultural output. Of course there are many countries in Africa where rainfall is too low and irrigation water too limited to permit the use of chemical fertilizer. In such areas chemical-fertilizer based agriculture will not develop.

### 10.4.8. Answers

6. C: The U.S. Conservation Reserve Program encourages conversion of highly erodible cropland to grassland or woodland and penalizes farmers who do not manage their soil properly. The program was put into effect in the mid-1980s. It is estimated that in 1987, this contributed to reducing U.S. soil losses by 460 million tons (Brown *et al.*, 1989, p. 186).
7. C: They are like other cancer-causing chemical agents. Their impact, if any, on health may not show until 20 to 30 years after exposure.

### 10.4.9. Answers

8. E: Triage is a French word meaning picking and choosing. It refers to an army hospital practice of sorting the wounded into three groups and giving immediate attention to those who will survive if and only if immediately treated, giving low priority to those who will survive without immediate treatment and those who will die no matter what.

### 10.4.10. Answers

9. B.: Only rough estimates are available. According to World Bank's *World Development Report*, 1990, cited in Durning 1991, 23.6% of the world's population are "meat eaters" thus defined.

10. E: Most of the grain consumption is through meat—grain is used to fatten the livestock.

11. E.: To produce one pound of beef, several pounds of grains are needed as animal feed. As for transportation cost, note that North Europeans eat lettuce trucked from Greece, Japanese eat turkey transported from the United States, and a substantial fraction of the grapes consumed in the United States comes from Chile. As for choice D, note that health-conscious affluent people eat more than they need and then spend time and money to deal with the consequences of over-indulgence, e.g. participate in weight-reduction programs; pay through pain, suffering, and hospital bills when afflicted with heart disease, stroke, and the like. (See Durning, 1991, for a development of these points.)

12. E.: The per capita consumption of soft drinks in the United States in 1989 was 176 liters, which was more than the corresponding water intake (141 liters). (See Durning, 1991, for the source citations.)

CHAPTER 11

# Population Growth and Economic Development

Implications of population dynamics for economic development have received considerable attention in the literature—perhaps more than any other population "problem." What is economic development? What is the distinction, if any, between economic development and economic growth? To what extent does population change affect economic development and vice versa? Is the empirical evidence on these relationships clear cut? Have the views about these relationships changed over time, and if so, in what direction?

## 11.1. CONCEPTS

A common definition of economic development is that it involves growth in income per person, in output per worker, and in the goods and services that reach people's consumption basket. Another definition emphasizes the creation of an environment for people to enjoy long, healthy, and creative lives. A distinction is usually made between economic growth and economic development. Economic growth refers to an increase in the wealth of a nation, whereas economic development is presumed to involve an increase in per capita income or output (*The MIT Dictionary of Modern Economics*). This distinction is not always emphasized in the writings on economic development. For example, examine the following: "Economic development involves evolution from a predominantly agrarian peasant economy to an economy with a greater division of labor, using more elaborate tools and equipment, more urbanized, more oriented to the market sale of its products, and characterized by rapid and pervasive changes in technique ... [and]

improvements in transportation, communications, and productivity ]..." (Coale and Hoover, 1958, p. 10), or "modern economic growth, or development ... may be defined as a rapid and sustained rise in real output per head and attendant shifts in the technological, economic, and demographic characteristics of a society" (*International Encyclopedia of Social Sciences*, entry on economic growth by Easterlin).

## 11.2. THE RELATIONSHIP BETWEEN POPULATION GROWTH AND ECONOMIC CHANGE

As is well known, the conventional view of economists at the time Malthus wrote his *An Essay on the Principle of Population* (1798) was that a large and increasing population was synonymous with wealth. Challenging that position, Malthus argued that in the absence of prudential checks, population's natural proclivity to grow in geometric progression would outpace food production and constrain economies to remain stagnant at a subsistence level. In the 1930s, however, the very low fertility levels in many of the Western nations prompted a number of experts to blame slow population growth for the prolongation of the Great Depression. The pendulum swung to the other end during the period 1950–1980. The popular view then was that rapid population growth hindered economic development in low-income countries (Coale and Hoover, 1958). This view has been the primary rationale for the starting of the national family planning programs in many less-developed countries with assistance from one or more of the more-developed countries. In 1974 at the World Population Conference in Bucharest, the Western countries, including the United States, expressed strong support for family planning programs. Many of the less-developed countries, including India and China, however, argued at that conference that economic development would "naturally" bring fertility down and that what was really needed was transfers of capital and technology from the more-developed to the less-developed countries. The 1980s saw the population-impact pendulum swing again. At the 1984 World Population Conference in Mexico City, the United States, departing from its earlier position, declared that "The relationship between population growth and economic development is not necessarily a negative one." Julian Simon's (1981) book *The Ultimate Resource* expounded the position that population growth in the long run could actually help accelerate the pace of economic development. These declarations prompted new assessment of the relationship in question. The National Academy of Sciences appointed a working group to look into the matter (National Research Council, 1986). The World Bank's staff wrote a special report (World Bank, 1984) on the issue. The general tone of the conclusions of these studies was less pessimistic and less dogmatic.

## 11.3. POPULATION GROWTH AS A HINDRANCE TO ECONOMIC DEVELOPMENT: A CLOSER LOOK

Those who saw a negative association between population growth and economic development in low-income countries emphasized the following: (i) For an economy, addition of people involves expenses (a demographic overhead) in terms of providing food, clothing, housing, and other goods and services. The greater such expenses the lower the ability to save and invest in developmental efforts (building factories, roads, irrigation networks, and the like). (ii) To accomplish a given percent of growth in per capita income, the economy has to grow faster if the population growth rate is high than if it is low, and there is little, if any, in the rapid population growth itself that helps the economy grow faster. A typical LDC is already overpopulated, and in such a situation, high growth rate in population size contributes nothing to stimulate economic growth—whatever stimulus a large population can provide has been present in such countries for a long time. (iii) Most low-income countries already suffer from underemployment and unemployment and under such conditions it is extremely difficult, if the population continues to increase rapidly, to bring capital formation sufficiently high to keep the work force productive (see Coale and Hoover, 1958).

In this discussion the dependency ratio enters the argument as follows: At any given level of output per worker, greater number of dependents increases consumption and reduces savings. Although theoretically this appears to make sense, empirical support for it had been difficult to find (World Bank, 1984, p. 42).

Regarding the creation of employment opportunities, it has been argued that when population growth is slow, chances are that the number of new job seekers in any year would be roughly the same as the number of people who leave the labor force (e.g., through retirement) that year. When population grows rapidly, however, the number of new job seekers is likely to be higher than the number of those who leave the labor force and investment must grow fast enough to create the required additional number of new jobs to absorb the growing number of new job seekers. Furthermore, consumption expenditures must grow fast enough to keep misery (starvation, malnutrition, etc.) down.

## 11.4. POPULATION GROWTH AS A STIMULUS TO ECONOMIC DEVELOPMENT

Ester Boserup (1965; 1981), Colin Clark (1967), and others have argued that in the long run, a growing population, rather than a declining or a stationary one, leads to economic development. Simply put, the argument is that population growth is the motivating force that prompts communities to change their methods and in the long run transform themselves into more advanced and productive entities (Clark, 1967). Support for this position is drawn from the history of Europe. Boserup (1965) pointed out that the reduction of fallow, the major means of increasing the area under cultivation in Western Europe during the 18th and 19th centuries, was stimulated by population growth. Julian Simon (1981) argued that the larger the population, the greater the number of people trying to solve problems and the greater the resulting growth of innovations, provided, of course, that the socio-economic system promotes free enterprise. Simon's view in this respect is not shared widely among demographers. Most of them argue that innovation comes from persons who have time and resources at their disposal to experiment.

## 11.5. ECONOMIC DEVELOPMENT AFFECTING POPULATION CHANGE

According to the classic version of the demographic transition theory economic development was a stimulus to population change. As Coale and Hoover (1958, p. 10) put it, economic change "had the effect (notably in Europe, the United States, Canada, Australia, and New Zealand and later in Japan) of bringing a striking reduction in death rates. The reduction in death rates may be ascribed partly to greater regularity in food supplies, to the establishment of greater law and order, and to other fairly direct consequences of economic change." The economic change that lowered death rates also motivated couples to lower birth rates. Closer look at the demographic history of Europe and the experiences of the currently less-developed countries, however, have clearly shown that economic development is not a necessary condition for demographic transition to occur.

## 11.6. CURRENT POSITIONS

The following are explicit or implicit in the conclusions of the 1986 National Academy of Sciences study of the relationship between population change and economic development. (i) There are both important positive and negative impacts of population growth on economic development in low-income countries. (ii) Whether the net impact is strong or weak cannot be determined, let alone an assessment of the actual size of this impact, given current evidence. (iii) Only the direction of the impact can be discerned—a slower population growth would be beneficial to economic development of developing countries. (iv) The net impact of population growth on economic development varies from country to country—in some it may be negative, in some positive, and in others neutral (see National Research Council, 1986).

Kelly's (1988) conclusions, based on his review of the literature on the relationship between population change and economic development, include the following: (i) Economic development (as measured by increase in per capita output) in many LDCs would have been more rapid if their populations had grown slower, although in some countries the impact of population growth was probably negligible, and in some it may have been positive. (ii) Population's impact is likely to be negative in countries where arable land and water are scarce, where property rights to land and resources are poorly defined, and where government policies are biased against labor-intensive programs. (iii) Population's impact is likely to be positive where natural resources are abundant, where possibilities of scale economies are substantial, and where markets, government, and other institutions allocate resources efficiently over space and time. (iv) Assessment of the impact of population growth on economic development is a highly complex matter, and an emphasis on policies of slowing population growth without simultaneously confronting the other fundamental causes of problems such as unemployment, famine, and malnutrition may well lead to disappointing results.

The World Bank's (1984) study concluded that at rates of less than 2%, living standard can continue to rise, perhaps more slowly than it would otherwise, that the conclusion that rapid population growth has slowed economic development in low-income countries is by no means straightforward or clear cut from the available evidence, and that the link between savings and dependency burdens is weak.

## 11.7. QUESTIONS AND ANSWERS*

**FOR EACH OF THE QUESTIONS IN SECTIONS 11.7.1 TO 11.7.3, STATE TRUE OR FALSE AND EXPLAIN.**

### 11.7.1. Concepts

1. Economy of scale (scale economy) is a measuring instrument for assessing the success and failures of a government's efforts at economic development.
2. Capital, in the context of economic development, stands for the geographic location of the central government where the planning for economic development takes shape.
3. The gross national product is the total output of goods and services available for the nation from economic activity.

*Answers start page 276.

4. Economic development implies that the economy must be growing at a faster rate than the population.

### 11.7.2. The Population-Economic Development Relationship

5. Among those writing on the subject there is agreement about the nature of the relationship between population growth and economic development.
6. The thesis that a growing human population is the "ultimate resource" is Julian Simon's.
7. The 1974 World Population Conference at Bucharest adopted the view that rapid population growth was indeed an impediment to improving the standard of living and that high priority should be given to reducing population growth.
8. At the 1984 World Population Conference in Mexico City, the United States took a position inconsistent with the one it took at the 1974 World Population Conference at Bucharest.
9. The higher the rate of population growth, the higher the rate of investment needed to attain a given level of per capita output.
10. There is no empirical support for the thesis that population growth is beneficial to economic development.
11. In economic development, the less-developed countries of today are following the same path traversed by the Western countries.
12. Rapidly growing population, through its young age structure and consequent high young age dependency, puts severe strains on the economy's ability to generate the needed savings for economic development.
13. The fact that the world appears to be better off economically with close to 6 billion people than it was when there were only 1 billion people supports Julian Simon's thesis that human population is the ultimate resource in the search for economic development.
14. Low population-growth-rate is a sure indication that the population involved is economically well off.
15. The impact of population on economic growth and development has been a controversial topic in economics for a very long time.
16. The empirical evidence is weak or nonexistent for the often-emphasized negative net impact of population growth on economic development.
17. The Third World nations have benefited from scale effect of larger populations.
18. The "investment-diversion" hypothesis has been challenged in the literature.

19. Diminishing returns to labor due to a limited supply of land reduces labor productivity.

### 11.7.3. The Context of Economic Development

20. As they try to improve economically, the less-developed nations face a set of world circumstances different from the one the Western nations faced when they were trying to do the same thing.
21. *The Club of Rome Study* (Meadows *et al.*, 1972) concluded that the world is already overpopulated.

**FOR EACH OF THE QUESTIONS IN SECTIONS 11.7.4. TO 11.7.5., FOUR ANSWERS ARE SUGGESTED, AT LEAST ONE OF WHICH IS CORRECT. IDENTIFY THE CORRECT ANSWER(S) AND EXPLAIN.**

### 11.7.4. Concepts

1. Economic development:
   A. Is the process of improving the standard of living and well-being of the population
   B. Implies the creation of an environment for the people to enjoy long, healthy, and creative lives
   C. Is usually achieved by industrialization
   D. Is measured by growth in net national product

### 11.7.5. Relationships

2. Scholarly opinion on the extent to which population change affects economic development has been like a pendulum, swinging from one end to another.
   A. Malthus (1798) argued that in the absence of prudential checks, starvation, vice, and misery would be the order of the day and the economy would stagnate at the subsistence level
   B. In the 1930s, scholars saw in the slow population growth a culprit responsible for the insufficient expansion of aggregate demand and the prolongation of the Depression
   C. During 1950–1980, the prevailing view was that rapid population growth hindered economic development in low-income countries
   D. The 1980s saw the emergence of a less pessimistic view regarding the impact of population change on economic development
3. In the literature one could find a whole range of opinions on the effect of population growth on economic change. Among these are:

A. In any free-market system, population growth stimulates economic growth
B. More people means more power
C. No cause–effect relationship exists between population growth and economic change
D. Rapid population growth is detrimental to economic development, particularly in low income countries

4. Which of the following statements apply to empirical studies of the relationship between population change and economic development?
   A. Most models taken for empirical testing predict a negative, albeit small, impact of population growth on economic development
   B. Typically, such empirical studies use correlational analysis
   C. No strong relationship between the two variables has been found in empirical studies
   D. Most of the investigations ignore the complexities of the relationships

5. Which of the following belong together?
   A. Population problems will disappear when exploitation of one group (workers) by another (business owners) stops
   B. A society's initial response to population growth is to have its people work harder
   C. If the more-developed countries would stop exploiting the less-developed countries and instead help the latter to develop economically, the population problems would be solved automatically
   D. Population growth would stimulate economic growth if adequate resources are available and the appropriate institutional structure is in place

6. Which of the following statements are part of the argument that rapid population growth is detrimental to economic development?
   A. Rapidly growing population creates high demographic overhead and hence makes savings for investment extremely difficult
   B. Rapid population growth requires higher rates of economic growth to maintain a given level of standard of living, while nothing in the rapid population growth itself helps increase the rate of economic growth
   C. A typical low-income country is already overpopulated, hence a larger population is not needed to stimulate economic growth
   D. The number of new entrants to the labor force is increasing rapidly, swelling the ranks of the unemployed and underemployed, making it all the more difficult to increase the labor-force productivity

7. How does age-dependency figure in the discussion of the impacts of population growth on the pace and form of saving and capital formation?
   A. An additional child is presumed to raise the household consumption, and hence, reduce household saving

B. When the dependency is high, each earner in the household will have to produce more goods and services just to maintain the same standard of living
C. With the same levels of resources and capital available, a population with lower fertility would have higher per capita output and higher per capita income as a direct result of having a higher fraction of the population in the working age groups
D. With the same size labor force, one population with a long history of high fertility would have lower saving and investment than one with a history of lower fertility

8. Which of the following are explicit or implicit in the conclusions of the National Research Council (1986) report on the relationship between population growth and economic development?
A. Population growth has both positive and negative impacts on economic development in low-income countries
B. The actual size of the net impact cannot be determined given current evidence
C. Slower population growth is beneficial to economic development of most developing countries
D. Family planning programs may not make a poor country rich, but they can help it to become less poor

9. Which of the following are among the conclusions of Kelly's (1988) review of the literature on the impacts of population growth on economic development?
A. In most LDCs, economic development would have been more rapid if their population had grown slower
B. The population impact is likely to be negative in countries with scarce natural resources, poorly defined property rights to natural resources, and governmental policies biased against labor
C. Population impact is likely to be positive in countries with abundant natural resources, substantial possibilities of scale economies, and efficient allocation of resources
D. The relationship between population change and economic development is a complex one and any policy that ignores the complexity is likely to produce disappointing results

10. Which of the following are among the conclusions of the World Bank's (1984) review of the relationship between population growth and economic development?
A. At population growth rates less than 2% per year, living standards can continue to rise
B. From available evidence one cannot straightforwardly conclude that rapid population growth has slowed economic development in low-income countries

C. The link between savings and dependency burden is weak
D. Dependency burden has little, if any, impact on educational expenditures

**IN EACH OF THE QUESTIONS IN SECTIONS 11.7.6 TO 11.7.8., FIVE ANSWERS ARE SUGGESTED, ONLY ONE OF WHICH IS CORRECT. IDENTIFY THE CORRECT ANSWER AND EXPLAIN.**

### 11.7.6. Concepts

1. Which of the following is inconsistent with the definition of economic development? Economic development:
   A. Is a process by which the standard of living of a population is improved
   B. Is usually measured by increases in per capita income
   C. Broadly conceived, includes the creation of an environment in which people enjoy long, healthy, and creative lives
   D. Is usually achieved by an increase in industrialization relative to reliance on the agricultural sector
   E. Begins with mass production of goods and services
2. Which of the following is inconsistent with the definition of economic growth?
   A. Typically, economic growth is measured by the increase in the real level of the net national product
   B. Economic growth and economic development are synonyms
   C. Economic growth is to be distinguished from "human development" as defined in United Nations Development Program (1990)
   D. Economic growth can occur without improvements in the well-being of a substantial segment of the population involved
   E. Economic growth implies transition from an agrarian to an industrialized society
3. The term "real wages" stands for:
   A. Goods and services wages can buy
   B. The take-home pay (after withholdings at source)
   C. Average wage earnings or wage rates for a given job
   D. Wage rates or wage earning in a normal year
   E. Wage earnings of real estate agents

### 11.7.7. Characterization of Less Developed Countries

4. The population growth rate of a typical low-income country is:
   A. Relatively high
   B. Relatively low

C. The same as the current population growth rate of a typical more-developed country
D. Zero
E. Negative

5. Which of the following definitely applies to a typical low-income country of today with a rapidly growing population?
A. No escape from mass starvation and misery in the foreseeable future
B. High young-age dependency
C. Civil war
D. 75 years of life expectancy at birth
E. Military dictatorship

6. The literature on the effects of rapid population growth on labor and employment emphasize:
A. That rapid population growth hinders the growth of income per capita, and thereby reduces rates of savings and investment, causing mass underemployment, unemployment, and poverty
B. That population growth stimulates technological change and the adoption of techniques that realizes economies of scale and thereby promotes economic growth
C. That despite unprecedented population growth in developing countries in the 1960–1980 period, the countries were generally able to absorb the new labor supply at increased levels of productivity
D. That cross-country correlations between growth in income per head and the rate of population growth are weak
E. All of the above

7. In their 1958 study of Mexico's demographic future, what did Coale and Hoover suggest as likely to occur in that country, given sustained population growth over subsequent decades?
A. Difficulty in maintaining agricultural self-sufficiency
B. Drop in exports
C. Increase in imports of consumer goods at the expense of capital goods
D. Decline in foreign investments
E. All of the above

### 11.7.8. Attempts to Peak into the Future

8. The *Global 2000 Report* (Council of Environmental Quality, 1980) concluded that:
A. The less-developed countries will before long attempt to subjugate the

more-developed countries, given the disparity between them in population growth rate
B. Population is the ultimate resource
C. Dependency burden severely depresses economic development
D. In the 21st century, the world in all likelihood would reach its carrying capacity
E. Human ingenuity will find ways to accommodate an indefinitely growing population

9. *The Club of Rome Study* (Meadows *et al.*, 1972) through a computer simulation predicted which of the following, based on their most optimistic assumptions regarding the paths of population growth and capital investment?
   A. Zero population growth will eventually be reached and the average income per person would then be equal to the 1970 level of U.S. per capita income.
   B. After a while, things would take a turn for the worse.
   C. Eventually industrial growth will be halted and food output would start declining.
   D. Death rate will rise.
   E. All of the above

### 11.7.1. Answers

1. False. Economy of scale refers to reductions in average cost of a product in the long run, resulting from an increased volume of output. The average cost of building a car is much less when thousands of cars are being built. At higher population densities, per unit costs of transportation and communication, extension services, and the like, would be lower (see Kelly, 1988).

2. False. Capital represents produced goods that serve as inputs for further production. Land and labor are not regarded as capital goods, since they are not ordinarily regarded as being themselves produced by the economic system. However, the term "human capital" has been in use for the human resources developed by making investment in education and the like, anticipating future returns.

3. True. There are three approaches to measuring the money value of the goods and services that become available to a nation from economic activity: (i) as the sum of the incomes (from profits and employment) derived from economic activity, (ii) as the sum of expenditures (consumption and investments), and (iii) as the sum of the products of the various industries of the nation. The last approach aggregates the sum of the values added at each stage of production by the industries. This gives the gross domestic product. To this is added the

net property income from abroad to obtain the gross national product. It does not measure the value added by unpaid domestic labor. Another weakness is that it does not reflect the national differences in purchasing power. A dollar may go much further in India than in the United States, for example.

4. True. If by economic development one refers to an increase in per capita output, and by economic growth one means an increase in national output, then it follows that for the former to occur the latter must have a growth rate exceeding that of the population.

### *11.7.2. Answers*

5. False. There are those who hold that population growth is a stimulus to economic development. They use as evidence the early phases of demographic transition in the West, when in most countries population growth occurred hand-in-hand with increase in the standard of living. Another view is that population growth is detrimental to economic development. This view was dominant during the 1950s and 1960s. It was argued that low income countries will not be able to climb out of poverty unless the runaway population was brought under control (Coale and Hoover, 1958). Currently the dominant view is that there is no simple relationship between economic development and population growth (Kelly, 1988).

6. True. In 1981 Simon popularized this thesis through his book *The Ultimate Resource*. His argument was that resources are limited only by humanity's ability to invent them and that the more people there are the more fertile minds there will be to invent solutions to problems such as developing new resources. As a source of energy, coal replaced wood, and later oil replaced coal. Maybe solar or some other type of energy is next in sequence, if only the human inventive genius succeeds in harnessing it.

7. False. Initially the draft of the "world plan of action," contained such as view, but in the final version, the idea was not underscored (see Weeks, 1994, pp. 380–381).

8. True. In 1974, the U.S. position was that rapid population growth was detrimental to economic development and that high priority should be given to family planning programs in the low income countries. In 1984, the U.S. took the position that population growth and economic development were not inextricably linked to each other, and that the crucial factor is whether constraints on free market economy are all removed.

9. True. Consider two populations A and B, similar to each other in size, accumulated capital, and output. "Assume that population A is growing at

a rate of 1 percent per annum, and population B at 3 percent. If the ratio of capital stock to current annual output is 3 to 1, population A must invest 3 percent of current output to maintain its per capita income, while population B must invest 9 percent of current output" (Coale and Hoover, 1958, p. 20). The question arises whether faster growing populations would also raise savings and investments. Coale and Hoover (1958, p. 20) argued that "There is nothing about faster growth per se to lower consumption and raise savings ..."

10. False. Some historians hold that economic development in Europe and North America was in fact stimulated by population growth (see Clark, 1967, for a review). Disappearance of plague and the introduction of the potato reduced the death rate in Europe, which resulted in population growth, which, in turn, created a demand for more resources. In the United States, it has been argued (Fishlow, 1965) that railroad development, which helped accelerate the economic development of the western states, followed population westward.

11. False. The level of living in most of the LDCs has been markedly below the level of the Western countries on the eve of the Industrial Revolution. The populations of the Western countries were not growing as fast as they have been recently in the LDCs. Furthermore, the LDCs have been able to borrow technology from the MDCs, whereas the latter had to develop them on their own. The LDCs are in competition with the MDCs for the world's resources—a competition in which the MDCs usually win, partly because of their economic superiority.

12. False. But note that this was the major theme of the Coale–Hoover (1958) study: With a very young age structure, resources are siphoned off to consumption, leaving little for investment. In a pioneering study, Leff (1969) reported negative effect for young, old, and total dependency on saving. That study stimulated a considerable debate on the subject. Many analysts examined the same relationships using different data and methods. They failed, however, to uncover notable dependency effects. Statistically significant results, when found, were often weak (Kelly, 1988). The widely shared current view seems to be that there is no solid evidence for the age-dependency effect. The World Bank's *1984 World Development Report* (p. 82) concluded that "recent empirical studies find only minor support" for the effect. For citations of other studies sharing the same view see Kelly (1988).

13. False. It is true that the world appears to be better off economically now (with almost 6 billion people) than it was when there were only about 1 billion people. But this does not necessarily prove that Simon's thesis is correct. It simply indicates that there is no simple linear negative relationship between economic standard of living and population size.

14. False. There are many relatively low income countries in Eastern Europe with very low population growth rates. The same may be said of parts of South Asia. Sri Lanka and Kerala state in India are prime examples. There is speculation that low birth rates in these populations have been a response to their low income conditions, as indicated by such things as a shortage of housing and low affordability of consumer goods.

15. True. The controversy can be traced to pre-Malthusian era, but the debate rose to prominence with the publication of *An Essay on the Principle of Population* by Malthus in 1798. In his book Malthus argued that food production could not keep pace with population growth; starvation, vice, and misery would be the order of the day in the absence of prudential restraint and the economy would stagnate at a subsistence level of income.

16. True. Typically one examines the correlation between per capita output growth and population growth, using countries as units of analysis. One difficulty with the usual correlation analysis is that it does not shed light on causal relationships. Another difficulty is the causal relationship may run in both directions, population growth influencing and being influenced by economic development. A third difficulty is that the usual analysis does not take into account the role of other factors (e.g., resource abundance/scarcity).

17. True. It is in the agricultural sector where the benefits of population density have been frequently discussed. The National Research Council's (1986) study concluded that the advantage of population size was not large in Third World manufacturing; or in any case, not as large as in the agricultural sector. Higher population densities can decrease per unit costs and increase the efficiency of transportation, irrigation, extension services, markets, and communications (Kelly, 1988, and references cited therein). These economies may be substantial where modern agricultural technologies require large infrastructural investments. "Green Revolution" technologies would not have produced the same advantage in sparsely settled regions as it has in densely settled regions. Empirical studies yielding quantitative assessment of the relationship between population size and scale are, however, rare (Kelly, 1988).

18. True. The hypothesis in question holds that rapid population growth prompts (mainly governmental) spending to be diverted from growth-enhancing forms (e.g., physical-capital investment) to allegedly less productive forms such as schooling. In a detailed study of governmental spending on schooling, T. Paul Schultz (1987) concluded that the relative size of the school-age population exerted no independent effect on the shares of GNP expended on education. This finding is not consistent with the investment-diversion assumption of the Coale–Hoover (1958) study.

19. True, theoretically speaking. This reduction can be offset by improved technology and expansion of land in quality and/or quantity and by realizing economies of scale (e.g., economies in transportation). The question is whether, and if so how much, such offsetting takes place as a result of population pressure. There is consensus among economists that the net impact of population change on agricultural productivity can be determined only empirically rather than theoretically (Kelly, 1988). For most of Asia population pressure seems to have encouraged the movement toward adopting new technologies that are exceptionally productive. But country-specific experiences vary considerably. Where institutional factors (markets, land-tenure patterns, government policies) are favorable, the new technologies seem to flourish, especially in densely settled Asia (Kelly, 1988). The potential gains from the new technology have generated an effective demand for such institutional changes as land reform (Hayami and Ruttan, 1987). But there is no empirical basis to determine the impact of population pressures on such institutional changes as land reform (Kelly, 1988).

### 11.7.3. Answers

20. True. When the Western nations started to develop economically the world's resources were plentiful and underdeveloped. Frontiers were waiting to be discovered, conquered, or colonized. Emigration was an unrestricted option. The technological level was low and, hence, development required relatively lower capital investment. The world that the less-developed countries face today is different in all such respects.
21. True. The study used an elaborate computer model and came to the conclusion that even under the most optimistic scenario, the world's population cannot long retain improvements in living conditions that might be achieved. Eventually prosperity will give way to misery. Of course, the model does not do justice to the complexities of the real world and hence its output should not be treated as a prediction. Also, remember that some things, such as future technology, are nearly impossible to predict. Thus, while one might be able to forecast more or less accurately when the world would have used up all of its coal deposits, it is not as easy to foresee the discovery and development of new forms of energy.

### 11.7.4. Answers

1. A, B, and C: Economic development is usually measured by change in per capita output and economic growth by change in net national product. The multidimensional nature of economic development is clear from choice B.

### 11.7.5. Answers

2. A, B, C, and D: Regarding choice B, see for example Keynes (1937); Hansen (1939); and Reddaway (1939). Regarding choice C, see Coale and Hoover (1958). Regarding choice D, note that several developments helped to produce this reorientation. Empirical studies had shown that technological change, especially in agriculture, could offset the effects of diminishing returns. Also opposition to government sponsored family planning programs grew in strength. Julian Simon's (1981) controversial book, which argued that population growth in fact could in the long run enhance the pace of economic growth and development in low-income countries, stimulated further empirical research and evaluation of the work already done (see, e.g., National Research Council, 1986; World Bank, 1984).

3. A, B, C, and D: Colin Clark (1967), among others, argued that in the long run a growing population is more likely than a declining or stationary one to stimulate the economy (also see Keynes (1937); Hansen (1939); Reddaway (1939); Simon (1981)). As for choice B, see Hendershot (1973) for an analysis of 1970–1972 data from 83 developing countries, leading to the conclusion that "population size is a major determinant of military power." The usual Marxian position is captured in choice C. Marx believed that economic development is related to political and economic structure, not at all to population growth. Choice D is the well-known Coale–Hoover (1958) thesis.

4. A, B, C, and D: Typically the empirical analysis of the relationship in question involves a bivariate correlation analysis of per capita income growth and annual population growth rate, using countries as the units of analysis. See Kelly (1988) for a representative graphical display. Such analysis has been characterized as simplistic and difficult to interpret (Kelly, 1988). The problems with such analysis include the following: (i) causation is not revealed, (ii) institutional variations among countries may mask the relationships, and (iii) the relationship runs in both directions (population growth affects and is affected by economic development) and this cannot be captured by simple bivariate correlations. It has been suggested that the observed weak association between the two variables results from the positive and negative effects of population cancelling each other. As for choice D, in addition to the points already made, note that writers tend to work with assumptions that suit their pessimistic or optimistic position, as the case may be, rather than paying attention to all considerations simultaneously (Blanchet, 1991).

5. A and C: The first one is the Marxist position. The third one is espoused by those who believe that the more-developed countries are exploiting the less-developed countries by using the latter as the source of raw materials and a

market for manufactured goods. The other two statements do not emphasize exploitation of one group by another.

6. A, B, C, and D: These are developed in Coale and Hoover (1958).

7. A, B, C, and D: These are all different ways of saying the same thing: Higher young-age dependency implies less savings and hence slower economic development, other things being equal. Obviously, the argument is based on a narrow conception of the role of children. No attention is given to the possibility that children may contribute to household income, that they may stimulate parents to work harder, or make it difficult for them to work at all, that children may prompt their parents to accumulate wealth, or mortgage them, and so on. The point is that, theoretically speaking, the impact of expanded family size on household saving can be negative, negligible, or positive (Kelly, 1988). Few empirical studies have investigated the subject using data from less-developed countries. Leff (1969) found that age dependency exerted a negative impact on saving. Other studies that reexamined the Leff model generally failed to uncover notable dependency effects. "In short, the evidence does not support the hypothesis of a quantitatively important negative impact of population growth (through age-dependency effects) on saving" (Kelly, 1988).

8. A, B, and C: The National Research Council's (1986) report contains the following conclusion: "On balance, we reach the qualitative conclusion that slower population growth would be beneficial to economic development of most developing countries" (p. 90). The phrase "on balance" implies choice A and the phrase "qualitative" implies choice B. The report does not include choice D as one of its conclusions, but it is a conclusion arrived at by Preston (1986, p. 95).

9. A, B, C, and D: Kelly (1988) emphasized that it is not possible to make a quantitative assessment of the population impact on economic development. One could speak of only the direction of the impact. The impact may be positive or negative, and it may vary from country to country and over time within the same country. It may also vary with the rate of population growth. With respect to choice D, Kelly (1988) pointed out that problems such as unemployment, famine, and malnutrition have multiple causes (including rapid population growth in many instances) and that an emphasis on one cause (e.g., population growth) exclusively may not produce the desired insights. Note that Kelly's assessment is consistent with that of the National Academy of Sciences Working Group on Population Growth and Economic Development (National Research Council, 1986) as well as that of the World Bank (1984).

10. A, B, and C: In the World Bank's assessment, at a population growth rate of 2% per year, economic development can continue, albeit at a slower pace. This assessment also recognized that under certain conditions, "moderate population growth" can have positive impact on economic development. This happens with improvement in the quality of the labor force; stimulation of aggregate demand; economies of scale in transportation, communication, social services, and production; technological innovation and reduced investment risks; and economic and military power. As for choice D, the World Bank's assessment is that there may be adverse impacts of dependency on educational expenditures.

### 11.7.6. Answers

1. E.: According to a well-known economic model (Rostow), high mass consumption is the characteristic feature of the fifth and last stage of economic growth. During this stage, the population is affluent and consumer goods and services are mass produced. See *The MIT Dictionary of Economics.*
2. B: According to the United Nations Development Program's (1990) definition, human development is the process of enlarging people's choices and the people's level of achieved well-being. Particular emphasis is given to people's choices concerning (i) a long and healthy life, (ii) the acquiring of knowledge, and (iii) access to resources needed for a decent standard of living. Life expectancy at birth, literacy rate, and real GDP per capita are used as indicators of the degree of choices people actually have in respect to the areas just mentioned.
3. A. In practice real wage rates or wage earnings are obtained by dividing actual wage rates or wage earnings by the retail price index.

### 11.7.7. Answers

4. A: Relatively high.
5. B: High young-age dependency.
6. E: Bloom and Freeman (1987) called choice A the pessimists's view and choice B the optimists's view, and advanced choice C as their own view. See Kuznets (1973, p. 43) regarding choice D. Kuznets reported a rank correlation of 0.11 between the rate of population growth and per capita product for underdeveloped countries.
7. E: All of the above

### 11.7.8. Answers

8. D: In the 21st century, the world in all likelihood would reach its carrying capacity.

9. E: All of the above. The optimistic assumptions the investigators incorporated in their model included the following: Full exploitation of resources, recycling of 75% of used resources, reduction of pollution generation to 25% of the 1970 level, doubling of the 1970 rate of land productivity, and the universal availability of effective methods of birth control.

# CHAPTER 12

# *Population Policy*

Population policies are explicit statements about goals regarding population size, structure, and change, and the specification of measures and programs to attain the goals. Most countries with such policies today developed them during the second half of the 20th century. But if the concept is broadened to include all governmental actions with demographic impacts, then population policies have a longer history. Examples of actions prompted by non-demographic reasons, but nonetheless with demographic consequences, include planned economic development, land reform legislation, and programs emphasizing equal employment and educational opportunities that enhance the standing of disadvantaged sections of a population beyond the level attainable by them otherwise. There is some evidence that reduction in inequalities, enhancement of educational attainment, and the like have significant impacts on fertility, mortality, and migration rates.

Recognizing that increasing the per capita income, enhancing the level of education, etc., are easier goals to accomplish if the population is increasing at a slower rate, it is natural to ask whether population growth, composition, or geographic distribution can be altered by direct intervention. For example, can the fertility level of a population be lowered by educating the public on contraception and supplying them with contraceptive devices free or at affordable prices? Or can the congestion in an area be reduced by encouraging people to shift residence to a sparsely settled area? These are examples of population policy questions.

Among the main features of population policies are the following: (i) they are usually formulated by national governments, (ii) they have explicit goals and often clearly specified plans to pursue those goals, (iii) they are sometimes aimed at increasing or maintaining population growth, but in many of the current LDCs they are aimed at restraining population growth rate. As mentioned, direct policies are specifically aimed at altering demographic features of populations, while indirect policies are those not necessarily so designed but nonetheless have that effect.

Many countries (e.g., India and China) have direct population policies, many do not (e.g., the United States). A United Nations survey conducted in the late 1980s showed that, of the 170 countries that participated in the survey, 71 had a policy of no intervention, 60 had a policy to lower growth rate, and 39 a policy to maintain or increase the growth rate (United Nations, 1989).

To redirect the population growth pattern, a government can (i) try to influence people's demographic behavior in the desired way by communicating with them, (ii) change the balance of incentives and disincentives to behave in the desired way and provide services as necessary, (iii) manipulate social institutions, and/or (iv) apply coercion (Berelson, 1974).

Theoretically, population growth can be manipulated by controlling one or more of the components of change in population size. But controlling some components may be more practical than controlling others. Raising mortality is not an attractive, practical option, for example. International migration in volumes that makes a significant impact on the growth rate of a large sending country is impractical. Birth control is thus the most practical means to control population growth.

## 12.1. U.S. POLICIES AND PROGRAMS

The United States does not have an official policy aimed at directing population growth rates. Efforts to formulate a population policy have been resisted by the legislative and executive branches of the U.S. government (Weller and Bouvier, 1981, p. 280). Thus, for example, the government under the Nixon administration did not accept a Presidential Population Commission's recommendation that a "no-growth" policy be adopted. The U.S. government, however, has a long history of immigration laws and other policies and program with demographic consequences. Two examples are mentioned below.

The U.S. urban policy aimed at revitalizing the economies of older central cities is well known. For decades since the Housing Act of 1949, funds were funneled into the renewal and rebuilding of the economic and housing bases of the neediest older cities. One of the implicit goals of such policies had been to slow, if not halt, the middle-class exodus to the suburbs. In some cases the goals included arresting the drift of jobs and population from older Frost Belt cities to the Sun Belt. Critics of such policies have argued that instead of propping up declining places, urban policies should be redesigned to help the poor and the unemployed to migrate to places where job opportunities are expanding (Palen, 1987, pp. 428–429).

The United States also has a long history of policies and programs aimed at the promotion of health and the prevention of disease. For example, in the 1990 publication *Healthy People 2000: National Health Promotion and Disease Pre-*

*vention*, the Secretary of the Department of Health and Human Services presented a comprehensive plan to attain the following three broad goals: (i) to increase the span of healthy life of Americans, (ii) to reduce health disparities among Americans, and (iii) to achieve access to preventive services to all Americans. The publication specified 300 specific and measurable objectives which, when accomplished by the year 2000, should lead to the achievement of the three broad goals just mentioned.

## 12.2. OPPOSITION TO POPULATION POLICIES AND PROGRAMS

It is well known that the Catholic Church is opposed to the use of contraception, abortion, and sterilization. The influence of this position on the actual behavior of people has, however, been not universally strong. Historically, France, a predominantly Roman Catholic country, was way ahead of other countries in regard to fertility transition, thus serving as a major exception to the common perception that the precepts of the dominant religion in a country determine the reproductive behavior of its people.

Early Christian writers used the biblical phrase "be fruitful and multiply" to combat the 1st- and 2nd-century belief that procreation amounted to imprisoning divine soul in evil bodies. St. Augustine, the great 5th century bishop, declared that, procreation being the aim of marriage and of each conjugal act, it was a sin to engage in coitus for any other purpose (Thomlinson, 1975, pp. 125–127). Roman Catholics were explicitly forbidden by the 1968 encyclical "Human Vitae" from using contraception, abortion, or sterilization for birth control. For a discussion of the Papal encyclical and its effect on family planning practice and attitudes in the United States, see Ryder and Westoff (1971).

According to a fertility survey in 1955, 30% of the U.S. Catholic women reported using contraception not approved by the Church, the corresponding figure in a 1960 survey was 38%, in 1965 it went up to 53% and by 1969, the year after the 1968 encyclical, to 76% (Ryder and Westoff, 1971).

Opponents of birth control have advanced various arguments in support of their position (Thomlinson, 1975, pp. 126–127). Some people in the United States believe that those who support the birth control movement in the country do so with black genocide in mind. In the 19th century, the U.S. Society for the Suppression of Vice pushed for the legal prohibition of manufacture or sale of contraceptives and the banning of dissemination of birth control information. In 1877 Annie Besant and Charles Bradlaugh were tried in England for publishing Charles L. Knowlton's book on birth control, the charge being that they corrupted the morals. In some countries, members of the majority group oppose family planning movement, on the ground that if just the majority group were to practice birth control, the minority would eventually become the majority.

## 12.3. PRONATALIST POLICIES

The following are examples of pronatalist policies, programs, or actions. In 1920 France prohibited the distribution of birth control propaganda and devices. In November 1966, the Rumanian government introduced severe restrictions on induced abortion. A Spanish edict in 1623 granted tax exemptions to those who married young and raised large families. In Singapore, substantial tax rebates have been offered to encourage women to have a third child. (Weller and Bouvier, 1981, p. 282; Weeks, 1994, pp. 468–469).

Following the Rumanian government's introduction of severe restrictions on access to abortion in November 1966, the crude birth rate tripled in nine months from 12.8 per 1000 persons to 39.9 per 1000 persons (David and Wright, 1971, cited in Weller and Bouvier, 1981, p. 283). After that fertility started its downward course. By 1989 the total fertility rate had dropped to 2.3. (The Rumanian policy changed in 1989 with a change in government. The new government legalized abortion and by 1993 the Rumanian TFR had declined to 1.6.) The lesson that one may draw from the Rumanian experience is that in those situations involving almost exclusive reliance on a single means of birth control, severely restricting access to it (as well as to other methods of birth control) can produce a sharp rise in fertility level; but if this occurs when the preference for small families is strong, any reversal in fertility resulting from changes in laws is likely to be temporary. (See Weller and Bouvier, 1981, pp. 283–285; Weeks, 1994, p. 471.)

## 12.4. POLICIES, PROGRAMS, AND ACTIONS AFFECTING MORTALITY OR MIGRATION

Millions of human beings have been killed as a result of international warfare, more than 50 million during World War II alone, and over 6 million Jews were put to death in Germany in a deliberate attempt to eliminate an entire ethnic group from the face of the earth. Most governments pursue policies aimed at lowering mortality and improving health.

Many governments have explicit policies restricting immigration. A few examples follow. In 1990 Sweden began turning back refugees from Somalia and other African nations. In the 1950s the Indonesian government started experimenting with a program for persuading landless peasants residing in Java, the crowded, main island, to shift residence to other less crowded islands. In the mid-1980s, the Mexican government started to move some government offices out of the capital into other cities (Weeks, 1994, pp. 451–455; see United Nations, 1990a, for other examples.)

## 12.5. FAMILY PLANNING PROGRAMS

Family planning programs involve government-sponsored efforts to give interested persons information, supplies, and services pertaining to modern fertility control. (i) In some countries in which social and economic development has been occurring, family planning programs have accelerated fertility decline. Examples are Taiwan, Hong Kong, China, and Mexico. (ii) In some countries such as those in some parts of Africa, family planning programs have been too poorly organized to produce any impact on fertility. (iii) In some countries (e.g., India) family planning programs have been in place for a long time but it is hard to estimate the impact of the programs on fertility decline. (iv) In some countries fertility transition occurred long before the invention of the modern family-planning programs. The present-day MDCs fall under this last category.

Family planning programs are said to be guided by the so-called "knowledge and service" theory, which holds that if you inform people about the methods of birth control and give them good service, a large proportion of them will adopt family planning (Bogue, 1966; Weller and Bouvier, 1981, p. 285). An appealing feature of such a program is its emphasis on voluntary behavior. Another appealing feature is that the program is presented as a health measure with demonstrable humanitarian benefits. Such features make the family planning programs politically acceptable (Weller and Bouvier, 1981, pp. 285–286).

Among the shortcomings of most family planning programs are the following: (i) Many of them concentrate on certain particular methods of contraception (e.g., sterilization) to the exclusion of others. Contrast this with the so-called "cafeteria approach." (ii) Almost all family planning programs place undue faith on the validity of the responses to the desired-family-size question. (iii) All family planning programs assume that decisions about family size made by millions of couples in their own interest will automatically produce the desired level of population control. (iv) Most family planning programs exclude unmarried persons from their reach. (See Weller and Bouvier, 1981, p. 286).

### 12.5.1. Family Planning Movement

Donaldson and Tsui (1990) identified four stages for the family planning movement. The first stage, extending from the late 19th century to the end of World War II, was characterized by a women's movement that advocated voluntary motherhood and the right of wives to use contraception. The second stage, which started after World War II, emphasized disassociating the movement from eugenic interests and linking it more to economic development. The International Planned Parenthood Federation (IPPF) was founded during this period. During the third stage, which began in the early 1960s and lasted until the early 1980s, many developed countries included family planning support in their foreign aid budget. The United Nations Fund for Population Activities was created as a central agency for population matters within the United Nations. Many universities created population studies centers. The first U.N. intergovernmental conference on population was held in 1974 in Bucharest and a World Population Plan of Action was adopted at the conference. During the fourth stage, which started in the early 1980s, family planning programs received increasing attention in the less-developed countries, but some of the developed countries, especially the United States, began to withdraw or reduce support of family planning programs.

These developments have been called the family planning movements because they represent the coming together of a number of bodies aimed at bringing about certain specific changes (e.g., fertility reduction) by direct intervention. Among the bodies that joined hands in this endeavor have been United Nations agencies, national governments, philanthropic groups, and affiliates of the International Planned Parenthood Federation.

## 12.6. BEYOND FAMILY PLANNING

Modernization, improving women's status, increasing female participation in the labor force, and population education in schools have been among the measures proposed to produce fertility decline in less-developed countries. Note, however, that fertility may increase temporarily with modernization, but it is believed that the long-term effect will be to reduce fertility. In the short-term, fertility rate may go up because of morality decline and improvement of general health resulting in an increase in the monthly probability of conception and a reduction in the chance of pregnancy wastage, and because of alterations such as a reduction in breast-feeding and nonobservance of traditional behaviors, e.g., abstinence during certain periods.

It is known that women who participate in the labor force in industrial setting tend to have lower fertility. Hence increasing the labor-force participation of women has been regarded as a reliable way to bring fertility decline. The Program of Action adopted by the 1994 World Population Conference emphasizes the importance of drawing women into the mainstream of development. Better health, education, and freedom to plan their family's future widen women's choices, liberate their minds and spirits, and empower them to be involved in making decisions that affect them and their families (Sadik, 1994, p. 5).

There are differences of opinion concerning how effective population education could be as a means of producing fertility decline. The proposal usually discussed is to include population education at the junior and senior high school levels. The assumption is that since a great deal of demographic behavior is the result of socialization and training, people who are taught the advantages of small families and the disadvantages of large families would practice birth control. One problem is the time-lag involved—children in junior and senior high school reach peak reproductive ages only years later. But, of course, the introduction of population education at the school level can be coupled with the same at the level of adult education.

## 12.7. POPULATION POLICIES IN THE CONTEXT OF POPULATION THEORIES

The draft Plan of Action of the 1974 World Population Conference emphasized that family planning should be the focus of population policies. The U.S. government subscribed to this view. This has been interpreted (see, e.g., Weeks, 1995, pp. 540–541) as tantamount to emphasizing Ansley Coale's (1973) thesis that knowledge and mastery of effective techniques of birth control is one of the preconditions for marital fertility decline. Similarly the U.S. government's emphasis on development at the 1984 World Population Conference, in Week's opinion, amounted to emphasizing Coale's thesis that the perception of advantages from reduced fertility is a precondition for fertility decline. And finally, the U.S. government's position at the 1994 World Population Conference, namely that couples, especially the women, must be empowered to take control of their reproductive decisions was a way of emphasizing that the acceptance of calculated choice as a valid element in marital fertility is a precondition for sustained fertility decline.

The focus on development at the 1984 World Population Conference can also be seen in the context of the classical demographic transition theory, according to which, socioeconomic development alters the incentives for childbearing because in the industrialized, modernized setting couples with small families are better able than their counterparts with large families to achieve economic mobility.

Pointing out linkages between policy statements and parts of one or another theoretical framework is not the same as demonstrating that a given set of policy statements is firmly founded on a clear-cut theoretical framework. Generally speaking, population policies are seldom derived directly from any well-developed theoretical formulations. This is because theoretical frameworks in the population field are not usually developed with population policies and programs in mind, and those responsible for formulating population policies and programs are not necessarily well informed of population theories.

## 12.8. QUESTIONS AND ANSWERS*

**FOR EACH OF THE QUESTIONS IN SECTIONS 12.8.1 TO 12.8.5, STATE TRUE OR FALSE AND EXPLAIN**

### 12.8.1. Types of Population Policies

1. The United States does not have an official "no-growth" population policy because the country's constitution prohibits it.
2. In the United States, abortion is legal.
3. The United States has passed several laws with a view to regulating immigration.
4. Many countries encourage the repatriation or departure of groups of non-national residents.
5. A significant number of countries have policies designed to integrate (absorb) current non-national residents.
6. In the United States, for many decades since the Housing Act of 1949, there used to be an emphasis on funneling funds to revitalize the economies of older central cities.
7. Several European countries have introduced measures designed to boost fertility levels.

### 12.8.2. International Efforts to Influence Population Policies

8. The consensus at the 1994 International Conference on Population and Development (ICPD) in Cairo, Egypt, was that making family planning information and services available to all people is necessary and sufficient to slow population growth.
9. Abortion is a very divisive issue that policy makers and planners face today.
10. The issue of teenage sexuality has become a hotly debated item at international meetings on population policies.

### 12.8.3. Impact of Family Planning Programs

11. Family planning programs were primarily responsible for the fertility decline in Taiwan in the 1960s.

*Answers start page 299.

12. The government's implementation of a family planning program in China has had a major impact on the country's fertility decline.
13. India's national family planning program has been severely criticized for its failure to produce significant fertility decline, particularly in the northern part of the country.
14. Indonesia provides an example of a country in which rapid fertility decline is occurring as a result of a combination of social and economic development and an effective family planning program.
15. Pakistan has made significant progress with respect to fertility reduction.
16. Bangladesh is a good example of a country showing that a strong family planning program can be effective even when the level of social and economic development is very low.

### 12.8.4. The Role of Factors Other than Family Planning Programs

17. Once fertility transition gets underway, there is no stopping or reversal, until low levels are reached.
18. Muslim countries are unlikely to experience fertility transition any time soon because Muslim women are secluded and family planning programs are unlikely to reach them.
19. A precondition for fertility transition is the demise of all traditional family values.
20. Once fertility falls below the replacement level, it is easy to raise it to the replacement level by means of strong incentive programs.
21. The role of government is unimportant in making family planning programs effective in low-income countries.

### 12.8.5. Policies in Regard to Matters Other than Fertility

22. One aspect of immigration policy-making in the United States has been the extent to which decisions have been driven by political considerations rather than information gained from research.
23. Planned suburban towns, compared with conventional towns (of approximately the same age, location, housing types, etc.), have higher degrees of residents' satisfaction, lower rates of population turnover, and greater participation of residents in community life.

24. The question, "Are the known facts used honestly and objectively to inform policy decisions?" has been repeatedly raised by social scientists.

**FOR EACH OF THE QUESTIONS IN SECTIONS 12.8.6. TO 12.8.10., FOUR ANSWERS ARE SUGGESTED, AT LEAST ONE OF WHICH IS CORRECT. IDENTIFY THE CORRECT ANSWER(S) AND EXPLAIN.**

### *12.8.6. Variations in Population Policies*

1. Strategies for influencing fertility levels include:
   A. General economic and social development
   B. Family planning programs.
   C. Communication (education) programs
   D. Family allowance programs

2. In regard to immigration policies, a 1987 survey by the United Nations indicated that:
   A. Countries with policies designed to maintain current levels of immigration formed a majority
   B. Those with policies designed to decrease immigration was about half as many as those of the category mentioned in choice A
   C. A very small percentage of countries pursued policies designed to increase immigration
   D. None had a non-intervention policy

3. Commonly adopted strategies of governments to influence population distribution within the country include:
   A. Slowing primate city (metropolitan) growth
   B. Promoting small towns and intermediate cities
   C. Developing rural areas to retain or attract rural populations
   D. Making migration permit a requirement for residential shift over a given distance

4. The specific goals set for the year 2015 by International Conference on Population and Development (ICPD) in Cairo, Egypt, include:
   A. Providing universal access to a full range of safe and reliable family planning methods and related reproductive health services
   B. Substantially reducing infant, child, and maternal mortality rates
   C. Increasing life expectancy at birth to more than 75 years
   D. Achieving universal access to primary education and improve female educational attainment beyond primary level

5. The 1994 International Conference on Population and Development in its Program of Action called on governments to take which of the following steps to end discrimination against women?
   A. Ensure that women can own property equally with men, obtain credit and negotiate contracts in their own names, and exercise their rights of inheritance
   B. End male-female gaps in hiring, training, and wages
   C. End exploitation, abuse, and violence against women
   D. Enact laws and implement programs enabling both men and women alike to organize their work around their family responsibilities.

### 12.8.7. *Impact of Family Planning Programs*

6. What do we know about the impact of family planning programs? The observed fertility decline (during 1960–1965 to 1980–1985) was:
   A. Greatest in countries with strong "program effort" and high levels of "development"
   B. Very weak or absent in countries where development was low and program effort was very weak or nonexistent
   C. Was weak when program effort was very weak or nonexistent, no matter whether development was high
   D. Was positively associated with program effort if the developmental level was "high" or "upper middle."

### 12.8.8. *Population Policies in China*

7. Which of the following apply to China's population policies?
   A. China had no campaigns for population planning prior to 1970.
   B. At first the approach advocated in the 1970s was to lower birth rates through later marriage, longer spacing of births, and fewer children.
   C. China's emphasis was all along on population education in schools.
   D. The well-known one-child-per-couple policy was adopted in the 1970s.

8. In China heavy reliance for birth control was put on:
   A. IUD
   B. Female sterilization
   C. Male sterilization
   D. The Pill

### 12.8.9. *The Role of Factors in Addition to Family Planning Programs in Fertility Transition*

9. Which of the following are among the explanations for the rapid fertility decline in China?
   A. China's significant progress in health and education.
   B. Rapid urbanization.
   C. The success of the political system in mobilizing family planning services for over 300 million women of childbearing age.
   D. Rapid economic development.

10. Which of the following are among the explanations why the rate of fertility decline and that of contraceptive prevalence has been considerably lower in the Philippines than in neighboring Indonesia and Thailand?
    A. The Philippines is far behind the two neighbors in social and economic development.
    B. The Philippines is less urbanized than Indonesia and Thailand.
    C. The mortality level is higher in the Philippines than in the other two countries.
    D. The Philippine family planning program is relatively ineffective.

### 12.8.10. *Impact of Population Policies on Population Structure*

11. High sex ratios at birth have been reported in China. The explanations advanced in the literature for the unusual sex ratios at birth include:
    A. Under-reporting of births of daughters
    B. Reporting the birth of a girl as a stillbirth prior to private adoption arrangements
    C. Sex-selective infanticide
    D. Sex-selective abortion

**FOR EACH OF THE QUESTIONS IN SECTIONS 12.8.11 TO 12.8.13., FIVE ANSWERS ARE SUGGESTED, ONLY ONE OF WHICH IS CORRECT. IDENTIFY THE CORRECT ANSWER AND EXPLAIN.**

### 12.8.11. *Concepts*

1. The term "unmet need" in the context of family planning programs refers to:
   A. The degree to which the supply falls below the demand for a specific contraceptive device or service
   B. The percentage of married women, of age 15–49, who say they want to prevent or postpone births but are not using any contraception

C. The degree to which information dissemination fails to reach the target population
D. The long waiting time for anyone to obtain a sterilization operation
E. The lack of sufficient number of personnel working in rural areas

2. The term "status of women" refers to:
   A. Autonomy
   B. Resources
   C. Well-being
   D. The degree of equality between men and women, within each class or stratum
   E. All of the above

### 12.8.12. *Policies and Programs and Their Changing Contexts in the Less-Developed Countries*

3. Changes in social policy producing a depressing effect on fertility include:
   A. Legalizing abortion
   B. Introducing a social security system
   C. Legally restricting child labor
   D. Raising the age at marriage
   E. All of the above
4. The fertility transition is completed or underway in how many of the four major Asian regions: West, South Central, Southeast, East?
   A. All four
   B. Three
   C. Two
   D. One
   E. None
5. Which of the following countries has a strong family planning program, low mortality, and high literacy?
   A. China
   B. India
   C. Bangladesh
   D. Nepal
   E. Pakistan
6. Which of the following countries experienced the least fertility decline between the late 1960s and the late 1980s?
   A. China
   B. India

C. Bangladesh
D. Pakistan
E. Sri Lanka

7. Which of the following non-program factors contributed to the fertility decline in rural China?
A. Reduction in mortality
B. Gains in female education
C. Erosion of traditional family values
D. Economic liberalization
E. All of the above

8. The percentage of married women using contraception is least in which of the following major regions of the world?
A. Africa
B. Asia
C. North America
D. Latin America
E. Europe

9. How much do family planning programs in the developing countries cost annually, on the whole?
A. $15–20 billion
B. $25–30 billion
C. $50–60 billion
D. $60–70 billion
E. Over one trillion

10. Which of the following is true of family planning programs in general?
A. Universally common structure, theme, and strategies
B. Emphasis on changing family size norms
C. Tendency to work within the social and cultural setting of the country involved
D. Focus on married as well as unmarried women
E. Heavy reliance on external funding

### 12.8.13. *Evaluation of Family Planning Programs*

11. It is difficult to separate the fertility effects of the family planning programs from those of modernization and development because:
A. The fertility effects observed are usually the joint effects of the two sets of factors confounded with the effects of other, usually unobserved, factors

B. The observed effects in a country are influenced greatly by particular features of the country involved
C. The programs vary in style
D. Measurement problems are serious
E. All of the above

### 12.8.1. Answers

1. False. The U.S. Constitution neither requires nor prohibits any official population policy. The explanation seems to be that neither the legislative branch nor the executive branch has felt a need for promulgating a population policy.

2. True, according to a 1973 ruling of the U.S. Supreme Court.

3. True. Examples include the 1798 Alien Act, the 1882 Chinese Exclusion Act, the 1921 Quota Act, the 1965 Immigration Reform Act, and the 1986 Immigration Reform and Control Act. See the chapter on migration for a brief discussion of these legislations.

4. True. For example, Belgium, Finland, the Netherlands, and Switzerland all had, as of the late 1980s, policies to encourage repatriation. Sri Lanka has a policy of encouraging repatriation to India of Tamils who migrated from India and who do not hold citizenship in Sri Lanka. The government of Bangladesh had sought assistance from international organizations to repatriate to Pakistan an estimated 260,000 people, originally from Bihar.

5. True. According to the responses to the *Sixth Population Inquiry*, 1987, of the United Nations, the Netherlands reported that foreigners with a history of continuous residence in the country for five or more years were given voting rights in municipal council elections. Other countries with policies of integration include Belgium, Canada, Norway, United Kingdom, and Switzerland. (See United Nations, 1990a, p. 234).

6. True. See text.

7. True. Among the measures are maternity/paternity leave, maternity and child allowances, tax benefits, expanded opportunities to combine household functions and labor-force activities (part-time work, work sharing, and flexible time schedules). For example, in 1984 Greece adopted a policy of granting a three-month paternal leave, Bulgaria increased maternity benefits and family allowances (1985), in Finland a parent could choose between a municipal daycare center and a home-care allowance (1985), in France an infant home-care allowance was introduced to help working mothers with at least three children

(1986), Austria raised maternity benefits, birth allowances, and family allowances (1987) (see United Nations, 1990a, p. 116). Note, however, that it is not clear whether any such measures were effective in raising fertility levels (see Demeny, 1986).

### 12.8.2. Answers

8. False. The consensus was that a combination of a number of social interventions will have to be sustained over a period of time to bring fertility levels down. The recommended policies include: sustainable development, education and empowerment of women, improved literacy, increased availability of contraceptives, and high-quality health care, particularly that related to reproduction.

9. True. Reproductive-rights advocates argue that abortion is an important option for women if their contraceptive method fails or if a pregnancy poses a high risk of complications. On the other side, anti-abortion activist organizations in the United States, for example, have attempted to block or overturn the legalization of abortion. In many countries, strong opposition on religious or ethical grounds has prevented abortion services from becoming widely available. At the 1994 International Conference on Population and Development (ICPD) in Cairo, the abortion issue was hotly debated. For a while it looked as though no compromise was possible between the opposing sides. In the end, however, the delegates adopted a compromise language, which included the statement that "in no case should abortion be promoted as a method of family planning."

10. True. One position is that imparting information on sexuality and reproductive health services will encourage early sexual activity among teenagers. The other position is that sexual education is an integral part of general education aimed at making young people responsible decision makers. In respect to the latter position it is also held that young people in many societies face pressures to engage in sexual activity and that they need information on reproductive health services to prevent unwanted pregnancies and sexually transmitted diseases. On average, in the less-developed countries teenage fertility rate is about 70 per 1000 teenage girls. The corresponding U.S. level is about 60. In the United States information about sexuality is more widely available as is reproductive health services than is typically true of the less-developed countries. Yet the U.S. level of teenage childbearing is not much different from that of typical developing countries. The question therefore arises whether the level of teenage child bearing is a simple matter of the availability of information about sexuality and the availability of reproductive health services.

### 12.8.3. Answers

11. False. The emphasis is on the word "primarily." An island-wide family planning program with unofficial government backing was begun in 1964. Before that time a local program was introduced in the city of Taichung. The government adopted an official population policy in 1968 with a family planning program as an integral component. Toward the end of the 1950s, the TFR in Taiwan was about 6 per woman. By 1963 it had dropped to 5.4 and by 1968 to 4.3. Obviously the fertility decline had stated before any organized family planning program (official or unofficial) was in place. In the early phase of the fertility transition, the major factor responsible for fertility reduction was postponement of marriage. It is not valid therefore to claim that the family planning programs were primarily responsible for the fertility decline during the 1960s. One third of the decline in the crude birth rate from 44.8 per 1000 persons in 1956 to 20.6 per 1000 persons in 1983 has been attributed to lower nuptiality (non-marriage and delayed marriage, mostly the latter) and the remaining to lower marital fertility (Freedman, 1995, p. 22).

12. True. In 1970, the government started its national family planning program. Within 12 years TFR had fallen 54%, and in the following decade China reached replacement-level fertility. It should be emphasized that the fertility decline in China was also to a significant extent facilitated by forces other than the government program, particularly in the urban areas. Fertility decline in urban areas began before the launching of the national family planning program. Among the significant non-program factors were prior declines in child and adult mortality, rising education levels, labor force participation of women, a severe housing shortage, and existence of old-age pension (Freedman, 1995, p. 9). But the family planning program is believed to have accelerated the fertility decline.

13. True (see, e.g., Freedman, 1995, p. 12). In 1989, the then-Prime Minister Rajiv Gandhi stated that the Indian program had fallen short of expectations because of bureaucratic bungling. But singling out the family planning program as the villain in the drama of fertility dynamics in India is an oversimplification. India is characteristically a heterogeneous country, with its 18 states differing widely in cultural, social, and economic features. In such a setting, it is no wonder that there are variations among the states in the starting time and pace of demographic transition. For a detailed comment on India's family planning program, including its history, see Cassen (1978, pp. 145–209). The complexity of the Indian situation is illustrated by the fate of a National Population Policy that the government announced in 1976. Family planning performance was accepted as one of the criteria for allocation of federal funds to states. Two

specific measures attracted wide attention: moves in some of the state legislatures to pass legislation for compulsory sterilization and the federal government's position that its employees were expected to adopt the small family norm. In 1976 only one state (Maharashtra) legislature actually passed a compulsory sterilization bill. Several states prepared such bills but chose to wait to see the outcome of the Maharashtra bill. The approach was so inconsistent with the existing political structure that it failed miserably—the political party that was behind the approach was voted out of office in the general election that followed and the whole family planning movement dropped into a dormant state for a considerably long time thereafter.

An often-mentioned explanation for the north–south difference in fertility in India has been based on the presumed higher female social status in the south than in the north (see Basu, 1992, and Dyson and Moore, 1983, p. 195). Basu (1992) compared migrants to New Delhi from a southern state (Tamil Nadu) and a northern state (Uttar Pradesh) and found that women in the former group had greater "autonomy," higher education, and lower fertility on average than the women in the latter group. Visaria (1993), however, did not find convincing evidence for the hypothesized north–south differences in female autonomy, which she defined in terms of "the ability to make one's own decisions about what to do" (e.g., with one's income or with natal-kin contacts). Neither did the study reveal any significant association between fertility and female autonomy.

14. True. Between the late 1960s and 1990, fertility fell by 46%. The 1994 Indonesian TFR was 3.0 per woman. Like China, Indonesia was able to produce effective action at the grassroots level for development activities as well as family planning. A study by Freedman *et al.* (1981) showed that in 1976 family planning program was able to reach remote, backward communities. Contraceptive use was at that time highest among the upper and the lowest income classes (Freedman, 1995, p. 10).

15. False. The 1994 TFR in Pakistan was 6.1 (PRB World Population Data Sheet, 1994). Pakistan's organized national family planning program dates back to the 1960s, but, in the opinion of many experts, it never was effectively implemented. Some experts (e.g., Mauldin and Ross, 1991) consider Pakistan's family planning effort as "moderately strong," while others (e.g., Freedman, 1995, p. 11) consider it to be "weak." The coverage of the family planning services does not exceed one-third of the population according to the 1992 report of the Demographic and Health Surveys.

16. True. Bangladesh ranks low on any index of social and economic development. In 1992, per capita income in Bangladesh was about U.S. $220. As of

1994, infant morality rate was very high at 116 per 1000 live births and overall mortality level was moderately high, with a life expectancy at birth of 53 years (PRB 1994 World Population Data Sheet). But between 1975 and 1994 the TFR fell from 7.0 to 3.4 (Kantner *et al.*, 1995, p. 11). The main factor responsible for this decline was a strong national family planning program (Freedman, 1995, pp. 13–14). Some elements of modernization must have also been influential to an unknown degree (Cleland *et al.*, 1994).

### 12.8.4. Answers

17. False. The case of Malaysia is an example (Freedman, 1995). During 1965–1978, the total fertility rate fell from 5.3 to 4.3 among the Malays, from 5.6 to 3.4 among the Chinese, and from 6.7 to 3.5 among the Indians; during 1978–1986, however, the TFR rose from 4.3 to 4.6 among the Malays, and continued to fall reaching 2.4 among the Chinese, and 2.9 among the Indians. The rise in fertility for the Malays during 1978–1986 has been attributed to a strong pronatalist initiative and political movement organized by Muslim religious forces. In a 1984–1985 fertility survey, a substantial proportion of Malay women reported that they revised their fertility expectations upward in response to the campaigns. In the post-1986 period, however, the total fertility rate fell among all the three major ethnic groups, to 4.1 by 1992 among the Malays, 2.1 among the Chinese, and 2.5 among the Indians.

18. False. Indonesia, the most populous Muslim country in the world, has an effective family planning program and rapidly declining fertility. Significant levels of contraceptive use exist in Muslim countries such as Egypt and Tunisia. Turkey, another Muslim country, has experienced rapid fertility decline. Bangladesh is another example. The hypothesis that links fertility transition to the secluded status of Muslim women should be considered within the context of political and cultural forces that modify the influence of religion in society (Obermeyer, 1994; Freedman, 1995, p. 19).

19. False. The history of fertility transition in Taiwan illustrates the point that traditional family values can coexist with high contraceptive use, low fertility levels, and high levels of socio-economic development (Freedman, 1995, pp. 21–22). Thus, the traditional preference for sons is still strong in Taiwan. In the early 1980s, when the TFR had fallen below the replacement level, about two-thirds of couples married during that period (1980–1985) had stayed a significant part of the beginning years of married life in the household of the husband's parents. The extended family consisting of one married son, his wife and children, and his parents, is still common in Taiwan, the only major

difference being that whereas traditionally the young wife did all the housework, the current pattern is for the mother-in-law to do such chores while the educated young wife works away from home.

20. False, judging from the evidence available so far. Demeny (1986) concluded that pronatalist policies in Europe had little effect, but Büttner and Lutz (1990) reported some success in East Germany in raising fertility through a strong incentive program. There are those who believe that by reducing the incompatibility between having children and working outside home it might be possible to encourage women to have more children. But there is not enough evidence to assume that this is possible.

21. False. A comparison between China and Indonesia on the one hand and Pakistan on the other provides an illustration of the point.

### 12.8.5. Answers

22. True. Fuchs (1992, pp. 1069–1076) refers to a number of examples of the kind, including the decision to end the *bracero* (guest-worker) program in 1964; the 1965 ending of the national origin system for allocating immigrant visa; and the 1976 decision to place restrictions on foreign medical school graduates coming to the United States for practice or training in the medical profession.

23. False. A study by Burby and Weiss (1976), in which the investigators compared 17 planned suburban towns with an equal number of conventional towns, found no significant difference with respect to any of the items mentioned.

24. True (see, e.g., Hawley, 1971, chapter 11). Consider, for example, attempts by despotic governments to prevent change by prohibiting migration in and out, the assumption being that exposure to ideas and experience from outside are likely to develop into a threat for the existing system. But such attempts fail because some external contacts are unavoidable, any external contact tends to bring with it innovative ideas, and also because with improvements in communication, external contacts become easier without physical movement across space. Referring to the attempts by many of the less-developed countries to stem internal migration to their metropolitan centers through such policies as requiring residential permits for settling in destination cities, Simmons (1979) argued that the lack of success of such attempts is traceable to ignorance of migration principles.

### 12.8.6. Answers

1. A, B, C, and D: The demographic transition in the West has demonstrated that general social and economic development is a sufficient condition to bring mortality and fertility levels down. One of the basic assumptions of family planning programs is that the program would help bring fertility down independently of social and economic changes. Communication (education) programs aim to convert people to small family orientation so that they would want to adopt birth control practices. The target population may be adults in the reproductive age groups or children in schools. Family allowance programs have been tried in some of the more developed countries with a view to encouraging people to have higher fertility. The success of the programs described in choices B, C, and D vary from very little to significant, depending upon the circumstances and the nature of the program.

2. A, B, and C: Fifty-six percent of all countries (with 77% of the world's population) reported that their policies were designed to maintain the current level of immigration, 19% reported policies aimed at decreasing immigration, 4% reported policies designed to increase immigration (United Nations, 1990a, p. 226).

3. A, B, and C: The Republic of Korea has, for example, put priority on promoting secondary cities as a means of reducing the dominance of Seoul. The government also emphasizes the development of rural areas, partly as a means of reducing out-migration. To encourage urban-to-rural migration the government uses resettlement allowances for the urban poor. In addition, the government exerts control over industrial location. The government of Bangladesh is creating 470 *upazilas* (subdistricts) to serve as the major local government unit, with functions and staff transferred from higher levels of government. See United Nations (1990a).

4. A, B, C, and D: The average level of infant mortality rate for the less-developed countries in 1993 was 69 per 1000 live births, and the corresponding child (under 5 years of age) mortality rate was 102 per 1000 children. These rates are to be reduced to 35 and 45, respectively, by the year 2015. The maternal mortality rate in the less-developed countries is to be reduced to 60 maternal deaths per 100,000 live births by 2015. For the world as a whole the 1994 life expectancy at birth was 65 years, which is very close to that of the less-developed regions (63 years). Hence to increase it to 75 years by the year 2015, the mortality situation in the less-developed regions will have to be considerably improved. See Ashford (1995, p. 33).

5. A, B, C, and D: These four steps are in addition to providing equal employment and educational opportunities for men and women. The idea that men and women are to be viewed as equal partners in all aspects of public and private life, as contained in these recommendations, was subscribed to by almost all delegates. See Ashford (1995, p. 22).

### 12.8.7. Answers

6. A, B, C, and D: See, for example, Bongaarts *et al.* (1990), in which the authors report the analysis of fertility decline during 1960–1965 to 1980–1985 in 78 low income countries. They classified the countries according to family planning program effort (based on measures of policies, resources, "stage setting," services, record keeping, and availability of birth control supplies and services) and according to development level (based on per capita gross national product, infant mortality, school enrollment, and a communication measure). They used four classes for program effort: "strong," "moderate," "weak," and "very weak or none" and four for development: "high," "upper middle," "lower middle," and "low."

   For countries in the "high" category of development, the total fertility declines were 3.1, 2.4, 2.4, and 0.8, respectively for the four program effort categories ("strong" to "very weak or none"); for countries in the "upper-middle" category of development level, the corresponding figures were 2.7, 2.4, 1.4, and 0.8. For those in the "low" development category, the TFR decline was negligible or nonexistent.

### 12.8.8. Answers

7. B and D: There were short-lived campaigns for population planning in the 1950s and 1960s; they emphasized mainly maternal and infant well-being. The efforts that started in the 1970s, however, had lowering birth rates as the major goal. The slogan was birth rates are to be lowered through *wan*, *xi*, *shao*, meaning later marriage, longer spacing between births, and fewer children, respectively. The one-child-per-couple was adopted in 1978–1979 to keep the population from growing beyond 1.2 billion by the end of the 20th century. The political muscle was heavily used in the implementation of the policies (Tien *et al.*, 1992).

8. A, B, and C: In 1982, over 80% of people using contraception in China were using the IUD, male sterilization, or female sterilization. Abortion was a backup method.

### 12.8.9. Answers

9. A and C: China is not yet an urbanized country. Only 28% of its population live in urban areas. Economically China still remains a poor country. The 1994 per capita income was about the equivalent of U.S. $380. In urban areas fertility had begun to decline before the starting of the national family planning program, but it was accelerated by an intensive urban family planning program during 1964–1967. Among the significant nonprogram factors that contributed to the rapid decline in urban fertility in China were: (i) prior declines in child and adult mortality, (ii) rapidly rising education levels, (iii) the employment of women in non-home-centered activities, (iv) a severe housing shortage, (v) the existence of old-age pensions, (vi) parents' strong aspirations for their children's education, and (vii) more recently, rising consumerism (Freedman, 1995, p. 9).

10. D: With respect to economic development, the three countries belong to the same class. With respect to urbanization, the Philippines is somewhat more advanced than the other two countries. With respect to mortality levels also the three countries belong to the same class, roughly speaking (the 1994 life expectancy at birth was 60 years in Indonesia, 64 years in the Philippines, and 69 years in Thailand). The percentage of married women who wanted to space or limit births but were not using contraception was higher in the Philippines in 1988 than in her two neighbors (Freedman, 1995, p. 16). The family planning program in the Philippines has been judged to be weaker than those of her neighbors (Indonesia and Thailand). After a careful examination of the available information, Freedman (1995, p. 17) came to the conclusion that the Philippines was significantly behind Indonesia and Thailand in fertility transition because its family planning program has been relatively ineffective, in part due to the strong opposition from the Catholic Church.

### 12.8.10. Answers

11. A, B, and C: The 1990 census confirmed high sex ratios for children born in the 1980s. In the urban areas the sex ratio for children under one year of age was 109 and for children of age 2–4 years was 107–108. In rural areas the corresponding numbers were 112 and 109–110 (Tien *et al.*, 1992, p. 16, citing Chinese census publications.) The results of two fertility surveys show a clear increase in the sex ratio during the 1980s, the decade that followed the introduction of the one-child-per couple policy. The high sex ratio among the live births during the 1980s has been attributed to the government's one-child policy. Some analysts have suggested sex-selected abortion as an explanation

in light of the one-child-per-couple policy. But sex-selective abortion is illegal and it is doubtful that the technology for the determination of sex was within the reach of the ordinary people. Another explanation is that births of girls were misreported, especially those meant to be given away for adoption. This explanation was prompted by the increase in the number of cases of adoption during the 1980s. Higher infant mortality among girls than among boys has been suggested as yet another explanation. Female infanticide has also been considered as a plausible explanation. Hard evidence for any of these explanations is difficult to obtain.

### 12.8.11. Answers

1. B: In some countries the "unmet need" is as high as 36% (see Ashford, 1995, p. 25).
2. E: There is no standard definition of the term "status of women." A commonly accepted definition of "status" is "relative rank in a hierarchy of power, privilege, and prestige." When women are compared to men the question is whether, other things (e.g., class membership) being equal, women have the same status as men. Autonomy, resources, and well-being are various dimensions of status. Sometimes the term "women's situation" is used as a synonym (see, e.g., Mason, 1995). Educational levels and literacy, employment status and occupation, age at marriage in relation to that of the spouse, and life expectancy at birth have commonly been used as indicators of status.

### 12.8.12. Answers

3. E: Abortion is an effective means of birth prevention when contraception fails. A social security system can take away one of often-mentioned motivation to have several children, namely old-age security. Similarly, restricting child labor takes away one of the benefits of having children, often mentioned in less-developed countries. In northern India, for example, carpet weaving used to be primarily done by children. Raising age at marriage significantly above the beginning of reproductive period will depress fertility, other things being equal.
4. A: Freedman (1995, p. 7), noted that in 1992, 24 countries accounting for 95% of Asia's population, belonged to one or other of the following four categories: (i) eight countries (China, India, Indonesia, Bangladesh, Pakistan, Nepal, Sri Lanka, Vietnam) accounting for 81% of Asia's population with a contraceptive use rate of 60% and TFR ranging from 2.1 to 6.0; (ii) two countries (Malaysia and the Philippines) accounting for 2.6% of Asia's population, with rather ineffective family planning programs or under distinctive pronatalist pres-

sures; (iii) eight countries of West Asia, with high TFRs but with clear indication of the onset of fertility transition; and (iv) six wealthy or moderately wealthy countries of East and Southeast Asia accounting for 8% of Asia's population, with almost universal contraceptive use and TFRs at or below replacement level.

5. A: China. Joining China in the category are Indonesia, Sri Lanka, and Vietnam. India's family planning program is rated moderately strong. Bangladesh has a strong program but high mortality and high illiteracy. Nepal and Pakistan have weak programs and high mortality and high illiteracy (Freedman, 1995, p. 7).
6. D: Pakistan experienced about 4% decline in fertility, while Sri Lanka experienced 43% decline, India and Bangladesh about 26%, and China 60%. (Freedman, 1995, p. 7).
7. E: With respect to choice C, note that the recurrent government campaigns against traditional family values must have had some effect, although no one has quantified it. With respect to choice D, note that the reference is to a recent development and therefore its presumed effect is based on the supposition that the so-called consumerism must have fostered small-family mindedness and fertility control.
8. A: According to the estimate published in PRB's 1994 World Population Data Sheet, 21% of married women in Africa use contraception. The corresponding figures for the other major regions are: North America 74%, Latin America 58%, Asia 60%, and Europe 72% (1991 figures).
9. A: According to the U.N. estimate, by the year 2000 the annual cost of family planning and related reproductive health programs will reach about $17 billion. (The estimate has been derived as follows: Using a model, the number of users of family planning is projected. The projected number is then multiplied by the cost per user.) The cost of family planning program is thus a small fraction of the estimated health-care cost of $848 billion (see Ashford, 1995, p. 34).
10. C: Family planning programs vary greatly in their structure, theme, and strategies. The main emphasis of all programs is to meet the existing demand for family planning supplies and services. One seldom finds a program that aims to change family size orientation or family size norms of the population. An exception is the Chinese family planning program, which has been criticized for neglecting human rights. "In response to stringent national and village targets, many local family planning efforts became coercive, forcing abortions and inducing premature deliveries ..." (Ryan and Flavin, 1995, p. 129). Regarding choice D, note that most of the national programs focus on

married couples. The exclusion of young people has been pointed out as a weakness of the usual family program. The assumption that only after marriage does one need family planning supplies or services is invalid in many modern setting. As regards choice E note that while some programs are heavily dependent on external funding (e.g., Bangladesh with 79% external dependence), there are programs such as that of Indonesia and the Philippines that are funded mostly from within (82% in the case of Indonesia and 69% in the case of the Philippines (Ashford, 1995, p. 36).)

### 12.8.13. Answers

11. E: A common procedure to estimate the impact of family planning programs on fertility involves a classification of countries by socio-economic development and family planning efforts (Bongaarts *et al.*, 1990; Mauldin and Ross, 1991; Entwisle, 1989). The focus then turns to a comparison of fertility changes of countries in different categories of program effort, controlling for socio-economic development. The effects of other factors that are excluded muddy the inferences drawn from such comparisons. Classification errors are also problems. Mauldin and Ross (1991) regarded Pakistan's family planning program as "moderately strong," but Freedman (1995, p. 11) classified it as weak. Both socio-economic development and family planning program effort are multidimensional variables. Reducing each of them to a single dimension by haphazard procedures, such as having a panel of people rate each, is bound to invite measurement errors. Moreover, such cross-country comparisons fail to give due attention to particular features of individual countries, which may be highly influential as far as fertility changes are concerned. Warwick (1986), for example, has identified several critical cultural factors facilitating the implementation of family planning programs and has pointed out that these were present in Indonesia but not in Kenya. Hull (1986) has enumerated a number of specific features of the Indonesian scene, which were claimed to have had significant impact on the outcome of the family planning program in that country. Note the difference between the authoritarian approach of China and the more educational approach of Indonesia.

# Glossary

**Abortion** Termination of pregnancy during the early part of the gestation period (typically the first 3 months); it may be spontaneous or induced.

**Abortion rate** The number of abortions in a given year per 1000 women of reproductive age (15–44 years or 15–49 years), using the mid-year estimate for the denominator.

**Abortion ratio** The number of abortions in a given year per 1000 live births in that same year.

**Achieved characteristics** Traits (e.g., the level of education one attains or the kind of occupation one chooses), which, to a certain degree, are regarded as open to one's choice; these are distinguished from ascribed characteristics.

**Administrative area** Geographic units, such as counties in the United States and districts in India, created for administrative purposes.

**Age structure** Classification of a population by age, presented in terms of absolute numbers (counts) or in terms of percentages.

**Age at marriage** The age at which a person is formally married.

**Age** (1) Time interval that has elapsed since birth; interval (in completed years) between birth and the time of observation. (2) Number of years completed as of the birthday anniversary nearest to the time of observation. (3) One plus the number of New Year's passed since birth (an oriental practice).

**Age-adjusted rate** See **standardization**.

**Age pattern of fertility** The way in which age-specific fertility rates vary with age: The rates increase sharply with age at first, reach a peak in the twenties, and then decline gradually.

**Age-sex pyramid** A graphic device for depicting the classification of a population by age and sex, consisting of two histograms, one for males oriented to the left of the vertical axis and the other for females oriented to the right of the same axis, age being represented vertically (with the youngest at the bottom), each bar having its area proportional to the number of persons in the corresponding age-sex category.

**Age-sex structure** Classification of a population by age and sex. *Syn*: age-sex composition.

**Age-specific rate** A rate that relates age-specific annual number of demographic events, e.g., deaths, to the corresponding at-risk population. The latter is usually approximated by the mid-year population of the specified age group.

**Age-standardized rate** See **standardization**.

**Age stratification** Status differentiation, hence inequality in power and privilege, in a society based on age.

**Aging of a population** Change in the age structure of a population involving an increase in the relative number of older persons (e.g., those of age 65 years and older), resulting usually in an increase in the average age of the population.

**Agricultural Revolution** Change in food production that occurred about 10,000 years ago when people began to domesticate animals and plants and establish relatively permanent settlements.

**Alien** A resident of a country who is not a citizen of that country.

**Antinatalist** (1) A person who is pro-birth control. (2) A policy aimed at birth control.

**Arable land** Tilled or tillable land.

**Area of destination** In the context of migration, the area where the migration ends. *Syn*: place of destination; host area.

**Area of origin** In the context of migration, the area from which the migration starts. *Syn*: place of origin; donor area.

**Ascribed characteristics** Traits one is born with or over which one has no control (e.g., sex); these are distinguished from achieved characteristics.

**Asylee** A person who is given asylum (protection from arrest and extradition) by a country.

**At-risk population** A set of people who are liable to experience (exposed to the risk of experiencing) a given type of event, e.g., getting pregnant.

**Average** In statistical usage, a measure of central tendency of a distribution, examples being arithmetic mean (total divided by the number of cases) and median (above which and below which 50% of the cases fall when arranged in ascending or descending order of values).

**Baby boom** The dramatic rise in fertility during the post-World War II period. This was more prolonged (from 1946 to 1964) in the United States than in other countries.

**Baby bust** The decline in fertility that followed the post-World War II "baby boom" in countries such as the United States, Canada, and other more-developed countries.

**Balancing equation** The mathematical equation that expresses change in population size as the sum of two components: (i) natural increase, i.e., births − deaths, and (ii) net migration, i.e., in-migration − out-migration (or immigration − emigration, in the case of national populations). Population size at a given point in time = population size at a previous point in time + births in the interim − deaths in the interim + in-migration in the interim − out-migration in the interim.

**Birth** The complete expulsion or extraction from the mother of a product of conception, irrespective of the duration of pregnancy, which product, after such separation, breathes or shows any other evidence of life, such as beating of the heart, pulsation of the umbilical cord, or definite movement of voluntary muscles.

**Birth control** As applied to couples, conception-preventing actions (e.g., abstinence, contraception) and post-conception measures (e.g., induced abortion) that prevent the pregnancy from resulting in a live birth. Some writers, equating birth control to conception control, do not regard induced abortion as a means of birth control.

**Birth interval** Interval between two successive births or that between marriage (entry into sexual union) and the first birth.

**Birth order** The number of previous births to the mother + 1.

**Brain drain** Emigration of a significant proportion of a country's highly educated, highly skilled professionals to other countries that offer them better social and economic opportunities.

**Capital goods** In economics, produced goods (e.g., machinery, tools, factories, roads) used in the production of other goods or services. The word capital is also used as a term for financial assets.

**Capitalism** An economic system characterized by (i) private or corporate ownership of property including capital goods, (ii) private or corporate rather than government decisions controlling investments, and (iii) competition in free market determining production, distribution, and pricing of goods and services.

**Capitalistic society** Society practicing or advocating capitalism.

**Cardiovascular disease** A disease of the heart or blood vessels.

**Carrying capacity** The number of people who can be sustained at a given standard of living by a particular land area at a specified technological level.

**Cause of death** Condition certified by a physician or a responsible authority in the registration process as having contributed to a person's death, the most critical condition (disease or injury that initiated events resulting in death) being regarded as the underlying cause. Final disease or condition resulting in death is called the immediate cause. The U.S. Standard Death Certificate has provision for listing a sequence of causes, beginning with the immediate cause and ending with the underlying cause.

**Celibacy** The state of not being married; prolonged abstention from sexual intercourse.

**Census** The total process of collecting, compiling, evaluating, analyzing, and disseminating population data pertaining to all persons in a specified geographic territory as of a specified time.

**Center of population** The point at which an imaginary flat, weightless, rigid map of the area inhabited by a population of interest would balance if the people were represented by weights placed on the map at their respective locations. In practice one assumes that people are clustered in certain locations (e.g., points representing cities, towns, villages) and are all of equal weight.

**Central city** The largest city of a metropolitan area.

**Childhood mortality** Mortality during childhood, i.e., during the age interval from 1 until 5.

**Children ever born** The number of live births to a woman until the time of observation, including non-surviving offspring.

**Child-woman ratio** The number of children of age below 5 years per 1000 women of childbearing ages (15–44 or 15–49 years).

**Chronic disease** Disease that persists for a long time.

**Circular mobility** Movement(s) to a geographic location and return (e.g., from a primary residence to a secondary residence at back).

**Civil registration** See **registration**.

**Clan** A kin group whose members claim descent from a common ancestor.

**Cohabitation** Persons of opposite sex living together without having gone through formal (civil or religious) marriage rites. *Syn*: consensual union or common-law marriage.

**Cohort** A group of people experiencing a demographic event such as birth or marriage at a common time point or interval, e.g., a calendar year. Those born, for example, in the calendar year 1990 form the 1990 birth cohort; those who got married in the calendar year 1994 form the 1994 marriage cohort.

**Cohort analysis** Demographic analysis using cohort as the unit of study, emphasizing the experience (e.g., with respect to reproduction) of a single cohort or the comparison of the experiences of different cohorts.

**Cohort measure** Demographic indexes calculated for true (as opposed to hypothetical or synthetic) cohorts.

***Coitus interruptus*** Withdrawal of penis before ejaculation occurs during sexual intercourse.

**Common-law marriage** See **cohabitation**.

**Communicable (infectious) disease** A disease capable of being transmitted from one person to another.

**Commuting** Movement between home and activity location, such as school or work.

**Complete life table** A life table in which all quantities pertaining to a time point are shown for each birthday anniversary and all quantities pertaining to an interval of time are shown for the interval between each successive birthday anniversaries.

**Completed fertility** The number of live births to a woman by the time she reaches a given age; if the age is the end of childbearing period, the term "terminal completed fertility" applies.

**Components of population change** Births, deaths, geographic mobility, and social mobility. If change in size is the focus, then only births, deaths, and geographic mobility are relevant.

**Conceptual framework** A body of concepts and a set of propositions that are logically and systematically interrelated, developed with a view to explaining a broad category of phenomena.

**Consensual union** See **cohabitation**.

**Consequences of population change** Outcomes produced by or necessarily following a given population change.

**Content error** An error in data, such as an inaccuracy in age, produced at the stage of reporting, editing, or tabulating.

**Contraception** Voluntary prevention of conception or impregnation when sexual intercourse takes place.

**Contraceptive** An agent that diminishes the likelihood that sexual intercourse results in impregnation. An oral contraceptive is a hormonal compound taken orally in order to block ovulation and prevent the occurrence of pregnancy. A contraceptive device is something contrived to prevent conception from occurring when sexual intercourse takes place, e.g., a diaphragm or condom to prevent entrance of spermatozoa into the uterine cervix, or an intrauterine device (a coil, loop, T, or triangle of plastic or metallic substance) inserted into the uterus to prevent conception.

**Coverage error** Omission of or counting more than once anyone who should be included, in a census or survey.

**Crowding** Having a large number of people in close proximity to each other in a given space.

**Crude birth rate** The number of live births in a population during a given year per 1000 persons, using in the calculation the mid-year population count for the denominator.

**Crude death rate** The number of deaths in a population during a given year per 1000 persons, using in the calculation the mid-year population count in the denominator.

**Crude rate** The number of annual events such as births or deaths in a population in a given year per 1000 persons, using in the calculation the mid-year population count in the denominator.

**Cultural community** A community whose members share a common cultural tradition.

**Culture** (1) A common heritage of a group of people, consisting of customs, values, ideas, beliefs, social forms, and artifacts. In a society this heritage is transmitted from one generation to the next through socialization and training. (2) Symbol systems and the information they convey in a society or group.

**Cumulative cohort fertility** Average number of live births to a birth cohort of women prior to a given age, e.g., prior to 25 years.

**Customs** Informal norms that define acceptable behavior in a society or a part of it.

***De facto* population count** Count of people present on the census moment in a specified geographic territory.

***De jure* population count** Count of people who "belong" to (are the usual residents of) a given area, no matter whether they are there at the census moment.

**Death** Permanent disappearance of all evidence of life any time after birth has occurred.

**Demand for children** A couple's desired number of surviving children.

**Demographic transition** A model of population change focusing on the transition from high levels of fertility and mortality to low levels. According to the classical version of this model, mortality levels start to decline first to which fertility levels respond with a lag prompted by the industrial-urban setting that undermines traditional values. The same model pictures mortality as fluctuating and fertility as stable at pre-transition high levels and vice versa at post-transition low levels. During the transition, population grows rapidly, whereas before and after the transition, the growth rate is low.

**Demographics** A popular term for population as a factor, affecting such things as business matters.

**Demography** Systematic study of population, focusing on population size and structure (the composition, and spatial spread) and the nature, components (fertility, mortality, spatial movement, and social mobility), causes, and consequences, of population change. The term demography is derived from two Greek words, δῆμος, the people, and γράφειν, to draw or write.

**Density** The average number of individuals or any other elements per space unit (e.g., a population density of 500 persons per square mile; a housing density of 4 houses per acre).

**Dependency ratio (age-dependency ratio)** The ratio of the number of dependent people (e.g., those outside the age group 15–64 years) to the number of economically active people (e.g., those in the age range 15–64 years).

**Descriptive analysis of population** An analysis that focuses on discernible patterns in population data without going into explanations regarding why the data are patterned as they are.

**Desired family size** The number of children one would choose to have if one could have exactly the number thus chosen.

**Determinant** A factor that establishes the nature of an entity or event or conditions an outcome. (Mathematicians use this as a technical term to represent an entirely different thing—a number associated with a square matrix).

**Developed countries** Technologically advanced countries with industrialized, urbanized economies.

**Developing countries** Countries in the process of becoming technologically advanced, industrialized, and urbanized.

**Differentials** Between strata differences in demographic parameters, when people are stratified according to demographic, social, or economic characteristics, e.g., differences in fertility by educational level.

**Disability** Limitation imposed by physical or mental handicap on the performance of activities such as self care and locomotion (e.g., climbing a flight of stairs).

**Disease** A condition of a living entity or of one of its parts that impairs the performance of a vital function.

**Distribution** (1) Spatial spread of people. (2) In statistics, the frequency of occurrence of the values of a variable.

**Divorce** Formally (legally) ending marriage with one's spouse.

**Donor area** In the context of spatial movement of people, the area from which movement starts.

**Doubling time** The time a population takes to double its size at a given annual growth rate. A formula commonly used for calculating it is the following: The natural logarithm of the ratio of population size at a given moment to that at a previous moment equals the annual rate of growth times the interval (in years) between the two moments. According to this formula, the doubling time (in years) is 100 times the natural logarithm of 2 divided by the percent annual growth rate. The natural logarithm of 2 is 0.6931. Therefore, at 2% annual growth rate, the doubling time is 69.31/2 or 34.7 years. A very close approximation to this result is given by the easy-to-remember formula: 70 divided by the annual percent growth rate.

**Economic development** The process of improving the standard of living and well-being of a population by raising per capita income through industrialization rather than relying on the agricultural sector.

**Economic growth** Typically an increase in the real level of net national product (see national income) without regard to the total number of people involved.

**Ecosystem** A community and its environment viewed as a single interdependent whole.

**Educational attainment** The highest level of education attained by a person, commonly measured by the number of years of schooling completed.

**Emigration** Migration of persons out of a country.

**Emigration rate** The number of emigrants from a country during a given year per 1000 mid-year population of that country.

**Employment** Activity in which one is engaged or employed.

**Environment of a population** All the external conditions, physical or sociocultural, affecting or affected by the lives of the members of a population.

**Enumeration** The information-gathering phase of a census. Enumerate means count.

**Epidemic** An outbreak of a disease affecting or tending to affect many people.

**Epidemiologic transition** Long-run shifts in health and disease patterns in a population.

**Epidemiology** The systematic study of the incidence, prevalence, distribution, and control of diseases in a population.

**Ethnicity** A person's identification with respect to national origin, race, language, or culture.

**European marriage pattern** Late marriage and a high proportion of people never marrying. This pattern was a distinguishing feature of Western Europe during the 18th and 19th centuries.

**Event** A change in state (e.g., from never married to married, from unemployed to employed).

**Ever-married** A collective term used for those who are currently married, divorced, separated, or widowed.

**Expectation of life** The average remaining life time, according to a life table, at any age for those who survive to that age.

**Expected family size** The number of children a person expects to have in all, those already born + the additions expected in the future. Usually the reference is to live births.

**Explanatory analysis** Data analysis that emphasizes explaining the patterns observed in the data, using a conceptual framework.

**Exponential growth of population** A model of population growth reminiscent of the compound interest formula, with compounding done at each instant. The formula is $P_1 = P_0 \exp(rt)$, where $P_0$ is the initial size of population and $P_1$ that after an elapse of $t$ years and $r$ the annual growth rate. Another way of expressing the formula is the following: the natural logarithm of the ratio of $P_1$ to $P_0$ is equal to the product of $r$ with $t$: $\ln(P_1/P_0) = rt$.

**Exposure to risk** The condition of being liable to experience an event (e.g., pregnancy).

**Family** Two or more persons related by birth, marriage, or adoption and residing together.

**Family life cycle** Successive stages from formation until dissolution that a family goes through. Traditionally, marriage marks the formation; childbearing and child-raising constitute the growth stage; and loss of members due to migration, divorce, or death characterizes the dissolution stage.

**Family planning** Deliberate attempts by couples to regulate the number or spacing of births. See **birth control**.

**Family planning program** Organized (usually government-sponsored) effort to reduce fertility levels in a population by providing interested people with information, supplies, and services pertaining to modern fertility control.

**Family size** (1) The number of surviving children of a couple or a person. (2) The number of live births to date to a couple or a person.

**Fecundity** The physiological capability of an individual or a couple to produce a live birth.

**Fertility** The childbearing performance of individuals, couples, groups, or populations, more commonly of the last two.

**Fertility control** Regulation of reproduction using birth control (contraception or abortion) or other means such as controlling exposure to intercourse, e.g., by postponement of marriage.

**Fertility cycle** Increase or decrease of fertility level of a population and subsequent return to the original level.

**Fertility differentials** Between strata differences in fertility levels in a population when people are stratified in accordance with their social, demographic, economic, or other characteristics.

**Fertility orientation** General inclination with respect to family size. The commonly used indicators include ideal family size, desired family size, intended family size, and expected family size. Typical interview questions concerning these are the following: "What do you think is the ideal number of children for the average (American) family?" "How many children would you want in all, if you could have just the number of children you want?" "How many more children do you intend to have?" "How many children do you expect to have in all (counting those you now have)?"

**Fertility rate** See **general fertility rate**.

**Fertility schedule** The sequence of age-specific fertility rates covering all ages.

**Fertility transition** Long-term shift from high levels of fertility to low levels in a population.

**Fertility trend** The long-run direction of movement of fertility level.

**Fetal death** Loss of life to a fetus. Stillbirth, miscarriage, or abortion.

**Fetus** The unborn product of conception in the post-embryonic period, i.e., after major structures have been outlined. In humans the period just mentioned is from seven or eight weeks after fertilization until birth. Some analysts take this period to be from the end of the third month of pregnancy until birth.

**Forced migration** (1) In modern times, a type of migration in which individuals are compelled by a government to move. (2) Historically, movement of slaves and often that of indentured laborers. "Shanghaiing" was once a widespread practice to secure sailors for voyages to the Orient. This involved putting someone aboard a ship by force, often with the help of liquor or a drug.

**Foreign-born** Those members of a country's population born in another country.

**Formal demography** Demographic analysis emphasizing mathematical or stochastic models of demographic phenomena.

**Frailty** Relative strength or weakness of the human body to resist disease and illness.

**Free migration** A type of migration in which the initiative and free choice of the migrant play a significant role. *Syn*: spontaneous, voluntary migration.

**Gainful employment** Activity engaged in by a person for pay or remuneration. This was the basic "work" concept before the introduction of the labor-force concept.

**Gender** The social meaning attached to being male or female in a society.

**General fertility rate** Annual number of births per 1000 women of childbearing age, using mid-year estimate of women 15–44 or 15–49 years of age for the denominator. Sometimes this measure is termed simply "fertility rate."

**Geographic mobility** Change of residence from one address to another, no matter whether it involves crossing a migration-defining boundary.

**Gestation (period)** The period from conception to parturition. *Syn*: pregnancy.

**Gravity model** The hypothesis that migration is directly proportional to the product of the sizes of the relevant origin and destination populations and inversely proportional to a positive function (e.g., the *n*th power) of the distance between the two.

**Green Revolution** A dramatic increase in agricultural output resulting from the use of "miracle strains" (high yield varieties) of grain and increased use of fertilizers, pesticides, and irrigation.

**Gross migration** In-migration plus out-migration (or immigration plus emigration, in the case of national populations).

**Gross reproduction rate (GRR)** Average number of daughters born to a group of women who reproduce in accordance with a given schedule of age-specific fertility rates, i.e. who complete the reproductive period, bearing children at each age at the rate for that age indicated in a given schedule of age-specific fertility rates. The GRR may be thought of as the average number of daughters per woman at the end of the reproductive age group in a hypothetical population where the given age-specific fertility rates (considering only daughters) remain time-invariant and no woman dies before the end of the reproductive age group.

**Growth rate (percent)** Percent change in population size per year. This may be negative in the case of population decline.

**Head of household** That person in the household who is acknowledged as the head of the unit by the other members of the household. In recent years opposition to the term has led to replacing it with other terms (e.g., reference person, householder) in several censuses (e.g., the United States and the United Kingdom). Relationship to head of the household ("reference person" or "householder") is a basic item of information that censuses and surveys routinely collect. This information helps to classify households into different types (e.g., family and non-family households).

**High-growth potential** A characteristic of a pre-transition population.

**High-yield varieties (HYV)** Strains of grain producing dramatically higher yields if cultivated using modern farming methods.

**Historical demography** Demographic analysis of historical source material such as parish registers of baptisms, weddings, and burials in an effort to improve the understanding of the demographic history of a particular population or to shed light on patterns discernible in contemporary demographic data.

**Host area** In the context of migration, the area in which migration ends.

**Household** One or more persons residing in a separate housing unit.

**Householder** A term that replaced the "head-of-household" concept; usually the household member who owns or in whose name the housing unit is rented.

**Hutterites** An anabaptist religious sect residing mostly in North and South Dakota in the United States and neighboring regions of Canada. This group is well-known for its high fertility in the early decades of the 20th century.

**Hypothetical cohort** A theoretical concept (involving the imaginary follow up of an imaginary group of people) using which certain demographic rates such as the total fertility rate can be given a cohort interpretation. *Syn*: Synthetic cohort.

**Ideal family size** See **fertility orientation**.

**Illegal immigrant** A person entering a country without proper government approval. *Syn*: undocumented alien.

**Illegitimacy** The state of being born to parents not formally married to each other.

**Illegitimacy rate** The number of illegitimate births in a year per 1000 unmarried women of reproductive ages (15–44 or 15–49 years), using mid-year estimate for the denominator.

**Illegitimacy ratio** The number of illegitimate births in a given year per 100 live births in that year.

**Illegitimate birth** Birth to parents not married to each other.

**Illness** An unhealthy condition of the body or mind.

**Immigration** The act of entering a country with permission to reside there permanently.

**Immigration rate** The number of immigrants during a given year per 1000 mid-year population of the receiving country. Note the analogy to the crude birth rate.

**In-migrant** An in-mover who crosses a migration-defining boundary.

**In-mover** A person who moves into an area to reside there.

**Incidence rate** In epidemiology, the number of new cases of a disease occurring in a population during a given year per 1000 persons, using the mid-year population estimate in the denominator.

**Incipient decline** A characteristic of a population at the end of or after the demographic transition.

**Income** The amount of funds, goods, or services received by an individual, corporation, or economy in a given time interval.

**Index of aging** The number of persons of age 65 years and older per 100 persons of age under 15 years.

**Induced abortion** Abortion following a deliberate attempt to terminate pregnancy.

**Industrial Revolution** The complex of social and economic changes that began late in the 18th century in England, and later in other countries, marked by the introduction of power-driven machinery, the growth of large factories, and the decline of home and small-shop industry.

**Industrial society** A society in which production of outputs uses machines powered by inanimate energy sources (e.g., coal, petroleum, natural gas, hydroelectric power).

**Infant mortality** Death of live-born infants before reaching the first birthday anniversary, measured usually by the number of such deaths in a given year per 1000 live births in that year.

**Infecundity** The inability to produce a live birth.

**Institutions** A system of social relationships and cultural elements that develops in a society to address basic problems. Education, the family, the economy, the polity, and religion are five major institutions in a society. The term is also used for establishments and established organizations, such as a university.

**Institutional population** Persons who reside in dwelling places that are not households. Examples are children at boarding schools, hospitalized patients, residents of nursing homes, and prisoners. Such persons are enumerated separately in censuses.

**Inter-censal period** The interval between two consecutive censuses in a population.

**Intermediate (fertility) variables** Physiological and social factors that directly influence the reproduction process: age of entry into sexual union, coital frequency, contraception, abortion, separation of spouses, abstinence, etc., through which, and only through which, social and economic background factors can affect fertility.

**Internal migration** Migration within a country.

**International migration** Migration from one country to another.

**International Classification of Diseases (ICD)** A list of diseases and causes of death prepared by the World Health Organization. The list has undergone numerous revisions. Several countries have prepared tables to derive comparable groupings over time. Many countries use the ICD for vital registration purposes.

**Intervening opportunities** A concept introduced by S. A. Stouffer (1940) suggesting that the number of migrants from one place to another will be proportional to the number of opportunities at the destination and inversely proportional to the number of opportunities between the origin and the destination.

**Intervening obstacles** In the context of migration, factors such as distance, natural barriers, and difficulties of transportation between two places that discourage migration from one to the other, even when other considerations encourage it.

**KAP survey** Survey regarding knowledge, attitude, and practice with respect to contraception. Beginning in the 1950s a whole series of such surveys were conducted throughout the world in an effort to measure the spread of family planning. It became fashionable in the 1960s and 1970s for population experts in the rich countries and international agencies to interpret the results of KAP survey to mean that the provision of cheap family planning and abortion services would quickly reduce fertility in the less-developed countries. This led to the inclusion of family planning support in the foreign-aid budgets of a number of national governments.

**Kin** People who are related to one another through birth, marriage, or common (social or biological) ancestry.

**Labor force** Persons employed, whether full time or part time, plus those unemployed (i.e., out of work, but looking for some), age 16 (less in some countries) and older. A problem with this concept is that it treats the same activity differently depending upon whether the person engaged in it is a paid worker or not. For example, a homemaker or housewife is not in the labor force but a domestic servant performing identical tasks is.

**Less-developed countries (LDCs)** Low income countries in the process of industrialization and modernization. *Syn*: developing countries; Third World countries.

**Life course** Sequential changes in the lives of individuals or families over time, beginning with birth and ending with death for individuals and beginning with formation and ending with dissolution in the case of families.

**Life-cycle perspective** (1) As applied to individuals, a perspective that focuses on the stages (e.g., adolescence, adulthood, etc.) that a person goes through from infancy to old age. (2) As applied to the family, changes from formation to dissolution—intermediate stages involve births of children; departure of grown children to be on their own; dissolution of marriage because of divorce or widowhood; death of the surviving spouse.

**Life expectancy** See **expectation of life**.

**Life span** Maximum number of years a person can expect to live under ideal conditions.

**Life table** A tabular presentation showing various statistics including the attrition due to deaths in the size of a hypothetical cohort as its members advance in age subject to the mortality experience represented by a given schedule of age-specific death rates.

**Life table functions** The various statistics given in a life table.

**Literacy** Ability to read and write at least a simple statement in a language.

**Live birth** See **birth**.

**Local mover** One who changes residence, but does not in the process cross any migration-defining boundary.

**Longevity** The length of life, often measured at the population level by the life expectancy at birth.

**Macro perspective** A perspective that focuses on larger entities such as societies or communities and on the regularities discernible at such levels.

**Malthusian component of the fertility transition** That part of fertility decline attributable to delay in marriage and/or nonmarriage.

**Malthusian** In the context of population studies, one who subscribes to **Malthusianism**, a theory of population based on or inspired by the writings of Thomas Robert Malthus (1766–1834).

**Marital dissolution** Ending of marriage by divorce, marital separation, or widowhood.

**Marital fertility** Fertility considering only married persons.

**Marital status** Classification of a person into single (never married), currently married, divorced, separated, or widowed.

**Marriage** Sexual union formalized legally and/or religiously. Sociologists used to view marriage as a contract between a man and a woman that legitimates their offspring.

**Marriage cohort** People married at the same time (e.g., during a given calendar year).

**Marriage squeeze** An imbalance between the numbers of males and females available for marriage. Such imbalance may be caused, for example, by excess male mortality in war, sex-selective migration, or fluctuating fertility rates, the last because there is usually a tendency for women to marry men slightly older than themselves. Fertility fluctuations usually affect the relative sizes of successive birth cohorts—when fertility is rising there will be fewer eligible (older) males per female and when fertility is falling there will be fewer eligible (younger) females per male.

**Marxist** In the context of population studies, one who subscribes to a theory of population based on or inspired by the writings of Karl Marx (1818–1883).

**Maternal deaths** Deaths to women resulting from conditions associated with pregnancy or child birth.

**Maternal mortality rate** Number of maternal deaths in a given year per 100,000 lives births during the same year.

**Mean age at marriage** The average age at which individuals marry. Demographers pay more attention to the mean age at first marriage than that of subsequent marriages.

**Median age** The age that marks the fifty-fifty (percent) divide of a population arranged in ascending or descending order of age.

**Menarche** The beginning of menstrual function.

**Menopause** The permanent cessation of menstruation.

**Metropolitan area** In the United States, a county with a large city and the adjoining counties with which the central city is socially and economically integrated. Typically, a metropolitan area has a population of at least 100,000 and contains one or more centers with 50,000 or more inhabitants. *Syn*: urban agglomeration.

**Metropolitanization** Increase in the metropolitan areas' share of the total population of a country.

**Micro perspective** A perspective that focuses on regularities discernible by analyzing characteristics of lower-level observable units (e.g., individuals).

**Migrant** One who shifts residence and crosses a migration-defining boundary in the process.

**Migration** A shift in residence that involves crossing a migration-defining boundary.

**Migration-defining boundary** The boundary of a political area such as a county in the United States, crossing which when shifting residence makes a person a migrant.

**Migration-defining interval** In the context of defining migration by comparing residence at two points in time, the interval between those two time points.

**Migration differentials** Between strata differences in migration rate, when people are stratified by social, economic, or demographic characteristics.

**Migration push** Factors or conditions in a given place that encourage residents to migrate.

**Migration pull** Factors or conditions in a given place that draw migrants from other areas.

**Migration stream** People who migrate from a given area of origin to a given area of destination during a given period of time; those who migrate in the opposite direction in the same period form the **counterstream**.

**Mismatched qualifications** Lack of correspondence between a worker's qualifications and those required for the work involved.

**Misreporting of information** Giving or recording inaccurate information (e.g., in censuses or sample surveys).

**Mobility** In population studies, shift in residence (e.g., from one neighborhood to another) or change in status (e.g., from married to widowed). The former is geographic mobility whereas the latter is social mobility.

**Modernization** Replacing traditional ways of thinking and doing things with new ways, usually associated with industrialization and urbanization.

**Momentum of population growth** The increase or decrease in population size that would occur if the net reproduction rate were to become one immediately and remain so indefinitely, other things remaining unchanged and migration ruled out.

**Moral restraint** In Malthusian theory, a desirable preventive check involving the avoidance of sexual intercourse prior to marriage and the postponement of marriage until a man can afford a wife and the children she might bear.

**Morbidity** The state of illness and disability in a population (from Latin *morbidus* meaning diseased).

**More-developed countries (MDCs)** Industrialized, urbanized, modernized countries (currently the countries of Europe and North America, the former U.S.S.R., Japan, Australia, and New Zealand).

**Mortality** The process by which deaths deplete population size.

**Mortality differentials** Between-strata differences in mortality indexes, when a population is stratified with respect to social, economic, and demographic characteristics.

**Mortality trend** Long-term direction in which mortality level moves.

**Mortality transition** Change from high and fluctuating mortality levels to low and stable level in a population.

**Mover** One who shifts residence.

**Multiple causes of death** All the conditions contributing to the death of a person reported by an authorized person (e.g., a physician).

**Natality** See **fertility**.

**National income** A measure of the money value of the goods and services available to the nation from economic activity. There are several approaches to measuring this. One of these, called the output approach, involves obtaining gross national product—gross domestic product, i.e., the sum of the values added at each stage of production by the industries and productive enterprises in the country, plus net property income from abroad.

**Natural fertility** (1) Marital fertility when couples do not control their reproductive behavior according to the number of children already born. (2) In practice, marital fertility in the absence of contraception or induced abortion.

**Natural increase** Births − deaths.

**Natural resources** All the freely given material phenomena of nature within the boundaries of human activities, including fertile land, oil, coal, ores and mineral deposits, natural forests, rivers that can be harnessed to produce hydroelectric power, rainfall, wind, and solar energy, some of which are renewable and some not.

**Naturalization** Process by which alien immigrants can acquire citizenship.

**Naturalized citizen** An immigrant who has been granted citizenship of the country of immigration.

**Neo-Malthusian** One who believes in the Malthusian position that population tends to outstrip resources but (unlike Malthus) accepts birth control practices as appropriate checks on population growth.

**Neo-Malthusian component of fertility change** That part of the transition from high to low levels of fertility attributable to declining marital fertility.

**Neo-natal deaths** Infant deaths during the first 28 days of life.

**Net migration** In-migration minus out-migration, or immigration minus emigration in the case of national populations.

**Net reproduction rate (NRR)** The average number of daughters that a birth cohort of women would bear during their lifetime if they experienced given sequences of age-specific fertility rates and age-specific death rates. The NRR is also the average number of daughters per women at the end of the reproductive age group in a hypothetical population having the given age-specific fertility rates (considering only daughters) and the associated mortality schedule for females remain time-invariant.

**Never-married** Single in marital status.

**Non-marital fertility** Fertility of persons who are not currently married.

**Norms** Rules binding upon the members of a group and serving to guide, control, or regulate proper and acceptable behavior. Sometimes the term "social" norm is used instead (e.g., social norm concerning family size). Norms may be formal (e.g., laws) or informal (e.g., customs).

**Nuclear family** A family consisting of husband, wife, and unmarried children.

**Nuptiality** The formation and dissolution of marriages (and other sexual unions) in a population.

**Old-age dependency** Number of old persons (usually of age 65 years and older) per 100 persons of working ages (usually 15–64 years).

**Opportunity cost** With reference to an action, the value of the foregone alternative action.

**Optimum population** The population size consistent with the attainment of a particular set of specific objectives, e.g., maximize per capita income or welfare given fixed resources.

**Out-migrant** In the context of internal migration, referring to a specific area, a person who migrates from that area to another. In the context of international migration the corresponding term is emigrant.

**Out-mover** In the context of local movement (e.g., within a county in the United States), referring to a specific area, a person who shifts residence from that area to another.

**Parity** Referring to women, the number of children ever born (e.g., "two-parity women" have had two live births; "zero-parity women" have had none).

**Parturition** The act or process of giving birth to offspring.

**Per capita** Per head (e.g., per capita national product = gross national product divided by the size of the population).

**Percentage** A part of a whole expressed in hundredths.

**Perinatal deaths** Fetal deaths occurring after 28 weeks of pregnancy plus infant deaths occurring during the first week of life.

**Period measure** A population parameter pertaining to a specified point or period of time (e.g., annual number of births or deaths per 1000 persons in a country for a specific calendar year).

**Population** All the people inhabiting a specified geographic area at a given time.

**Population change** Change in the size, composition, or geographic distribution of a population.

**Population composition** Makeup or classification of the members of a population by one or more characteristics such as age, sex, marital status, educational attainment, occupation, residence, or income.

**Population density** (1) The relationship of the size of a population to the size of the geographic area occupied by it (measured by the ratio of the population size to the area of the territory inhabited). (2) The relationship of population size to the resources in the territory occupied (measured, for example, by population per unit of arable land).

**Population distribution** Spatial spread of a population (e.g., by region; in rural and urban areas).

**Population dynamics** (1) Change in population size, composition, or geographic distribution brought about by mortality, fertility, spatial movement, or social mobility. (2) Any demographic feature susceptible to change.

**Population explosion** A popular term referring to the rapid increase in world population size, particularly in the post-World War II period.

**Population growth** Change (usually increase) in population size.

**Population growth rate** Population growth in relation to the initial size (commonly measured by percent growth, which is 100 times the ratio of population growth to the initial size).

**Population growth rate cycle** Any departure from, and subsequent return to, an initial population growth rate (e.g., starting from a zero growth rate an increase and then a decrease in the growth rate taking it back to zero).

**Population momentum** See **momentum of population growth**.

**Population policy** Explicit statements (usually by a government) about goals concerning population size and structure (composition and distribution) or changes therein, and action programs aimed at achieving those goals.

**Population problem** (1) A perceived consequence of population structure or change that causes concern to many people. (2) Any demographic condition that many people consider as undesirable and want to have eliminated. (3) Any social problem with population structure or change as a contributing factor.

**Population program** Project implemented with the objective of attaining one or more goals in a population policy statement.

**Population projection** Estimate of population size, composition, or distribution for a future date.

**Population pyramid** See **age-sex pyramid**.

**Population register** A system of data collection in which demographic and socio-economic characteristics of a population are continuously recorded.

**Population studies** See **demography**. When a distinction is made between demography and population studies, the former refers to the study of fertility, mortality, nuptiality, and migration and their interrelationships and consequences such as shifts in age-sex structure; population studies covers the whole field of population structure and the components, nature, causes, and consequence of population change.

**Population theory** Any conceptual framework dealing with the causes and consequences of population trends, particularly the relationship between population trends and social and economic change.

**Positive checks** A term used by Malthus to refer to mortality.

**Post-censal local review** A practice of the U.S. Bureau of the Census allowing local authorities, such as city officials, to review for accuracy preliminary census results pertaining to their area of jurisdiction.

**Post-enumeration survey** A sample survey conducted after a census, mainly to estimate the completeness of enumeration and secondarily to evaluate the quality of the data collected in the census.

**Poverty** As defined by the U.S. Bureau of the Census, state of having income below a certain level, which is estimated based on an economy food plan, taking into account such factors as family size, sex of the family head, number of children under 18 years of age in the family, and farm/nonfarm residence.

**Pregnancy** (1) The condition of having a developing embryo or fetus in the body after conception (the union of an ovum and spermatozoon). The product of conception is referred to as embryo for the first few weeks after conception, and thereafter as fetus. (2) The period between conception and the expulsion or extraction of the product of conception from the mother.

**Pregnancy history** A record of details of all pregnancies a woman has experienced, including the date at which each began and ended and the outcome.

**Pre-natal care** Regular medical check up and care of pregnant women.

**Prevalence rate** A measure of morbidity during a specified period for a specific disease, expressed as the number of persons with the disease per 1000 persons, using the mid-period population count for the denominator.

**Preventive checks** The term Malthus used in his essay for fertility control.

**Primate city** Among the cities of a country, the one that dominates the others in size and is an educational, political, industrial, and commercial center.

**Primitive migration** The type of group migration prompted by the inability of a group to cope with environmental forces.

**Pro-natalist** One who is in favor of encouraging, rather than controlling, births.

**Proportion** (1) A ratio in which the numerator is part of the denominator (e.g., in 1991, children of age below 15 years constituted a third of the world's population). (2) In algebra, the equality of two ratios, the common value of the ratios being called the constant of proportionality.

**Proximate variable** In a causal chain or causal nexus of a phenomenon, the most immediate cause.

**Push-pull theory** A migration theory according to which there are circumstances that push people out of a place and there are factors that attract migrants to the place. Factors that discourage outsiders from moving in are also push factors; similarly, those circumstances that keep current residents from moving out are pull factors.

**Race** Identification of a person by physical characteristics that are hereditary.

**Rate** A statistic that relates a flow volume of something during a period to another quantity (e.g., births during a calendar year to the mid-year population).

**Ratio** The result of dividing one quantity by another (e.g., the number of males in a population divided by the corresponding number of females gives the sex ratio of the population).

**Refugee** One who flees to a foreign country to escape danger of persecution, unable or unwilling to seek protection of his or her own country. A modified definition includes people who live under "refugee-conditions" in their own country.

**Registration** Continuous recording of events such as births and deaths for legal or statistical purposes.

**Registration system** A system for registration of events such as births and deaths on a continuous basis.

**Replacement level fertility** (1) The level of fertility at which a cohort of women, on the average, bear only just enough number of daughters to replace themselves in the population at the current level of mortality. (2) Net reproduction rate of one or the equivalent level of the total fertility rate (approximately 2.1 children per woman).

**Residence** Where one usually lives.

**Residential mobility** Shifts in residence (see **mobility**).

**Return migration** Migration that takes the migrant back to the place where he or she originally came from.

**Rural area** An area that has not been classified as urban (in the United States, a place with less than 2500 inhabitants or an area sparsely populated).

**Sample survey** A research strategy of collecting information usually through interviews from a part of a population with a view to drawing inferences about the whole.

**School dropouts** Persons who leave school before completing a critical level such as secondary school.

**School enrollment** Persons registered in a school system and assigned to a particular grade or level, as distinguished from school attendance, which refers to those who are present in school on a particular day.

**Secularization** Imbued with secularism, i.e., indifference to or rejection of religion or religious considerations.

**Separation** In the context of marital status, living apart from one's spouse.

**Sex** Biological division of individuals into males and females.

**Sex composition** Population makeup according to sex.

**Sex ratio** Number of males per 100 females in a population. Some countries, e.g., India, use the inverse, number of females per 100 males.

**Sexual union** A term that covers marriage and cohabitation. A heterosexual relationship that presumes free coital access for each partner to the other.

**Single** Never married.

**Size of population** Number of members of a population.

**Social demography** The branch of demography that focuses on the interaction of population structure and dynamics with other social process.

**Social stratification** Class or status differentiation and hence inequality within a population.

**Socialization** Training of potential members of society in regard to acceptable behavior in various contexts.

**Socioeconomic status (SES)** (1) A person's social standing based upon his or her social and economic characteristics. (2) A classification of an individual, household, or family according to income and/or other indicators of social or economic standing.

**Specific rate** Any rate calculated for a subset of a population such as those in a particular age group.

**Stable population** A population, closed to migration, that has a time-invariant age-sex structure (in percentage form) and a time-invariant rate of change in size.

**Standardization** A method to compute summary measures from a sequence of specific rates (e.g., age-specific death rates) for use in comparative analyses. For example, a weighted average of a population's age-specific death rates for a given year using the age composition of a "standard" population as weights is an age-standardized death rate for that population for that year. The comparison of the age-standardized rates calculated for two populations using the same "standard" population is unaffected by the differences in the age compositions of the two populations. The comparison of the crude death rates of the two populations, on the other hand, is influenced by the between-population differences in age composition—of two populations with the same age-specific death rates, the one with an older age structure is likely to have a higher crude death rate than the one with a younger age structure.

**Stationary population** A population, closed to migration, that has an unchanging age structure and a growth rate that always remains zero.

**Statistical areas** Geographic areas demarcated for statistical purposes, but not recognized as administrative or political units.

**Sterilization** In the context of birth control, a surgery performed on a person (man or woman) that makes the person incapable of producing any more children with any partner.

**Subfecundity** Diminished capacity to reproduce.

**Suburbs** The residential area on the outskirts of a city.

**Sun belt** The area in the southern part of the United States.

**Synthetic cohort** See **hypothetical cohort**.

**Teenage births** Births to women below 20 years of age.

**Terminal cumulative cohort fertility** Average number of children ever born to a real cohort by the time the survivors of the cohort reach the end of childbearing period.

**Theoretical framework** A set of general principles developed, on the basis of a consistent system of assumptions, with a view to interpreting observed patterns in one's data as particular instances of the general principles.

**Timing of birth** Controlling the interval between successive births or between marriage and the first birth.

**Total fertility rate (TFR)** The average number of children a group of women would bear by the time they reach the end of the childbearing period if they reproduce, as they age, in accordance with a given schedule of age-specific fertility rates. The TFR is also the average number of children per women at the end of the childbearing period in a population having the given age-specific fertility rates unchanged over time and no deaths among women in or below the reproductive age group.

**Triage** The sorting of patients, especially war and disaster victims, to determine priority of needed and appropriate treatment so as to maximize the number of survivors.

**Typologies** Categories formed by combining (crossing) two or more discrete variables (dichotomies, trichotomies, etc.). For example, Petersen (1975, p. 325) proposed a typology of migration consisting of eight categories defined by crossing "class of migration" (primitive, impelled or forced, free, mass) with whether the move resulted in a new way of life (innovating) or a continuation of the old (conservative). Thus slave trade is forced migration resulting in a new way of life; group migration involves free choice on the part of the individual members and has the aim of retaining the old ways.

**Underdeveloped areas** See **less-developed countries (LDCs)**.

**Underemployment** Persons whose work requires fewer hours per week than what is considered full-time work.

**Underenumeration** As applied to population census, failure to count people who should have been counted.

**Undocumented alien** Persons who enter a country illegally.

**Unemployment** State of being out of work but seeking work.

**Urban areas** In the United States, places with a population of 2500 or more and densely settled areas adjoining large population centers. The size cut-off varies by country.

**Urban growth** Growth in the urban component of a country's population.

**Urban agglomeration** A term used in many countries analogous to the U.S. term "metropolitan area."

**Urbanism** Having a lifestyle characteristic of people in urban places.

**Urbanization** An increase in the urban share of a country's total population resulting from rural–urban difference in growth rate, rural–urban migration, rural places acquiring urban characteristics and hence becoming reclassified as urban, or annexation of outer rings by cities.

**Urbanized area** In the United States, a city of population 50,000 or more combined with the densely settled territory surrounding it, to be contrasted with a metropolitan area, which is defined in terms of the county in which the central city is located and the adjoining counties with which the central city is integrated socially and economically.

**Vital registration** See **registration**.

**Vital statistics** Data on vital events (births, deaths, marriage, etc.).

**Wealth** In economics, anything that has a market value and can be exchanged for money or goods.

**Wealth flow** A term introduced by J. Caldwell to refer to intergenerational flow of resources, including economic goods, anything (e.g., money) that could be exchanged for goods and services, and other things such as deference and obligation.

**Widowhood** The state of being a widow or widower. Sometimes a distinction is made between widowhood (the state of being a widow) and widowerhood (the state of being a widower).

**Working age population** The population in the age groups (usually 15 to 64) from which the labor force is drawn.

**Youth dependency** Young people of age under 15 years per 100 persons of working age 15–64 years.

**Zero population growth (ZPG)** A situation in which a population's size remains unchanging because addition by births and immigration equals attrition by deaths and emigration.

# References

Ahlburg, D. and De Vita, C. J. New realities of the American Family. *Population Bulletin*, 1992, *47*(2). Washington, D.C.: Population Reference Bureau.

Ahlburg, D. and Schapiro, M. Socioeconomic ramifications of changing cohort size: an analysis of U.S. postwar suicide rates by age and sex. *Demography*, 1984, *21*, 97–105.

Alter, G. Theories of fertility decline: a nonspecialist's guide to the current debate. In J. R. Gills, L. A. Tilly, and D. Devine (Eds.), *The European Experience of Declining Fertility, 1850–1970: The Quite Revolution.* Cambridge: Blackwell, 1992, pp. 13–25.

Ashford, L. S. New perspectives on population: lessons from Cairo. *Population Bulletin*, 1995, *50*(1). Population Reference Bureau.

Axinn, W. G. and Thornton, A. The relationship between cohabitation and divorce: selectivity or causal influence? *Demography*, 1992, *29*, 357–374.

Basu, A. M. *Culture, the Status of Women, and Demographic Behavior.* NY: Oxford University Press, 1992.

Berelson, B. An evaluation of the effects of population control programs. *Studies in Family Planning*, 1974, *5*, 2–12.

Blanchet, D. On interpreting observed relationships between population growth and economic growth: a graphic explanation. *Population and Development Review*, 1991, *17*, 105–114.

Bloom, D. E. and Freeman, R. B. Population growth, labor supply, and employment in developing countries. In D. G. Johnson and R. D. Lee (Eds.), *Population Growth and Economic Development: Issues and Evidence.* Madison: University of Wisconsin Press, 1987, pp. 105–147.

Blum, D. Youthful professionals without any children transform city areas. *Wall Street Journal*, 1982, *1 February*.

Bogue, D. J. The demographic breakthrough: from projection to control. *Population Index*, 1964, *30*, 449–454.

Bogue, D. J. Family planning research: an outline of the field. In B. Berelson *et al.* (Eds.), *Family Planning and Population Programs.* Chicago: Chicago University Press, 1966, pp. 721–735.

Bogue, D. J. *Principles of Demography.* NY: Wiley, 1969.

Bogue, D. J., Arriaga, E. E., and Anderton, D. L., eds. *Readings in Population Research, Volume 4: Nuptiality, Migration, Household and Family Research.* Chicago: Social Development Center (published for the United Nations Population Fund), 1993.

Bongaarts, J. A framework for analyzing the proximate determinants of fertility. *Population and Development Review*, 1978, *4*, 105–132.

Bongaarts, J. The fertility-inhibiting effects of the intermediate fertility variables. *Studies in Family Planning*, 1982, *13*, 179–189.

Bongaarts, J. and Potter, R. G. *Fertility, Biology and Behavior: An Analysis of the Proximate Determinants*. NY: Academic Press, 1983.

Bongaarts, J, Mauldin, W. P., and Phillips, J. The demographic impact of family planning programs. *Studies in Family Planning*, 1990, *21*, 299–310.

Boserup, E. *The Conditions of Agricultural Growth*. Chicago: Aldine, 1965.

Boserup, E. *Population and Technological Change: A Study of Long-Term Trends*. Chicago: University of Chicago Press, 1981.

Boulding, K. Man's march to "the summit." Presented to the Warner-Gren International Symposium on Man's Role in Changing the Face of Earth. Princeton, NJ: June 16–22, 1955. Reprinted in *Population Today 23* (December 1995). Population Reference Bureau.

Bouvier, L. F., Shryock, H. S., and Henderson, H. W. International migration: yesterday, today, and tomorrow. *Population Bulletin*, 1977, *30*, 3–24.

Boyd, M. Immigration policies and trends: a comparison of Canada and the United States. *Demography*, 1976, *13*, 83–104.

Braidwood, R. J. Domestication: the food producing revolution. In D. L. Sills (Ed.), *International Encyclopedia of Social Sciences*. NY: Macmillan, 1968, pp. 245–250.

Brinkmann, C. Demographic Aspects of the Labour Force and Employment. Strasbourg: Council of Europe, 1987.

Brown, H. Introduction: the growth and distribution of human population. In H. Brown and E. Hutchings, Jr. (Eds.), *Are Our Descendants Doomed?* NY: Viking, 1970, pp. 3–12.

Brown, L. R. Population and affluence: growing pressures on world resources. *Population Bulletin*, 1973, *29*(2). Population Reference Bureau.

Brown, L. R. Reexamining the world food prospect. In L. R. Brown *et al.* (Eds.), *State of the World 1989*. NY: W. W. Norton, 1989, pp. 41–58.

Brown, L. R. The new world order. In L. R. Brown *et al.* (Eds.), *State of the World 1991*. NY: W. W. Norton, 1991, pp. 3–20.

Brown, L. R. Fertilizer use keeps dropping. In L. R. Brown, H. Kane, and D. M. Roodman (Eds.), *Vital Signs 1994: The Trends that are Shaping Our Future*. NY: W. W. Norton, 1994, pp. 42–43.

Brown, L. R., Flavin, C., and Postel, S. Outlining a global action plan. In L. R. Brown *et al.* (Eds.), *State of the World 1989*. NY: W. W. Norton, 1989, pp. 174–194.

Bumpass, L. L. and Sweet, J. A. National estimates of cohabitation. *Demography*, 1989, *26*, 615–625.

Bumpass, L. L. and Sweet, J. A. Cohabitation, marriage, nonmarital childbearing, and union stability: preliminary findings from HSFH2. Paper presented at the Annual Meeting of the Population Association of America, San Francisco, 1995.

Bumpass, L. L. and Westoff, C. F. *The Later Years of Childbearing*. Princeton: Princeton University Press, 1970.

Burby, R. J. and Weiss, S. F. *New Communities: U.S.A.* Lexington, MA: Heath, 1976.

Burch, T. K. Household and family demography: a bibliographic essay. *Population Index*, 1979, *45*, 173–195.

Büttner, T. and Lutz, W. Estimating fertility responses to policy measures in the German Demographic Republic. *Population and Development Review*, 1990, *16*, 539–555.

Butz, W. P. and Ward, M. P. The emergence of countercyclical U.S. fertility. *American Economic Review*, 1979a, *69*, 318–327.

Butz, W. P. and Ward, M. P. Will U.S. fertility remain low? A new economic interpretation. *Population and Development Review*, 1979b, *5*, 663–668.

Cain, M. Risk and fertility in India and Bangladesh. *Population Development Review*, 1981, *7*, 435–474.

Caldwell, J. Toward a restatement of demographic transition theory. *Population and Development Review*, 1976, *2*, 321–366.

Caldwell, J. C., Reddy, P. H., and Caldwell, P. *The Causes of Demographic Change: Experimental Research in South Asia.* Madison, WI: The University of Wisconsin Press, 1988.
Campbell, A. Changing patterns of childbearing in the United States. In National Institutes of Health, *The Family in Transition.* Washington, D.C. Government Printing Office, 1969.
Cartwright, F. F. *Disease and History.* NY: Thomas Y. Crowell, 1972.
Cassen, R. H. *India: Population, Economy, and Society.* NY: Homes and Meier, 1978.
Census of India. Paper No. 2, 1954: Life Tables—1951 Census. New Delhi: Government Printing Office, 1954.
Chatterjee, M. Indian women: their health and economic productivity. World Bank Discussion Paper, No. 109, Washington D.C.: World Bank, 1990.
Cho, L.-J. Population dynamics and policy in China. *Annals of the American Academy of Political and Social Science*, 1984, *476*, 111–127.
Clark, C. *Population Growth and Land Use.* NY: St. Martin's Press, 1967.
Clarke, J. I. *Population Geography* (2nd edition). Oxford: Pergamon Press, 1972.
Cleland, J. and Wilson, C. Demand theories of the fertility transition: an iconoclastic view. *Population Studies*, 1987, *41*, 5–30.
Cleland, J., Phillips, J. F., Amin, S., and Kamal, G. M. The determinants of reproductive change in Bangladesh: Success in a challenging environment. Washington, D.C.: The World Bank, 1994.
Coale, A. J. Factors associated with the development of low fertility: an historic summary. In *Proceedings of the World Population Conference*, 1965, Vol. 2. NY: United Nations, Department of Economic and Social Affairs, 1967, pp. 205–209.
Coale, A. J. The demographic transition. *Proceedings of the International Population Conference, Liège*, Vol. 1: 53–72, 1973.
Coale, A. J. and Hoover, E. M. *Population Growth and Economic Development in Low-Income Countries.* Princeton: Princeton University Press, 1958.
Coale, A. and Watkins, S. C., eds. *The Decline in Fertility in Europe.* Princeton: Princeton University Press, 1986.
Coleman, R. and Rainwater, L. *Social Standing in America.* NY: Basic Books, 1978.
Commission on Population Growth and the American Future. *Population and the American Future.* Washington, D.C.: Government Printing Office, 1972.
Cooley, C. H. Theory of transportation. In R. C. Angell (Ed.), *Sociological Theory and Social Research.* NY: Holt, Rinehart and Winston, 1930, pp. 75–83.
Cox, P. R. *Demography*, 5th ed. Cambridge: Cambridge University Press, 1976.
Council of Environmental Quality. *The Global 2000 Report to the President*, Vol. 1. Washington, D.C.: Government Printing Office, 1980.
Curtin, P. D. *The Atlantic Slave Trade.* Madison: The University of Wisconsin Press, 1969.
Dalrymple, D. G. *Development and Speed of High-Yielding Rice Varieties in Developing Countries.* Washington, D.C.: U.S. Agency for International Development, 1986.
DaVanzo, J. Why families move: a model of the geographic mobility of married couples. In Rand Report No. T-1972-DOL. Santa Monica, CA: Rand Corporation. 1976.
David, H. P. and Wright, M. H. Abortion legislation: the Romanian experience. Studies in Family Planning, 1971, *2* (October), 205–210.
Davis, K. The world demographic transition. *The Annals of the American Academy of Political and Social Science*, 1945, *237*, 1–11.
Davis, K. Malthus and the theory of population. In P. S. Lazarsfeld and M. Rosenberg (Eds.), *The Language of Social Research.* Glencoe, IL: Free Press, 1955, pp. 540–553.
Davis, K. The theory of change and response in modern demographic history. *Population Index*, 1963, *29*, 163–170.
Davis, K. The urbanization of the human population. *Scientific American*, 1965, *213*, 40–53.
Davis, K. The migration of human populations. *Scientific American*, 1974, *231*, 92–105.

Davis, K. and Blake, J. Social structure and fertility: an analytical framework. *Economic Development and Cultural Change*, 1956, *4*, 211–235.
DeJong, G. and Gardner, R., eds. *Migration Decision Making*. NY: Pergamon Press, 1981.
Demeny, P. Observations on population policy and population program in Bangladesh. *Population Development Review*, 1975, *1*, 307–321.
Demeny, P. Pronatalist policies in low fertility countries: Patterns, performance, and prospects. *Population Development Review*, 1986, *12* (Supplement): 335–358.
Denton, N. and Massey, D. Patterns of neighborhood transitions in a multiethnic world: U.S. metropolitan areas, 1970–80. *Demography*, 1991, *28*, 41–63.
Devaney, B. An analysis of variations in U.S. fertility and female labor force participation trends. *Demography*, 1983, *20*, 147–162.
Donaldson, P. J. and Tsui, A. O. The international family planning movement. *Population Bulletin*, 1990, *45*(3). Population Reference Bureau.
Dumont, A. Depopulation et civilisation; etude démographique. Paris: Lecrosnier et Babe, 1890.
Durand, J. D. Mortality estimates from Roman tombstone inscriptions. *American Journal of Sociology*, 1960, *65*, 365–373.
Durand, J. D. Demography's three hundredth anniversary. *Population Index*, 1962, *28*, 333–338.
Durand, J. D. The modern expansion of world population. *Proceedings of the American Philosophical Society*, 1967, *111*, 136–159.
Durning, A. Asking how much is enough. In L. R. Brown *et al.* (Ed.), *State of the World 1991*. NY: W. W. Norton, 1991, pp. 153–169.
Dyson, T. and Moore, M. On kinship structure, female autonomy, and demographic behavior in India. *Population Development Review*, 1983, *9*, 35–60.
Easterlin, R. A. Economic growth: overview. In D. L. Sills (Ed.), *International Encyclopedia of Social Sciences*, Vol. 4, 1968, pp. 395–408.
Easterlin, R. A. Relative economic status and the American fertility swing. In E. B. Sheldon (Ed.), *Family Economic Behavior: Problems and Prospects*. Philadelphia: J. B. Lippincott, 1973, pp. 170–223.
Easterlin, R. A. An economic framework of fertility analysis. *Studies in Family Planning*, 1975, *6*, 54–63.
Easterlin, R. A. *Birth and Fortune*. NY: Basic Books, 1980.
Ehrlich, P. *Population Bomb*. NY: Ballantine Books, 1968.
England, P. and Farkas, G. *Households, Employment, and Gender: A Social, Economic and Demographic View*. NY: Aldine De Gruyter, 1986.
Entwisle, B. Measuring components of family planning program effort. *Demography*, 1989, *26*, 53–76.
Espenshade, T. J. Marital careers of American women: a cohort life table analysis. In J. Bongaarts, T. K. Burch, and K. Wachter (Eds.), *Family Demography: Methods and Their Applications*. Oxford: Clarendon Press, 1987, pp. 150–167.
Evans, S. M. and Nelson, B. *Wage Justice: Comparable Worth and the Paradox of Technocratic Reform*. Chicago: University of Chicago Press, 1989.
Fawcett, J. T. and DeJong, G. F. Reasons for moving and migration behavior. In *National Migration Surveys X, Guidelines for Analysis*. NY: United Nations, Economic and Social Commission for Asia and the Pacific (ESCAP), 1982, pp. 109–131.
Feldman, J. J., Makuc, D. M., Kleinman, J. C., and Cornoni-Huntley, J. National trends in educational differentials in mortality. *American Journal of Epidemiology*, 1989, *129*, 919–933.
Feng, Z.-H. and Chen, C. H. C. Induced abortion in Xian city, China. *International Family Planning Perspective*, 1983, *9*, 81–85.
Fishlow, A. *American Railroads and the Transformation of the Antebellum Economy*. Cambridge: Harvard University Press, 1965.
Foner, A. Age in society: structure and change. *American Behavioral Scientist*, 1975, *19*(2), 144–165.

Food and Agricultural Organization. *Provisional Indicative World Plan for Agricultural Development*, Vol. 1. Rome, Italy: FAO, 1970.

Food and Agricultural Organization. *Agriculture: Toward 2000*. Rome, Italy: FAO, 1987.

Frank, O. Infertility in sub-Saharan Africa: estimates and implications. *Population and Development Review*, 1983, *9*, 137–144.

Freedman, R. The sociology of human fertility: a trend report and bibliography. *Current Sociology*, 1961–62, *X/XI*, 35–121.

Freedman, R. Family planning programs today: Major themes of the conference. In B. Berelson, R. K. Anderson, O. Harkavy, J. Maier, W. P. Mauldin, and S. J. Segal (Eds.), *Family Planning and Population Programs: A Review of World Developments*. Chicago: University of Chicago Press, 1966, pp. 811–825.

Freedman, R. Asia's recent fertility decline and prospects for future demographic change. *Asia-Pacific Population Research Reports*, No. 1., January 1995. East-West Center, 1995.

Freedman, R., Khoo, S.-E., and Supraptila, B. *Modern Contraceptive Use in Indonesia: A Challenge to Conventional Wisdom*. World Fertility Survey Scientific Reports, No. 20. London: World Fertility Survey, 1981.

Friedlander, D. Demographic responses and population change. *Demography*, 1969, *6*, 359–381.

Frey, W. Metropolitan America: beyond the transition. *Population Bulletin*, 1990, *45*(2).

Fries, J. F. An introduction to the compression of morbidity. *Gerontologica Perspecta*, 1987, *1*, 5–7.

Fuchs, L. H. Migration research and immigration policy. *International Migration Review*, 1992, *24*, 1069–1076.

Furstenburg, F. F., Jr. Good dads–bad dads. In A. J. Cherlin (Ed.), *The Changing American Family and Public Policy*. Washington, D.C.: The Urban Institute Press, 1988, pp. 193–218.

Furstenburg, F. F., Jr. and Cherlin, A. J. *Divided Families: What Happens to Children When Parents Part*. Cambridge, MA: Harvard University Press, 1991.

Gibbs, J., ed. *Urban Research Methods*. NY: Van Nostrand, 1961.

Glass, D. V. John Graunt and his natural and political observations. *Proceedings of the Royal Society*, Series B, 1963, *159*, 2–37.

Goldscheider, C. *Population, Modernization, and Social Structure*. Boston: Little, Brown, 1971.

Goldstein, D. and Goldstein, A. Surveys of migration in developing countries: a methodological review. *Papers of the East-West Population Institute*, No. 71, 1981.

Goldstein, D. and Sly, D., eds. *Basic Data Needed for the Study of Urbanization*. Belgium: International Union for the Scientific Study of Population. Ordina edition, 1974.

Grauman, J. V. Orders of magnitude of the world's urban population in history. *Population Bulletin of the United Nations*, 1976, *8*, 16–33.

Graunt, J. 1662 (1973). *Natural and Political Observations Made Upon the Bills of Mortality*. Reprinted with an introduction by P. Laslett in *The Earliest Classics: Pioneers of Demography*. Farnborough, Hants.: Gregg International, 1973.

Gray, R. H. The impact of health and nutrition on natural fertility. In R. Bulatao and R. Lee (Eds.), *Determinants of Fertility in Developing Countries, Volume 1: Supply and Demand for Children*. NY: Academic Press, 1983, pp. 139–162.

Grigg, D. B. E. G. Ravenstein on the laws of migration. *Journal of Historical Geography*, 1977, *3*, 41–54.

Guillard, A. Éléments de statisque humaine ou démographie comparée. Paris: Guillaumin, 1855.

Guzman, J. M. Trends in socio-economic differentials in infant mortality in selected Latin American countries. In L. Ruzicka, G. Wunsch, and P. Kane (Eds.), *Differential Mortality: Methodological Issues and Biosocial Factors*. Oxford: Clarendon Press, 1989, pp. 131–144.

Hajnal, J. European marriage pattern in perspective. In D. V. Glass and D. E. C. Eversley (Eds.), *Population in History*. London: Arnold, 1965, pp. 101–143.

Hall, P. *World Cities*. NY: McGraw-Hill, 1977.

Hansen, A. H. Economic progress and declining population growth. *American Economic Review*, 1939, *29*, 1–15.

Hauser, P. M. and Schnore, L., eds. *The Study of Urbanization*. NY: Wiley, 1965.

Hawley, A. H. *Human Ecology: A Theory of Community Structure*. NY: Ronald Press, 1950.

Hawley, A. H. *Urban Society: An Ecological Approach*. NY: Ronald Press, 1971.

Hayami, Y. and Ruttan, V. W. Population growth and agricultural productivity. In D. G. Johnson and R. D. Lee (Eds.), *Population Growth and Economic Development: Issues and Evidence*. Madison: Wisconsin University Press, 1987, pp. 57–101.

Hendershot, G. E. Population size, military power, and antinatal policy. *Demography*, 1973, *10*, 517–524.

Henry, L. Some data on natural fertility. *Eugenics Quarterly*, 1961, *8*, 81–91.

Henshaw, S. K. Induced abortion: a world view, 1990. *Family Planning Perspective*, 1990, *22*, 85–88.

Hirschman, C. Why fertility change? *Annual Review of Sociology*, 1994, *20*, 203–233.

Hull, T. H. Socio-demographic change in Indonesia. In K. Mahadevan (Ed.), *Fertility and Mortality: Theory, Methodology, and Empirical Issues*. New Delhi: Sage Publications, 1986, pp. 197–217.

Immigration and Naturalization Service. *1992 Statistical Yearbook of the Immigration and Naturalization Service*. Washington, D.C.: Government Printing Office, 1993.

Jacobson, J. L. Closing the gender gap in development. In L. R. Brown *et al.* (Eds.), *State of the World 1993*. NY: W. W. Norton, 1993, pp. 61–79.

Johnston, D. F. An analysis of sources of information on the population of the Navaho. *Bureau of American Ethnology Bulletin*, No. 197. Washington, D.C., 1966.

Kantner, A., Lerman, C., and Yusuf, M. What can we say about fertility trends in Bangladesh? An evaluation of the 1991 population census. *Asia-Pacific Population Research Reports*. Number 5 (June). East–West Center, Hawaii, 1995.

Kaplan, G. A. Epidemiologic observations on the compression of morbidity: evidence from the Alameda County Study. *Journal of Aging and Health*, 1991, *3*, 155–171.

Keely, C. B. U.S. Immigration: a policy analysis. Public Issues Paper PI-02. NY: The Population Council, 1979.

Keely, C. B. *Global Refugee Policy: The Case for a Development-Oriented Strategy*. New York: The Population Council, 1981.

Kelly, A. C. Economic consequences of population change in the Third World. *Journal of Economic Literature*, 1988, *26*, 1685–1728.

Keyfitz, N. *Applied Mathematical Demography*. NY: Wiley, 1977.

Keyfitz, N. Our demographic future: predictions for the next 50 years. *Population Today*, 1995, *23*. Population Reference Bureau.

Keynes, J. M. Some economic consequences of a declining population. *Eugenics Review*, 1937, *29*, 13–17.

Kiser, C. V. and Whelpton, P. K. Resume of the Indianapolis Study of social and psychological factors affecting fertility. *Population Studies*, 1953, *7*, 95–110.

Knodel, J. Natural fertility: age patterns, levels, and trends. In R. A. Bulatao and R. D. Lee (Eds.), *Determinants of Fertility in Developing Countries*, Vol. I, pp. 61–102. NY: Academic Press. 1983.

Kols, A. and Lewison, D. Migration, population growth, and development. *Population Reports*, Series M, No. 7. Baltimore: Johns Hopkins University, 1983.

Kritz, M. M. and Keely, C. B. Introduction. In M. M. Kritz and C. B. Keely (Eds.), *Global Trends in Migration: Theory and Research on International Population Movements*. Staten Island, NY: Center for Migration Studies of New York, 1981.

Kunitz, S. J. Speculations on the European mortality decline. *Economic History Review*, 1983, *36*, 349–364.

Kuznets, S. J. Population and economic growth. *Proceedings of the American Philosophical Society*, 1967, *3*, 170–193.

Kuznets, S. *Population, Capital, and Growth: Selected Essays*. NY: W. W. Norton & Company, 1973.

Lee, E. A theory of migration. *Demography*, 1966, *3*, 47–57.

Leff, N. H. Dependency rates and savings rates. *American Economic Review*, 1969, *59*, 886–896.

Leibenstein, H. *Economic Backwardness and Economic Growth*. NY: Wiley, 1957.

Lenski, G. E. and Lenski, J. *Human Societies: An Introduction to Macrosociology*, 5th ed. NY: McGraw-Hill, 1987.

Leridon, H. *Human Fertility: The Basic Components* (translated by J. F. Helzner). Chicago: Chicago University Press, 1977.

Lesthaeghe, R. *The Decline of Belgian Fertility, 1800–1970*. Princeton: Princeton University Press, 1977.

Lieberson, S. and Carter, D. A model for inferring the voluntary and involuntary causes of residential segregation. *Demography*, 1982, *19*(4), 511–526.

Liesner, T. *Economic Statistics 1900–1983*. NY: Facts on File Publications, 1985.

London, K. A. Cohabitation, marriage, marital dissolution, and remarriage: United States, 1988. Advance Data from Vital and Health Statistics of the National Center for Health Statistics No. 194. Hyattsville, MD: National Center for Health Statistics, 1–3, 1991.

Long, L. *Migration and Residential Mobility in the United States*. NY: Russell Sage Foundation, 1988.

Longman, P. Social security and the baby boom generation. *Journal of Aging & Social Policy*, 1989, *1*, 131–153.

Lopez, A. D. Causes of death: an assessment of global patterns of mortality around 1985. *World Health Statistics Quarterly*, 1990, *43*, 91–104.

Lopez, A. D. and Ruzicka, L. T. Introduction. In A. D. Lopez and L. T. Ruzicka (Eds.), *Sex Differentials in Mortality: Trends, Determinants, and Consequences*. Canberra: Australian National University, 1983, pp. 1–5.

Lorimer, F. *Culture and Human Fertility*. Paris: UNESCO, 1954.

Lynge, E. *Socio-Economic Differences in Mortality in Europe*. Population Studies, No. 9. Strasbourg: Council of Europe, 1984.

Macura, M. The influence of the definition of urban place on the size of urban population. In J. Gibbs (Ed.), *Urban Research Methods*. NY: Van Nostrand, 1961, pp. 21–31.

McFalls, J. and McFalls, M. *Disease and Fertility*. NY: Academic Press, 1984.

Malthus, T. R. *An Essay on the Principle of Population*. NY: Augustus Kelley, 1798.

Malthus, T. R. *The Principles of Political Economy*, 2nd ed. Tokyo: International Economic Circle, 1936.

Mandelbaum, D. *Human Fertility in India*. Berkeley, CA: University of California Press, 1974.

Manton, K. G. and Tolly, D. Rectangularization of the survival curve: implications of an ill-posed question. *Journal of Aging and Health*, 1991, *3*, 172–193.

Martin, P. and Midgley, E. Immigration to the United States: Journey to an uncertain destination. *Population Bulletin*, 1994, *49*(2). Population Reference Bureau.

Marx, K. *Capital: A Critical Analysis of Capitalist Production*. Translated from the third German edition by S. Moore and E. Aveling. Two volumes. London: Swan, Sonnenschein, Lowry, 1887.

Mason, K. O. Is the situation of women in Asia improving or deteriorating? *Asia-Pacific Population Research Report*, 1995, Number 6 (September). East-West Center, Hawaii.

Mauldin, W. P. and Ross, J. A. Family planning programs: efforts and results, 1982–1989. *Studies in Family Planning*, 1991, *22*, 350–367.

Maynes, M. J. *Schooling in Western Europe*. Albany, NY: State University of New York Press, 1985.

McKeown, T. *The Modern Rise of Population*. NY: Academic Press, 1976.

McNeill, W. H. *Plagues and People*. NY: Doubleday, 1976.

McNamara, R. S. *One Hundred Countries, Two Billion People: The Dimensions of Development*. NY: Praeger, 1973.

Meadows, D. H., Meadows, D. L., Randers, J., and Behrens, W., III. *The Limits to Growth*. NY: New American Library, 1972.

Molho, I. Theories of migration: A review. *Scottish Journal of Political Economy*, 1986, *33*, 396–419.

Monnier, A. and de Guibert-Lantoine, C. The demographic situation of Europe and the developed countries overseas. An annual report. *Population, An English Selection*, 1994, *6*, pp. 203–222.

Mosher, W. D., Williams, L. B., and Johnson, D. P. Religion and fertility in the United States. *Demography*, 1992, *29*, 199–214.

Murray, C. *Losing Ground: American Social Policy 1950–1980*. NY: Basic Books, 1984.

Muzhen, L. Distribution of Chinese population. In D. L. Poston, Jr. and D. Yaukey (Eds.), *The Population of Modern China*. NY: Plenum, 1992, pp. 83–113.

Nag, M. How modernization can also raise fertility. *Current Anthropology*, 1980, *241*, 571–587.

Nag, M. Sex preference in Bangladesh, India, and Pakistan and its effects on fertility. *The Population Council Working Papers* No. 27, 1991.

Nam, C. B. *Understanding Population Change*. Itasca, IL: E. E. Peacock, 1994.

Namboodiri, N. K. Some observations on the economic framework for fertility analysis. *Population Studies*, 1972, *26*, 185–206.

Namboodiri, N. K. Review symposium. T. W. Schultz (Ed.), Economics of the family: marriage, children, and human capital. Chicago: University of Chicago Press, 1975, *Demography*, 1975, *12*, 561–569.

Namboodiri,K. *Methods of Macrosociological Research*. San Diego: Academic Press, 1994.

Namboodiri, K. and Suchindran, C. M. *Life Table Techniques and Their Applications*. Orlando, FL: Academic Press, 1987.

Nathanson, C. A. and Kim, Y. J. Components of change in adolescent fertility, 1971–1979. *Demography*, 1989, *26*, 85–92.

National Center for Health Statistics (NCHS). *Health, United States, 1993*. Hyattsville, MD: Public Health Service, 1994.

National Center for Health Statistics (NCHS). *Health, United States, 1994*. Hyattsville, MD: Public Health Service, 1995.

National Research Council. *Population Growth and Economic Development: Policy Questions*. Washington, D.C.: National Academy Press, 1986.

Northam, R. M. *Urban Geography*. NY: Wiley, 1975.

Notestein, F. W. Population: the long view. In T. W. Schultz (Ed.), *Food for the World*. Chicago: University of Chicago Press, 1945, pp. 36–57.

Obermeyer, C. M. Reproductive choice in Islam: gender and state in Iran and Tunisia. *Studies in Family Planning*, 1994, *25*, 41–51.

O'Connel, M. and Bachu, A. Who's minding the kids? Child care arrangements: winter, 1986–1987. *Current Population Reports P-70*, No. 2, 1990.

O'Hare, W. P. America's minorities—the demographics of diversity. *Population Bulletin*, 1992, *47*(4). Population Reference Bureau.

O'Hare, W. P. Poverty in America: trends and new prospects. *Population Bulletin*, 1985, *40*(3). Population Reference Bureau.

O'Hare, W. P., Pollard, K. M., Mann, T. L., and Kent, M. M. African Americans in the 1990s. *Population Bulletin*, 1991, *46*(1). Population Reference Bureau.

Omran, A. A. The epidemiologic transition: a theory of the epidemiology of population change. *Milbank Memorial Fund Quarterly*, 1971, *4*, 509–538.

Omran, A. R. Epidemiologic transition in the United States. *Population Bulletin*, 1977, *32*(2). Population Reference Bureau.

Oppenheimer, V. K. The interaction of demand and supply and its effect on the female labor force in the United States. *Population Studies*, 1967, *21*, 239–259.

Oppenheimer, V. K. *The Female Labor Force in the United States*. Berkeley, CA: University of California Institute of International Studies, 1970.

Pakrasi, K. and Malakar, C. The relationship between family type and fertility. *Milbank Memorial Fund Quarterly*, 1967, *45*, 451–460.
Palen, J. *The Urban World*, Third edition. NY: McGraw-Hill, 1987.
Pearce, D. W., ed. In *The MIT Dictionary of Modern Economics*, 3rd ed. Cambridge, MA: MIT Press, 1989.
Pendleton, A. *Young Adult Literacy and Schooling*. National Center for Education Statistics, Analysis Report CS 88-604. Washington, D.C.: Government Printing Office, 1988.
Perrenoud, A. Mortality decline in its secular setting. In T. Bengtsson, G. Fridizius, and R. Ohlsson (Eds.), *Pre-Industrial Population Change: The Mortality Decline and Short-Term Population Movements*. Stockholm: Almquist and Wicksell International, 1984, pp. 41–69.
Perry, D. D. and Watkins, A. J., eds. *The Rise of Sunbelt Cities*. Beverly Hills, CA: Sage, 1977.
Peter, K. *The Dynamics of Hutterite Society*. Alberta, Canada: University of Alberta Press, 1987.
Peters, G. L. and Larkin, R. P. *Population Geography*, 4th edition. Dubuque, IA: Kendall/Hunt, 1993.
Petersen, W. A general topology of migration. *American Sociological Review*, 1958, *23*, 256–266.
Petersen, W. *Population*, 3rd edition. NY: Macmillan, 1975.
Petersen, W. International migration. *Annual Review of Sociology*, 1978, *4*, 533–575.
Population Reference Bureau. *1993 World Population Data Sheet*. Washington, D.C.: The Population Reference Bureau, 1993.
Population Reference Bureau. *1994 World Population Data Sheet*. Washington, D.C.: The Population Reference Bureau, 1994.
Population Reference Bureau. *1995 World Population Data Sheet*. Washington, D.C.: The Population Reference Bureau, 1995.
Postel, S. Halting land degradation. In L. R. Brown *et al.* (Eds.), *State of the World, 1989*. NY: W. W. Norton & Company, 1989, pp. 21–40.
Postel, S. Facing water scarcity. In L. R. Brown *et al.* (Eds.), *State of the World, 1993*. NY: W. W. Norton & Company, 1993, pp. 22–41.
Poston, D. L., Jr. and Yaukey, D. eds. *The Population of Modern China*. NY: Plenum, 1992.
Pressat, R. *Demographic Analysis*. Translated by J. Matras. NY: Aldine, 1972.
Presser, H. B. Can we make time for children? The economy, work schedules, and child care. *Demography*, 1989, *26*, 523–543.
Preston, S. H. Are the economic consequences of population growth a sound basis for population policy? In J. Menken (Ed.), *World Population and U.S. Policy: The Choices Ahead*. NY: W. W. Norton & Company, 1986, pp. 67–95.
Preston, S. H. The decline of fertility in non-European industrialized countries. In K. Davis, M. S. Bernstam, and R. Ricardo-Campbell (Eds.), *Below-Replacement Fertility in Industrial Societies: Causes, Consequences, Policies*. London: Cambridge University Press, 1987, pp. 26–47.
Pryor, R. J., ed. *The Motivation of Migration*. Canberra: The Australian National University, 1975.
Ravenstein, E. G. The laws of migration. *Journal of the Royal Statistical Society*, 1885, *48*, 167–235.
Ravenstein, E. G. The laws of migration. *Journal of the Royal Statistical Society*, 1889, *52*, 241–305.
Reddaway, W. B. *The Economics of a Declining Population*. London: Allen & Unwin, 1939.
Riley, J. C. and Alter, G. The epidemiologic transition and morbidity. *Annales de Demographie Historique*, 1989, 199–213.
Rindfuss, R. R. and Vanden Heuvel, A. Cohabition: Precursor to marriage or an alternative to being single. *Population and Development Review*, 1990, *16*(4), 703–726.
Robinson, W. C. Another look at the Hutterites and natural fertility. *Social Biology*, 1986, *33*, 1–2, 65–76.
Root, B. D. and DeJong, G. F. Family migration in a developing country. *Population Studies*, 1991, *45*, 221–233.
Russell, J. C. *Late Ancient and Medieval Population*. Philadelphia: American Philosophical Society, 1958.

Ruzicka, L. Problems and issues in the study of mortality differentials. In L. Ruzicka, G. Wunsch, and P. Kane (Eds.), *Differential Mortality: Methodological Issues and Biosocial Factors*. Oxford: Clarendon Press, 1989, pp. 3–17.

Ryan, M. and Flavin, C. Facing China's limits. In L. R. Brown *et al.* (Eds.), *State of the World 1995*. NY: W. W. Norton, 1995, pp. 113–131.

Ryder, N. B. and Westoff, C. F. *Reproduction in the United States*, 1965. Princeton, NJ: Princeton University Press, 1971.

Rystad, G. History and the future of international migration. *International Migration Review*, 1992, *26*, 1168–1199.

Sabagh, G. The fertility of the French-Canadian women during the 17th century. *American Journal of Sociology*, 1942, *47*, 680–689.

Sadik, N. The Cairo consensus: changing the world by choice. *Populi*, 1994, *21*(9), 4–5.

Sawers, L. and Tabb, W. K., eds. *Sunbelt/Snowbelt*. NY: Oxford University Press, 1984.

Schnore, L. F. On the spatial structure of cities in the two Americas. In P. Hauser and L. F. Schnore (Eds.), *The Study of Urbanization*. NY: Wiley, 1965, pp. 347–398.

Schoen, R. and Weinick, R. M. The slowing metabolism of marriage: figures from 1988 U.S. marital status life tables. *Demography*, 1988, *33*(4), 737–746.

Schultz, T. P. School expenditures and enrollments, 1960–1980: The effects of income, prices and population growth. In D. G. Johnson and R. D. Lee (Eds.), *Population Growth and Economic Development: Issues and Evidence*. Madison: Wisconsin University Press, 1987, pp. 413–476.

Schultz, T. W., ed. *Economics of the Family: Marriage, Children, and Human Capital*. Chicago: University of Chicago Press, 1975.

Shank, S. E. Women and the labor market: the link grows stronger. *Monthly Labor Review*, 1988, *111*, 3–8.

Sharma, O. P. and Retherford, R. How female literacy affects fertility: the case of India. *Asian-Pacific Population & Policy*, No. 15. Honolulu: East–West Population Institute, 1990.

Shyrock, H. and Siegel, J. *The Methods and Materials of Demography*. U.S. Bureau of the Census, Washington, D.C., Government Printing Press, 1971.

Simmons, A. B. Slowing metropolitan growth in Asia: policies, programs, and results. *Population and Development Review*, 1979, *5*(1), 87–104.

Simon, A. *Bread for the World*. NY: Paulist Press, 1975.

Simon, J. *The Ultimate Resource*. Princeton: Princeton University Press, 1981.

Skeldon, R. Circulation: A transition in mobility in Peru. In R. M. Prothero and M. Chapman (Eds.), *Circulation in Third World Countries*. London: Routledge & Kegan Paul, 1985, pp. 100–120.

Smith, D. P. *Formal Demography*. NY: Plenum, 1992.

Snipp, C. M. *American Indians: The First of This Land*. NY: Russell Sage Foundation, 1989.

Soltow, L. *Distribution of Wealth and Income in the United States in 1798*. Pittsburgh: University of Pittsburgh Press, 1989.

Spengler, J. J. The economist and the population question. Presidential address at the seventy-eighth annual meeting of the American Economic Association. *American Economic Review*, 1966, *56*, 1–17.

Stolnitz, G. J. Mortality declines and age distribution. *Milbank Memorial Fund Quarterly*, 1956, *34*, 178–215.

Stolnitz, G. J. Mortality: Post-World War II trends. In J. A. Ross (Ed.), *International Encyclopedia of Population*. NY: The Free Press, 1982, pp. 461–469.

Stouffer, S. A. Intervening opportunities and competing migrants. *Journal of Regional Science*, 1960, *2*, 1–26.

Tanaka, T. *Demographic Transition and Development in Asian Countries*. Tokyo: Asian Population and Development Association, 1989.

Tarrant, J. R. World food prospects for the 1990s. *Journal of Geography*, 1990, *89*, 234–238.

Teitelbaum, M. S. Right versus right: immigration and refugee policy in the United States. *Foreign Affairs*, 1980, *59*, 21–59.

Thomas, D. S. *Research Memorandum on Migration Differentials*. NY: Social Science Research Council, 1938.

Thomlinson, R. *Demographic Problems: Controversy Over Population Control*, 2nd edition. Encino: Dickenson Publishing Company, 1975.

Thomlinson, R. *Population Dynamics: Causes and Consequences of World Demographic Change*, 2nd edition. NY: Random House, 1976.

Thompson, W. Population. *American Journal of Sociology*, 1929, *34*, 959–975.

Thornton, R. *American Indian Holocaust and Survival: A Population History Since 1492*. Norman: University of Oklahoma Press, 1987.

Tien, H. Y., Tianlu, Z., Yu, P., Jingneng, L., and Zhongtang, L. China's demographic dilemma. *Population Bulletin*, 1992, *47*(1). Population Reference Bureau.

Tomasi, S. M. Sociopolitical participation of migrants in receiving countries. In M. Kritz, C. B. Keely, and S. M. Tomasi (Eds.), *Global Trends in Migration: Theory and Research on International Population Movements*. Staten Island, NY: Center for Migration Studies, 1981.

United Nations. *Populi: The UNFPA Magazine*, 1995, *22*(8).

United Nations. *Methods for Population Projections by Sex and Age*. Manuals on methods of estimating population. Manual III. NY: United Nations, 1956.

United Nations. *Demographic Yearbook, 1962*. NY: United Nations, 1962.

United Nations. *Population Bulletin of the United Nations*, No. 6. NY: United Nations, 1963.

United Nations. *Principles and Recommendations for a Vital Statistics System*. NY: United Nations, 1973.

United Nations. *Trends and Characteristics of International Migration Since 1950*. NY: United Nations, 1979.

United Nations. *Principles and recommendations of population and housing censuses. Statistical Papers*, Series M, No. 67. NY: United Nations, 1980.

United Nations. Women's employment and fertility. *Population Studies*, No. 96. NY: United Nations, 1985.

United Nations. World population policies, Vol. 1. *Population Studies*, No. 102. NY: United Nations, 1987.

United Nations. Trends in population policy. *Population Studies*, No. 114. NY: United Nations, 1989.

United Nations. *Results of the Sixth Population Inquiry among Governments*. Population Policy Paper, No. 31. NY: United Nations, 1990a.

United Nations. *World Population Monitoring 1989*. NY: United Nations, 1990b.

United Nations. *World Urbanization Prospects*. NY: United Nations, 1991a.

United Nations. The sex and age distributions of populations: the 1990 revisions of the United Nations global population estimates and projections. *Population Studies*, No. 122. NY: United Nations, 1991b.

United Nations. *World Population Prospects: The 1991 Issue*. NY: United Nations, 1991c.

United Nations. *The World's Women: Trends and Statistics 1970–1990*. NY: United Nations, 1991d.

United Nations. *World Population Prospects: The 1992 Revision*. NY: United Nations, 1993.

United Nations Development Program. *Human Development Report 1990*. NY: Oxford University Press, 1990.

United Nations Secretariat. Statistical definitions of urban population and their uses in applied demography. In S. Goldstein and D. Sly (Eds.), *Basic Data Needed for the Study of Urbanization*. Dolhain, Belgium: Ordina edition, 1974, pp. 15–32.

UNESCO. *Statistical Yearbook*. Paris: UNESCO, 1989.

UNESCO. *Compendium of Statistics on Illiteracy*. 1990 Edition. Paris: UNESCO, 1990.

U.S. Bureau of the Census. *Current Population Reports*, Series P-20, No. 193. Washington, D.C.: Government Printing Office, 1969.

U.S. Bureau of the Census. *Historical Statistics of the United States, Colonial Times to 1970*, Bicentennial Edition. Parts 1 & 2. Washington, D.C.: Government Printing Office, 1975.

U.S. Bureau of the Census. Geographical mobility March 1975 to March 1978. *Current Population Reports*, Series P-20, No. 331, 1978.

U.S. Bureau of the Census. *Statistical Abstract of the United States 1989*. Washington, D.C.: Government Printing Office, 1989.

U.S. Bureau of the Census. Household and family characteristics: March 1990 and 1989. *Current Population Reports*, Series P-20, No. 447, 1990.

U.S. Bureau of the Census. *Statistical Abstract of the United States: 1991*. Washington, D.C.: Government Printing Office, 1991a.

U.S. Bureau of the Census. Money income of households, families, and persons in the United States: 1990. *Current Population Reports*, Series P-60, No. 174, 1991b.

U.S. Bureau of the Census. Marital status and living arrangements: March 1990. *Current Population Reports*, Series P-20, No. 450, 1991c.

U.S. Bureau of the Census. Geographic mobility: March 1987 to March 1990. *Current Population Reports*, Series P-20, No. 456, 1991d.

U.S. Bureau of the Census. Marital status and living arrangements, March 1991. *Current Population Reports*, Series P-20, No. 461, 1992a.

U.S. Bureau of the Census. Educational attainment in the United States: March 1991 and 1990. *Current Population Reports*, Series P-20, No. 462, 1992b.

U.S. Committee on Refugees. *World Refugee Survey: 1972 in Reivew*. Washington, D.C., 1973.

U.S. Council of Economic Advisors. The economic effects of immigration. *Economic Report of the President*. Washington, D.C.: Council of Economic Advisors, 1986.

U.S. Department of Commerce. *Fertility Tables for Birth Cohorts by Color: United States, 1917–1980*. National Technical Information Service No. PB84-22052. [Machine-readable data file.]

U.S. Senate Committee on Aging. *Aging America: Trends and Projections*, 1987–88 edition. Washington, D.C.: Government Printing Office.

van de Kaa, D. J. Europe's second demographic transition. *Population Bulletin*, 1987, *47*(1). Population Reference Bureau.

van de Walle, E. and Knodel, J. Europe's fertility transition: new evidence and lessons for today's developing world. *Population Bulletin*, 1980, *34*(6). Population Reference Bureau.

Verbrugge, L. Longer life but worsening health? Trends in health and mortality of middle-aged and older persons. *Milbank Memorial Fund Quarterly*, 1984, *62*, 475–519.

Visaria, L. Regional variations in female autonomy and fertility and contraception in India. *Gujarat Institute of Development Research Working Paper Series 50*. Ahmedabad, India, 1993.

Warren, R. Estimates of the unauthorized immigrant population residing in the United States, by country of origin and state of residence: October 1992. Paper presented at the California Immigration 1994 Seminar, Sacramento, California. April 1994.

Warwick, D. P. The Indonesian family planning program: Government influence and client choice. *Population and Development Review*, 1986, *12*, 453–490.

Weeks, J. R. *Population: An Introduction to Concepts and Issues*, (updated 5th edition). Belmont, CA: Wadsworth, 1994.

Weeks, J. R. *Population: An Introduction to Concepts and Issues*, 6th edition. Belmont, CA: Wadsworth, 1995.

Weintraub, S. Implications of Mexican demographic development for the United States. In F. Bean *et al.* (Eds.), *Mexican and Central American Population and U.S. Immigration Policy*. Austin, Texas: Center for Mexican-American Studies, 1989.

Weller, R. H. and Bouvier, L. F. *Population: Demography and Policy*. NY: St. Martin's Press, 1981.

Westoff, C. F. The changing focus of differential fertility research: the social mobility hypothesis. *Milbank Memorial Fund Quarterly*, 1953, *31*, 24–38.

Westoff, C. F. Perspective on nuptiality and fertility. In K. Davis, M. S. Bernstam, and R. Ricardo-Campbell (Eds.), *Below-Replacement Fertility in Industrial Societies: Causes, Consequences, Policies*. London: Cambridge University Press, 1987, pp. 155–170.

Westoff, C. F. and Rindfuss, R. R. Sex preselection in the United States: some implications. *Science*, 1974, *184*, 633–636.

Westoff, C. F., Potter, R. G., Jr., Sagi, P. C., and Mishler, E. G. *Family Growth in Metropolitan America*. Princeton: Princeton University Press, 1961.

Wilkens, J. and Fried, D. Critics challenge census findings on the homeless. *San Diego Union*, 22 April, 1991.

Willis, R. J. A new approach to the economic theory of fertility behavior. *Journal of Political Economy*, 1973, *81*, S14–S69.

Wilson, C., ed. *Roland Pressat: The Dictionary of Demography*. NY: Blackwell, 1985.

Wood, J. W. *Dynamics of Human Reproduction: Biology, Biometry, Demography*. NY: Aldine De Gruyter, 1994.

World Bank. *World Development Report, 1984*. NY: Oxford University Press, 1984.

World Bank. *World Development Report, 1986*. NY: Oxford University Press, 1986.

World Bank. *World Development Report, 1990*. NY: Oxford University Press, 1990.

World Bank. *World Development Report, 1991: The Challenge of Development*. NY: Oxford University Press, 1991.

World Bank. The World Bank and Indonesia's population program. In *World Bank, Population and the World Bank: Implications from Eight Case Studies*, Annex 2. Washington, D.C.: World Bank, 1992.

Woytinsky, W. S. and Woytinsky, E. S. *World Population and Production*. NY: The Twentieth Century Fund, 1953.

Wright, R. *Address Unknown: The Homeless in America*. Hawthorne, NY: Aldine de Gruyter, 1989.

Xenos, P. and Gultiano, S. A. Trends in female and male age at marriage and celibacy. *Papers of the Program on Population*, No. 120. Honolulu: East–West Center, 1992.

Yaukey, D. *Demography: The Study of Human Population*. Prospect Heights, IL: Waveland Press, 1990.

Zelinsky, W. The impasse in migration theory: a sketch map for potential escapees. In P. A. Morrison (Ed.), *Population Movements: Their Forms and Functions in Urbanization and Development*. Liège, Belgium: Ordina Editions, 1983, pp. 19–46.

Zimmer, B. Suburbanization and changing political structure. In B. Schwarts (Ed.), *The Changing Forces of the Suburbs*. Chicago: Chicago University Press, 1975.

Zinsser, H. *Rats, Lice, and History*. Boston: Little, Brown, 1934.

Zopf, P. E., Jr. *Population: An Introduction to Social Demography*. Palo Alto, CA: Mayfield, 1984.

# Geographical Index

# Name Index

# Subject Index

ISBN 0-306-45338-X
EAN
9 780306 453380
90000>